THE RUSSIAN ADVANCE

PRAEGER SCHOLARLY REPRINTS

Source Books and Studies
in Russian and Soviet History

Harry Schwartz, *General Editor*

John Quincy Adams
JOHN QUINCY ADAMS IN RUSSIA

Albert J. Beveridge
THE RUSSIAN ADVANCE

Ivan Golovine
RUSSIA UNDER THE AUTOCRAT NICHOLAS THE FIRST

George Kennan
SIBERIA AND THE EXILE SYSTEM

Johann G. Kohl
RUSSIA: St. Petersburg, Moscow, Kharkoff, Riga . . .
and the Interior of the Empire

Sir Donald Mackenzie Wallace
RUSSIA

THE RUSSIAN ADVANCE

BY

ALBERT J. BEVERIDGE

WITH MAPS

PRAEGER PUBLISHERS
New York • Washington • London

PRAEGER PUBLISHERS
111 Fourth Avenue, New York, N.Y. 10003, U.S.A.
5, Cromwell Place, London S.W.7, England

Published in the United States of America in 1970
by Praeger Publishers, Inc.

Library of Congress Catalog Card Number: 70–104916

Printed in the United States of America

INTRODUCTION

Albert J. Beveridge's THE RUSSIAN ADVANCE was paid one of its highest compliments recently, almost seventy years after its publication, when Professor Theodore van Laue wrote:

> [A] contemporary American might best approach Imperial Russia at the turn of the century by way of Indianapolis. . . . Indianapolis was the home of an up-and-coming member of the United States Senate, Albert J. Beveridge. . . . In 1901, two years after his election, Senator Beveridge crossed the Pacific to the Far East and traveled over the Siberian railroad, then in the last stages of completion, to St. Petersburg; he kept his eyes and ears wide open and made notes for a book that he published after his return, entitled *The Russian Advance.**

In these days of jet planes flying at 600 miles per hour, there is nothing exceptional about a U.S. senator's visiting Moscow. At the turn of the century, however, when the great distances involved had to be covered by relatively slow land and sea vehicles, a visit to Russia by any American was rare. Rarest of all was a trip such as Senator Beveridge's across the vast Eurasian sweep of the Czar's land. There had, of course, been American antecedents—for example, George Kennan's travels in the 1860's and

* Theodore van Laue, "Problems of Industrialization," in T. G. Stavrou, ed., *Russia Under the Last Tsar* (Minneapolis: University of Minnesota Press, 1969), p. 120.

1880's—but, even in 1901, this kind of tour was far from usual, especially when undertaken by a full-fledged voting member of the U.S. Senate.

At present, Senator Beveridge's book is of special interest for several important reasons. First, it gives the reaction of an intelligent and perceptive Midwestern American to the realities of Czarist Russia at the height of its power in 1901. Second, it provides an illuminating eyewitness picture of the situation in Russian-occupied Manchuria at the time. In these days of extreme Sino-Soviet tension, with speculation rampant about the possibility of a war between China and the Soviet Union, Senator Beveridge's observations on relations between Russia and China at the turn of the century are particularly relevant. Certainly no one can accuse Beveridge of being blind to Russia's imperialist strain of thought, to aspirations that have survived the transfer of power from the Romanovs to the Communist Czars. As Beveridge wrote, "To the Russian mind, China is to be Russian, Persia is to be Russian, India is to be Russian. It is Russian power which is to restore the cross to Jerusalem. It is Holy Russia that is to bring the authority of His faith to the lands where the Saviour of mankind walked and talked and was crucified." Soviet Russia does not talk in terms of bringing the cross to Jerusalem, but that nation's intense interest in extending its power throughout the Middle East is today clearer than ever.

Finally, of course, there must now be great interest in Beveridge's picture of Russia itself. Was there any other American in this period, one wonders, who had conversed at length with Tolstoy, Witte, and Pobedonostsev, whose very different personalities represented such different aspects of the Russian reality? Beveridge saw and understood many important facets of the Russian scene, facets with enormous consequences for that country's future. He saw the "lethargy" and "lack of initiative" of the ordinary Russian peasant and worker and predicted, correctly enough, that these qualities would have to be replaced by "popular practices distinctively and characteristically non-Russian." He saw the influence of collectivist forms and practices on Russian life and warned, "No student or observer of Russian character with whom this writer ever talked believes that the time will ever come when the Russian people will proceed upon anything but communistic lines either in their social living or in their industrial efforts." This passage was written when Lenin was unknown and a Russian Marxist a rare type indeed.

As a politician, Beveridge was both a populist in domestic affairs and a jingoist and imperialist in foreign affairs. These aspects of his political personality are neatly summed up in two slogans he formulated that achieved some currency: "Pass prosperity around" and "America first, and not only America first but America only." Readers of this book will see here his eagerness for the United States to step up its commercial penetration of Asia, and they will not be surprised that, as a senator, he supported a strong navy. To Beveridge—as to his close political associate Theodore Roosevelt—it seemed a truism that the United States had to create an American empire to compete with and ultimately, perhaps, replace the British Empire. Later in his career, Beveridge hotly opposed U.S. entrance into the League of Nations. Yet, simultaneously, Beveridge was a domestic progressive, drafting the federal meat-inspection law, leading the fight against child labor, opposing high tariffs and concentrations of industrial power, and supporting both public-utility regulation and conservation of national resources.

Albert Jeremiah Beveridge was born on a small farm in Highland County, Ohio. His family was quite poor, and Beveridge was forced to go to work when he was only twelve. However, his verbal ability made itself apparent early, and he was able to enter high school at age sixteen and college at nineteen. At what is now De-

Pauw University in Greencastle, Indiana, he financed much of his education with his winnings in oratorical contests. He subsequently practiced law and, in the 1880's and 1890's, made many speeches for the Republican Party. In 1899, at the youthful age of thirty-six, he won, first, the Republican nomination for senator from Indiana and, then, the election. He was reelected to the Senate in 1905, but, in 1911, he was defeated in his try for a third term.

After joining with Theodore Roosevelt to found the Progressive Party, Beveridge was the keynote speaker at its 1912 national convention, in Chicago. Although he ran for public office several times thereafter, he was never again elected. Frustrated as a politician, Beveridge turned, first, to journalism—he was a war correspondent in Germany in 1915—and, then, to scholarly writing. His biography of John Marshall won the very highest praise when its four volumes appeared—two in 1916 and two in 1919. When he died, on April 27, 1927, he had completed two volumes of a projected four-volume biography of Abraham Lincoln. The *New York Times* editorial writer, discussing the Marshall biography, declared:

> Those who watched his [Beveridge's] political as well as his extra-political achievement will remember with what incredulity many of his Republican and Democratic opponents regarded the first two volumes on their appearance in 1916. Nothing in his other books had prepared them for it. They had built up for themselves a legend of an impulsive, rhetorical Beveridge, lacking solidity, lacking judgment.

But those who had conjured up this image had obviously never read THE RUSSIAN ADVANCE, whose permanent importance is attested to by the fact that ample interest in it still endures to justify its being reprinted here.

HARRY SCHWARTZ

THE RUSSIAN ADVANCE

BY

ALBERT J. BEVERIDGE

WITH MAPS

NEW YORK AND LONDON
HARPER & BROTHERS PUBLISHERS
1904

Published November, 1903.

CONTENTS

CHAP		PAGE
I.	Russia on the Pacific	1
II.	Russian Empire-Building in Manchuria	16
III.	Other Methods of Russian Advance	33
IV.	Types of Civil Agents of the Russian Advance	48
V.	The Overlords of the Czar's Advancing Power in the Far East	57
VI.	Results of Russian Railway Advance	68
VII.	Manchurian Railway Results and Methods	81
VIII.	A Diplomatic Game for an Empire	93
IX.	How Russia at Last Reached the Unfrozen Sea	110
X.	Collision of Russia's Advance with Japan	122
XI.	The Soldier of the Russian Advance and the Soldier of Japan	138
XII.	The Russian Advance Paralleled by the German Advance	152
XIII.	A Chapter of Digression: American Needs in the Orient	173
XIV.	A Second Chapter of Digression: American Progress in the Far East	187
XV.	Siberia: The Highway of Russian Advance	208
XVI.	High and Low Water Marks of Siberian Progress	224
XVII.	The Red Day of Blagovestchensk	242
XVIII.	Russian Capital and Labor	254
XIX.	The Russian Working-man	272
XX.	The Labor Laws of Russia	285

CONTENTS

CHAP.		PAGE
XXI.	The Independent Peasant Artisan	302
XXII.	February 19, 1861, the Birthday of Russian Industrial Freedom	319
XXIII.	Holy Russia, the Orthodox Nation	338
XXIV.	Priest, People, and Church	354
XXV.	Russian National Ideals	367
XXVI.	Russian Points of View—Russian Opinions of American Institutions	385
XXVII.	Things Casually Observed	401
XXVIII.	The Russian Common School and Country Hospital	416
XXIX.	Three Russians of World Fame	426

APPENDIX

Treaty of Shimonoseki, by which Southern Manchuria was Ceded to Japan	463
Mikado's Rescript Withdrawing from Manchuria	468
The (Reputed) Cassini Convention	469
The Russo-Manchurian Railway Agreement	473
Anglo-Russian Agreement Respecting Spheres of Influence in China	481
Treaty of Offensive and Defensive Alliance between Great Britain and Japan	482
Specimen of the Regulations concerning Foreign Joint Stock Companies Operating in Russia	483

MAPS

Historic Russian Advance	*Facing p.*	1
Russia, and the Remainder of Europe and Asia	"	367

PREFACE

ON the author's return from a journey made in 1901 through Manchuria and the Far East, preceded by a visit to Russia and Siberia, a series of articles was published in the *Saturday Evening Post*, of Philadelphia, setting out things seen and observed in the regions of Russia's latest Asiatic advance.

A description was also given of the apparent situation of China as affected by the operations there of two or three European nations; and what then seemed to be the probable conflict between Russia and Japan was particularly pointed out, with the causes of it.

These articles form a considerable portion of this volume; and, indeed, the seeming advisability of their publication in book form, and certain requests therefor, are the occasion and apology for this work. They are reproduced practically without change.

It was believed that a more comprehensive understanding of the whole subject might be given if other chapters were added briefly describing Siberia and certain conditions and tendencies in Russia itself. These form the remainder of the book.

It has been the earnest endeavor to treat the subject with impartiality. Indeed, nothing has been essayed except to give the reader a faithful report of what any inquiring traveller may see and hear for himself if he should take the same journey.

ALBERT J. BEVERIDGE.

INDIANAPOLIS,
October 1, 1903.

THE RUSSIAN ADVANCE

ARCTI
SPITZBERGEN
BARENTS SEA
NOVA ZEMBLA
KARA SEA
C.Sterligov
GULF OF OB OR OBI
Khatan
Borodino
Dudinsk
Turukhansk
Yenisei R.
Varanger Fiord
Kolguev I.
C.Kanin
KARA STRAIT
Pustosersk
Obdorsk
WHITE SEA
Mezen
Tornea
Uleaborg
Kem
ARCHANGEL
Berezov
Onega
L. Onega
Vasa
Surgut
Abo
ST. PETERSBURG
Revel
Riga
Novgorod
Tobolsk
Narym
Yenisei
RUSSIA
MOSCOW
Perm
Ural Mts.
Ob R.
Omsk
Tomsk
Vilna
Kaluga
Kursk
Warsaw
Volga R.
Orenburg
Saratov
Kiev
Ural R.
Sergiopol
L. BALKASH
AUSTRIA-HUNGARY
Odessa
Azov
Astrakhan
ARAL SEA
Urumtsi
CASPIAN SEA
Turkestan
BLACK SEA
CONSTANTINOPLE
KHIVA
Tashkend
CHI
Batum
Baku
Krsnovodsk
BOKHARA
TURKEY
Smyrna
ATHENS
Lar
AFGHANISTAN
TEHERAN
MEDITERRANEAN SEA
PERSIA
EMP
Himalaya Mts.
Nepal
Bhotan
Bushire
PERSIAN GULF
ARABIA
INDIA
AFRICA
RED SEA
ARABIAN SEA
Calcutta
BORMAY & CO., N. Y.

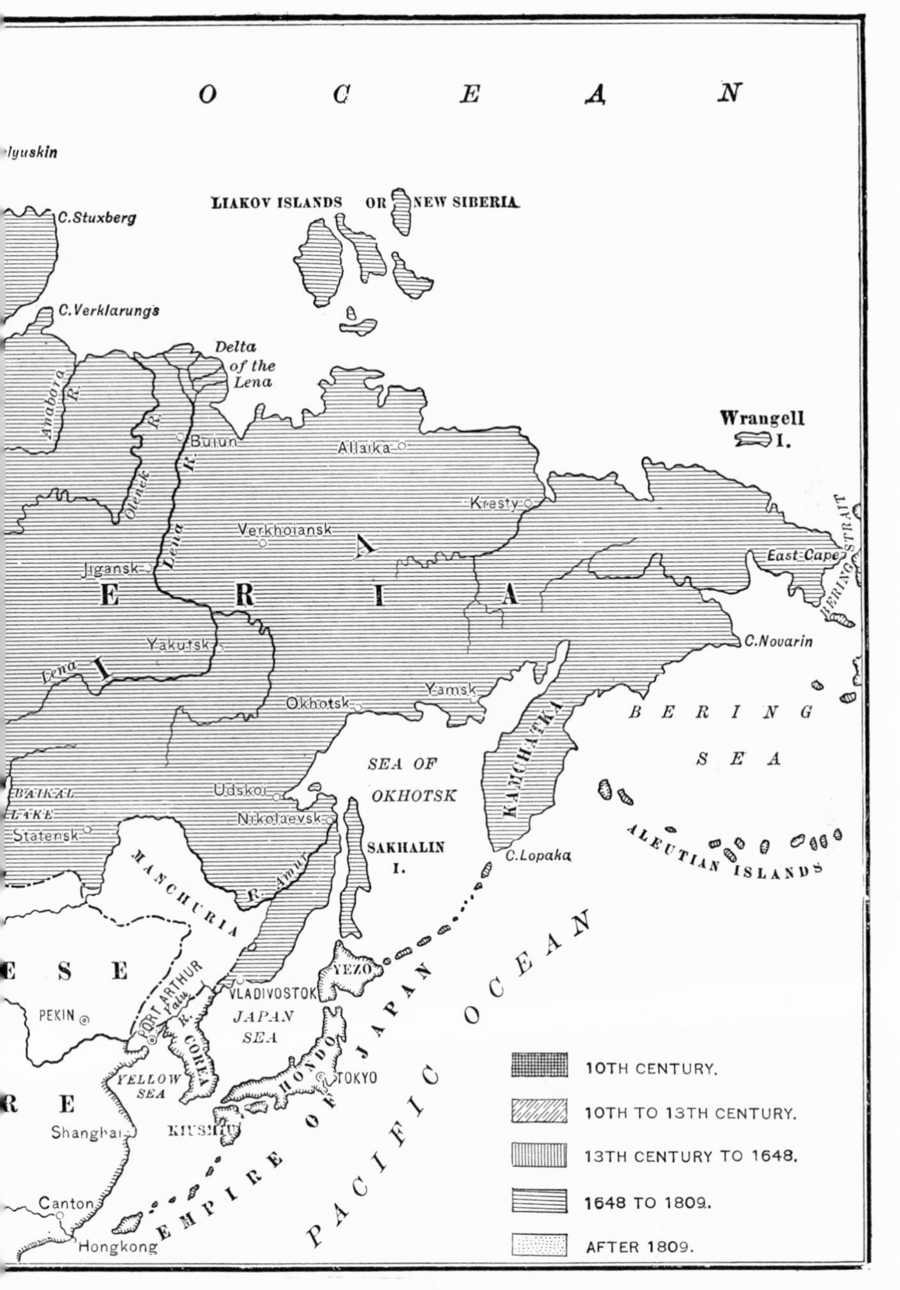

HISTORIC RUSSIAN ADVANCE

THE RUSSIAN ADVANCE

I

RUSSIA ON THE PACIFIC

THE Russian has arrived on the Pacific. For decades, of course, the world has been dimly conscious of a gray-clad, militant figure standing on the frozen shores of that ocean. But while gigantic in its proportions, its outlines were vague and indefinite. Surrounded by arctic fogs, it was apparently nothing more than a maritime sentinel of the ice-imprisoned harbors of the Czar. Only England, with inherited apprehension, gave much attention to the apparition, and even England's attention amounted to nothing more than instinctive fear. Occasionally, it is true, far-sighted thinkers divined the real significance of the Russian on the north seas, but their interpretation of the phenomenon fell on ears deaf to their message. The world, and especially the American people, went on without a thought of the spectre which, after the first surprise at its appearance, became a mere commonplace, without meaning or interest.

But within the last five years the Russian's presence upon the Pacific has claimed the acute attention of every cabinet in Europe and of every thoughtful American citizen; for he is now manifest on the Asiatic shores of that ocean in other guise than that of the uniformed bayonet - bearer of the Czar. He is there as Russian soldier and officer, it is true, and in portentous numbers and power. He is there on the merchant vessels of one of the great ship-lines of the world. More important still, he is there as the builder and operator of modern railways. Still more important, he is there as the actual administrator of dominions so vast that they may of themselves be called an empire. Most important of all, he is there as the Russian peasant; and that means that he has arrived in the form of the Russian people themselves.

In the summer of 1901, a single ship of the "Russian Volunteer Fleet," which the writer inspected at Port Arthur, Russia's Manchurian stronghold on the ice-free sea, had landed at another port 1500 Russian peasants. These were but a single shipment from the congested agricultural districts of southern Russia to such destination in eastern Asia as the statesmen of the empire thought advisable.[1] And these agricultural peasants came with their wives and their children, their beds and their furniture, their tools and their implements. Severed from the land of their birth and the ancient tombs of their ancestors by thousands of miles of ocean, they had all the appearance of men and women determined and equipped to plant permanently new seeds of Slav empire on the fresh fields of the extending Russian dominions.

The agriculturalist and the artisan, the husband and the wife, the mother and the daughter, young men and young women, boys and girls, babes new-born, were following so closely upon Russian military advance that the world hardly noticed it. So swiftly was the humble hut of the Russian peasant constructed beneath the shadow of the newly unfurled Russian flag that even the keenest statesman lost sight of this permanent and meaningful fact in his amazement at the planting of that flag itself. No one but diplomats and statesmen, who must deal with temporary situations, need be deeply concerned

[1] These peasants were not sent into Manchuria, of course; they were settled in the Ussuri littoral back of Vladivostock, and practically on the Manchurian frontier.

with the purely military advance of any nation, but when a people move forward it is a circumstance of world-wide significance and it is of especial and practical concern to every people upon whose interests that advance impinges or whose future in any direction that advance affects.

Three Russian war-ships lay in the beautiful harbor of Nagasaki, Japan, in the late summer of 1899. "Oh yes; we are getting used to that," said an English merchant, whose attention was called to the Russian colors. And it was natural enough, for Nagasaki is a coaling-station, and very convenient for many purposes. But in 1901 the sea-flag of the Czar floated from a ship in the roadstead from which the Woosung River leads up to Shanghai, the commercial clearing-house of China.

"Ten years ago that flag was seldom—in fact, hardly ever—seen in these waters." Again it was an English merchant who spoke, and a man who had spent his entire life since boyhood in commercial enterprises in the Far East. "It is a multiplying circumstance," he went on, "and it has its counterpart right here among our business houses. The most active, aggressive financial institution in Shanghai to-day is the branch at this place of the Russo-Chinese Bank. It is not yet so great as some of our other banks, but is making itself felt very effectively. Decidedly, Russia, which formerly was a subject of speculative conversation, is getting on our nerves in a very tangible and irritating way."

In Yokohama, five years ago, the only representative of the Autocrat of all the Russias was the Russian consul; yet in 1901 the Russo-Chinese Bank had been established, and was already doing a considerable business there. Not only so, but the ground had already been purchased, the plans of the architect drawn on his blue-prints, and the foundations laid for a building of this financial corporation. And this building, it was said, was to be by far the finest and most costly of all the banking establishments in this principal port of the Mikado's Empire.

"What—not in Hong-Kong, and already?" exclaimed an American traveller when told by an officer of a certain banking corporation of the Far East that the Russo-Chinese Bank had established a temporary agency in some little offices in Hong-Kong itself; for Hong-Kong is purely English. Moreover, it is in the extreme south of China; and here, amid surroundings of tropical beauty, and in the very centre of foreign commercial activities in the Orient, beats the heart of British influence in the Chinese Far East. It appeared too audacious for belief that the financial arm of the Russian government should so soon invade Hong-Kong; for the Russo-Chinese Bank was not in existence even in Russia itself five years before.

"Yes, even here in Hong-Kong, and at this early hour," repeated the English banker, "the Russo-Chinese Bank is doing business right before our very eyes; and while as yet it does not do much business or attract much attention, nevertheless it is here!" Still this branch of the Russo-Chinese Bank is competing for business, and, if reports be credited, getting it. But Hong-Kong's great British banks have nothing to fear from this Russian competition.

So the Russian advance is a commercial and financial movement; from Gibraltar-like Vladivostock, on the north, all along the shores of the Pacific, into the very citadel of English power on China's extreme south. It is a diplomatic advance, too, throughout every province of the Flowery Kingdom as well as on the Chinese seaboard. It is an advance by merchant vessels and war-ships from Odessa to Port Arthur; by railways through Manchuria even to the gates of Pekin; by Russian peasantry, cultivated farms, and permanent homes over the rich grain-fields of the Ussuri littoral, and even within the borders of Manchuria; by towns and cities and all the activities of peace into the very centre of Manchuria, which until this very moment the world's wisest statesmen have insisted and believed, though with the faith of fear, was permanently Chinese territory. And this advance, the methods of it, the people who are making it, their nature, characteristics, and development, are to-day, and for decades to come will continue to be, the most engaging subject of observation to the student of the movement of races which the contemporary world affords, as well as the most insistent and important foreign problem with which European and American statesmen must henceforth deal.

Let us, then, consider the phenomenon itself, and afterwards look somewhat into its sources. Let us, first of all, observe the Russian at work in Manchuria. Let us look upon his actual deeds and achievements there. Let us see him in the visible and material work of Russian empire-building within a new dominion. Then let us follow, as well as we can, the rough outlines of his Oriental statesmanship and policy—as well as we can, because it is not possible for any one to know with minute accuracy the processes of statecraft by which the Russian prepares the way for his subtle, and yet solid and masterful, advance. Then let us note the tangible effects of his activities upon the other great powers now making themselves felt in a physical way in the Orient. And then let us hark back on the mighty trail the Slav has made across Siberia, enter his hitherto suffocating, though vast, original home, and observe him in the fields, villages, and factories of Russia itself.

First, then, of Manchuria. Within the last two years everybody has heard of Manchuria. Even before that time the popular mind had a vague idea that something or other of more or less importance was going on in Manchuria. Later the American man in the furrow and in the shop learned that the Russians were building a railway in Manchuria. Recently our newspapers and magazines have been filled with editorials and articles on our diplomacy as it affects Manchuria. But just what Manchuria is, just where it is, and just what is being done there which is creating this world-wide curiosity, are not generally known. Even the few students who have some general understanding of the events transpiring there are not accurately informed of them.

The modern scientific method, first developed in the German universities and now adopted by all great institutions of learning, rejects the more or less imaginary accounts of what used to be considered the world's historians, and requires the student himself personally to examine original manuscripts, delve into archives, and write anew, from first-hand investigation, corrected chronicles of the past. This method not only sends archæologists to uncover the hidden cities of antiquity and replace with a description of real discoveries the legends of them handed down through generations, but in our own country the student of the germ of our government—the New England town-meeting—is no longer satisfied with inaccurate accounts of the old writers; he must go to the interior of some New England State where the town-meeting may still be seen, and, observing its workings with the naked eye and absorbing its spirit by actual contact, describe the facts as they are, and, after having learned the truth, to state it, and then, and not till then, deduce his conclusions. If this is the true method of studying the institutions of by-gone centuries, of course it is much more the true method of observing the weighty occurrences of the present day.

It is with something of this spirit—though, of course, without any pretension to the thoroughness and accuracy required by the modern scientific method — that the following observations on the Russian advance in the Far East, and particularly Russia's operations in Manchuria, have been made and are here set down.

What is Manchuria, and what are the Russians doing there? In answer to the first part of the question, more or less accurate accounts are already in existence; but in answer to the second part of the question, no one who is not a Russian has up to the present time made original investigations with a free hand. It is claimed by some that no opportunity has existed; and Manchuria certainly was "closed" to the world during the Russian operations in settling the disturbed conditions following the Boxer insurrection. While you may now board a vestibuled train of sleeping-cars at Port Arthur and go directly through the centre of Manchuria into Siberia and on to Moscow without change, no one even now appears to have attempted to do more, and it is declared that no one has been permitted to do more.

An English officer, as we are informed, who attempted to make such investigations, upon taking an independent excursion into the country, was arrested by the authorities and sent over the frontier. Several accounts have been given of the great difficulty in penetrating Manchuria before the road was "opened" to passengers; but it is believed that proper measures were not taken in advance to assure freedom of observation. Certainly the writer experienced no such difficulty, and on a frank statement to the proper minister in St. Petersburg, was accorded unqualified and absolute liberty to see what was to be seen, and to hear what was being said within Manchuria itself. So far as could be detected, no seal was put upon the lips of any one, from Chinese railroad laborer up to the highest representative of the Czar. Absolutely no restrictions of any kind were imposed. No guards of Cossacks or other soldiery were even suggested; the authorities advised no particular route of travel, and neither offered nor refused any aid. Not a single obstacle was thrown in the way. No excuses or evasions were made. With as full liberty as is accorded a foreigner on a tour of observation throughout the United States, the journey through Manchuria, of which these pages are the imperfect narrative, was made during the year 1901.

Let us see, then, where Manchuria is, how big it is, and what kind of a country it is.

If you will take Germany and France together, you will have a territory scarcely larger than the three great Chinese provinces combined under the general term Manchuria.

England, Scotland, Ireland, and Wales are not one-third so large as Manchuria.

If you will take Indiana, Illinois, and Iowa, their combined area is less than half that of Manchuria.

Pennsylvania, New York, New Jersey, and all New England are less than one-half the size of Manchuria, and no richer in resources.

We thus see that Manchuria is, in territorial extent, itself an empire. It is an empire more favorably situated as to its climatic conditions than any part of Asia. It is in the same latitude as southern Canada and the northern portion of the United States. Its northern limits are about the same as the northern limits of Quebec. Its southern limits are about the same as the southern limits of Maryland. It is bounded on the north by the richest portions of Siberia, which not many years ago was itself a part of the dominion of the Manchus; for several hundred miles on the east by the grain-fields of the Ussuri district of Russian Siberia, also until recently a part of the Chinese Empire; on the east and south by Korea, over which the world's next great war will probably be fought, and soon; on the west by Mongolia, and on the south by Korea, China, and the gulfs and extensions of the Yellow Sea, which touches or commands much of that empire. On these gulfs are two of the finest military and commercial ports of Asia, or the world—Port Arthur and Talienhwan, or, as the Russians call it, Dalni.

This enormous territory is fertilized by rivers running generally both north and south. Portions of the valleys of these rivers and the plains beyond the valleys are as fertile as those of the Sangamon in Illinois or the Miami in Ohio. Mountains traverse the northwest and southwest, and again the northeastern portion of this great region. The northern mountains are rich in gold, possibly richer than the gold-fields of that portion of Siberia which is just across the river from them, and of the wealth of which the world at large seems to be in ignorance. The mountains to the southeast and south are said to be rich in iron and coal. The coal now being turned out in quantities at Shanhaikwan, just beyond the southwestern borders of Manchuria and directly on the Gulf of Liao-Toung, is equal for all purposes to the coal produced in the United States.

Here, then, is an empire capable of sustaining fifty millions of people, and with scarcely more than fifteen million inhabitants at present; an empire with two of the best ports in the world for commercial and military purposes, with coal of a high quality immediately at hand; an empire which, in its strategic situation on the Pacific and in all Oriental affairs is second only to the commanding position of Japan itself.

And all over this territory Russia has spread her tangible influence in less than seven years, with the loss of scarcely a man, and the expenditure of hardly a dollar outside of her investment in railways and fortifications. Indeed, it may be accepted as a settled fact that Russia has already acquired Manchuria, if she concludes to remain there, although it is still nominally Chinese, and not Russian, and its governors are still appointed by the Chinese Emperor. For, no matter what treaties say, no matter what may be the statements of diplomacy regarding Manchuria, the fact exists that its fate is practically in the hands of Russia. It may continue as a province of China; but, if so, it will be of Russia's grace and not of Russia's necessity. Its ports may remain open to the trade of the world; but if they do, it will not be because of the limitations of Russia's power, but as a matter of Russia's policy.

For Russia, for all practical purposes, holds every foot of Manchuria in her firm, masterful, intelligent grasp.

Russian law, in the sense that all shall have justice regularly administered; Russian order, in the sense that murder and outrage by robber bands and savage clans shall cease; Russian system, in the sense that regularity and method shall succeed continuous social, political, and commercial disturbance — Russian law, order, and system, as thus understood, are there, and, it appears to the observer, are there forever. Chinese law still exists in Manchuria; but it is now promptly and impartially administered. Forever is a long time; but it is not extravagant to use the word with reference to Russia in Manchuria, because it is a fact, to which attention will be hereafter given, that Russia has seldom, if ever, permanently retreated from any spot where her authority has been established, except Alaska, which she believed she was selling to a permanently friendly nation. But whether she remains or departs will be a sheer question of what she wants to do, and not a question of what she must do. Even temporary evacuation will mean little as to her ultimate purposes; for she will leave behind her foundations of permanent occupation, to which at any time she can return. An achievement so vast, so quietly accomplished, so cheaply secured, so easily consummated, so important in itself, and so beyond calculation in its influence upon the rest of the world, compels the admiration of every thinking mind, no matter whether you regret or whether you applaud while you admire.

The methods by which it was accomplished are as engaging as they are instructive. Their interest to an American will increase to appreciation when he reflects that for the Philippines we paid twenty million dollars before beginning our occupation of the islands, and have expended hundreds of lives and many millions of dollars since then. To the Englishman, the story of Russian expansion in Manchuria should teach something more than mere inflammatory protest, when he reflects on his decades of blunder — bloody and costly blunder — in learning the lessons of colonial government in India. To the German, with his declared policy of *Drang nach Osten*, and the development of the German mixed military-commercial-diplomatic programme in Asia, the process of the Russianization of Manchuria should be most valuable. To the student of human progress everywhere something will be presented of greater moment than the story of the civilizing movements of races in the past; because here is the historic movement of a race in the present. And, to the American farmer, to the American manufacturer, to the American producer of every class to whom the hard and practical consideration of where to sell his goods has become, and will more and more become, the pressing problem, the recent occurrences in Manchuria are of immediate importance.

In investigations of this kind, quite as much as in the scientific examination of any subject, we must reason back from the smaller facts to the larger ones, and from all of them to general principles. The Baconian system of induction is the only scientific method of thought in the science of States as well as in the science of matter. Let us, then, begin with the small and apparently incidental observations of a journey.

First of all, for hundreds of miles along the northern border of Manchuria not a Chinaman was visible two years ago. Three years ago, Chinese villages, though not numerous, nevertheless existed on the southern bank of the Amur. To-day, not one can be seen, and even the ruins of only one can be detected along the banks of that great but vexatious waterway of northern Asia. But the Cossack is there. He is not there in large numbers. The Cossack is never in any place in large numbers. One Cossack is as valuable for thrusting forward the boundaries of Russian dominion as a hundred ordinary soldiers; and yet the Russian ordinary soldier is superb.

But the Cossack has inherited from father to son, through generations running back for hundreds of years, the instinct of the frontier. He knows intuitively how to inspire with fear or affection the senile or savage tribes with which his ancestors have for centuries been coming in contact. He impregnates the very atmosphere with the authority of Russia. And so not many of him are necessary, and not many of him are used along these interminable stretches of frontier which he sentinels and safeguards. Sometimes you will see him standing alone, silently gazing at you from the Chinese shore.

Sometimes you will see him with two or three comrades. At two points only in many days' journey will you find a larger number of him than half a dozen at one single place. One of these spots is opposite Blagovestchensk, where, in 1901, a hundred Cossacks were encamped; another is near Aigun, ten miles down the river, where barracks have been erected on the Manchurian shore, as the general headquarters of the entire military of that region. Without further than noting that the northern frontier of Manchuria is patrolled by Cossacks, let us pass this most dramatic figure of Russia for the present, in order to observe him more adequately hereafter.

Though Russia's natural and most employed road into Manchuria is by the Sungari River, navigable for hundreds of miles from the Amur into the interior, the real door to Manchuria is Nikolsk, the centre of the grainfields to the north of Vladivostock. It is over fifty miles from the Manchurian frontier, but it is the point where the Vladivostock branch of the Manchurian railroad joins the Ussuri railroad into Vladivostock. You will find American ploughs, reapers, and threshing-machines for sale in Nikolsk. It is the local commercial centre of the district. It is the rendezvous for immense military forces, and it was the general administrative headquarters of the great Manchurian railway, under construction when the author made the journey through Manchuria, and now completed.

"Yes," said an intelligent Russian commercial man, referring to the prairies north of Vladivostock, "these fields were all once occupied by Chinamen; but now, as you see, they are as fully occupied by the Russian peasant, his wife and children, as if this land had always been a part of Russia. That has not been so very long ago, either. It is quite impossible to explain the retirement of the Chinese. There was no friction between the people and the Russian peasant."

This singular fact, which repeats itself in many different phases, is one of the most significant truths in the peculiar progress of Russian expansion—"never any friction between the Russian and the native." The Russian moujik, stupid and ignorant man and ruinous agriculturist as he is, yet wins his fields from man and nature by two invariable qualities—his fixedness to the soil and the stolidity of his good-nature.

The merchant who pointed out the fact of the disappearance of the Chinaman and the appearance of the Russian agricultural peasant throughout the grain district surrounding Nikolsk was a German. That is a fact which has nothing to do with the Russian problem we are examining, but a great deal to do with the general situation of the Orient and the world. It is a fact to which the American business man must give almost, if not quite, as great attention as to the steady advance of Russian influence over the only remaining unexploited markets of the world—the markets of China. The principal merchants of Nikolsk are German; the principal merchants of Vladivostock are German; the principal merchants of Blagovestchensk are German. In the heart of Manchuria, the manager of one of the commercial establishments which supplies the railroad with provisions of every kind was a young German, twenty-four years of age, handsome in appearance, American in alertness, brilliant in speech, encyclopædically informed. These are no accidental illustrations. All over the Orient they exist; all over Siberia they exist; all over the world they exist. It is sufficient for the moment to glance at this commercial phenomenon as we pass, that we may return to it with the seriousness its importance deserves when we reach it later.

About Nikolsk are military barracks and storehouses. Whatever you think of the policy and character you cannot but respect the power and strategical far-sightedness of the men who erected on this spot the tremendous and substantial military buildings that exist there. From Nikolsk, Russia can pour her warriors into Manchuria, Korea, Japan, with almost equal facility. At Nikolsk Russia's martial thousands can be fed more easily than elsewhere in her Far Eastern dominions. And so Nikolsk is full of barracks. And these barracks are full of soldiers.

And these soldiers are drilling, drilling, always drilling. Drilling, that is, when they are not on active duty. You may drive to one side of the city until you emerge upon a great open, surrounded by barracks and arsenals, and on every side there is preparation — practice. From one building come the strains of music of a military band—it is practising. From another a company of white-capped soldiers are issuing and falling into line—they are practising. Yonder comes the artillery with all the haste of battle—it is practising. Scatter and skirmish line, close order for cavalry attack, sudden whirl from one position to another—all the evolutions of actual fight are before your eyes.

But where is that stern secrecy, that black and forbidding hand which thrusts the observer from out her gates or blindfolds him while he remains inside, which the Anglo-Saxon world has been taught to associate with Russia and all things Russian? You have asked no permission to drive upon this field of Mars. You have shown no permit. Yet your appearance is taken quite as a matter of course. Officers attend to their martial duties without appearing even to notice you. No frowning policeman asks your business. No polite messenger requests you to retire. Observe to your full; make notes to your full; the Russian bear is very clearly asleep.

But to find out whether he is really asleep is more valuable even than the privilege of undisturbed observation. Let the interpreter take a pocket-camera and try to photograph them; surely that will be forbidden. But they do not appear to notice him. Go up to an officer now, call his attention to the fact that you have a camera, and that you would like to photograph these warlike manœuvres, these throngs of soldiers, these barracks, this astonishing permanent camp. With a pleasant smile he tells you to photograph what you please and as much as you please, and the illusion of the black and forbidding hand begins to fade. The bear is not sleeping then; so far as this incident reveals him, he is merely a very good-natured, a very sensible, and a very powerful creature, whose consciousness of his power makes him welcome your observations, and smile at your criticism and the world's.

There must be a meaning in all this. But, if you ask what that meaning is—if you ask why all these preparations, why these storehouses, why these drilling hosts—you must again look at the map of the Far East and write across the whole of it the words of Washington, "To be prepared for war is one of the most effectual means of preserving peace," and then reflect that, perhaps, the same thought has occurred to Russian statesmen, too. Yes, study the map of Asia, and run back over Russia's far-sighted and patient policy, which has always looked ahead and considered the needs of the Russian people a century beyond the immediate moment, and perhaps an explanation will spring from these combined considerations.

II

RUSSIAN EMPIRE-BUILDING IN MANCHURIA

STRANGE companies were they that, during the summer of 1901, proceeded daily from Nikolsk towards the Manchurian frontier; strange companies that, during the same period and for three or four years before, floated down the broad and treacherous Amur. But that is another tale. Going into Manchuria from Nikolsk, the observer might, any day during the summer of 1901, have witnessed Russian soldiers, of course—not in troops or companies, but in twos and threes, or in little clumps of a dozen, perhaps; Russian officers, of course; here and there a Chinaman; and, most significant of all, and perhaps most numerous of all, the wiry-framed, contemptible-looking Koreans.

And you are struck by the fact (nay, if you be Anglo-Saxon, you are startled by it) that all of this mingled motley of humanity get along in perfect harmony. The bronzed Korean, the queued Chinaman, and the blue-eyed, yellow-haired Russian soldier arrange themselves on an open flat-car in a human mosaic of mutual agreeableness. There is no race prejudice here then! Superior to all the world, as the Russian believes himself, he shows no offensive manner towards the other races with which he so picturesquely mingles. It is a thing you must have noticed up in Siberia, where the Russian peasant is also coming in contact with semi-Oriental peoples. But, with the blood of racial bigotry coursing through your veins, here this social fusion of races startles you. It is a strange page suddenly opened before you.

And it is a page you will read again and again every day as long as you are in Manchuria. And from a reading of it a lesson may be learned, and part of Russia's secret of dominion revealed.

Grodekoff is the name of the pleasant little Russian town which stands at the frontier of Manchuria, so styled in honor of the Governor-General. Its streets are broad —broad as the streets of an American frontier town. Its surveying is regular—regular again as that of an American town. Common features, these, of Russian towns with American towns. But for the speech of the people, the white-uniformed officers, and the touch of Orientalism which every cottage suggests, a town of Russia or Siberia might be an American town; and this is repeated on the borders of Manchuria. Civilization, then, is pushing forward by forced marches into northern Asia. You can see that easily enough; for here, at the gates of Manchuria, near a region which ten years ago was the haunt of robbers, are a modern town, modern commerce, modern order, and that modern safety which comes from regular laws regularly enforced. The word enforced may be repeated, for, with all his defects, and he has many of them, the Slav administers his laws. He does not administer them brutally, as is supposed, nor even sternly, except when he must.

For example, under the electric lights of the railway station at Grodekoff two Chinamen were fighting fiercely. Chinamen are very quick in wrath, and fights among them are frequent. The Russian soldier acting as policeman did not separate them with bayonet, did not use a club, or even a whip. He sprang forward, and, with his open hand, slapped one of the Chinamen on the cheek, whirling the other one with his other hand away from his fellow-combatant. That was all. It was the prompt stopping of a row that might have ended in a riot. In Hong-Kong or other English-governed portions of China a cane on the back of a Chinese jinrikisha man who insists on what is thought too large a fee is a common occurrence. On a first visit to the Orient, five years ago, one of the first European business men of the Far East, in the presence of ladies, was seen caning a clump of Chinese jinrikisha men who had irritated him by clamoring for his patronage.

But inside Manchuria we shall surely see deeds of real cruelty, for we all know that Russia is establishing her authority there. And is it not the understanding of every one that Russia plants her power in the soil of desolation and fertilizes it with blood? She is successful, however, all will admit; and, since she is gradually extending her control over the future unoccupied markets of the world, it is interesting to observe the processes by which she advances her influence.

There are large numbers, and of various nationalities, on the construction-train which through the night creeps towards the Manchurian frontier, but a few miles away. You do not understand this, for has not every one heard that Manchuria was "closed" to the world during the period of railroad building and military settlement, of insurrection and disturbed conditions generally? Still, nobody has been put off the train as yet. To be sure, scores of Chinamen are doing work on the railway, and the other scores of Koreans appear to go where they wish within the limits of Russian authority. All these, you are informed, are being conveyed thither for particular purposes.

But there are other people on that train, too. Three men, very well dressed, of some foreign nationality, but certainly not Russian, attract your attention. There are several women, too. To be sure, all these are sitting on the railway material piled on the flat-cars; but, nevertheless, they appear to be going right into Manchuria. So this forbidden land does not seem to be so very much "closed" after all. But the train stops at a point where there is a single station building; high hills, which in the moonlight seem mountainous, are on every hand. At this point you find out how much Manchuria was "closed" during 1901; for every human being not especially authorized to proceed is ordered from every car. The protestations of the well-dressed, non-Russian foreigners fall on deaf ears. The pleas of the women, emphasized by their tears, are utterly unheeded. Off they go, and there in the night, without shelter, they are left. They should have remained at Grodekoff. But they took their chances of passing unobserved in the large throng through the gates of Manchuria, and they must suffer the consequences.

Men who were apparently foremen of the Chinese seem to be marshalling their groups of men and answering for them. Others do the same for the Russian peasant workmen. The soldiers pass, as a matter of course. But every one else is ejected in a very business-like and very rough, perhaps though not unkind, manner. Upon the refusal of one person to get off, he is peremptorily thrown off by a Cossack. Another person had hidden himself in one of a pile of great drainage-pipes with which a certain car was loaded. He was located by a soldier who was engaged in finding just such stowaways by thrusting his gun, with bayonet fixed, into every one of those drainage-pipes. Clearly, the Russians did not intend to take any chances on having their work in Manchuria disturbed by unknown persons going into that land at a time when they were settling its disturbed conditions and constructing their great steel highway.

And when you reflect upon the reign of terror which the Boxer uprising had spread all over Manchuria, and the difficulty which had thus been caused the Russians, your disapproval of this policy of "closing Manchuria to the world" was softened. They could hardly be blamed for taking every precaution to prevent the agents of those who wished to stir up further disorder from entering the very region where the Russians were bending every energy to restore order, and restore it permanently.

This incident, however, does not diminish your apprehensions as to what you will see in Manchuria.

But, in spite of your sanguinary expectations, the first thing that strikes you in the first beautiful valley through which you go, after you enter Manchuria, is cultivated fields and peaceful people. In China itself you will not observe greater liberty of action among an industrious population. As a matter of fact, the Chinamen who have returned to their fields are enjoying a peace and undisturbedness of industry never heard of before in this part of Manchuria.

Chinese towns are organized filthiness. They are quite impossible of description. The streets are rambling and sickening; in rainy weather they are miry, with a slime compounded from all the elements that might offend both sight and smell. You see mixtures being made on the soil in front of Chinese shops and stores in the ordinary Chinese commercial town (not in the great cities, although these are hideous enough, as the ordinary traveller will tell you, nor yet in mere rural villages) which will nauseate you if you do not pass by rapidly. The shops are poor structures of wood and earth; the homes themselves are of mud. This is the kind of town you will see all over Manchuria, and this the town you will see all over China.

But side by side with it in Manchuria you will behold something that you did not see in China—something so surprising that it seems almost unreal. And, indeed, it is a miracle—a modern European town planted adjacent to the congeries of hovels which comprise the Chinese towns just described. Brick buildings of substantial construction and not uninviting architecture stand completed, and others are rising by their side. Broad streets, regularly laid out — not paved yet, of course, for the town itself is only building — but streets with gutters along the sides and with hard-beaten gravel covering convex surface, and in far better condition than the streets of most of the cities of modern Russia.

It may be that the attractiveness of the Russian towns in process of erection in Manchuria in 1901 was unduly magnified by the hideousness of the native villages reeking with offensiveness which stood by their side. It may be, too, that the newness of the Russian's handiwork added an element of charm not permanently belonging to it, or that the atmosphere of pioneer occupation and achievement deflected accurate and steady judgment; but one can only set down exactly what one sees at the time he sees it, and certain it is that Russian town-building in Manchuria in 1901 was a comfort and a delight to behold.

It is more than a hundred miles into Manchuria that you encounter this striking material evidence of the Russianization of the country—a Russian town being built side by side with the decaying, germ-infected collection of hovels which compose the Chinese town. The residences of this Russian town are of wood perhaps, or stone, as taste determines. They are pleasant to look upon, too. Indeed, the homes of merchant or miner or officer, or even of moujik in Siberia are often much handsomer than those ordinarily occupied by the same class in Russia; and it would seem that this comparative superiority is to be repeated in Manchuria. Generous verandas circle the home of a railway official; cool awnings of blue, shifting with the sun, protect these porches from its rays. Young trees are planted along the new-made streets. Occasionally a block is reserved for a miniature park; and, again, there are trees fresh planted, and the color and fragrance of flowers. This, in contrast, is the order, the loveliness, the system, the cleanliness which Russia in Manchuria is building over against Chinese aggregations of corruption, disease, disorder, and all unsightliness. If the Russian is uncivilized, as it has been the fashion to declare, at least in Manchuria he is erecting precisely those very things which, in America, we look upon as the results and proofs of civilization.

You go into the Chinese town and ask for food. It is there in abundance, but you will not eat it. There is nothing familiar, nothing appetizing, nothing that suggests the food products of America. But you will find a European restaurant in the Russian town, and there you may have what you like; quite as much, indeed, as you can get in an American town of ten times its size—bread made from American flour, American sugar-cured ham, American canned fruits from the Pacific coast, and so forth. If you will go up the street to the Russian store, you will find American salmon from the Columbia, American canned meats from the Central West, and American condensed milk and cream from Illinois.

Clearly, American trade in Manchuria does not, as yet, seem to have been injured by this Russian invasion. If conditions could only continue as to the American observer they presented themselves in 1901, none of us could find cause for commercial alarm at the sight of the Russian flag in Manchuria, for it appears to the investigator who has in mind America's commercial interests that, for the moment at least, American markets have been increased by the forward movement of the Muscovite in Asia. It does not accord with our former notion, of course, but there is the fact, and it is from facts that we must reason to theories, and not from theories that we must reason to facts. It is a fact—deceptive, perhaps, and misleading, maybe—but such as it is, it is there.

"Why should you be astonished at these signs of peaceful activity?" said a Russian officer. "Why, man! peaceful activity is what we are after. Our soldiers clear the way for our families; they create conditions which make roads possible, towns possible, commerce possible. We have our notion of civilization; we think it is as good as yours, and you must admit that in its external features it is very like your own. The soldier helps to make it for the people of Russia; the people of Russia do not make it for the soldier." And much more to the same meaningful purport. "And," he added, with a trace of bitterness, "we do not march up and down with torch and sword, slaying, pillaging, desolating. That is not our purpose. What good would that do us or anybody? And yet that is the story which animosity tells of us. We have been misrepresented so long that we are used to it and are silent before it."

It is not intended in this noting of Russian peaceful activities to minimize the soldier in Manchuria. He is there, and there in large numbers. He is there with his gun, with bayonet always fixed (it is a singular circumstance, and more typical of Russia than any one fact I can select, that the Russian bayonet is always fixed). But the Russian soldier is in Manchuria, not with rifle and sword only, but with shovel, and pickaxe, and adz, and all the implements of toil, as indeed is the case in Siberia and in Russia itself; for the Russian soldier is more of a laboring man, after all, than he is a military man. He digs and builds and plants far more than he fights. Russian soldiers were seen digging a drain on the grounds of the excellent museum which Grodekoff has erected at Khabaroff.

Yes, the soldier is there, and his bayonet is there, and the shot which means death is there. But though all these signs are present in Manchuria, they are, combined, but the single crimson thread of the fabric of empire which Russia is weaving throughout that mighty domain. The martial note is not dominant. The thud of axe in forest and thump of drill in quarry, the grating swish of the mixing mortar, the click of mason's trowel on bricks of rapidly rising walls, the drone of the saw, and the drum of hammer from one end of Manchuria to the other—these are the sounds which greet you.

Again and yet again you are impressed with this—the Russian soldier in Manchuria is a laboring man first and a military man afterwards. It is an item not to be overlooked—indeed, the Russian soldier must be most carefully considered by those who are estimating the forces influencing the world at present. No toil is too heavy for him; no hardship is to him a hardship at all. He will fell trees, excavate ditches, build houses with the same good-humor with which he will go into action where wounds and death are his sure reward.

In Manchuria there are three classes of the Russian soldier: the Cossack first, then the railway-guard, and then numbers of that host of which the Russian army is composed, the common soldier of the empire. The railway-guards are of first importance in this connection, because they are the second visible instrument of the Russianization of this dominion, the first visible instrument being, of course, the railway itself. But, having the railway, it becomes necessary to guard it, and that not for to-day or to-morrow, but so long as danger exists; and of the existence or probability of danger to her investment Russia herself, of course, will insist upon being the judge.

Therefore in Manchuria there are tens of thousands of railway-guards. In 1901 the railway-guards with which Russia was protecting her railway construction formed a military force of sixty thousand men. M. Leroy-Beaulieu estimated that there were this number in Manchuria early in 1900. In certain particulars they are picked men. To a man, they are large men physically; almost to a man, they are below thirty years of age. Man for man, they are of higher intelligence and greater ability than either Cossack or common soldier, and, without exception, share with Cossack and common soldier the characteristic Russian indifference to danger and death. All soldier, each of them, and yet all farmer, each of them, and, by the same token, men of all work at your service, are these permanent makers of empire. Every man of them who is married has his wife with him and his children and all his earthly possessions. Every man who is not married is thinking of getting married; and one cannot resist the feeling that in its unseen and tactful way the government is encouraging each bachelor guard who sentinels the railway in Manchuria to take to himself one of those round-cheeked, broad-backed, deep-breasted peasant girls of Russia.

The Russian women in the interior of Manchuria are wives of those hearty, wholesome-looking, bearded giants, the railway-guards. Even at the dangerous period, when the journey was taken which these chapters chronicle, and at points hundreds of versts in the interior, these women-mates of Russia's workingmen-soldiers were seen at the scarce-erected stations of the railroad which was then being constructed. They were there selling milk or melons or berries or quass (a non-intoxicating Russian drink made out of black bread or berries). So far have Russian and Siberian conditions reproduced themselves in Manchuria that the only difference observed at the railway-stations was the unfinished nature of the road and the increasing number of Koreans and Chinese.

For the Russian peasant is there, as he is in western Siberia, and the Russian peasant's wife is there, as she is in Siberia, and the little, white-haired children, with the pale-blue eye of the Slav, are there, as they are in Siberia; and, as in Siberia and Russia, the little girls from eight to twelve are universally carrying in their arms infant brothers and sisters of as many months or even weeks, for Russian children are being born in Manchuria. And a land where a people's dead are buried, where a people's children are born, becomes to that people sacred soil. Russian homes, not for railway official only, but for the "peasant guard," are springing up throughout Manchuria. Manchurian fields are being languidly cultivated by Russian hands. It is all quite "temporary," of course; you can read it for yourself in the treaty. And, besides, the railway-guard's term of enlistment—or, rather, his contract—is for only five years. But the Slav root strikes quickly into new soil, and having struck, history tells us that, usually, it stays.

And so it is that, gradually, naturally, physically, plausibly, with appearance of entire good faith (not that it is denied that it is good faith), the master-mind that has planned this extraordinary semi-conquest of territory has provided the elements of permanent occupation and unbreakable control, should that course later appear to be dictated by events. For your Russian statesman is a great consulter of events, and so is every public man who deserves that large title—statesman.

The land occupied by the Manchurian railway-guards and their families is only, so far as could be found in 1901, along the northeastern and northwestern portions of the railway. It was vacant land. There was no external evidence of its having been previously occupied. A gentleman connected with the Chinese telegraph service, and familiar with every foot of Manchuria, said that many tens of thousands of acres of fertile land in Manchuria have not been occupied within his recollection, and his personal observation extended back over a period of forty years. It was a strange state of affairs. But one explanation exists, and that only partially accounts for it. That explanation is that all eastern and northeastern Manchuria was so terrorized by the robber bands which for more than a century have had free hand there that the farmer, trader, and merchant abandoned the soil. In lower Manchuria the robbers had, up to the time of the Russian occupation, licensed commerce so as not to kill the goose that lays the golden eggs for them, as their unrestrained outrages did in the territory now referred to. It is on this land, from which the inhabitants have long ago been driven by fear, that you may find the families of the Russian railway-guard established.

"How much land do each of you have?" was asked of one of them.

"All we can use. And why not? This is nobody's land."

And so it is. One of the most inviting valleys within the length and breadth of Manchuria was found to be uninhabited and with little trace that it had been inhabited within recent times. And yet that valley is a natural granary. Climate and soil make it equal, for agricultural purposes, to any part of the United States, and its charming frame of mountains, which, when you reach them, you find to rise abruptly from the level plain, gives to this natural home of industry an engaging and varied beauty.

We are now about one hundred and fifty miles into the interior of Manchuria. We find it rapidly undergoing the same process with which we in the Philippines were, with so much difficulty, engaged; with which Germany in Shan-Tung, with so much outlay of wealth, is engaged; with which England in South Africa was engaged with blood and bayonet, and burning villages, and conquering hosts, and ruinous expenditure, and dissolving prestige. We are one hundred and fifty miles into Manchuria, which is being Russianized under our very eyes; and the soldier appears, as yet, to be the least important instrument of dominion. Thus far the Russian elements of empire seem to be brick and mortar, shovel and wagon, quarry and wall, houses and homes, women and children, order and system.

And now, piled up by the side of the temporary track (one hundred and fifty miles into the interior, mind you), you behold another Russian element of empire. It is a great, white monument, covered with canvas. It is important that you should know what this is, for the traveller soon acquires the instinctive understanding that things vital and full of meaning must be looked for in the incidental and occasional. Some Chinamen, at an officer's request, remove the canvas which conceals this great pile, and you find that this monument of Russian progress in Manchuria is built of five thousand sacks of American flour. It is a strange feeling which steals over you when you read on the sacks the name of the mills and the name of the State, "Washington, U. S. A."—a strange feeling and a sense of confusion, for you are in Manchuria, that forbidden land, that region concealed from the eyes of the remainder of the world by black clouds of terrible rumor. But you have beheld nothing thus far but peace and industry; and perhaps an idea steals imperceptibly over your mind that you have been mistaken in your understanding of Russian methods of expansion. At all events, one thought repeats itself in your mind, whether you will or no, and that thought is that here, with all the outward necessaries of civilized life about you, among which are five thousand sacks of American flour from Washington, U. S. A., you stand in perfect security, where ten years ago you probably would have been murdered by bands of brigands.

Chinese working-men were building the railroad. There were hundreds of them, thousands of them, tens of thousands of them. Let us bring them before the eye. They are busy constructing grades, not with horses and scrapers and all of our modern labor-saving devices, but each man bearing two baskets of earth (each basket at the end of a bamboo pole across his shoulders), from where it is dug in the cut to where it is emptied on the fill. These Chinese laborers look good-humored; they appear well fed; they give all the evidences of happiness and contentment. They laugh at you, joke with you, say things to you rough and unrepeatable, but yet kindly and without meaning to offend.

They are at work on buildings, too. Excellent masons they make; and above all superb stone-cutters. In this last occupation their patience is invaluable. You cannot imagine how independent they are. It is said that the railroad company experienced a serious difficulty at one time because the Chinese laborers struck. These laborers were paid eighty copecks a day in winter and sixty copecks a day in summer (two copecks make a cent of our money). Such wages were never heard of before in this, or, indeed, any portion of China. It is many, many times the pay of the Russian ordinary common soldier, and almost equals the pay of the Russian-Manchurian railway-guard. It was too heavy a drain upon the railway resources, and in the summer of 1901 the company attempted to reduce the wages to forty copecks a day.

One hundred thousand Chinamen and more instantly quit work. The alternative was presented to the government of restoring the former, and as the Russians thought exorbitant, wages or abandoning work upon the road. The men won; the wages were restored and work was resumed. Astonishing, is it not?—a strike of Chinese laborers in Manchuria, and a successful one. Undoubtedly the desire to hurry the railroad to completion, the utter absence of all labor but Chinese labor, and, lastly, the care exercised by the Russians not to offend a people they have subdued, influenced the railway company to yield to the demand of the Chinese laborers. For such a strike in Russia itself would be put down by bayonet and ball.

All of these Chinese laborers, as before remarked, seemed contented and happy. They were found, among other things, building a church in the new town of Hmanpo, two hundred miles into Manchuria. And these same men only a year before were Boxers, frenzied fanatics, butchering without mercy man, woman, and child, slaying even their own kind who refused them active aid. It is a method worth considering—that of changing these furies, these demons (for such only twelve months before they were), into peaceful and happy laborers, apparently not only pleased with their lot, but, as it seemed to the looker on, rejoicing in it.

What, then, is that method? It is the simple and traditional method of Russia to strike when you strike, and to spare not when you are striking. It is to wage war while war exists, and to employ the methods of peace only when war is over. Skobeleff at Goek Tepe refused to accept the surrender of the heroic Tepens, who had terrorized Central Asia for centuries, and he slaughtered more than twenty thousand men, women, and children in twenty days. (The siege lasted exactly twenty days, and Skobeleff's estimate of the number slain is twenty thousand.) It seemed quite terrible, and was as terrible as it seemed; but it is hard to see that it is much worse to destroy twenty thousand men, women, and children in twenty days and secure peace for all time than it is to kill that number during twenty years, and in the process increase the irritation, the disorder, and the feud. For from the red day of Goek Tepe to this hour, order, law, safety to traveller, security of commerce, and all other things which help to make up civilization, have existed in Central Asia, as firmly guarded as they are in the United States. War is bad under any circumstances, but if it must be it should be thorough, that it may be brief and not fruitless.

And so in Manchuria, when the great Boxer uprising began (and it began in Manchuria with the historic attack on Blagovestchensk), the smiling Russian, with his mild blue eye and his kindly bearing, became, in truth, what rumor pictures him to the Anglo-Saxon world—a man of the sword and of blood. Russia was caught unprepared. The diabolism of some of the massacres by the Boxers does not admit of description; but Grodekoff at Khabaroff, Chichagoff at Vladivostock, and Alexieff at Port Arthur poured every available man into Manchuria. Five Russian divisions entered from different points, and, sweeping all before them, converged upon Kirin. It was fire and sword and death. It was war. There were no attempts to pacify or cajole while villages were burning. While the conditions of war lasted, Russia waged war. And she waged no "milk-and-water" war; she waged a war of blood. And when she had finished, she had finished, indeed, just as everywhere Russia's task has been finished when once she has concluded a border conflict.

For it is worth the attention of all men that when Russia has once inflicted her punishment there has seldom been any recurrence of insurrection. Where Russian law and order and system have been established they have remained, upheld not by the bayonets of the soldiers who established them, but by the hands of the very people among whom and against whose resistance they were planted. Among all the defects of Russia's civilization, its virtues are striking and elemental, and one of the chief of these is stability.

And so in Manchuria, thousands of men, who bear on their foreheads the scar which distinguishes the Boxer of the most ultra type (for, it is said, the radical, determined, genuine fanatic wears a peculiar scar made in the forehead next to where the hair begins to grow) are now smiling, chaffing, even jolly laboring-men upon the Russian railroad, constructors of Russian buildings, and, most striking of all in its antitheses, the builders even of a Russian church; for among the working-men who were building this church at Hmanpo were several Boxers. Thev confessed it cheerfully. "Why not? Everybody did it!" said one young former Boxer to the interpreter. Oh yes; everybody did it! Also, everybody knew, too, that they never would be Boxers again, or anything else but the loyal adherents of Russia. They understand her now. They understand that she is not to be trifled with, and that whoever touches Russian authority with violent hands has seized the currents of certain death. And, equally important, they understand that with Russia, when war is over, it *is* over, and that a kindly treatment, as natural, unobtrusive, pleasing as if they and the Slav had always dwelt together, is the characteristic of Russia and the Russian in time of peace, as death without mercy is the characteristic of Russia and the Russian in time of war.

For here again you are dazed by that phenomenon which startled you at Nikolsk and attracted your attention with less sharpness in Trans-Baikal Siberia: that Russian peasant and Chinese working-man and Korean laborer mingle together as though they were all of one race, one blood, one faith, and even of one nationality. It is a phenomenon to which attention will be called again and again, because it is fundamental; because it is one of the profound elements of Russia's power in Asia, with its curious causes running far back into Russian history and character.

III

OTHER METHODS OF RUSSIAN ADVANCE

GREAT railways through the heart of Manchuria, with bridges, Roman in their massiveness, with heavy grades and deep cuts, with buildings for engines and equipment solid as fortresses—all this looks as if Russia intends to remain in Manchuria (and, by the same token, all of this appears to indicate that Russia thinks Manchuria quite valuable). Brick and stone buildings, homes of officials, cottages of peasants, the blond wives of a majority of the sixty thousand railroad-guards; the tow-headed children brought with their parents, and the still younger ones born on the soil of Manchuria itself —all these things indicate permanency of Russian occupation. And, above all, Russian churches, raising their semi-Oriental spires to heaven in the centre of every Russian town, point to permanency of Russian occupation.

Let us not pass so hurriedly these Russian churches which former Boxers are building, not by compulsion, but for wages, in Manchuria; for with the Russian Church the Russian priest has arrived in Manchuria, too. He is not there in droves or flocks or communities of monks. He is there only very occasionally and very unobtrusively. He acts the part of the apostle of peace—and he looks the part. Clad in a long robe of black, his blond hair combed straight back from his forehead and falling in picturesque masses of yellow curls on his sombre-clad shoulders, his abundant golden beard covering half his breast, his mild blue eyes full of languid benevolence, the Russian priest in Manchuria is a circumstance as soothing as it is picturesque.

He appears to be attending only to the orthodox Russian flock of his Church. There is no irritating zeal for converts manifested by the priest which the national Church of Russia sends to her frontier. He is in no feverish hurry to convert the heathen. It is not necessary for him to be in a hurry. Seemingly—perhaps really—he respects the religious opinions of those among whom he is placed, as highly as he wishes them to respect his religious opinions. He is apparently very tolerant. A Mohammedan mosque does not offend the Russian priest, a chinese temple does not offend him. Nothing in the faith of others offends him. To the unconverted, to the followers of other religions, he is all consideration and courtesy and sweet agreeableness. Above all, he does not debate, contend, argue.

And yet the Russian Church, with methods such as these, succeeds in gathering communities, provinces, tribes, and peoples within her fold. It is done by the combined influence of those thousand incidentals which, united, are so irresistible in human thought and feeling. The beautiful service of the Russian Church; the semi-Oriental adoration of even the most highly educated and refined Russian worshipper; the unobtrusive kindliness of Russian priest towards the unbeliever, combined with a certain stately attitude of superiority—these and innumerable other circumstances create an atmosphere of gentle and reposeful and alluring Russian orthodoxy. Even the antagonism of the priests of other religions is lulled, first into quiescence, and then into actual friendliness.

Three hundred miles and more in the heart of Manchuria a converted Chinaman was met. He had become a member of the Russian Greek Orthodox Church. He had cut off his queue; he wore his hair like a European, dressed like one, and made the elaborate Russian sign of the cross on greeting you. And you observe a striking fact on looking into this converted Chinaman's case—his Christianization has not made him unpopular with his fellows. And this fact, when followed up, reveals the most remarkable situation of which there is any record; for, *mirabile dictu*, the Chinese Buddhist priest at this particular place comes to the Russian orthodox priest and gives him the name of any Chinaman who wishes to embrace the Christian religion. This was hard to believe, but inquiry tended to confirm it.

Here, then, is one clew to the secret of Russian success in "colonization." The apparent brotherhood of Russian peasant, soldier, and officer with all classes of other nationalities, which we have twice noted, is another clew. The progress of actual, material improvement — buildings, streets, parks, roads, railways—is still another and a greater. The intelligent ruthlessness of Russian warfare, when warfare must be waged, is a still more important clew.

But the conduct of the Church is even more enlightening. There is no preaching of the gospel to these Asiatic pagans as you would preach it to New-Englanders, any more than there are sentimental attempts to realize academic theories of government. There is nowhere profusion of words; there is everywhere profusion of deeds. There is the powerful teaching of example.

"You see," explained a Russian priest (far and away a superior man to the Russian priest you ordinarily meet in Russia), "we Russianize and Christianize, and, if you please, civilize by natural processes and silent influences. After they have been taught that there will be no trifling with interference to our authority (and we never teach the lesson more than once) the people come gradually to like us. We do not interfere in their worship of their god in their own way. In our Church affairs we do not offend the eye or ear or any of their elemental prejudices, and the Church gradually becomes pleasing to them. In precisely the same way they soon get accustomed to our railway, and are quick to catch its practical advantages. They find that if they are orderly and obedient to the common authority, their treatment is that of all the remainder of us. And so, gradually and by natural adaptation and adjustment, they become what you call 'Russianized.'"

It is merely observing a proper proportion, in examining the Russianizing of Manchuria, to give this much attention to the Russian Church and the Russian priest; for the Russian carries his Church, his religion, his wife, and his bayoneted rifle with him wherever he goes. It is idle to debate whether his religion is as genuine as yours. You certainly cannot answer the question whether it is a mere empty form or a profound fervor which each individual feels in common with the great race of which he is a unit. These refinements are not useful in considering the part it plays in the advance of Russian dominion; for, whatever its nature, it does the work expected of it. It is the centre of that social order which Russia begins to establish the very moment she lays the foundation of a building or surveys the line of a railroad. It is the centre from which radiates an indescribable but very real human gentleness, inferior to ours if you like to have it so, but a distinct improvement over the atrophied human conditions of Asia. And for the Russian himself, it is enough to say that at least he lives in its forms and observances, and in its articles he smilingly goes to his death.

Wherever Russian improvement may be seen in Manchuria, there may be seen also the wooden Greek cross which Cossack and guard and common soldier have planted above their slain comrades. Wherever a Russian home has risen, wherever a telegraph-office has been erected, wherever even the Cossack has built his watch-tower, from which by day and night he sweeps with watchful eye the surrounding country, wherever a Russian is housed, there hangs the holy icon. And before that sacred image every Russian, noble or peasant, general or common soldier, governor or servant, bows his head and makes the holy sign; for the Prince of Peace, wherever the sons of Russia have raised the empire's flag, is acknowledged Lord of all, even by the Czar himself. Whatever may be said of the Russian Church by its critics, it must be admitted that the religion it teaches has a certain carrying and sustaining power which bears the Russian up in his most desperate trials, and repels not the strange people among whom he plants his law, his authority, and his faith.

It had been a day of hardship and labor. The floods had cut us off from food. Temporary bridges had been swept away by a sudden rush of waters from a series of cloud-bursts in the near-by mountains. The deluge of the seventies, when thousands lost their lives, was repeated in Manchuria in the dreadful summer of 1901. One had to drink tea made from muddy waters, along which now and then a drowned Chinaman floated by. Rivers ran so swift and wide that it appeared impossible for a boat to be propelled from shore to shore. Once, when a too-daring party of three attempted the hurrying waters, the racing rapids snatched the boat from their control and death seemed near. High winds blew bits of sand into your face until the skin felt perforated as by a hundred needle-points, and the blazing sun stung and burned and blistered; to be succeeded at evening by currents of air so cold that you shook with ague as you lay down to rest on the rain-drenched earth.

But there was no note of impatience from any Russian tongue. Only a German, an American, and a Dane—acting as English, Russian, and Chinese interpreter—only these fretted, with the impatience of too highly organized nerves. Attempt after attempt is made to rescue this strange company. Attempt after attempt fails. And in the attempts some men are drowned. Still no disturbance of the Russian phlegm. Your Dane, your German, and your American may pace up and down and mutter and complain. The Russian sits stolidly on the great embankment, or firmly stands and patiently waits, patiently watches, good-humored, adaptable, imperturbable. Note well this characteristic, even in the folly of your impatience, German, American, Dane; for here is another source of Russian power which, in cooler moments and at greater leisure, it will pay you well to study, and deeply study, too.

At last a huge boat, hauled miles up-stream, is floated down and paddled steadily towards your shore; and half a mile below you the Cossacks who are bringing it to your relief succeed in running it into the marshes on your side of the river. With much pains, much patience, and in constant danger of being drowned, they finally bring it to your feet, and you embark. With exertions which make you fear for them, so mightily do they labor, so swelled and congested become the veins in their foreheads, the Cossacks finally reach the other side, a long distance below the point from which you started.

That night you sit exhausted at the Russian local headquarters, in the heart of the most troubled district of Manchuria. The headquarters consist of four long buildings, of a single story, with thick walls of hardened gray bricks, enclosing a court whose sward is green with often-watered grass and delicious with flowers, whose careful tending tells you of the supervision and directing hand of woman. It is very restful, secure from sun and protected from storm, and there are kindly mannered, travel-cultured Russian officers about you, conversing pleasantly and quite freely on any subject you like. The talk includes in its range even the respective merits and demerits of their government as compared with yours; the wisdom or the unwisdom, according to individual opinion, of the Russian programme in Manchuria; or the ecclesiastical policy of the Greek Church; or, strangest of all, the nature and meaning of our American industrial organizations known as "trusts." (The Russian is just as curious and keen an inquirer as the American.) Night falls. Heavy clouds shut out the stars. An occasional drop of rain spats upon the roof, and then descends the steady downpour of a Manchurian rainfall. All of you—Russian, German, American, and Dane—feel very far away from the world, very much cut off from your kind, very much surrounded by dangers—as, indeed, you are.

Suddenly, through the darkness, which the rain emphasizes, a bugle peals across the night a few martial and not untuneful notes, and then silence again closes on the sound. For a moment only the stillness, and then rises, strong and fervid and deep-toned, a solemn chant. The talk ceases. Every officer makes the sign of the cross, and the night is full of the feeling and atmosphere of prayer. A strange sound surely for such a place. You ask its meaning, and learn that it is the Cossacks in their barracks intoning their night-time appeal to the throne of God for His care and protection in toil and in battle, and, finally, for the salvation of these, His servants, when, their duty done, they shall stand before His face.

Go, you doubter of the sincerity of these bearded soldiers and behold the faces of these men as this song-prayer is chanted! Witness the attitude of adoration; see the looks of humility; behold shining from their eyes the light of a faith which is sufficient for them even unto death! And, however you reason it out, you cannot—resist it as you will—overcome the feeling that here is a vital element of Russian power and an efficient instrument of Russian policy. You sometimes feel that you cannot put this very real thing—this simple faith of these Russian soldiers—on the low plane of a mere agency of statecraft. Sometimes, in spite of yourself, the suggestion forces upon you that this unquestioning belief is quite as real as your own. And it is a curious confusion of thoughts that crowds upon your mind when you reflect that these are the men who, that very day, risked their lives, just to give you and others a little comfort—risked them gladly and with laughter. These are the men who meet, subdue, destroy those bands of robbers who for decades have so terrorized Manchuria that even their crimes have come to be licensed. Study it well, you German student of the elements of empire, noting, as you are, the smallest incident which passes before your watchful eyes. And study it well, too, you American, study it well every one, for here, it may be, is a force in the hands of Russian statesmanship with which the world must reckon.

Later on the contract with the Chinese government will be set out, under which the Manchurian railway, now completed, but then in course of construction, was being built. You can there read for yourself the administrative power given Russia under this contract. But at these Russian headquarters the actual execution of her powers was observed. Two Chinese vagabonds were brought in to the commanding officer. They were not brought in by the Russian soldiery; they were delivered by Chinamen doing police duty, perhaps under Chinese authority, but certainly under Russian pay. These offenders had already been rudely manacled. Very abject were they, very penitent they appeared. It seemed that they had stolen some kind of railway material. The Russian commander made very short work of it. He merely turned them over to the Chinese Governor of a near-by town for the administration of Chinese justice.

"What will be done with them?" was asked.

"Undoubtedly," came the answer, "old" (naming the Chinese Governor) "will execute them."

And so it is that theft and disorder are becoming very unpopular wherever Russian authority is influential in Manchuria.

Now for another phase of Russian treatment of the Manchurian native. Half an hour later three sick Chinamen, variously afflicted, followed these evil-doers who had been sent hence to their death. Two of these sick men were ill of some kind of a fever, and another one had been injured and required surgical attendance. On former visits to China it had been observed that the Chinese do not take kindly to the medical assistance of foreigners. It has required years for the missionary hospitals and dispensaries in the various treaty ports of China proper to get the confidence of the people. It appeared strange, therefore, that these Chinamen should come voluntarily to the Russian headquarters for medical treatment.

"But you see," explained the Russian physician, who at once took them in charge, "it is our policy to help the people among whom we have come, from the highest to the lowest, in every possible way we can. If I did not fear that you would think that I am trying to impress you with our good qualities I should tell you that we do this thing not only from policy, but also from our nature and disposition. Nothing pleases a Russian more than to help some other person who is in need. Apparently the Chinese feel this, for, as you see, they come on their own motion and very willingly. I shall treat each of these men just as carefully as I do any of our own soldiers or officers. They go away very grateful and tell the good news to their fellows. And so, imperceptibly, but with astonishing rapidity, there grows up a kindly feeling for us."

Greater credit was given to this statement from having observed, again and again, in Siberia, many instances of the same personal kindliness and helpful desire of the Russian nature. And so, once more, it appeared that, in his material advance into a dominion which he is absorbing, the hand of the Russian when opposed is a hard hand; but when opposition is crushed, a soft, soothing, and even caressing hand.

Again, it must be borne in mind that, although building roads, raising towns, constructing churches, and the other works of peace constitute the largest part of the method employed by the government in Russianizing Manchuria, military activity is not wanting; for, indeed, it is not wanting. But when you compare the expenditure of energy and money in the execution of her peaceful methods with the energy and money expended in her warlike activities the proportion is nine to one. This is true, too, in external appearance, in physical manifestations, and results.

Remembering this proportion, we can better appreciate at its true value Russia's military operations in constructing her new empire on the Pacific. Never forget that when Russia feels it necessary to employ her soldiers in the field she does not hesitate. She uses them with all the power and deadly effect possible. This is as true of a little campaign as a big one. It was true of the final campaign in south-central Manchuria, in the summer of 1901, as it was of the campaign made necessary by the Boxer movement. The robber bands, whose richest field of operations extended from the port of New-Chwang, in southwestern Manchuria, through Mukden to Kirin, in central-eastern Manchuria (a diagonal line of several hundred miles), had clung tenaciously to their criminal supremacy. Through this territory the trade of Manchuria, and even a portion of the commerce of Trans-Baikal Siberia, passes.

Over this commerce the robbers of Manchuria exercised such terrorism that merchants, Chinese as well as foreign, finally came to recognize the authority of these powers of pillage; and it is said that an office was actually established in the port of New-Chwang where persons desiring to import goods into Manchuria might secure insurance against molestation from robber hordes. When this insurance was paid for, the robber agent gave the merchant a document and a little flag, and with this document in his possession and this flag nailed to his carts or boats he travelled in safety.

This was the system of crime which Russia found in Manchuria, from the profits of which some thousands of criminals were living in unmolested insolence. These robbers were among the most relentless of the Boxers; and, after that fanatical movement had been suppressed, these Manchurian brigands did not cease for an instant their activity against the power whose firm establishment in Manchuria would mean the certain and permanent destruction of their practices.

Russia did not hesitate an instant. She sent no commission to treat with them. No honeyed methods, no moral suasion, no "sweet reasonableness" was employed. Russia understood the people she was dealing with. It is said that the forces she despatched to the scene of disturbance would not receive a flag of truce from the brigands and could not have sent one unless they had taken the white blouse of the common soldier for that purpose. "We never carry material from which flags of truce can be made," said a young officer, rather vaingloriously.

Mukden was instantly garrisoned with twelve thousand Russian soldiers (this garrison was still there in 1901, and has since been increased to twenty-five thousand men, as credible rumor reports); and a flying body (none but the Russian government knows how many) was placed in the field, commanded by picked officers, every one of whom had distinguished himself for courage and resource within the preceding twelve months, either in the Boxer uprising or in some of the frontier campaigns of Russia. And the whole was under the command of the Kitchener of Russia — General-Lieutenant Cierpitsky. This commander is Russia's field fighter. He has given his life to the business of war, and loves his profession with an enthusiasm which cannot properly be described by any other word than passionate. He took the field in person at the head of his troops. Three thousand robbers were killed in less than six weeks; two thousand were captured, and the rest scattered and hunted like beasts into the caves and fastnesses of the concealing mountains. The power of organized brigandage in Manchuria has been destroyed, it is hoped and believed, forever.

And do not forget that it was a formidable power of its kind. It could even be said to have had resources supplied by the fees of licensed spoliation. It was comparatively a well-organized power, with captains and chiefs. And now it is broken, crushed, scattered, obliterated, in a period of time ordinarily required to get ready for such a campaign. And this was accomplished by the simple process of making war when war was inevitable, just as though there were nothing else in the world to do but to make war; instead of conciliating one day and threatening the next; instead of entertaining insurgents on Monday and taking the field against them on Tuesday.

"You seem to work at this business, General," was a remark made to General Cierpitsky.

"Why not?" said he. "If it is the thing to do, it is the thing to do. Is it not?" That was a simple statement that put you in mind of Grant—so clear, so plainly true, so free from complexities, limitations, explanations. "And," added the Russian commander, "I think we have pretty high warrant for it. For what is that in the great book of the world's law" (rather a fine phrase, is it not?) "about doing whatever is necessary with all your soul—'Whatsoever thy hand findeth to do, do it with thy might.' Is not that the quotation?"

This remark of a fighting general of Russia was a key to the Russian system of pacification. Also it revealed the interesting circumstance that the field officer of the empire knew his Bible. Further and extended conversation with him disclosed the fact that he knew other books as well, and especially all that had been written on the science of war. Of course, everybody interested in bringing an end to armed conflict (and we are all interested in that) has read the third volume of Mr. Bloc's really great work on war, in which the author demonstrates, by mathematics and statistics, the impossibility of any more wars on a large scale between first-rate nations. No civilian can read this remarkable monument of reasoning and learning without becoming convinced that the day of organized slaughter on the fields of battle must soon end. What more engaging subject, then, could be suggested to this practical soldier than this book of his fellow-subject and servant of the Czar? However, being merely a soldier, he has probably not read it. Mention it to him timidly, then. You find that he has not only read the third volume, but the first and second volumes too, and he overwhelms Mr. Bloc's apparently irrefutable conclusions by pointing out practical facts of so simple and obvious a nature that, civilian though you are, you wonder why you never thought of them yourself. Test this rough-and-ready soldier a little further and you discover that there is not a work in the literature of war which you can name to him with which he is not familiar.

The most notable thing about General Cierpitsky is his devotion to his martial profession; the second thing to impress you is his enthusiasm in Russia's work in Manchuria. It is no forced ardor, no simulated interest.

The following is the way he spoke to a detachment of his soldiers at the close of the Mukden campaign, in August, 1901. As the soldiers saw General Cierpitsky walking swiftly down upon them, every hand of the long line came instantly and rigidly to the cap in impressive salute, and from a thousand throats in unison was shouted out their soldier-greeting to their commander, a free translation of which is, "Hail! our General!" or "Good-morning, our General!" or "We greet you, our General!" And here, in free translation, is the exact speech he made to them, with their responses:

General Cierpitsky. "Soldiers, I am glad to see you again."

Soldiers (in unison). "Thank you, our General."

General Cierpitsky. "You have overcome the robbers, armed with the best guns; you have overcome climate, floods, and heat; and you have overcome dysentery and every form of disease which vile water and viler surroundings create. And, soldiers, you ought to thank God for preserving your lives."

Soldiers (in unison). "We thank God, our General."

General Cierpitsky. "And, soldiers, you ought to pray to God to keep you strong to fight again for Him and for your country."

Soldiers. "We pray God, our General."

General Cierpitsky. "Now you are going home and you deserve rest; but you must always be ready to fight for your Czar, your country, and your God."

Soldiers. "We will always be ready, our General."

Can any one fail to see the significance of this brief address? Here was Russia's hardest field fighter, at the end of a bloody campaign made necessary for the protection of her railroad property, reminding his troops that they had been fighting "for God and their country," commanding them to "thank God for preserving their lives," and admonishing them to be ready always to serve "their God and their country." And there was not one bit of cant in it. It was spontaneous, natural, real.

And so the General closed; and, with a kindly wave of his hand to the troops, whom he in person and on foot, with sword in hand, had led on a hard excursion in a difficult country, he turned to leave them. Instantly the soldiers broke into the deep-toned, thrilling Russian huzza, and the air was filled with their caps, waved and tossed aloft in adieu to their leader. These soldiers had just returned from a merciless campaign, yet they did not look very blood-thirsty — on the contrary, quite mild-mannered, quite easy-going, and quite *en rapport* with the people themselves. This is a note touched before, but it must be touched again and again if you will understand Russia's success in extending her authority. The Russian army, as well as the Russian working-men and peasants, fraternize with the conquered people. They do it naturally and without effort. There is in the familiarity of their intercourse a suggestion of kinship. Perhaps, Russian understanding of the Asiatic is instinctive and congenital; for the Russian has a little Asiatic blood in his veins and much Asiatic traditions in his mind, inherited from the centuries of Tartar rule. But whatever the causes, it is certain the Russian does understand the Asiatic as no other people understands him; better than the German, better even than the Englishman.

Skobeleff sounded the key-note of Russian policy when he said: "My system is this—to strike hard, and keep on hitting until resistance is completely over; then at once to form ranks, cease slaughter, and be kind and humane to the prostrate enemy."

It is a system based on very simple common-sense, is it not? Certainly it is a system peculiarly adapted to Asiatics. At any rate, no man can deny that it has been successful wherever employed; for be it remembered that Russia has absorbed more territory, assimilated a greater number of different peoples, and fought more border wars than any modern nation; and that in the whole course of her ceaseless march there has never been a single serious uprising against Russian authority, once that authority has been established. That is a fact worth examining and reflecting upon.

IV

TYPES OF CIVIL AGENTS OF THE RUSSIAN ADVANCE

IN General Cierpitsky we observe the type of officer that Russia puts in the field to conduct actual operations at the front. What kind of men does she place in charge of the administrative functions of her forming dominions? What of the minds and characters that are constructing her railway, the mileage of which in Manchuria alone is nearly half the distance across the American continent? What of the subordinates in the force of constructive empire—the station-agents, the "masters of distance"? After all, the only three things worth studying in any country are the soil and its potentialities, the people and their capacities, and the few leaders and their inherent power. All that is ancient and monumental is of value only in interpreting these three elements of the present.

All Russian railroads are divided into what are called "distances," each distance having a master. This "master of a distance"—literal translation—is a cross between the division superintendent of an American railway and a section boss. The same system exists in Manchuria wherever the railroad is completed. Let us see what quality of mentality and force of character are in this type.

"I believe with all my soul in the Orthodox Greek Church, but I believe in it as an engine of national authority more than in a religious way." It is a great, big, bearded "master of distance" on one of the divisions of the Manchurian railway who is talking now, as the construction-train bearing materials proceeds slowly along the temporary track laid by the side of the substantial permanent grade. Let him talk. Every word is a measure of the men in whose hands Russia places her work of building what she calls and believes is civilization in Manchuria. "I believe in God, of course," he continued, "but not the individual God with parts and substance, who was the deity of my childhood days. As for immortality, I cannot figure that out. After a lifetime of meditation, it seems to me unthinkable. But there is the immortality of the race—a divine destiny and purpose for every nation. The Church of Russia is the highest interpretation of our national unity and of Slav dominion. And so I am as earnest a member of the Russian Church as I am a loyal subject of the Czar, and for much the same reason."

"What do you think of the divine destiny, as you call it, of the Russian nation?" was asked of this railway section-master.

"You mean, what do I think is the divine mission of the Slav race, as expressed through the forms of the Russian autocracy or nation?" was his answer (rather discriminating and analytical, I thought). "Well," continued he, "what do you say to the introduction of law, order, justice, and religion among the four hundred millions of China?"

Let us keep in mind this flash of imperial purpose from one of Russia's humblest instruments. What we are doing now is putting the tape-measure up and down the spine of Russian agents in Manchuria, finding the length of their arms and the stability of their legs and the size of their heads. And this extract from a fascinating conversation does that very well. But here, flaming up in the least expected of places, is an expression of Russian aspiration which must be followed with the same care with which the miner follows the first thin vein of gold that points to priceless and hitherto unsuspected deposits in the heart of the mountains. But that is for another chapter. It is enough for the present that we find this section-master discoursing, with sense and real depth of thought, upon those abstruse questions involved in the philosophy of the Greek Orthodox Church. And, far more significant, we find him stating a racial ambition with almost poetic power. Of course, upon the subject of the railroad in Manchuria he will talk with you by the rod; but that was to have been expected. For example:

"The railroad is much better than the Siberian railroad," said he. "It is more honestly built, for one thing. I do not think there has been any corruption in the construction of the Manchurian road; certainly not so much as in the Siberian, and particularly in the Ussuri road. You notice yourself that the line is as straight as it reasonably can be." And he went on about the railroad very entertainingly and very informingly.

"Ah!" said he, springing up as we came in sight of a thick-walled house built for the engineers and officers of the temporary work, "there is where they nearly got us." (Referring to the Boxers the previous year.) "They attacked us in force, and had rifles and some field-guns. It was a surprise, sure enough, I will admit. But we got our men together quickly, and I myself took command. We beat them off, but since the Turkish war I have seen no harder fighting. It was hand-to-hand sometimes. Six men I shot myself."

He was full of tales like this; whether they were true or not they were significant. Proud as he was of the railroad, he was prouder of his feats as a soldier. It was the soldier bubbling up in his blood from the hidden and profound sources of his very soul. It was that racial spirit not inherent in the Slav blood, but injected into it by generations of military assault from Europe on the west and barbaric invasion from Asia on the east; for, if from beneath the placid and languid manner of the Russian the world has now and then been astonished by volcanic eruptions of martial spirit, let the world remember that for many centuries the Turk on the south, the Tartar on the east, the Teuton and the Gaul on the west, and even the icy hosts of nature on the arctic north, have been battling the patient Slav. Why should the world be surprised if at every point of the compass Russia presents fixed bayonets ready for the thrust? For from every point of the compass Russia has for centuries been invaded and assaulted. We cannot take up too much space with conversations, of course, but this one is typical. A hundred others like it from men of inferior station might be given; and only brief points from this one are referred to, but their illumination is their apology.

"I make no doubt of the permanency of Russian occupation here," said he. "It is my intention to remain when my contract with the railroad has expired. My wife and children are on the way here now. The opportunities in a hundred lines are so alluring and substantial that I should feel as if I were insulting Fate if I did not improve them. And those opportunities are in every direction. There is mining in the mountains, there is commerce, there is everything. I will show you a young man about twenty-five versts from here who is getting rich with his little provision store."

At dawn of a morning full of rain, the interpreter routed out "the young man who is getting rich." He had a little store in a Russo-Chinese village clustered about a station. He was a typical, blond-haired, blue-eyed, light-skinned Slav. We bought meats canned by a Chicago packing firm, crackers made by another American firm. The store was well stocked, and every item of its merchandise was from Russia, Germany, and America, with proportions in the order named, except perfumery, which was from France as well as Russia. (No Russian store is so mean and humble that it cannot supply you with a half-dozen brands of perfumery.)

"I am getting a little Chinese custom," the man said. "They take best to American flour. Of course, most of my trade is Russian [he meant that he sold mostly to Russians—guards, officers, etc.]. It is hard to get any line started with the Chinese, but when it is started it steadily grows. But I cannot compete with the Chinese merchants once they take it into their heads to sell the same kind of goods I do. And it will not be long before they do that, but by then I shall, perhaps, have developed into a general merchant for the supply of foreign goods to local merchants."

Here, then, was a contribution to one of the most important of Oriental commercial studies—to wit, to get the Chinaman to buy your goods, you must induce him to like them; and to induce him to like them you must take the thing itself to his very table. When he uses it he acquires a taste for it, and when he acquires a taste for anything the Chinaman becomes a most persistent and generous customer. This observation is by the way, and as a reminder of a subject of immediate interest to Americans when we reach it.

Frequently a gang of a thousand Chinamen have but a single yellow-mustached Russian as their overseer, but this single overseer keeps them at work by a system of bosses. They are divided into companies, and these companies into squads, and each squad has its Chinese boss. These overseers you will find respectful, disciplined, of fair intelligence, but every one of them endowed with the personality of command. Certain it is that the multitudes of laborers are well managed. Go to their huts when the day's work is done, and have your interpreter engage them in conversation. Some are smoking tobacco—why do Chinamen never chew?—some smoking opium, some gambling. You are treated courteously, offered food and tobacco, and there is no unwillingness to talk freely with you.

"We are very contented, indeed, with our lot," was

the free translation of the interpreter, talking to a Chinese laborer, who, with more than a thousand comrades, was building an immense grade. "Many of us were Boxers. There is no use going into the reason why; maybe we were misled, and maybe we received orders. We like the way the Russian treats us. We have work to do, are told how to do it, and get paid for it. We don't know, and we don't care, who governs the country. All we want is to make money, so that we can buy food and tobacco and opium."

Connect this remark of the railway laborer in Manchuria with the observation of a highly educated, English-speaking young Chinese merchant of Shanghai, met as a fellow-traveller in Japan: "I don't care who governs us, and I don't know a single Chinese merchant who does care. All we want is an opportunity to do business and make money."

We have observed the soldier, the priest, the subordinate officials, the bosses, even the laborers. Let us now become acquainted with the constructive minds on the ground. At Nikolsk, Harbin, Vladivostock—wherever emergency or inclination calls him—you will find the engineer-in-chief in charge of the Manchurian railway, that most extraordinary example in the world of what is called "progress," recently constructed, on which the Russian government have expended more than one hundred and fifty million dollars.

Engineer-in-Chief Tugovitch is, perhaps, sixty years of age, of powerful physical frame, face glowing with intelligence, an eye dull in lustre but keen in suggestons of quick mentality. Tugovitch is the personal selection of Russia's master mind, Witte, Minister of Finance and now practical Premier of the Czar. For nearly forty years he has been in active service. He was a military engineer in the Russo-Turkish war. He was one of the engineers of the Trans-Caspian road. Again, he was employed in difficult engineering work in the mountains of Bessarabia.

There is not a practical feature of railway building, from the placing of ties or the bolting of rails to the planning of lines and the thinking-out of systems, of which Tugovitch is not master by experience as well as ability.

And, like nearly all the men who struggle to the top through the civil-service grades of Russia's administrative system, Tugovitch is a planner of empire, a moulder of the future, a suggester of material schemes for the seizure of power and opportunity by the Russian government. For example, Tugovitch many years ago proposed that the Czar should build the railway across Asia Minor to Bagdad, thus controlling the commerce of the Levant and holding Persia in the inextricable grasp of Russia. It is said that Witte approved the scheme, but he was then only the head of a department in the Ministry of Finance, and the cabinet rejected the Persian proposition. It was a mistake of which Germany took quick advantage, for German capitalists now have the concession for this railroad. It is a part of Germany's strategy, which has usurped the past power of England and the future possibilities of Russia in the Turkish Empire, across Asia Minor and through Persia, even to the gulf. If you ask what all this means, the answer is so simple as to be startling. It means some twenty million of consumers in Turkey, several millions more in Asia Minor, and some fifteen millions in Persia; and that is something to interest factory owners, factory laborers, agriculturists, and everybody else who has anything to sell.

Tugovitch is very frank and free in his expression of opinion. More than seven years ago he went through Manchuria on horseback over every possible line of the proposed road. He personally selected the routes which the various lines were to take.

"I know the road was not built for the purpose of seizing Manchuria," said he, "nor, as dreamers declare, for the purpose of ultimately controlling China. It was built for a plain engineering reason—namely, because of the impracticability of water transportation down the Amur and Shilka rivers. You have been over that route yourself. The rise and tall of water in those rivers make navigation impracticable." (It had taken me more than four weeks to go a distance on those rivers which was scheduled for eight days.)

"The engineering difficulties and financial cost of continuing the Siberian lines along the Amur River," he continued, "are plain to everybody who takes the journey. And yet, having built the Siberian railroad as far as we have, it was necessary to complete the line continuously to Vladivostock. Manchuria was between our line and Trans-Baikal Siberia on the west and our port of Vladivostock on the east. The plains, valleys, and passes of Manchuria afforded a route almost straight, and one which, in comparison with the difficult Amur route, is cheap and easy. This fact of physical geography and engineering science was the origin of the Manchurian railway. Of course, when it became possible to lease Port Arthur and Talienhwan for a short period, and thus have a railway outlet to the very thick and centre of the human activities of the Orient, common-sense suggested the extension of our line to those ports."

"That," he went on, "is absolutely all there is in the purpose and consequences of the building of this road. Russia cannot colonize this territory if she would. The Russian cannot compete with the Chinaman as merchant, laborer, artisan. Now that safety and order have been established as a necessary consequence of guarding our railroad, Chinamen are pouring into Manchuria literally by the hundred thousand. So far, then, from the Russian peasant crowding out the Chinaman in this country, the very much more serious question is: How shall we preserve Siberia, and even Russia, from Chinese competition? The contract with the Chinese government for the construction of the road provides that the Chinese government may take it off our hands in thirty years, and that in any event it shall become the absolute property of China in eighty years. I think, and all of the deeper students think, that exactly this will occur. You ask why, then, are we expending all this energy, all this money in constructing the road at all? It is to complete the Siberian road, as I tell you."

This same question was asked another official, who made a similar answer, but added: "I admit that is no sufficient answer to the question, nor to any of the schemes for the extending of Russian Empire. We are moving forward, always moving forward, in each particular and specific case, without knowing exactly why. The practical and immediate reasons against each of our advances for more than a century have been overwhelming, and most Russians, as individuals, have been opposed to them; and yet the command is, 'Forward!' still 'Forward!' and ever 'Forward!' It is as if we were impelled outward and onward by some unseen hand. And by 'we' I include the Czar himself; the Czar and his people are one."

Sure enough, nearly every Russian met in Russia and Siberia was against the acquisition of Manchuria, and yet all of them were willing to fight rather than abandon it.

V

THE OVERLORDS OF THE CZAR'S ADVANCING POWER IN THE FAR EAST

GENERAL GRODEKOFF, Governor of eastern Siberia and Manchuria, and Admiral Alexieff, executive representative of the Russian government in south Manchuria and upon the Oriental seas, were both very frank, very open, and astonishingly independent in their opinions—astonishingly independent, that is, from the Anglo-Saxon view-point, which is that all Russians, and especially all officials, have the same opinion, and that that opinion is formulated for them at St. Petersburg. Let us observe what manner of men are these overlords of the Czar's civil, military, and industrial forces in Manchuria.

You will hear about General Grodekoff a thousand miles before you reach the capital where he has his headquarters. He is one of those vital personalities about whom there is individual interest and mouth-to-mouth gossip. "He is a simple man," you will hear one remark. Another will say, "General Grodekoff is the hardest worker in all Russia." "A hard worker, yes; but not so hard as Witte, is he?" a third will interject. "General Grodekoff fought with Skobeleff," remarked a German-speaking Russian merchant, as our boat slowly paddled down the Shilka River. "He did more than that—he was one of Skobeleff's favorite officers," said another. (Skobeleff is the hero of all Russians. To have it said that "he fought with Skobeleff" is a greater distinction than a title.) "He is a bachelor; he has always been too busy to marry," said another, and much more of the like.

And so, from a medley of chance remarks, more of gossip and with gossip's inaccuracy, most of them praise, some of them censure, but all of them personal and full of color, the individuality of General Grodekoff, who wields all the absolute powers of the Czar throughout a territory as large as the United States east of the Mississippi River, grows upon you until it becomes a living thing. And how simple, how direct, how strong this man is you must lose no opportunity to observe.

Ask for an audience, then, the afternoon of your arrival at Khabaroff. It is customary to receive callers only in the forenoon, but audience is granted not for the next day, nor for that night, nor in an hour, but instantly. There is no "red tape" here, then, but an air of business curiously American. An adjutant meets you at the door and conducts you through an anteroom into an impressive audience-chamber, where the Governor-General receives deputations, delegations, commissions of every kind from any portion of the sub-empire which he rules for the Czar. At one end of this room is a raised platform, with three great chairs upon it, back of which hang the portraits of the Czar and Czarina. On either side and in front of this platform two quick-firing guns command the hall. The impression is that of naked power. You can understand that a deputation of Chinese received in the hall would go away with an idea of sheer force instantly available.

But you do not stop in this audience-chamber. You are taken through into a plain office, with plain desk and many papers in neatly arranged bundles. In a moment a quick step is heard, and through the door of an inner room General Grodekoff himself comes forward to greet you. He is short in stature, broad-shouldered, bald-headed, full-bearded, nervous of speech. He is dressed in uniform, of course, and wears his trousers inside his boots, according to the universal Russian custom. He talks quickly, with precision of idea and direction of manner. Force, energy, keenness, masterfulness—these are the impressions he makes upon you. He knows all about President McKinley. He knew all about President Roosevelt, too (then Vice-President), and speaks of incidents in his career. Both of them he admired. You get the notion, though, that Grodekoff has not been a great reader of books, and that the reason is that he has been too busy. He has been the maker of materials for books. He was an officer under Skobeleff. He knows all about Afghanistan from having tramped and ridden over and through it. The same is true of Persia. On all these subjects he has clear and vigorous personal opinions formed from actual experience.

Turn where you will, you will find this deputy of the Czar informed, usually at first hand and from personal observation. Where it has been impossible for him to see for himself, he has learned from the lips of those who have seen. He knows all about our situation in the Philippines, and is not reserved in his opinion. He is a master of Chinese conditions in comprehensive generality and in particular detail (the secret of this was learned later in China itself). Most of all, you note his unhesitating frankness. No matter what the subject, he does not pause for ready and full reply, and if there is hesitation he leads the conversation himself. Above all, there is no attempt to impress or to please or to do anything else than simply to meet you face to face on any ground of possible mutual interest. To sum it all up, you find that he is a man so absorbed in his work that he has given his whole life to it. And this is the quality of man whom the representatives of other nations must meet and overcome wherever their interest conflicts with that of Russia. It is a consideration worthy of as much thought as the subject of Oriental markets and Oriental statesmanship itself, for no nation will be permitted to have her own way on the Pacific or in the Orient until such highly equipped and devoted men as General Grodekoff are met and reckoned with. And Germany has just such men, too.

Two more examples of the intellectual agencies employed by Russia in Manchuria, and you have enough data from which to form a fair estimate. Admiral Alexieff, with headquarters at Port Arthur, makes upon you the impression of almost abnormal alertness. He, too, is a bachelor. His life also has been devoted, with the enthusiasm of a boy, to the growing power of Russia. He is perhaps fifty years of age, and instinct with nervous energy. His step is impetuous. The whole movement of the man is full of dash. His talk is the vocalization of force; his attitude, even when sitting in conversation, is that of bolt-upright intentness. Alexieff is informed, very frank, open, never hesitating to formulate a reply and giving you his opinion quite off-hand. He is as quick in speech as is Admiral Dewey, of whom again and again you are reminded when talking to him. His days are full of toil; indeed, most of his nights are full of toil also.

There appears to be something about these men whom Russia has set at the front of her advance which fascinates them into a passion for work. Perhaps it is that they are always doing something, and not merely talking about doing something. Each day things are to be settled. Ships are to be sent hither and yon; movements of bodies of troops are to be thought out and executed; information is to be daily, almost hourly, received on all kinds of important subjects; decisions are required on all manner of cases, many of them of far-reaching importance; delicate conditions, constantly changing and newly forming, are to be reckoned with, and reckoned with accurately. In short, the great heads of Russian administration have enough, and more than enough, to do all of the time. And the things which they do are tangible, definite. They are things which afford a man the consciousness, when he closes his eyes at night, that he can see where his energies have gone during the day. Whatever the reason, the activity, intelligence, alertness, and immense information of men like Admiral Alexieff strike you most powerfully. And when one who had come to take the measure of this man departs, he will find this one expression repeating itself again and again, "Equipped—well equipped."

In 1901, when the writer met Admiral Alexieff, he was in supreme command of the Asiatic Russian squadron, and also in command of all southern Manchuria. Into his hand, too, it was understood, were gathered all of the threads of Russian diplomacy and statecraft running out all through the Orient. It was at that time predicted that Alexieff would soon be the first and highest representative of the Czar throughout Manchuria and the entire Far East, and even in Trans-Baikal Siberia. His elevation during the present year to precisely that station has established the reality of the impressions formed in 1901. Whatever may be the future career of this uncommon man, whether he continues indefinitely to enjoy the exalted confidence of his sovereign, which is now his, or whether one of these strange revolutions of autocratic favor shall reduce him to an humbler place, all statesmen, of whatever nationality, who may during this period be called upon to meet in negotiations or otherwise Admiral Alexieff would do well to understand that they are dealing with a master mind, a master will, and altogether with a masterful man.

While Admiral Alexieff was perfectly unreserved in his conversation, while he talked with all the freedom of Tolstoi—as indeed was the case with General Grodekoff—the statement that the conversation was to be regarded as personal necessarily excludes a repetition of anything said by either, or even an intimation of their views, utterances of opinion, or assertions of fact; and none of the extracts of conversation given either heretofore or hereafter in this volume came from either of them in the remotest degree. Indeed, it may as well be stated here as elsewhere that significant utterances quoted in this book are, of course, given without the violation of any confidence. This statement is, no doubt, quite unnecessary, but is made out of excess of caution.

Interesting as are the personalities of General Grodekoff and Admiral Alexieff, so much space would not be devoted to them merely on their personal account; for this volume is neither biography nor character study, and either or both of these men may to-morrow be removed to other fields of duty, and at best, of course, as is the case with all of us, the period of human life will soon take them out of active work. But these careful descriptions of them are set forth because they are genuine types of the highest class of Russian administrators. Should either of them die or be removed their places will be filled with men so much of the same stamp, quality, and experience that, allowing for the difference of personality, their successors might be the same men. It is the *type*, the quality, the preparedness of the men whom Russia puts in charge of her foreign business that these sketches of Alexieff and Grodekoff are designed to bring to the mind of the reader.

You may credit all that you read in detraction of Russian officials, if you like; but you may credit it and still understand that, in her important positions, and particularly at her strategic outposts of empire, where she is coming in contact with the other powers of the world, Russia will have just such men as Alexieff and Grodekoff; for throughout the vast web of the Russian administrative system her agents undergo every possible test, are subjected to every possible temptation; and it appears to be the purpose of the government to place at critical points, like Manchuria, about which are swirling the ambitions, schemes, and physical activities of other nations, none but those whom experience has shown to be the strongest men in the whole administrative establishment, civil, naval, and military, throughout the dominions of the Czar.

Let us now take a typical railway administrator, who is neither governor or engineer or soldier, and yet who is every one of them in education, experience, and natural aptitude. An excellent type of the civil officer that Russia sends to do her work is Mr. Girshmann, the administrator of the southern divisions of the Manchurian railway. A very hearty, off-hand man you will find him. He, too, was a soldier in the Turkish war; he, too, has seen service in the Caucasus; he, too, has constructed other railroads for Russia; he, too, has read many books, and is instructed by personal experience. He gives you the impression of steady and informed intelligence, thoroughly awake and well in hand. Like Grodekoff and Alexieff, he is an incessant worker. Having had a hard day and night, the interpreter wanted a little rest.

"Why," exclaimed Mr. Girshmann, "I have not had a wink of sleep for two nights running, and I feel quite fresh."

The occasion for this unusual exertion was the destruction of his grades and bridges by the flood of August, 1901.

The energy of this administrator, his attention to details, and his comprehensive knowledge suggested inquiry concerning him. It was found that he was at work usually ten hours out of the twenty-four, every day of the year. Frequently he works as much as sixteen hours a day, a thing you will not understand until you see with your own eyes what he has to do. Every day, ten hours of work always, and sometimes much more—very much like an ambitious young American building his fortune in one of the great cities of the United States; and yet this man, more than fifty years of age, is an imperial railway administrator in south Manchuria.

Such energy and application are not characteristic of the Russian, however; the reverse is very much the rule. Indeed, his slothfulness is one of the striking characteristics of the Slav.

After learning about Mr. Girshmann, you would not be

surprised to find that, though the railway was then only in the process of construction, it was, nevertheless, hauling local traffic for more than two hundred miles, from its southern terminus at Port Arthur. Although the track was then given up to the construction and material trains, the income from this local traffic, for three months of the spring of 1901, was 700,000 rubles ($350,000). This gives you a hint of the paying possibilities of this property when completed. It gives you a hint, too, of what this railway will do for the development of the resources and the people of Manchuria. It gives you a further hint of what the road will do in the development of the commerce of the world.

"The road," said Mr. Girshmann, "will pay very heavily. You can see for yourself, on these southern divisions, how enormous the traffic will be. Look at that"—pointing to large piles of beans in bags, tobacco in bales, native wine in boxed bottles and casks—"and at that"—pointing to a side track crowded with cars, every one loaded to its utmost capacity with freight, all waiting to be moved. "Surely, you have noticed considerable passenger traffic on these southern divisions. You ask what will be the government's policy as to tariff duties on imports. That is not within my province. But there is, at the present time at least, no reason for it; for we are as yet an importing nation, so far as Manchuria is concerned. In fact, generally, Russia cannot be said to be an exporting nation yet. What our condition in that respect will be fifty or a hundred years from now is a different matter. What our final policy will be, who shall say? Russian history will show you that events have shaped our policy in spite of ourselves. A man like me must act—not dream. Here we are and here is my daily task. I am happy in it and I hope I am useful to my country and my Czar. What it will lead to is in God's hands." That expression is thoroughly Russian. From priest and peasant to the Czar himself it is always, "as God wishes," or "it is in God's hands."

The passenger traffic to which Mr. Girshmann called attention was, of course, almost exclusively Chinese. The German representative of the great German firm of Kuntz & Albers was observed; several Russian officers, of course, were present; but the great bulk of the passengers were Chinamen. Here was a Chinese merchant travelling to New-Chwang, there a Chinese official on his way to Pekin; for wherever the railroad has gone in a country peopled by the Chinese, they have taken very kindly to it, after they have failed to destroy it. On the road from Tien-Tsin to Pekin, for example, you may observe them waiting at the station, exactly as Americans do here; rushing for the cars, exactly as we do here; trying to get the best seats, just as an excursion crowd does in our own country. But the Russian management of them seems to suit them better than their treatment by any other Europeans which the writer has ever observed. Indeed, the hostility with which the Chinaman regards European physical encroachments, like the building of new railroads, etc., in any part of China (which hostility you feel in the very air), was not apparent in Manchuria. As has been observed, many Russian towns were building; and the Chinese appeared to take very kindly to it, even when they were not employed in the work.

The town of Harbin, in the exact centre of Manchuria, is by far the best illustration of Russian constructiveness in the interior. It has well-built houses. It is admirably laid out. Its streets have the characteristic Russian breadth and generosity. Its trade is already active. Even in 1901, when its building was not yet completed, it had well-equipped stores. The Russo-Chinese Bank was already there. The Greek Orthodox Church was there, too. To the person familiar with Russian methods in a new country it is, perhaps, unnecessary to mention that these financial and spiritual agencies of the Russian people had already established themselves. The Russo-Chinese bank, in 1901, was housed in some not-imposing Chinese-constructed buildings; but it is said that at this focus-point of constructive activity in Manchuria this branch of the imperial finance ministry was to have in a short season very handsome quarters. The Russian church also was a temporary affair — much more unsubstantial than the church edifices of other and comparatively unimportant Russian Manchurian towns. But as soon as the Russians can get a breathing spell at this point, about which at present their energies most actively play and swirl, a cathedral of the Greek Orthodox Church is to be erected, so that, in the centre of Harbin, an architectural spectacle will present itself with which every traveller within the Czar's dominions, whether in European Russia or Siberia or elsewhere, is familiar — a splendid church building, noble in dimensions and magnificent in equipment. What Harbin will be eventually was, in 1901, indicated by the extraordinary activity in the construction of brick buildings in New Harbin; for it must be known that there are two or three or more Harbins, all within a stone's-throw of one another. Eventually they will all be joined together. In short, at Harbin and at Dalni, and, indeed, in other towns in Manchuria, Russia appears to be doing with autocratic instantaneousness what other pioneer peoples do gradually.

The designers of Harbin have not forgotten the amusements of the people; and a piece of ground where, generations ago, the Chinese had planted a great row of trees, has been made into a park, with band-stands, children's swings, seats in the shade, and all of the conveniences of popular pleasure with which we equip our parks here in America.

Of course, Harbin is the railway headquarters in Manchuria. It is from here that the provisions and material for several divisions of the road, east, west, and south of

Harbin are distributed. And this may give Harbin a so much greater appearance of importance than it would otherwise have that perhaps we ought not to take it as a measure of the ordinary Russian urban achievement in Manchuria. On the other hand, this town will not appear very imposing to the American or European who now passes through it on the completed railway, coming, as he does, fresh from towns and cities long since built and administered. But it is nothing short of imposing in comparison with the condition which preceded it. It is an admirable work, when we bear in mind, as the observer of the Russian advance in Manchuria must always do, that on the spot where Harbin stands there was little safety, either to person or property, less than a decade ago.[1]

[1] Two considerable flouring-mills have been built in Harbin since the author was there, one of them, it is said, with a daily capacity of several hundred barrels.

VI

RESULTS OF RUSSIAN RAILWAY ADVANCE

THE results of Russian railway advance were, in 1901, by far the most general and absorbing subjects of conversation among non-Russian foreigners in the Far East. Indeed, from the beginning of the Siberian road, the consequences of this extraordinary enterprise have occasioned anxious thought in the minds of every careful student of the world's material activities. And, as will be seen, Russia's Manchurian railroad is only another step in her railway extension to the Orient, of which the Siberian railway was the first step. The purposes of the Manchurian railway, as given by Engineer-in-Chief Tugovitch, have already been set out, as have the comments of Administrator Girshmann. But, perhaps, an independent analysis, illustrated by various observations made on the ground, may also be helpful to an understanding of the meaning and effect of this greatest agency of civilization which the Czar has employed in the Russian advance upon the Pacific.

To what, then, will this railroad which Russia is building through Manchuria lead? What results will follow its completion and operation? He is a daring reasoner who would attempt to deduce all the consequences. The man would be called an immoderate dreamer who should suggest to the world, which looks upon this industrial phenomena from afar, what appear to be certainties to those who survey the ground itself. No one but two or three prophets of empire, such as Russia, with all her deficiencies, is so fortunate as always to have about the

Czar at St. Petersburg, understood the sure results of the great Siberian railroad. Most men regarded it as a military enterprise only; although why Russia should exhaust herself in military enterprises which in themselves would bear no fruit seems not to have suggested itself to most non-Russian thinkers.

But the Siberian railway was no sooner completed to Irkutsk than a steadily swelling volume of Russian emigrants began to pour all over the agricultural portions of western and central Siberia, irrigating that neglected land with the fertilizing fluid of human effort. No sooner was the railroad extended to Stretensk, at the head of the navigation of the Shilka and Amur rivers (hundreds of miles east of Irkutsk, and yet almost thousands of miles from the Pacific), than this current of Slav peasantry ran still farther eastward, spreading itself to right and left, until finally the Russian agriculturist and miner were slothfully at work, even to the very shores of the ocean.

Trade, which had been nothing but barter, rapidly increased to the dignity of commerce. Fields which for centuries had been only pasture-lands grew golden with grain, even under the negligent and wasteful methods of the Russian farmer. Mines which, since the days of Ivan the Terrible, had been little more than rumor became richly productive, notwithstanding the stupid legal restrictions and the sleepy Muscovite inertia which exploited them. Cities with beautiful homes, astonishing public buildings, commercial houses so considerable that you must see them to believe that they exist, and temples of worship magnificent in size, decoration, and design, sprang into being where not so long ago the nomad camped or the Chinaman revelled in his village dirt. Such had been the practical results of the building of the Siberian railroad. Such were the results of the building of our own transcontinental lines, except, of course, that the greater intelligence, greater energy, and higher general sum of modern qualities which distinguish the

American from every other people produced along our transcontinental lines consequences larger, higher, more miracle-like.

But, without entering into speculation which might be disputed, what are the obvious consequences, the small and immediate effects, which will be produced by the Manchurian railway? It is one of the few defects of our race and our present system that we look only to immediate results. We are intent only upon "the instant need of things," as Kipling puts it. It is one of our shortcomings, which many a temporary set-back must remedy, that we do not take thought for the morrow. The English look farther ahead in foreign matters than do we as a nation, but even the English do not have so much concern for distant results of her policies as do the Russians. A keen English observer records of an English Oriental merchant who, in response to the pointing out of the decline of British commerce in the Far East, unless improvement occurred in the out-of-date methods of English trade conditions, said: "What do I care for the future? We are not here for the benefit of posterity." But we Americans are already improving in this, and our foreign commercial necessity will some day make our foreign commercial policy rational, continuous, and far-sighted.

But we are examining the railway features of the Russian advance towards the Pacific. Let us, then, look at the immediate aspects of this railway, which is by far the greatest single work of construction recently accomplished anywhere in the world.

First of all, the road branches off from the Siberian railroad about one thousand miles from Vladivostock and takes a practically straight course, a little to the north of the middle of Manchuria, to Vladivostock. Thus the port of Vladivostock, on the Pacific, is directly connected with Moscow, St. Petersburg, Berlin, and Paris, without varying the mode of transportation, or even changing cars.

In the second place, this road, on its way to Vladivostock, cuts a great artery of Manchuria, the Sungari River, several hundred miles south of the point where this principal commercial tributary of the Amur empties into the larger stream. Thus, water communication is secured with the rich mining and agricultural Russian provinces north of the Amur River (for the Amur, impracticable for most of its course on account of sand-bars and rocks, is profitably navigable for several hundred miles from where this Manchurian river empties into it).

But the harbor at Vladivostock is frozen part of the year, and so, in the third place, the Russians were building, at the time of the author's investigations, and have now completed, another branch of this road from Harbin, the point where the Sungari River is crossed, almost due south to Port Arthur and Dalni, on the never-frozen sea. This branch passes through the most populous and productive portions of Manchuria, and connects Russia and all of Europe with splendid ports, on Oriental waters, open all the year round. Changed conditions have changed Russia's plans, and this new branch now becomes itself the principal line.

First of all, then, Oriental passenger travel to Europe is turned westward through the Russian Empire. A quick, comparatively pleasant, and comparatively cheap method of transportation is provided for all European business-men who want to reach Asia, and for all Asiatic business-men who want to visit Europe. Personal communication is established between the civilization of Europe, on the one hand, and the chaos of vital humanity and disintegrating institutions in the Orient, on the other hand. Think of the Oriental, for ages separated from the rest of the world, travelling from Pekin to Paris in a fortnight. A true *Arabian Nights* tale this, and more astonishing. The profound significance of this circumstance was probably not foreseen by its Russian creators. It is one of those larger meanings which always accompany any really great work of man; the achievement of that work always has results so vast and momentous as to startle those who undertook the original enterprise. Witness the immediate purpose and final results of Bismarck's plan of German federation; witness the original intention and the ultimate result of our late war with Spain; witness the development of all large and permanent national policies; witness the original purpose and final results of any of the great movements of history.

So of these Russian railways in Asia. Already passenger-trains running westward are well filled with European business-men returning home; and among them, even now, is a sprinkling of Chinese merchants on their way to the capitals of Europe. Even in 1901 the passenger-trains travelling eastward on the Siberian road were well filled with Russians, Germans, Frenchmen, an occasional Englishman, and sometimes an American journeying towards the Orient—this, too, when the road was uncompleted, and with days and weeks of vexatious discomfort on forest-fringed rivers. For remember that, until last year, a hard journey of many days on the Amur and Shilka rivers was necessary before you could board the Siberian train at Stretensk.

With the Manchurian line finished, nearly all the business-men of Europe and China will travel by this route. They can go from Pekin to Moscow in three weeks, in trains equipped with most modern conveniences and luxuries. Where, until now, one Chinese merchant visited European markets in person, hereafter one hundred will do so. Where, formerly, one European business-man investigated commercial conditions in China in person, a hundred will do so hereafter; and all of them who take this trip will pass through Russian dominion, breathe Russian atmosphere, be impressed with Russian influence and power.

A branch of the Manchurian railway has been built to the port of New-Chwang, hitherto the commercial door through which most imports into Manchuria were admitted. From this port a well-constructed railroad runs to the very gates of Pekin itself. This line was built by English engineers, under authority of the Chinese government, and its bonds were held by a British syndicate under a contract between the Chinese government and the Hong-Kong and Shanghai Banking Corporation, the great English financial institution of the Orient. Rumors were current in 1901 that this English syndicate was ready to sell its investments to the highest bidder, just as the owners of English ship-lines in the Orient seem to be willing to sell out to the highest bidder. We all know who that highest bidder will ultimately prove to be. It will be Russia.

The Chinese Emperor has a richly constructed special car on this railroad to Pekin. Immediately after the Boxer troubles the administration of this road was taken over by the allies, and its active operations intrusted by agreement to the English military forces. This military operation of the road by the English was still effective in the summer of 1901. In company with the English general in command of the British forces in China, a trip was made on this car from Tien-Tsin to Pekin. Recent from a journey over the Siberian railway from Moscow, fresh from the scenes attending the building of grades, the bridging of rivers, the laying of rails, and other incidents of the construction of the Manchurian railway, it was difficult not to associate this continued journey to Pekin with those great lines. Other passenger-cars were filled with English officers on leave of absence, going to Pekin from posts at which they had been recently stationed near Manchuria.

One could not help remembering that at the World's Fair in Paris a rolling panorama of the Siberian railway was exhibited by the Russian government, taking the travellers from Moscow directly by rail to the very gates of the Chinese capital. And it is not unreasonable to foresee a journey of the Chinese ruler to the courts and capitals of Europe. When this imperial journey takes place—indeed, when any man takes this trip—the first flag that greets his vision when he passes the Great Wall will be the colors of Russia. As he speeds upon his journey he will behold at every station the uniform of Russia; every hour he will hear the speech of Russia. For days and nights and nights and days he will pass through the unending territories of Russia. As he rolls rapidly westward, Russian conditions increase; Russian flags multiply; Russian atmosphere thickens, until finally, when he steps from his train in Moscow, he feels the very beat of the heart of the Russian nation.

It will be hard for that man ever to get away from the feeling that the great power of the future is Russia. No ordinary Oriental mind will be able to overcome the impression that the other nations of Europe are but inferior states compared with Russia and that the bearded Slav, notwithstanding his defects, is nevertheless the coming autocrat of all the Asias. And if that conviction is once fixed in the Eastern mind it will have an important if not determining influence not only upon the commercial conditions, but upon the destiny of the world. The first thing, then, that is the plain result of the Manchurian road is that the quickest—and in any case the only—overland business route to China is through the dominions under the protection and surrounded by the influences of the Czar.

An English merchant, a German investigator, and an American traveller were sitting under the tree before the English Club, looking out upon the charming bay of Chefoo. What were they discussing? Russia, of course. In the Far East everybody is discussing Russia wherever you go, and the Manchurian-Siberian railway as the most conspicuous illustration of her activity. The Englishman closed an intemperate assault on Russia as follows:

"She will flood Oriental markets with goods from Moscow and Tver, Smolensk and Lodz, and her other manufacturing centres, as she will flood China with her soldiers."

"That opinion seems absurd to me," said the German. "It is unprofitable for freight to be shipped to the Orient over the Siberian - Manchurian road. The distance is too great, and freight charges, if based on nothing more than operating expenses only, would be too heavy. The world's trade with the Orient, so far as European exports to China or any other parts of the Far East are concerned, must long continue to be by water."

The careful student of traffic who goes over the ground will be inclined to agree with this German opinion. The Siberian-Manchurian road will bring very little European merchandise into the Orient for some time to come. It is too long a haul. At lowest possible rates, the freight charge is so heavy that any thought of competition with ship-lines for that class of business does not appear possible, for the present at least. Large Oriental shipments of freight will go westward by the road to Europe, but not the reverse. For example, all of the finer brands of tea, which are so much injured by moisture when transported by ship, will hereafter be shipped very largely by this railroad. Indeed, heretofore a considerable part of this traffic has been by camel caravan across the desert for many weeks, until the Siberian railroad was reached, and then by rail.

As elsewhere, Oriental exports to Europe, and all kinds of freight requiring quick despatch, will also go by the Siberian railroad; but European exports to the Orient, in whose markets cheapness is an element of such moment, must for the present continue to be by water. This is a fact of first-class importance to America. We are less than five thousand miles from Oriental markets, and our competitors—Germany, England, Russia, and France—are, practically, eight or nine thousand miles away by water. Comparatively, Oriental markets are right at our door; and very far away, indeed, from our European rivals. And, for purposes of freight traffic, the Siberian-Manchurian railroad does not bring our European competitors any closer to the markets for which we are mutually contending.

"Why, then," said the Englishman, "is Russia building this road? Not for fun, I think!"

"Oh no, not for fun—certainly not!" responded the German, "but for very far-seeing, long-headed reasons, in which Russia surpasses us all. In the first place, Russia considers nothing hers which she does not control in a visible, tangible, material way; in the second place, she is always looking one or two centuries ahead; in the third place, the Russian people are hardly a people yet—they are still in the process of being compounded. Our children's children may find themselves worn out when these thick-skulled, hairy, no-nerved Slavs are just coming into their prime; and, similarly, our posterity may find themselves without markets when the future Russian may find himself in the actual possession of the only markets of the world now capable of seizure."

This bit of commercial philosophy is given for what it is worth. But, confining ourselves to the Manchurian road at present, it appears that it and the Siberian road will serve as highways for the introduction of European and American products into the very shops of the merchants and homes of the people in the interior of Manchuria, and into the markets of Siberia itself, until a point is reached where American merchants cannot afford to ship farther westward and where Moscow merchants can afford to pay the railway freights. And since America is thousands of miles nearer to the Orient by water than any European rival, including Russia itself, these Russian railways through Manchuria and Siberia would naturally become the principal distributing agencies for American goods.

But two circumstances can prevent this result: First, the placing of Port Arthur, Dalni, and New-Chwang under a Russian tariff so that American importers will have to pay heavy duties, whereas Russian importers will have to pay nothing at all on landing their goods at these Russian-Asiatic ports; or, second, a system of differential railroad rates by which, even if the ports remain open, the goods of every other nation except Russia will have to pay such extravagant freight charges that none but Russian merchandise can penetrate the interior along the line of the road. But if railway rates remain uniform and ports remain open, American commerce along the lines of these roads will not only be considerably increased, but actually multiplied manyfold.

"Do you not think that the long-hoped-for reform of internal communication in China will begin as a natural result of the railroad through Manchuria?" was a question asked of one of the deepest students of Oriental commerce. (The greatest practical difficulty, you know, in extending commerce among China's four hundred millions is to get the goods into the interior; an internal transportation tax on foreign goods—sometimes irregular, exorbitant, and corrupt—consumes all the profits before imports penetrate two hundred miles from any port.)

"Yes," was the reply, "I have thought of that myself, and, Englishman though I am, I will admit that if the Manchurian railway would break up the ruinous, foolish, and villanous obstruction to foreign commerce in the interior, the world should accept it as a blessing, notwithstanding its menace to the supremacy of other powers in the Orient; and no possible help to the Chinese could be of such far-reaching benefit."

Let us see just what this means. The Manchurian railway runs through about seventeen hundred miles of Chinese provinces, mostly populated. Over this region has spread that net-work of commercial obstruction which prevents internal foreign commerce all over China—that is to say, that heretofore the Chinese merchant who wanted to transport foreign goods from one point to another in China, has had to do it by carts over unimaginable roads (let us rather say imaginary roads), or by boats, or, what is more usual, on the backs of coolies; and he has been, and still is, literally "held up," every few stages, by collectors of transportation tax. (This is the famous "likin" tax.) This tax, even if it were legally charged and honestly collected, would be a serious enough burden on commerce to discourage trade for any great distance in the interior; but the "likin" tax serves as an excuse for numerous irregular collectors to still further burden all transportation of merchandise into the interior by exacting, under the guise of the tax, arbitrary, illegal, and corrupt charges.

But the irregular collector of corrupt transportation tax does not "hold up" the train of the Manchurian railroad; it thunders by him unheeding. Indeed, the traffic over the road is free from the regular "likin," as will be seen when we come to the railway agreement. The merchant gets his goods as quickly as possible to the railway, and, for a fixed and definite price, his merchandise is transported to distant points. Not by any other law, therefore, than the irresistible operation of practical progress, the reform of this ancient abuse of the whole Empire of China has begun. And when you reflect that, if transportation of imports were free throughout the Chinese Empire, foreign imports to the Chinese people would increase almost immediately, with little effort, from two hundred and fifty million dollars a year (the present amount) to a thousand million dollars a year (and this is the conservative estimate of the most conservative minds), you will understand what the working out of such reform would mean to the producers of America, who are many thousand miles nearer these markets than any of their competitors.

Think of America with a Chinese export trade of one hundred millions a year—of two hundred millions a year! And yet, unless our statesmanship is unequal to our opportunity, we shall ultimately have a greater commerce than that.

The stimulus to the commercial spirit of the people, on the one hand, and the deadening effect upon governmental obstruction on the other, which the railroad is producing already in Manchuria, are astonishing only because we do not think of these things till we are brought face to face with them. The local merchant who thought no market possible to him except that within the reach of his cart suddenly finds commercial limitations lifted, and a demand for his merchandise hundreds, even thousands, of miles away. The agriculturist or other producer who sold through his little merchant to this little market at no price at all, and with no demand, suddenly finds that his products are sought for, and at comparatively better prices. It would be a low order of mind which did not see the cause for this, and the Chinaman has not a low order of mind; commercially, he has a very keen mind. He finds the cause of this in a steel railway; from this it becomes clear to him that to get to that railway is the best thing for him.

Therefore he sees for the first time in his life the necessity for good roads. And although in 1901 the railroad was only in process of construction, and although freight was as yet hauled along the southern divisions only, and then merely as a matter of obliging merchants, and not as a matter of business, little branches of highway were already springing up and out from this steel spinal column of commerce like growing trade-nerves. As yet, of course, the improvement on these roads amounts to little. You would not notice it unless you were looking for it; but it is a safe prophecy that within ten years from the completion of the Manchurian railway fairly passable roads will lead from every station for distances into the interior; and from these roads others will gradually branch off. And so a people hitherto segregated from their fellow-men will be brought into contact with the other inhabitants of the earth.

Good roads in China! Free transportation of exports through the interior of China! Five years ago no serious thinker upon the development of commerce in the Orient would have even talked to you about those subjects, so impossible would he have declared them; for the roads of China (and Manchuria is a part of China) are impassable sloughs of mire in the rainy season and almost impassable rivers of dust when the weather is dry. Only in winter is transportation in Manchuria practicable, except by boats. In winter the solidly frozen earth makes a firm road-bed, and the snow gives possibility of speed. In this respect Manchurian roads are like Russian roads, but in all other seasons—well, an attempt was made to drive to a Chinese town three miles from the point where the Russians were building a railway grade, but it had been raining for two days, and the cart sank to its bed and the ponies to their bellies before the start was fairly made. The road was impracticable, and that town was cut off from the world.

"The theory of the Chinese government concerning roads has been that if there were no roads insurrection would be less probable and each community would be more firmly rooted to its own village," explained a gentleman of forty years' acquaintance with China and Manchuria. And the following patriotic reason was given by the Governor of one of the Manchurian provinces:

"If we had good roads, the Russians or any other invader could march right down into the very heart of our country. To build a fine road through Manchuria or any other part of China would be to invite invasion by our foreign enemies."

"So you see," said a European traveller in the Orient, "Chinese logic makes the building of fine highways the very substance of treason."

VII

MANCHURIAN RAILWAY RESULTS AND METHODS

"I CAN tell you one result of the Manchurian railroad," said the principal American agent for locomotives, steel rails, and the like, located at a certain treaty port of China. "America has sold the Manchurian road several millions of dollars' worth of engines, machinery, rails, and other railroad materials. In this respect, at least, the Russians are still buying in the best and cheapest market, and the best and cheapest market in the world is our own. It is not so with the Germans," he continued. "We underbid every one for the railway materials and other steel products for the German works at Kiaochou and the German lines in the province of Shan-Tung, but we did not get the contract. The German official explained to me that the German manufacturers demanded that preference be given to them, and it was." We shall see why this was true when we come to examine the German railway concession in Shan-Tung.

"Baldwin Locomotive Works, Philadelphia, No. ——, —1900." This legend on an American engine, running on American rails, spiked down to a Russian railway grade in Chinese Manchuria! Sordid or not, the feeling of national pride is strong within the American breast when this spectacle presents itself. It was seen many times in Manchuria during the summer of 1901. Now that the road is opened, you may see it for yourself; for most of the equipment for the Manchurian railway is American, a small percentage of it is French, very little is Russian.

Mature reflection will convince any man who has been through the locomotive works of Russia, and considered the extent of her railroad lines, that she cannot, for many years to come, supply her needed railway equipment. Certainly this is true of all the Manchurian and Trans-Baikal Siberian lines. After a while, maybe, she can supply her own needs. And it is the "after a while" that Russia is always thinking about. If Russia would think more about the present than the future, and if America thought more about the future than the present, the future condition of one and the present condition of the other would be bettered.

But what of the people of Manchuria? Just this of them, then. As has been noted, they are being brought into relation with the rest of the world. And they are being given work of which they never dreamed. Wants are being created in their breasts which the commercial activities of all mankind will ultimately be called upon to satisfy. Better clothing, better food, elbow-touch, and mind-contact with their fellows—so much for the people of Manchuria is this railway beginning to do. Fate, which is weaving its great web of civilization around the globe, has picked up at last this neglected strand of people, and the shuttle is already carrying it backward and forward and making it a part of the fabric of material human progress.

As we have seen, Russia in Manchuria appeared to be exercising care not to offend the people or their prejudices. Another example of this good sense was exhibited in her policy of paying for the land over which her railroad through Manchuria is built; for it is said not one foot of the right of way occupied by private persons was taken without compensation. Not only that, but the compensation was agreed to—often fixed—by the owner of the land. This fact is of interest because of the popular belief in America that Russia built her road through Manchuria by the forcible seizure of the right of way.

The railway company or the Russo-Chinese Bank (these are the ostensible builders of the road, and we shall come to this in a subsequent chapter) left the securing of the right of way to the officials of the Chinese government themselves. The Russians understand well these officials, and the officials understand well their people.

So the Russians came to an understanding with the Chinese officials; and even before that the Russian government had come to an understanding with the Chinese government (for this road is built under a contract to which the Chinese government is a party). And the Chinese officials, thus brought into sympathy with the Russians, remembering the intense prejudice of the people against railways, mindful of their vivid superstitions, satisfied, first of all, the pockets of the land-owners. It is said that not a foot of private land actually occupied has been touched by the Russians for which its full price has not been paid, and in some instances more than its full price. For example, it is stated that three thousand rubles were paid for one tract of thirty acres—that is, a hundred rubles, or fifty dollars in gold, per acre. Of course, special reasons may have influenced high payments. The average price paid for good land and bad land was twenty rubles an acre, or ten dollars in gold. Such was the apparently credible information, which, however, could not, of course, be verified.

Sometimes the railroad will make strange little deflections to avoid a clump of trees; but it is not the trees which the road is avoiding. It is the graves of which the little grove is the monument. (A Manchurian landscape is often made strangely attractive by clumps of trees scattered over it; and each clump of trees marks a burying-ground or a village. It is said to be the survival of an ancient and noble sentiment, neglected now in China, which makes the Manchurian wish to repose beneath the shades of the green foliage.) Sometimes, though, the expense of avoiding these burying-grounds was too great, and the railroad had to pay the family their own price for the land where their ancestors were sleeping. Then the remains were exhumed and placed elsewhere.

Of course, there are long stretches of the road through uninhabited plains and mountains for which nothing at all was paid. Parts of the line running through northwestern Manchuria, for example, traverse prairies whose soil is impregnated with alkali. Nobody lives there. Nobody lives in the northwestern or northeastern mountains, either. Nobody lives in some of the extensive valleys of northeastern Manchuria through which the road runs. Most of the fertile agricultural lands in these tracts are, and for decades (possibly centuries) have been, uninhabited. It is estimated by experts that not more than one-fifth of the cultivable land of Manchuria is occupied.

Russians are not so expert in railway building as Americans; they are not so expert in anything as Americans, except the art of establishing authority and maintaining it without friction after it is established. And though the Manchurian railway does not equal our great lines, as we know them at present, its construction, compared with that of the Siberian road, or even with any road of Russia, excepting only two, is very good indeed.

Of the corruption and fraud in the building of the Siberian road, and especially the Ussuri branch from Kharoff to Vladivostock, there can be no question, and the fact is not denied. In comparison, the Manchurian road is superior in solidity of construction, directness of route, and honesty of building. Both fills and cuts are well done. Even in 1901 short sections north of Port Arthur were ballasted with rock, and the bed for a new road is surprisingly good in these places. The bridges, particularly, were admirable. However, it must be admitted that there were signs of waste of power and material painfully apparent at many places. It is not said that the Manchurian road is ideally built; it is said, however, that its methods of construction are a distinct advance over those employed in the building of the Siberian road.

And this further and redeeming fact is noted also, that corruption in railway construction is being eliminated in Asiatic Russia as well as in Russia in Europe, and, indeed, throughout the whole world. Honesty of method is increasing because civilization is increasing all around the globe. Men are growing more and more upright from principle, and from policy also. And it is something of a defence of what some harshly call "commercialism" that fraud, dishonesty, and all financial unrighteousness are being eliminated, and gradually being made impossible even, by the highly complex organization of the commercial world.

Out of "the chaos and disorder of things" in Russia, as a keen, young Russian engineer brilliantly phrased it, business method, far more than moral improvement, is bringing regularity, accuracy, and therefore honesty. For example, Witte, Russia's finance minister and President of the Committee of Ministers, the master mind of the empire, has, it is said, applied to all expenditures a system of audit through which the smallest item of outlay must pass. The chief defect of this system is the cumbersome minuteness of its examination. Witte and other men of his quality of mind and will are the hope and salvation of commercial and constructive Russia.

Here again is noted that circumstance (perfectly natural, but which at first thought seems unnatural)—the beginning of reforms which extend to the home country by new work away from home.

Take, for example, a most obvious, simple, and striking instance. A Russian railway-train not only moves slowly, but it stops at all stations, and when it stops it stops for a long time. Officials go into the station with papers and telegrams and all manner of bureaucratic over-systemization. You would think that enough paper had been exchanged to start half a dozen trains. Suddenly an official with a whistle blows a loud shriek—a very needle-thrust of sound; but the train does not start and nothing is done, and nobody pays any attention to it. Then a loud-sounding bell is rung; still nothing is done, and no one pays any attention to it. In a few minutes (perhaps five) the bell is again rung, and again nothing is done, and no one pays any attention to it. And a third time the bell is rung four or five taps, and the people begin to move languidly to the cars; and then there is blowing of whistles. Finally, the whistle of the engine itself sends up its hoarse shout, and the passengers embark, and when all are on board the train sleepily moves off. On but three lines in Russia is there any more expedition than this.

It seems foolish, incongruous, that the reform of this non-modern leisurelyness of Russian transportation methods should begin in that Chinese Botany Bay—that fag-end of the world, called Manchuria. Yet this is precisely what is going on. In the two divisions north of Port Arthur Mr. Girshmann had regular passenger service inaugurated even in 1901. It was, of course, merely local and unimportant, and confined to carrying Chinese local merchants and Russian officers; and yet the train started off like an American train, with a single, sharp, swift signal. In two cases people who had been in Russia came near getting left. "I am doing away with that old practice," said Mr. Girshmann, "or, rather, I have never introduced it. We have new ground to work on here, you see, and it is easier to establish modern methods than it is where custom has already fixed and forfeited ancient abuses." And so it is that the reform of the transportation methods of the world's greatest empire has begun at its farthest extremity and upon its newest work.

There are other reforms which will be wrought by Russia's appearance on the Pacific; for this brings her face to face with the world's keen competition and its invigorating association, more even than does her railway connection with Europe. There is an indifference to promptness, a lack of enterprise and expedition, an acceptance of situations without speedy efforts to improve them, about Russian railway administration (except on two or three crack lines and trains), which are not in keeping with the spirit and methods of the present day. And when Russia comes in contact with American enterprise in the Orient (and American enterprise in the Orient will predominate in a very few years), and German enterprise in the Orient (and nowhere in the world is German enterprise so vivid and dynamic as in the Orient), Russia herself will catch the spirit of modern things and fall in step with modern methods in her entire commercial economy, but first of all in her railway administration. And she needs this badly.

But do not imagine that all is industry and punctual alertness in the Russian's work in Manchuria. Even there sloth and carelessness are in evidence. For example, a young engineer in charge of a bridge construction was found reading a French novel in a rather sumptuous private car on a siding in central Manchuria. The floods had impaired the temporary bridges some twenty miles ahead. Locomotives were in the yards, some of them with steam up. We had arrived on a little push-car, made by a platform, six feet by eight, lifted upon two sets of wheels and pushed by Chinese laborers. The "master of the distance" was asked to take the party to the break in the road with his locomotive. He refused, saying it was under the command of the young engineer. The young engineer refused because—"Well, because, what's the use?" said he; "you can't cross the river. You will have to go back and wait till the floods go down, and so there is no use disturbing myself for two or three hours to get you down the river, twenty miles away." Yet the river was reached and crossed, though with much hardship and some peril.

At another station the following incident occurred. Connection was refused because the assistant "master of the distance" had not ordered it, and the assistant "master of the distance" had not ordered it because he was not yet out of bed (it was eight o'clock in the morning). When he was awakened he declined because "the master of the distance" had not ordered it; and he had not ordered it because he was still in bed. When the "master of the distance" was aroused he declined because no special orders had been received subsequent to general orders, telegraphed three days before.

"Yes, it is quite true that the general orders to forward you when you wish are comprehensive and explicit, but that was three days ago. I must now have special orders to put these general orders into effect."

But when the methods of Mr. Girshmann are extended over the whole Manchurian system; when the Manchurian road makes its connections with the great American freight liners; when the current of commerce is switched on from all the world at Port Arthur and Dalni, these mediæval characteristics of Russian railway administration will disappear, because the conditions that permit them will have been destroyed.

Already the connection is beginning. Port Arthur is unsightly with its yellow hills and noxious with its streets of filth, and yet picturesque, too, in its cosmopolitan interminglings. It is a military and a naval port also. But while Russia is actually creating Dalni (it was said in 1901 that she had 25,000 laborers at work on buildings, breakwaters, piers, etc., and in the general construction of this port on Talienhwan Bay), Port Arthur serves as the commercial terminus of the railroad until Dalni is ready. Its harbor therefore was, as early as 1901, crowded with the ships of all nations. From Port Arthur you may go direct to Japan, Pekin, Cheefoo, Shanghai, Hong-Kong; sometimes direct even to Manila, and always direct to Singapore and Odessa. There are the crowding and bustle and jostle of commercial activity. Already there are three American commercial houses in Port

Arthur, conducted with vigor and push. The principal commercial establishments are German, as everybody who has been around the world would expect.

"If the Russians will only continue to let imports come in free, I ask nothing better," said a keen American merchant, who is making his mark in Port Arthur. "It is the best thing for them, too," continued he, "for even if we Americans and Germans do the most business temporarily these Russians after a while will get on to our commercial methods, which would be worth more to them than all the temporary rubles and copecks they could possibly make by monopolizing trade. Russia needs modern business system more than she needs anything else, and she will catch it from us if she rubs up against us long enough."

This young American was quite right, for within an hour a Russian railway official made this remark: "What we need is more of America's business method and system, more of Germany's cautious aggressiveness and laborious plan. We heartily dislike many things that seem characteristically American; they seem to us irrational. But one thing all men must admit, America is the business expert of the world, with Germany a close second, and, indeed, with some points of superiority over even America."

At the wharf in Port Arthur was a great ship of twelve thousand tons burden. It was flying the Russian flag: It is a member of that ambitious maritime undertaking, the "Russian Volunteer Fleet." Not many Atlantic liners have accommodations for first-class cabin passengers superior to this Russian ship running from Odessa to Port Arthur. She is fitted up to carry emigrants, too. This particular vessel had just landed fifteen hundred Russian emigrants, and her freight-carrying capacity is also fair. These astonishing ships—astonishing when you consider that Russia is a land nation, when you reflect upon the port they leave and the port they make—constitute one of the world's fast lines. There is not a modern device which they do not have. No twentieth-century comfort, luxury, or appliance of efficiency is neglected. They are fitted to be auxiliary cruisers in time of war—transports, commerce-destroyers, and what not. But, over all, their chief use is in commerce. They constitute Russia's water connection with the Manchurian-Siberian railway. They complete Russia's trade circuit around the world.

This "Russian Volunteer Fleet" deserves particular attention. It is not only Russia's first adventure in a large way in the fields of maritime commerce; it is also a great practical training-school for Russian seamen. Indeed, just that is its first and underlying purpose. Its officers are accomplished navigators, carefully educated. The crews of its vessels are young Russians taken from the shores of Russia's southern inland seas. The fleet draws a continuous stream of young men, carefully selected, educates them by means of practical service, and turns the best of them over to the already considerable and ever-growing Russian navy.

In this way Russia is preparing practical seamen for her navy and merchant marine, with which, in the course of time, she expects to become one of the first sea powers of the world, as she is already one of the very first land powers on the globe.

Russia's "Volunteer Fleet" is characteristic of the Slav race in three particulars — patient tenacity of purpose, aspiration towards the world's waters, and largeness of plan and execution. With her "Volunteer Fleet" on the sea the Russian nation is doing, as a government and a people, in the twentieth century what Peter the Great did at Saardam, Holland, in the latter part of the seventeenth century. This first of Russian rulers personified the silent instinct of the Russian people in his determination to place the flag of Russia on Russian vessels and launch them on the ocean highways of the world. Nobody in Russia knew how to build a ship, much less to navigate one. The Czar, who felt himself inspired not only to give the orders for progress, but actually to carry out his conception with his own hand, went to the yards of the best ship-builders in Holland, at that time the best naval constructors of Europe. He worked as a journeyman in the actual building of sea-going craft.

Everybody is familiar with this charming piece of biography, full of human interest and appealing in a peculiar way to all men of all races who feel in their blood the aptitude for the practical. Everybody knows, too, the story of the beginning of the Russian navy by this remarkable ruler. From the days of Peter until the present, Russian statesmen and the Russian people have steadily adhered not only to their great monarch's Far Eastern designs, but they have even more earnestly persisted in trying to realize his dream of Russia on the ocean. And exactly as the Russian Autocrat went to Saardam to work as a common laborer in the ship-yards of Holland two centuries ago, so the Russian people to-day are learning seamanship by real practice in the navigation of the deep, on voyages as hazardous as can now be made; for be it remembered that from port to port the regular journeys of the ships of the "Russian Volunteer Fleet" are the longest made by any line of the present day.

They start from Odessa, in southwestern Russia, and, sailing across the Black Sea, pass through the Dardanelles, the Sea of Marmora, and the Bosporus, traverse the Mediterranean, and, touching at but one Asiatic port, Singapore, make land no more, except for coal, until they tie up at the docks in Port Arthur, Dalni, or Vladivostock, hundreds of miles north of Japan. Two of these ships also start from St. Petersburg. It will be interesting and instructive to trace with your pencil on the world's map the course sailed by these modern Russian commercial leviathans of the deep. When you have traced such a line, and then remember the size of the ships, equal in tonnage at the time they were built to any ship afloat, you will begin to understand the comprehensiveness with which Russia lays out her plans. You will begin to discern also those contradictory elements in Russian policy—the element of national provincialism woven into world purpose.

For practical purposes, this remarkable fleet makes but two ports—Russian Odessa or St. Petersburg in Europe, the port of departure, and Russian Dalni, Port Arthur, or Vladivostock in northern Asia, the port of destination. Thus, practically without commerce except at Russian ports, Russia sails almost around the world to complete her circuit of empire.[1]

Largeness of design, comprehensiveness of purpose. The Siberian - Manchurian railway from the heart of Russia practically to the capital of China on the one hand; on the other hand the "Russian Volunteer Fleet," flying the colors of the Czar, from Russia's greatest commercial centre in Europe to the terminus of Russia's railroad on the waters of the Far East. So it is that the Russian sailor and Russian railway-man clasp hands in the Orient. Not that in this process they do not also touch shoulders with the rest of the world. Whether they will or no, these very agencies compel them to meet in commercial fraternity the keen minds and daring hearts of men of every other nationality. And so it is that these two agencies of commerce and communication are not only cementing Russian solidarity by land and sea, but are also bringing Russia into commercial brotherhood with the rest of mankind. And, finally, so it is that the revolution of Russian commercial methods is beginning where the hands of her commercial activities are joined at the farthest outposts of her dominions.

[1] Russia is now beginning local seafaring service in the Orient. For example, the East China Railway Company now have a regular line of steamers between Dalni and Nagasaki, just as Germany has between Kiaochou and Shanghai.

VIII

A DIPLOMATIC GAME FOR AN EMPIRE

"I THOUGHT that Japan took the lower part of Manchuria, including Port Arthur, as her price for ending her war with China," remarked a travelled American on board a great German liner bound for Hong-Kong. (Among the very finest ship-lines of the Orient are those of Germany.) "How, then, can Russia be occupying that same land?" he asked.

It is a pertinent question, and its answer relates to the most fascinating part of Russia's Manchurian advance on Asia. It is a story that can never be completely told, perhaps, by any one but Witte himself or the Russian Foreign Office. In a nebulous way, the external facts, however, are familiar to the diplomatic world, and careful inquiry and the sifting process of judicial impartiality give us a fair idea of those that are not in evidence. Entire accuracy is not claimed and is not possible; but general outlines may be drawn.

Attempts of any one to ascertain the foreign operations of the financial and diplomatic ministries of Russia are like the movements of a catfish in a muddy pond—it can never see clearly the details of its movements, and must be satisfied with locating the general boundaries of its home. So, in the financial and diplomatic plans of Russia, the world is kept admirably in the dark till results first announce the purpose of which those results are the accomplishment; and even then the real history leading up to them can be discovered only in large general demarcations. The same is true, though in less degree, of the diplomacy of the French Republic and of Germany, too; whereas the plans of the Amercan Republic (and almost equally of England) must be publicly debated before they are adopted. With this admission of our limitations, therefore, let us survey the head-lines of recent diplomatic history in the Far East.

First of all, everybody will recall how the triumph of China was universally predicted when the war between that country and Japan broke out. China was big, everybody said; her reserve strength was so enormous, her resources so inexhaustible, and so forth. Japan might win at first. It would take much time to arouse the giant of the Asiatic main-land. Yes, but once China was aroused, impertinent little Japan would be crushed. This was the belief of even the English Foreign Office. It seems incredible that the British ministry should have had no better information and reached no wiser conclusion than that of the rumor-fed crowd on the streets; but such appears, even to the warmest friends of England, to have been the fact. At the beginning of the war, therefore, England favored China, and, it is said, embarrassed Japan's naval operations on one or two signal occasions. Not till the world knew that China's defeat was certain and irretrievable did British statesmen appear to realize the situation; and then their change of front was ineffective.

On the contrary, in this great Asiatic crisis (world crisis it might properly be called) the intelligent, patient (her enemies say unscrupulous) work of Russia's bureaus of information throughout the Orient bore golden fruit. Russia knew that Japan would win. She reasoned that Japan would probably demand the cession of some portion of Chinese territory, most likely the lower part of Manchuria, which commands Korea; and on Manchuria Russia had long looked with desiring eyes. With that celerity and address which make Russia's foreign statesmanship as much superior to that of other nations as her internal and economic statesmanship previous to

Witte's administration had been inferior, the government of the Czar prepared for the result.

In this problem the Slav statesman had five factors to consider: China and Japan, of course, and England, Germany, and France. First, then, of France. Between the French Republic and the Russian Autocracy exist the most perfect and smoothly working governmental and diplomatic understanding of modern times. It is a singular illustration of the influence of hatred and interest in making a combination between two peoples unlike in temperament, ideas, and methods. Their alliance was born of their common fear and hatred of England and Germany—of the numerous conflicts of German and English interests with Russian and French interests. And so, in their foreign policy, and particularly in their Oriental diplomacy, they might almost be said to work as one government. So far as the rest of the world is concerned, French diplomatic agents in Asia operate in undersanding with Russia; and the reverse is also true. Russia, then, could count on the first trump in this game of empire.

Next, of Japan. Japan was, of course, the party whose purposes it was Russia's object to defeat; and her position, therefore, was clear, and her play in the game was well understood. She was a known and certain quantity. She would resist to the extent of her strength when the purposes of Russia were disclosed; but her statesmen could be depended upon to restrain the national passions and to prevent Japan from resisting beyond her power; and, at the close of the exhausting conflict, entering upon another war with a fresh power, her defeat would be certain. Russia knew, therefore, just how far she could go with Japan. And, in connection with Japan, she considered England as a quantity whose actions could be foretold with minute certainty, and the limitations of whose Far Eastern movements were as clearly defined as if they had been traced on a map. It was taken for granted that England would do nothing but protest.

"Oho," laughed a Russian official, when speaking about this very matter, "we knew very well that England would solemnly protest, but we also knew as well that she would also solemnly do nothing." (So far as that is concerned, no nation is anxious to go to war with any other first-class power.) "That is the reason why, from the day of her last statesman, Disraeli, until now, we have not counted, and do not count, on real opposition from England."

"If England had landed even a company of marines at Port Arthur when we took possession," said a Russian military authority, "we would have evacuated even after we took possession; for that would have shown that England meant to fight; and, of course, we are not going to fight a great power when we can get our ends just as well by waiting a few years."[1] And this is the picturesque way it was put by an Englishman, disgusted with his government's Chinese policy: "In counting upon the assistance of Great Britain, Japan believed she held a trump, when in reality it was but a trick card, whose apparent quality would disappear when it fell upon the table under the fierce illumination of impending conflict, like those manuscripts whose real writing is revealed only under a certain quality of light." And so Russia did not count England as a factor in the game.

But she did count Germany. Germany understood herself. Germany understood the Orient. Germany was the only European power, except Russia, that had a clearly defined Asiatic policy. Germany was pursuing that policy with material and physical methods and instruments. *Drang nach Osten! Drang nach Osten!* Steamship lines; increased fleets; pushing, growing, and gigantic commercial houses in the Orient; vast German investments in Chinese enterprises; German merchants,

[1] On May 4, 1898, in a speech to the Primrose League, Lord Salisbury actually said: "I think Russia has made a great mistake in taking Port Arthur. I do not think it is any use to her whatever."

German clerks, German traders; German the keenest commercial minds, and German the steadiest energy, even in Siberia itself; German the best consular service in the Orient and German the second best diplomatic service in the Far East; and, in Europe itself, the best army and the most highly organized system of transportation; the best-prepared net-work of mobilization which the world has yet developed; a vital people, the most assertive national spirit and the most vivid racial *esprit de corps* in Europe; German one of the ablest and most forcible rulers in the world; German the most highly trained corps of public men on the Continent! Germany must be reckoned with then.

Very well. Russia would reckon with Germany, and, when the time was ripe for it, Russia did reckon with Germany. Germany was brought to see that for Japan to seal her victory with a part of China's territory would be the beginning of Japanese supremacy throughout the whole Celestial Empire. Japan would follow up that victory with increasing influence in the affairs of China. Japan would dominate the Chinese court. Japan would reorganize China. Japan was herself Asiatic, and the natural agent of Chinese reorganization. Japan's superb statesman, Ito, was still in the meridian of his wonderful constructive vigor. And with Japan securely intrenched as the controlling power of China's four hundred million inhabitants, the commerce of the Far East would be forever dominated by the Island Empire. The Japanese problem of finding soil upon which they might live and resources which might be developed under their direction would be solved. All of this was pointed out to Germany, and all of this was believed to be true; and it was just as true that these facts spelled the commercial disadvantage of the German people in the Orient. And, therefore, Germany was brought to see that her interests and Russia's were identical. Thus reasoned Russia with Germany, and thus German commercial logic followed Russian diplomatic reasoning.

In all justice, it must be stated that Germany herself is said by many to have been the originator of this alliance.

The last card was the Chinese government itself. That government would be defeated. Russia knew that, and was the only power that did know it, so superior is her information concerning all Oriental conditions.

All that Russia had to do, therefore, was to await the inevitable defeat of China, the sure and profound humiliation of the Chinese government, the consequent and real danger of the overthrow of the present Manchu dynasty at the hands of the outraged Chinese people. All that Russia, had to do was to await the coming of all the circumstances which would make the government at Pekin crawl on its face to any power that would save its life. That power Russia prepared herself to be.

The end came. China was defeated. The hour was striking for the formation of the triple alliance of Germany, Russia, and France. Li Hung Chang, representing China, and that extraordinary intellect, Marquis Ito, representing Japan, met at Shimonoseki, and concluded the famous treaty of peace which bears that name. By this treaty Port Arthur, Talienhwan, and the entire Liao-Toung peninsula were ceded to Japan. It was not only a war indemnity to Japan, but it secured the very points of the Korean controversy which were the origin of the war itself.

But now, when Japan was in the full flower of her well-earned success, when the world applauded the diplomatic ability which had concluded one of the most ably conducted conflicts in history (little, though, that war was); now, when Japan stepped forth from the smoke of battle, amid the applause of nations, to her place among the powers of the world—a place earned by her civil and industrial revolutions at home and confirmed by glorious conduct in war by sea and by land: now, when

China was prostrate, humiliated, disgraced—at this supreme and psychic hour Russia made her carefully prepared play, which in an instant deprived Japan of the material fruits of her victory and the glory of her achievement, apparently rescued the Manchu dynasty from certain ruin, and bound it by the consideration of gratitude and every form of obligation to Russia.

A joint note of the Russian, the French, and the German governments was addressed to Japan, telling her, in the politest of terms, and with the cleverest of arguments, why the peace of the Orient would be permanently endangered by her retaining possession of the Chinese territory ceded to her, and expressing the hope of these "friendly" governments that the wise, the peace-loving, and the humane Mikado would save the situation by surrendering what his generals' skill and his soldiers' blood had won.

At the same time there were gathering ships of war between Japan and her prey. French ships came from the south, Russian ships came from the north, German ships hovered near. The Japanese navy was overmatched. The attitude of the Russians was that of immediate and determined action. Steam was kept up, decks cleared for battle, and every dramatic effect of war was introduced and employed with the skill of accomplished performers. It was, therefore, a lurid light by which the Japanese statesman Ito read the note of Russia, Germany, and France. He was out of money; he had just finished an exhausting conflict; his navy was outnumbered if not outclassed. It is said that the Japanese government in this gloomy hour of agony looked to England, her natural ally; but England's face was averted in indecision.

The Japanese nation clamored for war; but Japanese statesmen knew that war at this moment, without powerful aid, meant defeat, and defeat ruin. Therefore, the little empire broke her sword, submitted to her fate, and, with her hand held in the mailed fingers of the alliance which Russia had constructed, wrote the historic withdrawal of her claim to and authority over the territory China had ceded to her.

It was but two days after the ratification of the treaty by which Japan became the owner of the southern shores of Manchuria that she was forced to give them up, with such swift effect did the triple alliance strike. Apparently, in willing response to the note of the three powers, but in reality under duress of the alternative of war, the Japanese government issued to the world her withdrawal from every foot of land she had wrested from China. This reveals so fully the method of diplomatic operations of this kind that the most of the Mikado's proclamation is here reproduced:

"We recently, at the request of the Emperor of China, appointed plenipotentiaries for the purpose of conferring with the ambassadors sent by China, and of concluding with them a treaty of peace between the two empires. Since then the governments of the two empires of Russia and Germany, and of the French Republic, considering that the permanent possession of the ceded districts of the Feng-t'ien peninsula by the Empire of Japan would be detrimental to the lasting peace of the Orient, have called, in a simultaneous recommendation to our government, to refrain from holding these districts permanently.

"Earnestly desirous, as we always are, for the maintenance of peace, nevertheless we were forced to commence hostilities against China for no other reason than our sincere desire to secure for the Orient an enduring peace. The governments of the three powers are, in offering their friendly recommendations, similarly actuated by the same desire, and we, out of our regard for peace, do not hesitate to accept their advice. Moreover, it is not our wish to cause suffering to our people or to impede the progress of the national destiny by embroiling the empire in new complications, and thereby imperilling the situation and retarding the restoration of peace.

"China has already shown, by the conclusion of the treaty of peace, the sincerity of her repentance for her breach of faith with us, and has made manifest to the world our reasons and the object we had in waging war with that empire.

"Under these circumstances, we do not consider that the honor and dignity of the empire will be compromised by resorting to magnanimous measures and by taking into consideration the general situation of affairs.

"We have, therefore, accepted the advice of the friendly powers, and have commanded our government to reply to the government of the three powers to that effect."

The next move in the game was to secure from China authority to extend the Siberian road across Manchuria. In further preparation for the accomplishment of this end and object of Russian policy, the Czar's good offices to China secured a reduction of one-fifth of the interest on China's war debt and guaranteed the loan which the Pekin government was forced to make, and without which, or a similar guarantee, China could not have negotiated it at all. Indeed, you will be informed on high authority that this was the sole consideration for the concession by China to Russia for the building of the Manchurian railway; that the rescue of the Manchu dynasty had nothing to do with it; and that the "Cassini Convention" and all rumored secret understandings between Russia and China are purely mythical. But the course of events gives credit and plausibility to the other view, which well illustrates the ability of Russian foreign statesmanship to "sense a situation" and anticipate unborn conditions.

The enemies of Russia say that it was in anticipation of the difficulties, diplomatic and others, involved in such a grant of powers that the Russian government (and, if true, it shows how superb their resource is in foreign affairs) caused the famous Russo-Chinese Bank to be incorporated. The writer does not credit this statement; it is here given only because it is current. But, even if true, it does not appear that such a step is anything to Russia's discredit. If true, it would appear to unprejudiced minds to be quite the contrary, and to display a far-sightedness worthy of emulation by those who look only upon to-day and then complain if the conditions of to-morrow are not to their liking.

But it is not important whether the Russo-Chinese

Bank was evolved by Witte as a factor in this game or not; it existed when wanted, and that was enough. Apparently it is nothing but a private banking corporation with capital, stock, stockholders, board of directors, and all the other machinery of such a corporation. "In reality," said a credible banker of the Far East, "it is the financial agent of the Russian government throughout Siberia, and especially the Orient. In reality it is the financial end of the diplomatic machinery of Russia in the Far East. In reality it is the empire of the Czar engaged in the banking business."

All of this appears to be admirable rather than reprehensible; for Russia cannot be blamed for looking after her own interests, and such a bank is the most powerful of all agencies for the material advancement of Russian trade and prestige. This bank, therefore, secured from the Chinese government a contract by which to extend the Siberian railroad across Manchuria, the Chinese government giving the necessary authority. The foundation or beginning of this concession is said to have been the famous "Cassini Convention," negotiated by Count Cassini, present Russian ambassador at Washington. When the diplomatic world first heard rumors of the "Cassini Convention" there was something like consternation in the cabinets of Europe, and notes of inquiry were addressed to the Russian Foreign Office, which denied the existence of such a treaty. But while the "Cassini Convention" as reported may not have been concluded in the terms reported in the newspapers, the concessions were granted, and the road is now an accomplished fact.[1] Thus does Russia proceed, where her foes inquire and protest. It is not here stated that Russia ought to be checked; but if she ought, she must be confronted by a clearly thought out policy, continuously adhered to and backed by the certainty of something more than paper hostilities.

[1] See the reputed "Cassini Convention," in the Appendix.

You can hear all sorts of rumors concerning secret understandings between the Russian and Chinese governments; it was at one time said that Li Hung Chang had concluded a secret unwritten arrangement by which the Czar was to be suzerain of Manchuria. Of course, all reports of such secret understandings are rumors, and it is impossible to tell whether there is any truth in them. It may be said, however, that the observer becomes impressed with a sort of atmosphere of Russo-Chinese unity quite impossible intelligently to analyze. Despite Chinese protests against the Russian advance and all the hostile words exchanged between the two governments, things usually come out as Russia wishes. Of course this may be due to the superiority of Russian diplomacy, backed as it is by armed force; but the rumors of a secret understanding between the two governments are worth noting merely to fill in the general picture. It is again repeated that any unspoken, unwritten alliance is not stated to be the fact, but merely the suspicion of intelligent men familiar with the Far East.

Under concessions granted by the Chinese government to the Russo-Chinese Bank, this financial arm of the Russian government organized, under Russian laws, the East China Railway Company. This company is the builder of the road. It had a capital of 5,000,000 rubles ($2,500,000), practically all controlled by the Russo-Chinese Bank. But the actual capital for construction was raised by an issue of bonds guaranteed by the Russian government. Most of these bonds, it is believed, are held by the Russian government itself, either directly or through the instrumentality of government banks. Thus the money to build the road comes out of the Russian imperial treasury directly. The report of the Minister of Finance for 1900 contains the following:

The extraordinary expenditure is estimated at 192,945,424 rubles, including 25,195,258 rubles for the construction of the Siberian railway; 3,418,524 rubles for auxiliary undertakings in connection with that railway; 30.573.550 rubles for the construction of other railways; 43.758,092 rubles for the purchase of rolling stock for the Siberian and other railways; 85,000,000 rubles for loans to private railways, on security of bonds guaranteed by government, and 5,000,000 rubles for indemnities to private persons and institutions for loss of the exclusive right of selling spirits in retail.

Though it is not stated that any of this expenditure for that particular year was for the Manchurian railroad specially, it is known that a great part of it was; and the budget of 1900 states that the estimated expenditure on loans to private railway companies, on security of bonds guaranteed by the government, was 82,000,000 rubles (about $41,000,000). Moreover, the report accompanying the Budget of the Minister of Finance declared that

> The losses of the East China Railway Company are very great, owing to the destruction of a considerable part of the permanent way in Manchuria, and the delay in the completion of the unfinished line; these losses have had their effect on the budget of 1900 in the form of large grants, under the head of extraordinary expenditure, for loans to railway companies.

So it is not denied that the great Manchurian railway, built ostensibly by the East China Railway Company, and financed by the Russo-Chinese Bank under a contract with the Chinese government, is, in substance and in practical reality, built by the Russian government, under plans formulated in the office of the Russian Minister of Finance and upon disbursements made from the Russian imperial treasury. It is not clear where rational fault can be found with the Russian government for this method of procedure.

This railway company is also given certain mining monopolies in Manchuria. Mining rights are usual coincidents of a railway concession anywhere in the Orient, and often constitute its most valuable element. Accordingly, Russian mining-engineers are carefully and patiently investigating the mountains of Manchuria in search chiefly for coal and iron—gold is a secondary consideration—and, of course, for any other mineral riches which this possible addition to the Russian Empire may contain. More than one of these Russian engineers were met in the summer of 1901, and each of them freely told, with the enthusiasm of the discoverer, of valuable deposits which he had located. Coal, iron ore, and rich indications of gold have already been found, and no one need be surprised if oil and natural-gas fields, similar to those of Pennsylvania, Ohio, and Indiana, be developed on the other side of the globe.

The following are some of the items of the railway construction agreement (actual language of the agreement is here condensed):

First. The bonds of the railway company shall be issued as required, and only with the special sanction of the Russian Minister of Finance. The face value and real price of each separate issue of bonds, and all of the conditions of the issue, shall be directed by the Russian Minister of Finance.

Second. The payment of interest on and amortization of the bonds of the Manchurian railway shall be guaranteed by the Russian government when issued.

Third. The railway company must secure advances upon these bonds through the Russo-Chinese Bank, and not otherwise; but the government itself may directly, if it choose, take up the bond issue as a government investment, or upon loan, advancing on the bonds the ready money needed by the company from time to time.

Fourth. Money received by the company for these bonds, no matter whether it is received through the agency of the Russo-Chinese Bank or directly from the government, or in any other manner, must be kept at such places as are designated by the Russian Minister of Finance, and absolutely under his supervision and control.

Fifth. The ready money thus realized may be expended by the company in payment of various items of construction, and, of course, on interest on bonds as the same become due.

It thus appears that for all practical purposes the work is the direct work of the Russian government, and that the Russo-Chinese Bank and the railway company are nothing but agents.

The following are a few of the traffic and operating provisions of the railway agreement. (Again a condensation of the actual contract is given):

First. The gauge of the railway must be the same as that of Russian railways (five feet).

Second. If the Manchurian railway becomes inadequate to care for the traffic turned over to it by the Siberian and Ussuri railways or Russian ship-lines, it shall increase its capacity upon notification of the railway named. If the Manchurian and Siberian railways disagree about this, the Russian Minister of Finance shall decide the question, and if the Manchurian Railway Company has not money enough to make the improvements, the Russian Minister of Finance may supply the funds, if he think wise.

Third. Freight, passenger, and all other kinds of trains running upon the Trans-Baikal Siberian and Ussuri railway lines shall be received by the Manchurian railway as if these separate systems were one system, in full complement, without delay of any kind. The same rate of speed shall be maintained on the Manchurian lines as is maintained by the Siberian railways.

Fourth. The Manchurian Railway Company must build and maintain [it has done this already] a complete telegraph line connecting the same with the Siberian and Russian service.

It is thus seen that in the contract itself the railroad is made for all purposes a mere extension of the Siberian system.

Four more provisions of this contract are illustrative of the effect of the road upon transportation reform in China, already noted:

First. Passengers' baggage and goods carried in transit shall not be liable to any Chinese charges or dues.

Second. The tariff (or rates) for the carriage of all other commerce of the road shall be free from Chinese taxes or dues.

Third. The amount of import and export transportation taxes are fixed by special articles.

Fourth. The Russian postal service shall be extended over the entire Manchurian system, and the Russian letter and parcel post, together with the entire official machinery of the same, shall be carried by the railway company free of charge.

Finally, it is provided by this contract that the Chinese government may purchase the road from this railway company at the end of thirty years, and at the end of eighty years the whole property shall revert to the Chinese government without payment of any kind.

It is not intended at this point to set out technically and in detail the provisions of the contract under which the Manchurian railway is being constructed. Enough is given to show the financial character of the enterprise, its unity with the Russian railway system, the beginning of tax reform even before a rail was laid, and, in general, the legal outlines of the enterprise.[1]

Why, then, since the Russian government is in reality building this road, does it not build directly, without the intervention of the Russo-Chinese Bank as its financial agent and the East China Railway Company as its constructing agent? Why is not the construction agreement between the Russian and Chinese governments direct instead of through these agencies? There are many answers to these questions, known to those familiar with Russian railway construction, but there is one suggested which is of interest to other nations concerned in the trade of the Orient.

That answer is that, if Japan or any other power objects to the Russianization of Manchuria, the Russian government can, if it thinks expedient, reply that it is not the work of the government, but of a private corporation, whose interests, nevertheless, the Russian government has the right to protect, as Germany has the right to, and indeed does, protect the rights and property of her citizens and corporations.

Again, if Russia sees fit to extend her power still farther towards the Chinese capital, if she desires to proceed even farther southward, to the very centre of China, and meet the French lines advancing northward, thus making a

[1] The entire railway agreement is given in full in the appendix.

great Franco-Russian trunk-line throughout the length of the Chinese Empire (and that this is the intention is thought probable by most students of the Far East), she can do so through the agency above described, to whose methods the Oriental mind has become accustomed and in which the world has acquiesced.

And, in the third place, should it become desirable to exclude the goods of all other nations (except such a nation as Russia had entered into a private understanding with) from the interior of Manchuria it could be done by differential railway rates within the limits of the agreement, and, upon complaint by any other nation whose goods were thus discriminated against, Russia could reply that the fixing of these rates was a matter of business policy of the railway company. And so, though the closing of Chinese ports now controlled by Russia might be resisted by other nations vitally interested in the commerce of the interior, it is reasoned that those nations could not effectively object to differential railway rates, which would accomplish precisely the same result.

And so it is that the Russian statesmen are extending their net-work of power over Asia with a far-sightedness not exhibited in the foreign diplomacy of any other nation of the present day, except, perhaps, Germany. So it is that England may find herself helpless in the presence of accomplished facts and a series of impregnable diplomatic positions. So it is that quietly, plausibly, skilfully, and by the lasting methods of material constructiveness, Russia has achieved the first of her plans for the capture of the only remaining uncaptured markets of the world. So it is that, while England and America have been wasting time on academic argumentations about unsubstantial theories, Germany has been forging ahead towards the position of the first maritime power of the twentieth century, and Russia has been placing on the future the mortgage of her material dominion.

THE RUSSIAN ADVANCE

"Yes," said a Russian, "you may be stronger now, richer now, than we are, but we shall be stronger to-morrow than you—yes, and all the world; for the future abides with the Slav!" Such expressions you may hear again and again from young Russian gentlemen who have not become government haters. For example, take from another young Russian the following, which is striking: "Would you know another name for Russia? Very well, then, call her 'The Inevitable.'"

IX

HOW RUSSIA AT LAST REACHED THE UNFROZEN SEA

PREPAREDNESS is the secret of most successes in this world. Fate seldom makes league with the unequipped. Events come marching into every century, into every day, crying aloud for the nation or the man who is prepared. Russia's foreign statesmanship, admittedly the ablest of the present day, as her internal development has been admittedly the most backward, consists largely in reasoning out possible events from existing conditions, and then preparing for them. Her bloodless triumph over Japan, after Japan's bloody triumph over China, is an illustration of this. When the future of Manchuria looked most hopeless for Russia, she was in reality winning her right to build her railway and creating opportunities for permanent occupation, should that ever appear desirable. But the right to build the railway did not include the right to occupy the two coveted ports on the open and ice-free waters on the south Manchurian coast—Port Arthur and Talienhwan. She had merely secured the right to build her railway across Manchuria to her superb harbor of Vladivostock, which, however, is open to commerce during the winter months only by aid of ice-breaking devices. It was Russia's desire to secure ports where ice did not chain the feet of her commerce. It is believed that for decades her intentions have been firmly fixed on the two excellent Manchurian ports above mentioned.

Indeed, some outlet on the open oceans has been the determination of the Russian for centuries.

THE RUSSIAN ADVANCE

From the time of Peter the Great—he whom statesmen-for-a-day called mad, but whose vision embraced all future Russian policy, so far as the eye of man can now discern it—from the time of this marvellous mind and will till now, one vast purpose of Russia has become so fixed as to be almost a religion, and that is the determination of the Slav to reach the seas where summer skies await him and over whose waters the winds of commerce blow. There is something pathetic about the patient effort of the Russian to reach the oceans of the globe—to sail the seas that other men sail, to make the ports that his brothers make, and to meet his fellows face to face in all the harbors of the world. There is something that wins our sympathy in the Russian's almost instinctive attempts to escape from his vast and mighty cage, unequalled in its own extent though that cage may be.

For Russia is a cage and has always been a cage—the prison of a race. On the west, millions of gathering bayonets of Germany and all Europe, menacing the Slav with the perpetual possibility of war; on the south, the Turk turning Russia backward from the Mediterranean and the common highways of mankind; on the north, the frozen Arctic; on the east, the savage and remorseless tribes of Asia; and, later in time and farther in distance, India disciplined, armed, and fortified by England against the Russian's progress towards the Oriental seas. On the east, again, and farther south, between Siberia and India, the ancient empire of the Son of Heaven, mighty in its day, but now in the period of its decline and falling in pieces, yet forbidden to the Russian by the masterful policy and power of England in former days, and later by the jealousies and fears of other nations. Turn where he would, the Slav could discern in the far distance the world's common oceans, which he felt to be his common right as well as the right of other peoples, but from which man and nature had conspired to bar him.

And so, for this priceless privilege of the seas, the Slav

has for centuries been battling, until by sheer experience in the concentration of his energies and thoughts on foreign policy he has become the most finished diplomat in the history of negotiation, and the first in foreign affairs among the statesmen of the nineteenth and twentieth centuries.

Thus had he armed his hand with that skill which easily defeated Japan, easily discomfited England, and easily secured for himself permanent rights in a dominion which is itself an empire—an achievement so simply and so easily accomplished that, to readers of the world's affairs, it appeared to be sheer luck or else a very miracle. It was thus he took his first step in Manchuria, and, finally, it was thus that he found himself prepared to extend his advantages, his railroad, his power, his dominion southward through Manchuria, and to occupy and fortify the best ports for commerce and war, with only two exceptions, on all the coasts of China. Thus was realized at last a part of his passion and his dream—open ports on open seas. And so it is that the world beholds the beginning of the fulfilment of the imperial Peter's policy.

Remember, then, that the original railway agreement by which Russia began to throw her lines across Manchuria did not include that branch which has since become the trunk-line itself, running hundreds of miles through central Manchuria to Port Arthur and Talienhwan. But the Slav was on the ground. He was already building railroads, as contemplated in the initial agreement. He had already rescued China from its conqueror; he had already made the Manchu dynasty his debtor. Now he patiently built his railroad towards Vladivostock; and while he built he patiently awaited the development of events.

And events did not disappoint him. Once more the ancient tale was told of fate conspiring with him who is prepared. Some time before two German missionaries had been wantonly murdered in the province of Shan-

Tung. Germany demanded reparation. But the negotiations dragged their weary lengths along. The peculiar dilatoriness characteristic of Chinese diplomacy promised to make all effort fruitless. Finally, the Geman Emperor landed marines at Tsing-Tau, the port of Kiaochou, seized the latter town and the entire bay. No opinion is here expressed as to the right or wrong, the expediency or the inexpediency, of this bold move. Germany's friends pointed out, however, that her justification existed in the apparent impossibility of securing terms from China. Of course, the critics of Germany's action stoutly maintain that she was merely paying herself for her helpful attitude towards China in the past.

Confronted at last by the display of actual force, which most European statesmen believe to be the only thing the Asiatic anywhere understands, the Manchu Emperor made a definite grant to Germany of the entire bay of Kiaochou, including the city and port, and a coast boundary of land surrounding it. The salient features of this Kiaochou convention are as follows:

I. His Majesty the Emperor of China is willing that German troops take possession of the above-mentioned territory at any time the Emperor of Germany chooses. China retains her sovereignty over this territory, and should she at any time wish to enact laws or carry out plans within the leased area, she shall be at liberty to enter into negotiations with Germany with reference thereto, provided always, that such laws or plans shall not be prejudicial to German interests. Germany may engage in works for the public benefit, such as water-works, within the territory covered by the lease, without reference to China. Should China wish to march troops or establish garrisons therein, she can do so only after negotiating with and obtaining the express permission of Germany.

II. His Majesty the Emperor of Germany being desirous, like the rulers of certain other countries, of establishing a naval and coaling-station and constructing dock-yards on the coast of China, the Emperor of China agrees to lease to him for the purpose all the land on the southern and northern sides of Kiaochou Bay for a term of ninety-nine years, Germany to be at liberty to erect forts on this land for the defence of her possessions therein.

III. During the continuance of the lease China shall have no voice in the government or administration of the leased territory. It will be governed and administered during the whole term of ninety-nine years solely by Germany, so that the possibility of friction between the two powers may be reduced to the smallest magnitude.

Chinese ships of war and merchant ships, and ships of war and merchant ships of countries having treaties and in a state of amity with China, shall receive equal treatment with German ships of war and merchant ships in Kiaochou Bay during the continuance of the lease. Germany is at liberty to enact any regulations she desires for the government of territory and harbor, provided such regulations apply impartially to the ships of all nations, Germany and China included.

IV. Germany shall be at liberty to erect whatever light-houses, beacons, and other aids to navigation she chooses within the territory leased, and along the islands and coasts approaching the entrance to the harbor. Vessels of China and vessels of other countries entering the harbor shall be liable to special duties for repair and maintenance of all light-houses, beacons, and other aids to navigation which Germany may erect and establish. Chinese vessels shall be exempt from other special duties.

V. Should Germany desire to give up her interest in the leased territory before the expiration of ninety-nine years, China shall take over the whole area and pay Germany for whatever German property may at the time of surrender be there situated. In case of such surrender taking place, Germany shall be at liberty to lease some other point along the coast. Germany shall not cede the territory leased to any other power than China. Chinese subjects shall be allowed to live in the territory leased, under the protection of the German authorities, and there to carry on their avocations and business so long as they conduct themselves as peaceable and law-abiding citizens. Germany shall pay a reasonable price to the native proprietors for whatever lands her government or subjects require. Fugitive Chinese criminals taking refuge in the leased territory shall be arrested and surrendered to the Chinese authorities for trial and punishment, upon application to the German authorities, but the Chinese authorities shall not be at liberty to send agents into the leased territory to make arrests. The German authorities shall not interfere with the likin stations outside but adjacent to the territory.

In connection with this lease the German government secured from the Chinese government a railway and mining concession, the leading features of which, condensed, are as follows:

The Chinese government sanctions the construction by Germany of two lines of railroad in Shan-Tung. [Then follows a description of where the first line shall run and of an extension to the second line]. The construction of this extension shall not be begun until the first part of the line, the main line, is completed, in order to give the Chinese an opportunity of connecting this line in the most advantageous manner with their own railway system.

In order to carry out the above-mentioned railway work, a Chino-German company shall be formed, with branches at whatever places may be necessary; and in this company both German and Chinese subjects shall be at liberty to invest money if they choose, and to appoint directors for the management of the undertaking.

All arrangements in connection with the works specified shall be determined bv a future conference of German and Chinese representatives. The Chinese government shall afford every facility and protection and extend every welcome to representatives of the German railway company operating in Chinese territory. Profits derived from the workings of these railroads shall be justly divided *pro rata* between the shareholders without regard to nationality. The object of constructing these lines is solely the development of commerce. In inaugurating a railway system in Shan-Tung, Germany entertains no treacherous intentions towards China, and undertakes not to seize unlawfully any land in the province.

The Chinese government shall allow German subjects to hold and develop mining property for a distance of thirty li from each side of these railways and along the whole extent of the lines. [Here follows description of mining districts in detail.] Chinese capital may be invested in these operations, and arrangements for carrying on the work shall hereafter be made by a joint conference of Chinese and German representatives. All German subjects engaged in such work in Chinese territory shall be properly protected and welcomed by the Chinese authorities, and all profits derived shall be fairly divided between German and Chinese stockholders, according to the extent of the interest they hold in the undertakings. In trying to develop mining property in China, Germany is actuated by no treacherous motives against this country, but seeks alone to increase commerce and improve the relations between the two countries.

If at any time the Chinese should form schemes for the development of Shan-Tung, for the execution of which it is necessary to obtain foreign capital, *the Chinese government, or whatever Chinese may be interested in such schemes, shall, in the first instance, apply to German capitalists.*

Application shall also be made to German manufacturers for the necessary machinery and materials before the manufacturers of any other power are approached.

Should German capitalists or manufacturers *decline* to take the business, the Chinese shall *then* be at liberty to obtain money and materials from sources of other nationality than German.

The importance of this lease and railway and mining concession, is apparent on the face of the documents themselves, and in another chapter further remarks will be made concerning them. They are inserted at this point as necessary links in the chain of the story of Russia's occupation of south Manchuria, and of the military, naval, and commercial ports on the shores of the Chinese waters; also, they are believed to be of interest as an example of what a Chinese railway concession to a first-class power is like.

When Germany seized Kiaochou, Russia was not long in acting. Russia reasoned thus: Here was a seizure of territory by an empire which is already one of the great powers, and which has declared ambitions to become the first and chiefest power among the nations. Here was Germany throwing her influence across the path of Russian intentions in Asia, as she has so effectively thrown her financial and commercial power across the path of Russia, and of England too, in Turkey and Asia Minor. And here was this seizure of territory, an extension of physical and material influence into the very breast of China, sanctioned by the Chinese government.

The event for which Russia was prepared had occurred at last. Very clearly, if the seizure of a portion of Chinese territory by Japan, as her price of peace in closing her war with China, was a menace to the permanent peace of the Orient, Germany's seizure of territory in the very centre of the Chinese coast was equally a menace. True that Germany, Russia, and France had protested against

Japan's occupation of a portion of Chinese territory; true that Germany's seizure of Kiaochou and the extension of German railways into one of China's great provinces was inconsistent with the allies' protest against Japan's occupation of southern Manchuria; true that the implied understanding as to the integrity of China, necessarily involved in the allies' protest to Japan, had been broken.

But, said, in effect, the Russian statesmen, it was not Russia that had broken it. It was not Russia that had changed these conditions. Apparently, so far as the letter of the implied agreement was concerned, Russia had been faithful to the understanding. But now conditions were changed, and through no fault of Russia. She was justified in protecting her interests, then. Nobody could find any fault with that. She would protect her interests therefore. If Germany received a port, so should Russia receive a port. If Germany occupied Kiaochou, Russia should occupy Port Arthur and Talienhwan. So reasoned Russian statesmen. Such was her representation to China. Such was her case before the public opinion of the world. Like lightning, she carried this determination into effect. The German lease was dated March 6, 1898.

On March 27th of the same year a treaty was signed by the representatives of the Chinese and Russian governments, leasing Port Arthur and Talienhwan to the Czar, and extending all railroad construction rights from where the line of the road crosses north-central Manchuria on its way to Vladivostock southward to these ports.

And because the Russian lease, like the German grant and concession, is fundamental, because it, like the German lease, is an historical and political landmark, from which the beginning of the disintegration of China, in a physical, tangible, and material sense, may be reckoned, if that break-up ever occurs, it is here set out almost in full:

Article I.—It being necessary for the due protection of her navy in the waters of north China that Russia should possess a station she can defend, the Emperor of China agrees to lease to Russia Port Arthur and Talienhwan, together with the adjacent seas, but on the understanding that such lease shall not prejudice China's sovereignty over this territory.

Article II.—The limits of the territory thus leased, for the reasons above stated, as well as the extent of territory north of Talienhwan necessary for the defence of that now leased, and what shall be allowed to be leased, shall be strictly defined, and all details necessary to the carrying out of this treaty be arranged at St. Petersburg with Hsu Tajen so soon as possible after the signature of the present treaty, and embodied in a separate treaty. Once these limits have been determined, all land held by Chinese within such limits, as well as the adjacent waters, shall be held by Russia alone on lease.

Article III.—The duration of the lease shall be twenty-five years from the day this treaty is signed, but may be extended by mutual agreement between Russia and China.

Article IV.—The control of all military forces in the territory leased by Russia, and of all naval forces in the adjacent seas, as well as of the civil officials in it, shall be vested in one high Russian official, who shall, however, be designated by some title other than Governor-General (Tsung-tu) or Governor (Hsun-fu). All Chinese military forces shall, without exception, be withdrawn from the territory, but it shall remain optional with the ordinary Chinese inhabitants, either to remain or to go, and no coercion shall be used against them in this matter. Should they remain, any Chinese charged with a criminal offence shall be handed over to the nearest Chinese official, to be dealt with according to Article VIII. of the Russo-Chinese treaty of 1860.

Article V.—To the north of the territory leased shall be a zone, the extent of which shall be arranged at St. Petersburg, between Hsu Tajen and the Russian Foreign Office. Jurisdiction over this zone shall be vested in China, but China may not quarter troops in it except with the previous consent of Russia.

Article VI.—The two nations agree that Port Arthur shall be a naval port for the sole use of Russian and Chinese men-of-war, and be considered as an unopen port so far as the naval and mercantile vessels of other nations are concerned. As regards Talienhwan, one portion of the harbor shall be reserved exclusively for Russian and Chinese men-of-war, just like Port Arthur, but the remainder shall be a commercial port, freely open to the merchant vessels of all countries.

Article VII.—Port Arthur and Talienhwan are the points in

the territory leased most important for Russian military purposes. Russia shall, therefore, be at liberty to erect forts at her own expense, and to build barracks and provide defences at such places as she desires.

Article VIII.—China agrees that the procedure sanctioned in 1896, regarding the construction of railroads by the Board of the Eastern China Railway Company, shall, from the date of the signature of this treaty, be extended so as to include the construction of a branch line to Talienhwan, or, if necessary, in view of the interests involved, of a branch line to the most suitable point on the coast between New-Chwang and the Yalu River. Further, the agreement entered into in September, 1896, between the Chinese government and the Russo-Chinese Bank shall apply with equal strength to this branch line. The direction of this branch line and the places it shall touch shall be arranged between Hsu Tajen and the Board of Eastern Railroads. The construction of this line shall never, however, be made a ground for encroaching on the sovereignty of China.

It will be observed that Russia's lease of Port Arthur and Talienhwan is for the period of twenty-five years. But note also that the first article states that the lease is made because it is necessary for the due protection of Russia's navy in the waters of north China that Russia *shall possess* a station she can defend.

Also note, as with Germany in Shan-Tung, authority is given to *fortify;* and note, most of all, that Russia has acted upon this authority. The harbor at Port Arthur is deep and narrow and not over large, and is surrounded by high, almost mountainous hills. With all speed, day and night, Russia instantly began planting impregnably her power on these eminences. At the time the writer reached Port Arthur, at the end of the journey of investigation through Manchuria, work was still in progress. Trench and earthwork and guns—not frowning guns, but guns that hide their menace—and all the incidents of modern fortification were being perfected over this maritime terminus of her railroad. With the foundation of her physical authority planted deeply, even to the hearts of the everlasting hills, it is not likely that Russia will ever depart, at least from Port Arthur and Talienhwan. It is the last and most conclusive piece of evidence to sustain the proposition that she intends to remain in Manchuria, and permanently.

Statements to the contrary were made by the highest authorities in the diplomatic world. If, in 1901, you asked an English diplomat, an American diplomat, most of all a Russian diplomat himself, "Does Russia intend to occupy Manchuria permanently?" each of them would have assured you, and sincerely too, that she did not. An eminent American diplomatist in conversation, in the fall of 1901, ridiculed the statement that Russia was a fixture in Manchuria. The suggestion, made at the same time in published articles, was received with incredulity by the great body of the American press. You were told, too, that even then Russia was urging upon China a treaty providing for Russia's departure from Manchuria and for her evacuation of even Port Arthur. No doubt, such a treaty was being presented to the Chinese court, but also, no doubt, such a treaty will never be signed.

And if it be not, will it not become clear to the simplest mind that again Russia has made a paper record of non-aggression and of a willingness to surrender which all the world may read? And is not that a strategic position of commanding value in Russia's frontier negotiations upon the Pacific? Can she not point to the fact that it was not she who violated the spirit of the allied protest to Japan concerning the occupation of Manchuria, but another? that it was not she who was the first to seize Chinese territory, but another? that she secured the lease of Port Arthur and Talienhwan and adjacent territory only as a matter of self-defence? and that, finally, she has actually proposed a treaty for the withdrawal from every foot of Chinese territory?

For that is the case on the record which Russia has made to the world; and should the Manchu Emperor decline to sign such a treaty, has Russia not put the Pekin government under additional guarantee and bonds?

And so it appears improbable that Russia will withdraw from Manchuria. Her railroad is there, her ships are there, her mines are there. Coal, iron, silver, gold, and other treasures of mineral wealth—all Russia's under her railway agreement—are there. Soil which will grow any vegetable in the temperate zones and some of those of the semi-tropic countries are there. (You may see wheat, barley, oats, tobacco, potatoes, Indian corn, beans, millet growing in fields that look like miniature American farms, or, rather, like overgrown American gardens, in all the inhabited portions of Manchuria. The soil is so rich that many crops were seen, in the summer of 1901, already beginning to grow in the same fields from which the first crop had been gathered only a fortnight before.) All these are there. And, most of all, the command of all China, the point from which the sceptre of the Russian Autocrat may be extended over all the East, is there. The throne of the future of the Orient appears to be planted now upon the eminence that lifts above the waters of Port Arthur, and above it already floats the Russian flag.

X

COLLISION OF RUSSIA'S ADVANCE WITH JAPAN

THERE is but one agency which might dislodge the Russian from Manchuria; that agency is the sword-like bayonets of the soldiers of Japan, the war-ships of Japan, the siege-guns of Japan, the embattled frenzy of a nation stirred to its profoundest depths by the conviction that the Czar has deprived the Mikado of the greatest victory and the richest prize in all the history of the Island Empire—a history which reaches back not through centuries, but through millenniums. And that Japan is determined that Russia shall withdraw from Manchuria no careful student on the ground can doubt. No thoughtful student of geography can doubt it.

War between Russia and Japan is a serious probability. It is believed by the best informed that it would be raging now if Japan had the money. It came near breaking out in February, 1901, in spite of the Mikado's poverty. Only the financial situation muzzles the artillery of the England of the Orient. And Russia's financial situation is almost as bad. And so it is that both Russia and Japan will hesitate to give the other a *casus belli*. All statesmen are obliging, conciliatory, reasonable when confronted with the grim alternative of armed conflict before they are ready for it. But, however long the want of actual cash may postpone this conflict, it is hard to see how it is to be avoided in the end. If it is put off for five years, the causes for it will still remain; if it is put off for ten years, yet will those causes persist; if it is put off for a quarter of a century, nevertheless the elements of conflict will continue. What then are those enduring causes which time itself, as it now appears, cannot remove?

Look at your map. Just above Japan, within hardly more than a day's sail, is Vladivostock, one of the finest harbors for naval and military purposes in the world, and one whose only defect is its three months of ice. It is the Gibraltar of the East. And it is Russian. In its waters the Russian war-ships lie safe from all attack. From its wharves Russian railways run northward through Russian wheat-fields to the Russian capital of east Siberia.

Cross now, southward, a peninsula and reach the sea; and travel, still south, the shores of the sea till you come to the mate of Vladivostock, Port Arthur, of which so much has already been said. Here, again, the war-ships of Russia are within instant touch of Japan. Here, again, they lie in safety, secure from all attack. Again, from the wharves of this southern Vladivostock the Russian railway lines run northward; and though the territory through which these railway lines run is still nominally Chinese, the facts here presented show that, for all practical purposes, it may, in the future, become Russian, if the Russian wills it so.

North of this peninsula, then, are Russian ports, Russian ships, and Russian guns; a Russian railway, Russian commerce, the Russian people: Back of this peninsula, again, are Russian railways, Russian commerce, and Russian bayonets. South of this peninsula, again, are Russian harbors, Russian guns, Russian commerce, and Russian railways.

And this peninsula, running out from these Russian environments, almost touches Japan itself. As a Japanese statesman said, in speaking of this peninsula, "It is like an arrow, with the point aimed at our heart."

This peninsula is Korea, and it is inevitable that Korea shall become either Russian or Japanese. And if it be Japanese, it will be a powerful factor in preventing Manchuria from ever becoming Russian.

Let us listen again to the Japanese publicist just quoted. "The absorption," said he, "of Manchuria by the Russians, if completed, renders the position of Korea precarious. And Korea is a matter of first and last importance to us. Korea is life or death to Japan."

"Yes," said another Japanese publicist, of high intelligence, "if I were a Russian I might insist on Korea becoming Russian; but as I am a Japanese, for the safety of my country, I insist that it shall become Japanese, and upon that insistence every subject of the Mikado is willing to lay down his life."

"Ah," said a Japanese diplomat, in concluding an absorbing conversation upon the next great crisis of the world, "Korea must be Russian or Japanese, it is said. Yes. Well, in that case, it will become Japanese. Every one of Japan's two hundred and fifty thousand soldiers will die, if need be, to achieve this victory for his emperor—this act of international justice, this guarantee of the safety of the Japanese nation. And, after our soldiers are gone, the nation itself, man, woman, and child, will battle, forty millions of us, till the last yen is gone and the last life yielded. I mean what I say. It is with us no statesman's policy; it is with us the settled purpose and the burning passion of a people."

This is fervid language; but talks with merchants, with guides, with even the common people of Japan, will convince you that this Japanese diplomat's Oriental eloquence is quite within the limits of the truth.

Here, then, is reason enough, and there are other reasons still more profound. Japan is already seriously crowded for living-room for her people. During the past ages of her history, the birth rate was, no doubt, as great as now, but the death rate also was almost equally great. And so her population, during many centuries, was very steady, just as China's is to-day. But in recent years Japan has become a modern hygienic nation. The science of medicine has made no such progress anywhere in the

Orient as in this island-empire. Indeed, comparing her ignorance of the healing art, even in recent years, with the high position she occupies to-day, her medical progress is the greatest, relatively speaking, in the world. A conspicuous illustration of this is found in her quarantine system, which is far and away the most perfect in detail and careful in administration of any quarantine system on the globe.

Four years ago a certain ship entered the port of Nagasaki. The quarantine officers made that careful inspection of passengers with which all Oriental travellers are familiar. Finally, one man was taken from the ship who had some little indications of fever. By sunset that man was dead of the bubonic plague. The ship was accordingly quarantined for eight days. Its disinfection by the Japanese quarantine officers was as thorough as could possibly be done by any medical men in the world. During these eight days the writer, by special courtesies, was permitted to carefully inspect the whole quarantine establishment at this important place, and to have long talks with the medical authorities. Similar examinations were made elsewhere, and the perfection of Japan's quarantine system compelled heartiest admiration. So it is that, while the plague may ravage China, which is almost within sight of the Japanese shores, the Japanese millions have been made secure from its dread invasion. And medical advance in other directions is being made with astonishing rapidity throughout the little group of islands where live the forty odd millions of the Mikado's subjects.

The result, of course, will occur to any one. The birth rate continues as great as formerly, and in only two or three places in the world is it greater than in Japan; but the death rate daily decreases. The population of Japan, therefore, steadily and rapidly increases. Japan has no method of relieving this accession of numbers by emigration as Germany has, so we find her in the condition in which Germany would find herself if the millions of Germans who have come to America and the other millions who have gone elsewhere throughout the world had all been kept at home. So Japan is looking for some place to plant her surplus millions. This was one of the three or four great reasons for acquiring Formosa; it is one of the vital reasons for ultimately occupying Korea. Manchuria, with its comparatively scanty population, and climatic conditions like those of Japan, would have been an ideal spot for the planting of a Japanese empire with the surplus Japanese population.

On the other hand, in addition to the other reasons given why Russia considers Manchuria desirable, is the fact that she, also, feels that the natural pressure of her population requires Russian occupation of Manchuria. It is not a matter of future speculation, but only of simple arithmetic and of near-by certainty, that Siberia will be as thickly peopled as Russia itself. When that occurs, the overflow can go no place but southward, through the fertile valleys of Manchuria.

Still another fundamental reason for this conflict is that which gave rise to the triple alliance, whose diplomacy and menace drove Japan from southern Manchuria after her war with China. This is the fear entertained by every Russian, German, and French statesman, in common with every student of Oriental affairs, that Japan intends to undertake the reorganization of the Chinese Empire; and that Japan regards this as her "destiny" no one who has gone over the ground will deny. The reasons for it are powerful. They grow out of the elements of race and geography. The Japanese and Chinese are both Asiatics. Their written language is very similar, and for practical purposes the same; some of their religions are identical; their modes of thought are so much alike that the Japanese may be said to be the only people who understand the Chinese. In this, it is true, the Russian is a close second to the Japanese.

Furthermore, they are so close together that they may be said to be physically in elbow touch.

Indeed, Japan, it is said, has already begun work upon a far-sighted programme of China's reorganization. The reported employment of Japanese professors in the Imperial University at Pekin is an illustration. The employment of Japanese officers in the Chinese army in the place of European officers is still a more significant one. This plan is very great in its outlines. It comprehends the modernizing of all the schools of China, substituting for the study of the ancient classics the acquirement of modern scientific and useful knowledge; it includes the opening up of the country by the gradual construction of highways; it looks to a systematic policing of the entire empire.

Indeed, an entire chapter might be written, and upon respectable authority, describing the ultimate intentions which Japan entertains as to China. It sometimes seems that her statesmen do not take very much pains to conceal them. There is no doubt that up to the present she has earnestly hoped that she might be aided in this, her high dream of Oriental dominion, by an alliance with England and America; and although such an alliance would rob her of most of the fruit of her statesmanship, she would be only too glad to make the division for the invaluable aid of these two powers. It is believed, however, that she has abandoned hope of such a far-reaching, hard-and-fast compact, and that she has finally come to the consciousness that she must go it alone.

Of course, if Japan should thus become the dominant influence in China, her merchants and manufacturers would capture the lion's share of the vast future commerce of the Flowery Kingdom. Such Japanese predominance in China would also make of China a far more powerful barrier against Russian advance than Japan itself now is.

It is thus easy to see that the Japanese conception of the Oriental "destiny" of Japan and the Russian conception of the Oriental "destiny" of Russia come into a face-to-face conflict. On the one hand, Russia would be deprived of the markets which she hopes in the future (perhaps not for a century or two) to be able to as perfectly control physically as she now controls those of her own dominions; on the other hand, a halt would be called to the march of her alleged national ideal of setting up the cross over China's myriads of millions, of which ideal something will be said in a later chapter. Even if Japan's programme were carried out with the co-operation of England and the United States, the effect upon Russia would be precisely the same. So it appears that this dispute, whose springs are deep in the rocks and soil of circumstances, seemingly beyond the control of any human statesmanship, may have to be settled, in the final analysis, by trial of battle.

And if war does come, there are more contradictory elements of strength, more contradictory conditions, more premises upon which wagers for either side might be reasonably made than in any war of modern times—the Japanese navy, the Russian navy; Japanese preparedness, Russian preparedness; the Japanese soldier, the Russian soldier; the skill, valor, the staying powers of the flower of the people of the Orient, against the slowest, most undeveloped, but yet the most tenacious and most unexhausted race of the Occident. It will be a great drama, and when the curtain falls on its last desperate act the destiny of the East, and in a certain sense the future of the world, will be forecast by the flag which flies in triumph over the carnage of that final conflict.

This probable and prospective war between Japan and Russia will be a conflict not only of opposing interests but of singularly acute race antipathies. Tolerant as the Russians are of other races, their hatred of the Japanese is pronounced and apparently instinctive. Also, there is in it an element of contempt. At a Moscow dinner-table the progress of the Japanese was remarked and the word civilization applied to them. "Civilization!" quickly spoke up a banker, with an eager spirit not in keeping with his calm calling. "Civilization! You don't mean that. You mean imitation. Everything is on the surface. Everything is temporary—false!"

And this same harsh idea was voiced by Cierpitsky's common soldiers in the middle of Manchuria. An officer was indulging in an informal talk to several hundreds of his soldiers (this is a characteristic of the Russian army). Here is the conversation as it occurred, repeated verbatim and with literal accuracy. An officer leaning out of a window said to the assembled soldiers:

"Well, boys, are you glad this campaign is over?"

The soldiers answered in their customary chorus: "Yes, our colonel, but we are willing to fight again."

Colonel: "If the Japanese come, will you let them whip you or will you whip them?"

Soldiers, in chorus: "What! Those monkeys whip us? Never, our colonel!"

This same sentiment was found among the Siberian miners. "I cannot tolerate the Japanese," said a Siberian mine-owner, who has travelled very extensively. "They are such make-believe people, and there are other things about them." And then very unpleasant references were made to the Japanese.

These pages might be entirely taken up with similar expressions from business-men, bankers, soldiers, officers.

It is even denied that the Japanese are content with their evolution into European civilization. "They are not capable of it, and actually despise it," said a Russian diplomat in a certain Asiatic station. "They are already beginning to abandon the externalization of our European civilization as a child throws away a new toy. For example: In Tokio a very prominent public man and his wife adopted European modes of dress when that craze took them off their feet some years ago. Their daughters were reared in English clothes. Well, last year those daughters threw away their Paris-made gowns and resumed the native Japanese kimono; and instances like that could be given by the hundred."

The deep dislike of the Japanese for the Russian is even more passionate. "They cannot be trusted; they will violate any compact when their selfish interests dictate," was the expression of a Japanese of good birth, good education, and good condition. "They are the spoilers of the world," said another. "When has Russia kept faith? When has she ceased to slay and debauch?"

These expressions are given only to reflect the real mutual opinions of these opposing peoples. It may be that they are the utterances of mere temporary irritation, which will pass away, as French and German antagonism have so largely evaporated with the years. Indeed, many far-seeing men think that just this happy conclusion will occur. But at the present hour the war itself is taken for granted. One of the most conservative of Japanese statesmen said: "I admit that it looks like an appeal to arms, but I hope and believe that it will be settled peaceably. The immensely increased intercommunication of nations, the telegraph, the interwoven commercial interests, all conspire to aid us to a peaceful settlement."

Like the conservative men of all nations, the thoughtful statesmen of Japan are hoping and working for peace but preparing for war. "I admit that Russia is strengthening herself in Manchuria as fast as she can," said one of the weightiest minds of the island-empire, "and that she is doing it with ultimate intentions on Korea there cannot be the slightest doubt. We hope that the public opinion of the world will never permit further Russian aggression, but we are preparing as fast as she is. In such a war she will be helpless, because we command the sea, and she will never again be able to make the triple alliance which robbed us of our victory over China."

The expression of Russian public men, on the other hand, is even more pacific. You will never be able to get a Russian civil official to admit the possibility of war. "But," said a Russian diplomat travelling towards his station in the Far East, "if war is forced on us, we are ready this moment." And he meant it; but, from what was personally known, this is believed to be an over-statement. They were not ready "this moment," and neither was Japan.[1]

"Those brown fellows must strike first," said the head of a Russian civil commission. "We don't have to strike first; all we have got to do is to wait and strengthen ourselves."

"No, there will be no war between Russia and Japan," declared a high official of the Manchurian railway, "because it is perfectly hopeless for Japan, and her statesmen have sense enough to see that. Why, suppose they actually occupied Korea and defeated us at first; we would swarm back upon them whenever we got ready and sweep them into the sea. Besides, out of all this turmoil and confusion we will reach some common and peaceful ground at last."

But behind the individual expression of official opinion on both sides are the common, emphatic, clearly defined views of the masses—an open and racial antipathy and feeling of certain conflict.

And there is one chord which is struck by both sides, and struck again, and still again played by each side, and that chord is the favor of America. Each side insists that the interests of America are identical with its own. "Under existing conditions, it seems to me that the friendship of America should be ours; certainly our interests are the same." So spoke a Japanese statesman. "If

[1] All these conversations and observations occurred in 1901.

we ever do have a conflict with Japan," said a much-travelled and highly cultured Russian, "one thing is clear to all the world, and that is that the sympathy of America will be with Russia."

"We shall depend upon you in our conflict for our existence and for the integrity of the East," earnestly exclaimed a Japanese public man, educated in the universities of Europe. "The door through which the world enters Asia was first unlocked by an American. We are neighbors, and nature has made us partners to resist the aggression of the Slav in the Orient. We are more like you than we are like any other people, and your Mr. Curtis, in his fine book, has even called us 'the Yankees of the East.' And, aside from sentiment, the sheer question of commerce is enough to keep you with us."

Now listen to the counterpart of this from a Russian source: "There is only one nation upon whose abiding friendship Russia counts," said an eminent Russian, "and that nation is America. Our friendship is traditional and has never been broken. You had our sympathy in your War for Independence, our fleet at your gates, a menace to all the world, during your Rebellion, and we were the only people of the world who did not sympathize with the South in that mighty effort to split up your republic. We sold you the imperial province of Alaska for a song. Our industries are not developed, and while they are developing, it is from you that we shall buy more and more.

"And we are the only two peoples in the world who are alike—both young, both expanding, both developing. In all the fundamental elements of comparison we are the only two races in the world that are similar. As for our institutions—at bottom there is more resemblance than dissimilarity, and at the top the very antithesis suggests unity. We are different sides of the same shield. Autocracy on one side, democracy on the other—each developed by the two admittedly coming peoples of the world.

"Have you not a saying in your country, 'We will never

pull down the flag?' Well, let me remind you that our Emperor Nicholas said, when it was proposed to retreat from the mouth of the Amur, 'Where the Russian flag is planted once, there it shall remain forever.'"

And the Emperor Nicholas did say, substantially, just that, and just that is the common thought and determination of those many tens of millions of units of human inertia called the Russian people. An illustration:

The boat had stopped for the night in its tiresome progress down the Amur, and the peasants and soldiers swarmed ashore. For some reason the captain decided to change the location of the boat for the night, and ordered the gang-plank hauled in. All hands began to haul it in; a Russian common soldier had taken the first step upon it. "Back! Back!" shouted the boat officer (not in the military service). "Back! Back!" shouted the hands, continuing to haul in the gang-plank.

"Never! The Russian soldier never goes backward!" shouted the white-bloused private, rushing forward on the moving plank, and escaping by a hair's-breadth from falling into the river.

And the people on the boat and the peasants on shore applauded his somewhat melodramatic utterance.

Melodramatic it was, but significant it was also—significant of the giant race of which he was one. "Where the Russian flag is planted, there it remains forever!" speaks the Czar from his Winter Palace. "The Russian soldier never goes backward!" shouts the obscure private on the Amur. And between them, to the same militant purport, speaks and feels and believes the Russian people. This Russian soldier and his comrades on the vagrant Amur boat were good examples. Many days were spent in studying them. Observations of their brothers in Nikolsk and Khabaroff and throughout Manchuria revealed interesting facts; and nothing can be more interesting in forecasting the probable Russo-Japanese war than an estimate of the men who must do the fighting.

The good-humor of the Russian soldier is apparently his chief, certainly his most visible, characteristic. Song and laugh and joke; joke and laugh and song. There is a playfulness as of overgrown boys. Nothing seems to impair or discourage this wonderful cheeriness. The writer has seen them, drenched to the skin, lips blue with cold, laugh and talk in the greatest good-humor, their teeth chattering while they spoke. You never hear a complaint from them.

"I should say that the difference between our soldiers and yours," the Manchurian colonel above quoted added, "or Germany's or England's or any others, is that when they go through hardships they think it merely their duty; when they fight they think it nothing more than their duty, and when they die they consider it quite the proper thing because it is their duty. Every other country pays its soldiers a very fair sum for their service—you Americans, especially, pay very high wages. We pay our soldiers practically nothing—two or three dollars a year; but they are taught to believe, and do believe, that it is their duty—a part of their lives which they owe to Russia, to the Czar, and to the King of kings in heaven. We think it a mistake to pay soldiers. It puts the military service of the country on a mercenary basis. The theory should be that every man should be prepared to give not only three or four years of service, but his life, if need be, to his country; but the idea of pay debases the spirit of this service."

Associated with their conception of service as a duty, and not as something that the government compels them to do, or as something for which they are paid, is the element of obedience in a Russian soldier. He obeys, not because he must, but because it is his nature. There is an almost worshipful regard for officers—an unreasoning belief in them which is childlike. This obedience of the Russian soldier is not the obedience of discipline, as in the case of Germany, or of that of our own military establishment, or that of any other nation. It has its springs far down in the very nature of the Slav race and in the peculiar relationship between officer and men.

Indeed, the whole Russian system is based upon the idea of father and son. It is the Czar and his children in the empire, the governor and his children in the province, the marshal and his children in the district, the patriarch and his children in the family. And in the military establishment, again the soldiers of the Czar are the children of the Czar; the soldiers of any army are the children of the general; the colonel is father of his regiment, the captain of his company. Thus a paternal and filial relationship exists which you may see nowhere else on earth. A German officer would consider military discipline seriously violated if he did what, to the Russian officer, is a natural method of insuring discipline. An American soldier submits to discipline because, on the whole, he thinks it a good thing, and also because he must; a German soldier, almost wholly because he must; but the Russian soldier because his "father" commands, and it is his filial duty.

One night, in Trans-Baikal Siberia, the strange, weird notes of a Russian peasants' song came through the darkness. (Nothing can describe the Russian peasant and soldier songs—their wildness, their mingled sadness and joy. Towards the end of each verse, breaking in upon the deeper chorus, a high, shrill voice takes up the strain and dominates it to the thrilling end.) A Russian officer of very high birth exclaimed, "It is the Cossacks singing to their Mother Volga."

He gladly consented to go over to their company and ask them to sing their war-songs and translate them as they sang. They sat in a circle in the darkness, poor, mean, with little to eat or wear, as humble a cluster of privates as you can find among Russia's militant millions. But this heir of one of the noblest names in Russia approached them with the deference and courteous bearing of equality that he would have used in a St. Petersburg ballroom. He greeted them pleasantly. This was an American. Did they feel like singing more? And if so, would they kindly sing some of their Cossack songs? And they, on their part, as the child might to the father, responded. And as they sang their songs about the Volga being their mother, and the steppes their father, and their musket their brother, and their knapsack their wife, the camp-fire, lighting up their faces, showed this son of a hundred nobles and high officer in the Russian army gazing upon them with the kindly, courteous, even flattering attention that you might expect from a father looking upon children who were pleasing him. And when the song had closed he did not abruptly leave, but remained awhile in familiar conversation, and then bade them a courteous good-night.

Upon this being noted, he replied: "Oh yes! that is our system; that is out civilization. It is the element of affection of child for father which runs through our whole social and military organization. It is a source of strength, too, which no other nation has. All the rest of you, in your devotion to what the world calls manhood equality, have destroyed those fundamental relationships which nature has established. With you, the son is as good as the father, the soldier as the officer, and even God is hardly recognized as a superior." (You will often hear flings like that at our democratic ideas.)

Many war-ships of the Russian fleet were lying in the harbor of Vladivostock. While there the admiral came on board (acquaintance had been made two years before on his ship in Nagasaki Harbor). The captain, commander, executive officer, the whole official establishment of the ship down to lieutenants, came into the admiral's room quite freely; all smoked with him, all talked with him together, and when he left he shook hands with impartiality all around. And that is something you can see on the war-ship of no other nation except upon a Russian battle-ship. It is something which, however admirable it might be in the army, every American or English navy officer will tell you is impossible in the navy.[1] It is cited here as another illustration of the relationship between Russian officer and man, which is an element of such immense importance in understanding their semi-military, semi-industrial operations.

[1] Numerous stories of the brutality of Russian officers to their men both in the army and navy may be heard; and some of them are doubtless true. But the paternal and filial spirit predominates. Instances of common soldiers acting as body servants to officers were frequently observed; but no striking example of harshness was witnessed. On the other hand, more than once common soldiers were seen in familiar and even humorous conversation with a general.

[Since this volume went to the printer the Russo-Japanese crisis has become acute. At the present moment it appears impossible to determine whether there will be immediate war between Japan and Russia. The author does not think hostilities probable at the present time, because neither power is yet ready for the conflict and because the action of other nations, and particularly of England, is not yet definitely known. It is more probable that the present negotiations will have a temporarily peaceful conclusion, Japan agreeing not to interfere with Russia in Manchuria, and Russia agreeing not to interfere with Japan in Korea. It is possible that Russia may even agree to evacuate Manchuria at some future day. Any "evacuation," however, will be temporary. But no matter what agreement is reached between the governments of the Czar and the Mikado, by which war is put off, the causes for it will remain. The event itself can at best only be postponed, unless, indeed, Russia and Japan should agree to be permanent allies in all Asiatic operations; and this seems at the present time an unthinkable proposition. But anything short of this cannot, from the very nature of the situation, be more than a makeshift, the pacific results of which will at best last but a few years.]

XI

THE SOLDIER OF THE RUSSIAN ADVANCE AND THE SOLDIER OF JAPAN

PERHAPS the finest specimens of physical manhood personally observed at any place in any country were, on the average, the Russian Cossacks and the Russian common soldiers along the Amur and in Manchuria. They are big men — necks thick, shoulders powerful, chests deep, legs sturdy, great room for play of lung, great stomach capacity, heavy-skulled, ruddy-countenanced. Their physical vigor instantly attracts your attention. And there is an impression of hardness about them—iron men, steel men, granite men. And when, day after day, you note that their food is principally sour-cabbage soup, black bread, dried fish, and weak tea, you have discovered two elements upon which, you will find, if you will converse with educated Russians, the Russian military theorist largely counts in any conflict which hereafter may occur with any nation. Physical hardiness and endurance on the one hand, and little and simple food, easily transported, on the other hand. It reminds you of the stories you read of the Scotch soldiers in the time of Bruce carrying many days' provisions of oatmeal in a little pouch, or of the Swiss soldiers, or, indeed, of the soldiers of every country who first won for their respective lands the glory of military triumph.

"It is one of our chief points of excellence. The same thing is true of our horses. Now, Germany feeds her soldiers too much; also, Germany's horses are too richly fed. In war, therefore, if the German army should be cut off from supplies, or should its commissariat for any reason fail, their forces would be at a great disadvantage compared with ours. Our horses can live where other horses would languish and die; and, as you see, our soldiers thrive on the simplest and plainest fare. The Russian soldier can live on the country in any part of the world, and that is something no other soldier in the world can do, not even the Japanese." So reasoned a Russian officer.

Every Russian military man puts preponderating emphasis upon the Russian soldier's ability to endure. General Cierpitsky personally told of an assault which he himself led during the Boxer troubles, near Pekin, at the close of a march of fifty versts (thirty-five miles). His troops made the assault with but five minutes' rest. From another source, but illustrating the same point, came the following story, undoubtedly exaggerated, but descriptive of Russian endurance and spirit. It is related that a body of French troops were to make the charge with the Russians. The Frenchmen had joined Cierpitsky's men only fifteen versts from the point of attack. Yet, although the Russians had marched fifty versts and the Frenchmen only fifteen, the latter refused to join in the assault until they had thoroughly rested. It is said that the Russian commander, raging, bitterly rebuked the French commander, turned on his heel, and ordered the assault by the Russian column, who executed it alone.

Again, on another occasion, so the camp tale runs, a body of Russian infantry and English cavalry came to a stream in which ice was beginning to form. The English cavalry turned back rather than subject their horses to the cold; but the Russians, with shouts of scorn and derision, plunged bodily into the waters themselves and waded and swam across. This story appeared too dramatic to be true, but inquiry in two different and independent quarters suggested that there may have been some foundation for it.[1]

I have myself seen Russians go for two days practically without food, and also without complaining.

The Russian soldier's ability to make friends with the people with whom he mingles, and even with those whom he conquers, is one of his striking characteristics, and common to all Russians. The Russian soldiers in Tien-Tsin, on the way to Pekin, and in the Tartar capital itself, were able to communicate with the Chinaman quite as much as they did with the Germans and Americans, or even the French. A credible writer tells of having seen a Russian soldier, recently arrived in Manchuria, attempting to address a crowd of Chinamen in their own tongue, and making himself understood. Certain it is that the Russian soldiers and the Koreans who came over the border into Russian territory in ever-increasing numbers, in the summer of 1901, spoke to each other without much difficulty. The Muscovite's facility for language, and especially his

[1] Lieutenant F. V. Greene, U. S. A., in his charming sketches of "Army Life in Russia," relates the following incident which he observed in the Russo-Turkish War and which illustrates the Russian soldier's hardiness, his readiness to endure fatigue and cold, and his good-humor: "We were up before daylight the next morning, and just as the sun arose—a bright morning of intensely bitter cold—the troops which had come up during the night, and slept in the fields on the other side of the river, began crossing the stream. As they had to fight all day in the snow it was very important that their clothing should not be wet, and they were therefore ordered to strip naked, roll their clothes in a bundle and carry them on their heads. As they came out of the icy river they were as red as boiled lobsters, but made merry as they squatted about in the snow to put on their clothes. They then formed and marched through the village, where the general saluted them as usual.

"'Good-morning, my men.'

"'Good-morning, your Highness.'

"'Did you burn your feet coming over?'

"'No, indeed, your Highness!' they answered in shout, as a broad grin stole over their good-natured faces."

aptitude for Oriental tongues, is a valuable amalgam with which Russian policy knits and fuses alien peoples into the Slav metal.

So we see that Russia's human instrument of war with Japan—to wit, the Russian common soldier—is an elementally vital creature, with knotted muscles, and strong legs, and hairy breast, and doglike obedience, and child-like faith in his military "fathers" (his officers), a religious feeling so profound that it has no questioning, an adoration of God, and faith in his sincere if crude conception of the Word, woven into the texture and substance of his very being. I have never observed the Turkish soldier personally, but I should say that the religious faith of the Russian soldier is of the same quality as that said to be characteristic of the Turk, with Christ substituted for Mohammed and the Bible for the Koran.

How many of these living bayonets, then, has Russia on the ground? At the outbreak of the Chino-Japanese war she had scarcely any. At the beginning of the Boxer troubles she was still deficient. The best authorities estimate that, in 1900, she had sixty thousand in Manchuria. It can be stated, on the word of a very high military authority in the Far East, that Russia had, in August, 1901, within a fortnight's march of Korea, not less than one hundred and fifty thousand men. Personal observation suggests that this estimate was not extravagant. In Nikolsk alone it is believed that there were no less than fifteen thousand troops even as early as 1901, and the numbers have been greatly increased since then. Vladivostock, Khabaroff, Port Arthur swarm with them. Trans-Baikal Siberia is full of them, their number growing visibly greater as the Pacific is approached. Manchuria is garrisoned with them; and every boat that comes down the Amur brings from three to fifteen common soldiers. Our boat had twelve.

They travelled quite unostentatiously, mingling and sleeping with the peasants, who covered the lower floor of the boat as closely as your interlaced fingers. Other travellers when questioned recalled the same phenomenon. It is not said that there is any design in the inconspicuous transporting of this steady column of Russian soldiery towards the Korean frontier. The fact is noted. It may be that the same thing was occurring in the opposite direction; but no one was discovered who had seen it. If it be true that Russia is thus adding to her military strength, it is possible for her to have two hundred thousand troops within striking distance of Japan by the present time, without any one knowing it. Should war be declared within a year, it is believed that Russia will be found to have on the ground, ready for instant service, a quarter of a million men. "Of course," remarked a Russian officer, "we can just keep on bringing troops there or any place else. It costs us but very little, and our soldiers are absolutely inexhaustible."

You can know how true this is when you recall this notable fact: Over eight hundred thousand young men reach military age every year in Russia, and the government is able to avail itself of scarely more than two hundred thousand of these for active service. Other nations may have storehouses of coal and fleets and heavy armaments, but there is no nation of modern times that has such a magazine of human vitality to draw upon as has the Russia of to-day.

The universal feeling in the Far East is that if Japan ever meant to go to war with Russia, she should have struck her antagonist four years ago.

"Last spring was her final day," said an earnest friend ot Japan in Shanghai in September, 1901. "Had she struck then she might have had some chance. I fear that now it is too late."

The Japanese themselves admit that it would have been much better had they remained on the ground which they had won in Manchuria, thus compelling Russia to attempt their ejection by force; but, although Japan had right and possession and the opinion of the world on her side, she could not do this because she was overawed and outmatched by the allies, and because she was temporarily exhausted. For the latter reason, she has not been able to strike since then. To have entered upon war with the allies, or even with Russia alone, immediately after her conflict with China, would have meant her defeat. Tired from her war with China, and with scant financial resources remaining, a new conflict immediately was too large an undertaking. Well-informed men say that war must come within a few years—even presently. But all any one can hazard as to time is mere speculation. What, then, of Japan's preparedness, and especially what of her soldiers?

First of all, they are little men. In weight and strength and all the elements of physical preponderance, the Russian might almost be said to be the equal of two Japanese. "But," said a Japanese officer, laughingly admitting this, "the little man can shoot as straight as the big man, and the big man affords a better target."

The courage of the Japanese is admitted very willingly, even by the Russians themselves. "Yes, indeed, they will fight. There is no doubt about that," said a young Russian officer, returning from the Mukden campaign (a man, by-the-way, who, at twenty-nine, had won a distinguished decoration, and who was informed in the minutest details of the strategy of every one of Napoleon's battles, of Frederick the Great's battles, and of all the battles fought by Grant, Sherman, Sheridan, Lee, and Jackson in the civil war, and who pronounced Sheridan the ablest strategist of them all).

"I gladly admit the courage of the Japanese," said a Russian general, discussing the comparative merits of the world's soldiers as exhibited at Pekin during the terrible months of 1900. Everywhere, on all hands and by all nations, you will hear the praise of Japanese gallantry sounded high and loud, even by their worst enemies, and a bookful of stories can be picked up illustrative of their daring and even of their chivalry.

As well disciplined troops as I ever have seen are those of the Japanese army. Far and away the best-dressed, best-groomed, best-appearing soldiers observed in Pekin and Tien-Tsin and on the route between, in 1901, were the Japanese soldiers (and the "crack" soldiers of all the world were there). It was a pleasure to observe the policing of their quarters. And you might search for days to hear a story of Japanese brawling and not be rewarded, while fights with fists and even knives between other soldiers were daily occurrences.

Inspection of barracks after barracks in Japan itself, made when they were not expecting visitors, showed the policing of the quarters to be almost perfect. If the Russians at Nikolsk were drilling, drilling, drilling, the Japanese in Japan are doing all of that, and then again, in addition to it, still drilling, drilling, drilling. Their tactics are almost wholly German, even to the artificial and exhausting "goose step" on parade. Indeed, the Japanese army is a perfect machine, built on the German model, but perfected at minute points and in exquisite detail with the peculiar ability of the Japanese for diminutive accuracy and completeness. The Japanese army, regiment, company, is "built like a watch," and each Japanese soldier is a part of this machine, like a screw or spring or disk, with this exception—every soldier is capable of being transformed into another part of this complex yet simple mechanism.

They are hardy fellows, too—not apparently of a high intelligence as revealed in physiognomy or cranial development, but with suggestions of the bull-terrier. Of one company, for example, over two-thirds had the heavy jaw, broad at the jowls and protruding, that you associate with the pugilist or the bull-dog. You can well believe the tales of their ferocious courage. But it is not thought that they have the endurance of their Russian antagonists. For one thing, they are fed more than the Russian soldiers are fed. Inspection of their rations for each meal was a source of surprise, for it appeared that they eat almost as much as the American soldier, though, of course, not of so heavy and nutritious food. But their food is better and of greater quantity than the food of the Russian soldier. For this reason Russian officers assert that the Japanese soldiers are not so efficient in the stress of bitter campaigns.

Unlike the Russians, they have no religious services in quarters, and, in reality, no definite religious faith. The Japanese soldier goes into battle burning with the thought of dying in the service of the good Mikado, dying for the glory of the flag of the Crimson Sun. The Russian soldier goes into battle with the little metal cross next to his very heart. (Every orthodox Russian, noble and peasant, sleeping and waking, wears around his neck and on his breast, next to the flesh, the little metal cross.) He goes into battle believing not only that he is obeying his commander, not only that he is serving the Czar, but that he is fighting in the cause of Heaven itself, and that when he falls he will go to the sure rewards of a loving Father, in whose service he laid down his earthly life.

Space cannot be given for detailed description of Japanese discipline. Perhaps their method of desultory firing, mingled with fixing bayonets, preparatory to a charge, is the best single example to illuminate the whole subject which can be selected.

Suppose, then, that a Japanese regiment is to charge an enemy. They will kneel on one knee, and a general and continuous fire all along the line will be kept up, each man firing as fast as he can carefully aim, and quite at will; between shots, one man and then another, but not all at once, quickly draw their knifelike bayonets and fix them to the guns, and continue firing. When all the bayonets are fixed, the officers spring to position (the captains in front) so quickly that you hardly observe it;

the order to charge is shouted, and the whole line springs forward, first on a slow run, but quickening as they near the enemy, and bursting into a wild, high yell as they close upon their foe. It is reasoned that by this method no time is wasted; the enemy do not know that a charge is to be made; firing is continuous to the very moment of onset; and, principally and far above all, that by this continuous firing, mingled with the fixing of bayonets, the soldier is gradually worked up to a point of terrible eagerness, and that at the psychic moment the human engine of death is released upon its antagonist.

The impartial observer will conclude that, though the Russian soldier has points of superiority over the Japanese, nevertheless the Japanese soldier, man for man, is more nearly a match for his Russian antagonist than is generally supposed.

"We can mobilize our entire army of two hundred and fifty thousand men in thirty-six hours," declared one of the very highest military authorities of Japan. And there is no doubt of the truth of the statement. The Japanese believe that they can land an army corps in Korea in less than three days. But competent European officers think this impossible. It is believed by the most conservative men in Japan that a force of two hundred thousand men can be transported to the peninsula or to Manchuria in two weeks, and a line of provision transports established and defended. Perhaps this is not so far from the truth. Very moderate opinion is, that in three weeks Japan could have every man in her active military establishment landed at any point she pleased in Manchuria or Korea, and a line of commissary transports established and defended.

In the coming war, therefore, it is believed that Japan can get into position throughout the country she desires to absorb, and that it would then be for Russia to oust her. Anybody will understand the advantage of being in position and intrenched. When the conflict comes, the

Russian force and the Japanese force of available, active fighting-men will not be far from the same. Every day that Japan delays, Russia's numbers, of course, increase.

In this conflict the chief—perhaps determining—element will be the respective Russian and Japanese fleets. The Japanese navy, practically all of which is at home and instantly available for this war, is one of the best fighting naval organizations in the world. Indeed, for its size it is perhaps the best-equipped navy of any nation. But neither is the Russian navy to be sneered at. Steadily, slowly, almost stealthily, she is increasing her maritime armament in the Orient. The stories told about the mismanagement and neglect of the Russian war-ships are believed to be erroneous, and this belief comes from personal observation. It must not be forgotten that the pet and pride and hope of the Russian nation has been her navy ever since the time that Peter the Great established it. Russia herself makes her own guns for her war-ships. She makes most, nearly all, of her war-ships herself. They are well done. The ships were found in quite as good condition upon unexpected visits to them and on personal, but, of course, uninstructed and non-expert examination of all parts of them, as English and American ships were found under like circumstances; and no opinion is here ventured as to the respective fighting powers of the Japanese and the Russian ships in a combat to the death.

Finally comes the estimate of comparative resources, and it is plain that the subject cannot be exhaustively handled in a paragraph. Only a broad, general outline can be stated.

In the statement of that, it may be said that Russia has vast resources unorganized and only now in the process of modern arrangement by Witte. Russia has coal; Russia has iron; Russia has timber; Russia has admittedly the third richest, and many believe the richest, gold-mines in the world; Russia has a bread-producing area second only to that of the United States; Russia's manufacturers are making strides which, for the Slav race, are astonishing, but which for a highly systemized people like the Americans or Germans would be considered lethargic.

On the other hand, Japan, with no iron, with poor coal, with limited fields, with a crowded population jostling and elbowing one another into the sea, has as highly systemized industrial organization as any nation, and her manufacturing enterprises are progressing with almost American rapidity. Her sources of taxation are comparatively limited and meagre, but, to quote on this subject one of the coming men of Japan, "Organized little counterbalances unorganized abundance."

Japan, however, is hampered by a semi-democratic form of government, which most enlightened Japanese and every student of Japanese development now admits to be a disappointment. The representative assembly of Japan, so admirably arranged in theory, has more than once proved to be a vexatious interference with the far-seeing plans of the empire's real statesmen. The floors of the Diet have frequently been made rostrums from which demagogy has shouted to the masses—a stage upon which candidates for applause have outscreamed one another in playing the rôle of parliamentary conspicuity. This prevents Japan from making adequate preparation, although, so profound is the national feeling that, when the time arrives, it will be the representative assembly who will want to rush into war, for which meanwhile they refuse to prepare, and the conservative statesmen who will strive to prevent war, for which in the mean time they wish to prepare.

Russia, on the other hand, takes her measures far in advance. In addition to her ordinary sources of revenue, she has now taken over the monopoly of vodka. The taxation of vodka alone is said to have largely supported the army and navy, and, now that the government has itself become the distributer of intoxicants for one hundred and forty millions of Russian people, it will add to its former taxation the profits of hundreds of thousands of dealers. At the same time, the people will be taught moderation in drinking.

Again, for example, the one thing consumed by man, woman, and child in Russia is tea—in the homes, tea; on the streets, tea; in the trains, tea; in the camps, tea; on the boats, tea; among the squalid knots of ragged pilgrims, tea. Very well, says Witte; why should private dealers profit from the common and universal necessities of the masses? And so the government is perfecting plans for taking on the monopoly of tea. This will be an enormous and constantly increasing source of revenue. However, it is not yet being carried into practice.

Of course, as was pointed out by the Japanese statesman, in the conversation above quoted, there is the possibility that the very vastness of the struggle will prevent it. The effects of such a war would be so far-reaching and enduring, it may involve so many nations, that the powers, for very fear, may agree to prevent it. We have here, repeated, the situation so often presented during the nineteenth century, and still in evidence, of the dismemberment of Turkey, or its absorption by Russia, prevented by the rest of the world. And the judicial thinker must not omit the important factor also pointed out by the Japanese statesman above referred to, that the progress of civilization, as manifested in steam and electricity, and the constant weaving together of the advancing forces of the world, may have a delaying if not an absolutely preventive effect.

But, taking all of these into account, and giving them their just weight in balancing the forces which make for war and the forces which make for peace, one is forced, however much against his will, to the conclusion that the pacific influences may be too weak to prevail. Indeed, it may be that forces far greater and deeper than any of these pointed out are precipitating this conflict, and that it may be the beginning of the long-anticipated struggle between Occidental civilization on the one hand and Oriental civilization on the other hand.

Finally, there is a rare possibility that Marquis Ito (by the test of achievements entitled to be called the first constructive living statesman of the world) and Witte (the ablest commercial and financial mind in Europe, and certainly the best business-man the empire has produced, so far as the world has any data to judge from)—it is possible that these two great, conservative minds may prevent the inevitable, avert the impending, and answer with their moderation the syllogism of nature itself, whose probable conclusion is, as pointed out, the first great war of the twentieth century.

Witte is devoted to peace. Ito is devoted to peace. Each man has on his hands that noblest of tasks—the developing of an old people into a new people and of ancient conditions into modern system. And war, which costs so much money—war, which wrecks credit—war, which eats up resources, is to these two mighty men of Europe and Asia their mutual nightmare. They will avert it if they can; but to the observer who traverses the ground, and then, from afar, as from a high peak, surveys conditions, it looks as though two vast avalanches, moving towards each other on the same line, were steadily gathering momentum, and that the two giants' shoulders, braced against them in attempting to hold them back, will not be strong enough for that great task—Herculean though those shoulders are. To the impartial observer, whose business it is to see and not to dream, to deduce the probable from the actual, and not to call his hopes his facts, it would appear that sooner or later these two great bodies must meet.

Meanwhile, the hopes and prayers of the world will be with the master-minds of Russia and Japan—Witte and

Ito. But if, despite their wisdom and their will, war comes, it will be one of those issues of fate in whose progress and ending, as in all like elemental and unavoidable conflicts, men and history may see the hand of God.

XII

THE RUSSIAN ADVANCE PARALLELED BY THE GERMAN ADVANCE

ONLY two powers are making substantial headway in China, as evidenced by physical accomplishments on the ground. For ten years none but these two nations has accomplished permanent results which you can see with your eye, upon which you can put your finger. The first of these powers is Russia, a suggestion of whose material and constructive advance has been inadequately given. But the building of her Manchurian railroad is not the limit of her activity. When that enormous terminus of the Siberian road is completed Russia will have harnessed Asia to her chariot with traces of steel; but to make Asia move, to subdue, to train, to guide the Orient will require time, patience, and ceaselessly steady effort.

And these three elements are the very ones in which Russian character is richest. Russia knows the incomparable effect of carefully cultivated public opinion—the autocracy of precedent, even in the most absolute of autocracies; therefore her diplomatic and consular agencies, together with those of the French, are fountains of subtle influence all over the Celestial Empire. She knows the importance of banking institutions as fosterers of trade and power among Eastern peoples, and, therefore, the Russo-Chinese Bank is weaving a net-work of financial influence throughout the Far East. Starting from St. Petersburg, this golden nerve of empire stretches across Siberia with a ganglion at every town; spreads over Manchuria again with a centre at Harbin, one at Mukden, at

Port Arthur, at Dalni, at New-Chwang; enters Pekin, where it gathers fresh power and impetus from Mr. Posdneff, the remarkable head of the Russo-Chinese Bank at that place; stretches southward again to Shanghai, pausing at Chefoo on the way; crosses the Yellow Sea, and runs the circuit of Japan, with headquarters at Yokohama; doubles on itself, and finally ends with an aggressive agency at Hong-Kong, the very headquarters of England's Oriental power and activity. The Russo-Chinese Bank deserves a chapter to itself; the limits of this chapter permit no adequate analysis. It is mentioned here only in the summary of Russia's Oriental preparations.[1]

The other power making commercial and territorial progress in China is Germany. Its visible activity and apparent results are superior, at the present moment, even to those of Russia. Four years ago the writer was surprised and startled upon observing, on a careful trip through China, the seeming predominance everywhere of German commerce as manifested in immediate activity. In the summer of 1901 the increase in the externalization of German influence would not have been believed but for actual sight and hearing and the testimony of the physical senses—yes, and the testimony of that sum of physical senses, the witness of that indefinable psychic suggestion which we in America express by saying "the drift of things," or "it is in the air"; for all over China, Germany is "in the air."

Attention has been called to the fact that at Nikolsk

[1] The Russo-Chinese Bank now has branches at the following places: Andijan, Batoum, Biisk, Blagovestchensk, Bedaibo, Bombay, Bokhara, Calcutta, Chefoo, Dalni, Hailar, Hakodate, Hankow, Harbin, Hong-Kong, Irkutsk, Kalgan, Kachgar, Khabaroff, Khokand, Kiachta, Kirin, Kobé, Krasnoiarsk, Kouantchendze, Kouldja, Moscow, Mukden, Nagasaki, New-Chwang, Nikolsk, Ouliasoutai, Ourga, Paris, Pekin, Port Arthur, Samarcande, Shanghai, Stretensk, Tachkent, Teline, Tien-Tsin, Tchita, Tchougoutchak, Tsitsikar, Verchneoudinsk, Vladivostock, Werniy, Yokohama, Zeiskaia, and Pristan.

the principal merchants of that Russian commercial and military centre were Germans, and that Germans even supplied the builders of the Manchurian railroad with provisions. At Port Arthur the great German firm of Kuntz & Albers are said to employ a score of young Germans in their establishment. In Vladivostock Kuntz & Albers have enormous headquarters, and there is not a department store in Washington whose building surpasses the handsome structure which this German firm has in Blagovestchensk, Siberia.

The same thing is true of China itself. In Tien-Tsin perhaps the first foreign mercantile house — certainly the second—is the North China branch of the great firm of Carlowitz & Company. In Canton, at the other end of the empire, by far the most active, though possibly not the largest, commercial establishment is the South China branch of this immense trading establishment. In Shanghai, the clearing-house of the whole Celestial Empire, German activity is aggressive, omnipresent, persistent.

On a certain day in the late summer of 1901 more German flags were counted in the water-front before the bund at Shanghai than those of any other nation; and that was a spectacle which, only five years ago, an Englishman would have assured you to be an utter impossibility under any circumstances or at any time. The carrying trade of the Far East is passing into German hands with a rapidity which would alarm the former English monopolists of this great business were it not for the strange stupor which seems to have seized their minds and numbed their nerves. It is less than ten years ago—not more than five years ago—since the unrivalled passenger line of Eastern waters was the English Peninsular and Oriental Company. Nobody calls it unrivalled to-day. The vessels of few Oriental steamship lines equal to-day the ships of the North German Lloyd's Oriental fleet.

The Yang-tse River might as well be a narrow estuary of the ocean, so wide, so deep, so navigable for ships is it for almost a thousand miles into the heart of China. It is the artery of commerce, through which flows the blood of foreign trade into the richest and most thickly populated portion of the empire. The carrying trade upon this river was, until five years ago, almost exclusively in the hands of the English. To-day the Germans are rapidly overtaking their British competitors in the tonnage which they own on the Yang-tse River. English shipowners are selling their lines—their German competitors are buying them.

The above is only an index, the counting of a few items of German commercial activity in China. A full and careful description would require a volume in itself; but an examination of the causes, which are few and fundamental, may reasonably be given within the limits of these discussions. Before taking them up, however, let us notice Germany's territorial, diplomatic, and military activity on the ground.

Perhaps at no spot in any country could so picturesque an interior have been seen as the dining-room of the principal hotel at Tien-Tsin, in the late summer of 1901. It was the place where the officers of the European powers assembled for their evening dinner, and for their smoke and gossip and relaxation on the verandas afterwards. The English were there, of course, proud, clean, charming examples of that incomparable product—the Anglo-Saxon gentleman. The French were there, and the Italian (and Italy certainly sent the very pick and flower of her physical manhood—some of the Italian officers were superb to look upon), and the Austrian, and everybody else. But, over all, conspicuously the master figure, was the German. The whole atmosphere of Tien-Tsin was German. One or two German officers had brought their wives with them, beautiful, blond, vivacious creatures. Every German man and woman in the Orient is imperial in bearing, manner, and purpose. Their veins seem to be filled with the winelike blood of German supremacy. Every officer, every diplomat, every consul is the German Emperor in miniature.

"I tell you frankly," said a resident of Tien-Tsin, and one of the best-informed foreigners in China—"I tell you frankly, whatever the newspapers may say, and whatever the diplomatic phrases may be, the real, substantial powers here are Germany and Russia. The German's bearing of insolent superiority, with the constant reminder that the mailed hand is back of every demand, impresses the Chinaman far more than it angers him, for he respects nothing so much as power."

When he said that he gave the key which, in the opinion of German, English, and Russian, unlocks the secrets of the Oriental heart. It was not a discovery. It was merely saying over again what most foreign students of Asiatic peoples have said since the very beginning of Oriental investigation by modern peoples.

The barracks of the German "legation guard" at Pekin are permanent structures, large, numerous, and apparently sufficient for several thousand men. They impress the observer as garrison buildings more than as the quarters of the diplomatic guard. At Shanghai, in the summer of 1901, German officers and soldiers were conspicuously in evidence. It was even rumored that ground was to be leased by Germany for permanent barracks; but this has not yet been done, if, indeed, it was ever contemplated. Of course, the focus of German military and constructive activity is Kiaochou and the Shan-Tung province midway between Shanghai and Tien-Tsin. The story of this feature of German advance in China has been told in a previous chapter. The miracle wrought in the brief years of German occupation justifies, in the opinion of many informed European residents of China, the bold step taken by Emperor William.

No one in Shan-Tung province ever heard of a period of such prosperity, of a time of such good wages in that vicinity, as the inhabitants of Kiaochou and the surrounding country have enjoyed since the German came among them. For he came, not with his musket alone, not equipped with bayonet, sword, and cannon only, but, as with the Russian in Manchuria, he came with spade and adze and plane and saw, and all the building implements of peace. He has promised himself that he will reproduce England's miracles at Hong-Kong in Germany's miracle at Kiaochou. (In less than fifty years a barren rock, rising from the water, with a few huts of starving Chinese fishermen, clinging like crabs to its base, has been transformed into one of the greatest ports and one of the most beautiful cities in the world. Such has been the Englishman's work in Hong-Kong; and be it remembered, too, that when the work began, and while it was in progress, it was denounced by English statesmen in Parliament, and its failure predicted by economists of almost every other nation.)

In her Kiaochou concessions Germany has erected modern buildings, modern storehouses, modern everything. Perhaps the best hotel (but two) in the Orient, the Prince Heinrich Hotel, stands where filthy hovels, made of a paste of disease and mud, housed wretched Chinamen, less than eight years ago. The railroad runs around the Bay of Kiaochou itself. The sandy hills are being reclaimed with forests planted by the hands of scientific foresters from the Fatherland. A work of beauty, of cleanliness, of system, of industry is being wrought by the determined Teuton at this forbidding and unwelcome gateway to a province whose twenty millions of inhabitants are yet to be told of the great world outside, and yet to be brought into human, civilizing, saving contact with their brother human beings. Meanwhile, slowly, and yet quite as rapidly as the yellow hands can do the work, the iron and steel nerves of the railway creep into the interior towards the mountains, where, it is believed by the German investors, coal and iron and other minerals await the hand of enterprise to make these cliffs and hills of poverty a second Pennsylvania. And with the railroad goes the German soldier. Any interference with a bolt, the loosening of a plate that fastens rail to rail, the undermining of a single tie, means punishment, and that, thinks the German, is something the Chinaman understands. And so it is that, with the progress of this highway of commerce and civilization, order goes, and system and peace.

"The German people will soon sicken and tire of this disgusting enterprise. Think of the millions they have spent, think of the millions they must invest, and think of the trifling returns!" So spoke an English critic of the German enterprise in Shan-Tung.

When this was mentioned to a vigorous German merchant in Tien-Tsin he laughed his great, hearty, vital, German laugh, and said: "What nonsense! A factory has to establish its plant before it can make any goods, has it not? It must send out its advertisements before it can get others to buy its goods, must it not? And from the time of its establishment to the time the profits begin to come is always a long period. Well, Germany is establishing her plant in the Orient. Take the railroad in Shan-Tung. I am a merchant. I do not expect always to stay here. I am here to make money myself. Ah, yes, and to extend German trade wherever I can, too, I admit. Well, with this purely commercial end in view, I am investing my money in the Shan-Tung railroad. I am investing it because, after careful examination, I am confident of profitable returns; and I shall stay right with it till profitable returns come. I shall help them to come. All Germans will help them to come. The German government will help them to come."

This conversation occurred at six o'clock in the evening. A visit at five o'clock to the first English commercial office of Tien-Tsin found the office shut, clerks and managers gone for the day. But the German commercial house was not shut; the German clerks had not departed for the day. They were at their desks; they were about the "go-downs" (warehouses), and the manager of the great business, collarless, in shirt-sleeves, vast and brawny, a very riot of masculinity, sat, working away, with sweaty brow and moist face, in his little office.

"Yes, I think it, perhaps, is one secret of our success in the Orient," said he; "we never cease to work. The Englishman must have his time for tennis. You must not push him too hard during business hours, either. He must have his relaxation in the evening. He must drink at his club. He must spend his social hours in pleasant converse with the ladies. None of these for us Germans out here in the Far East. We are a humbler race. We are here for work. That is the first thing we are here for; and the second, third, fourth, fifth, and sixth thing that we are here for is work also."

Two years before, at Canton, an English and American house, the successor of the famous Russell & Co. (the American "merchant princes" of the Far East fifty years ago) closed at four o'clock. A pleasant excursion on the river was taken until about the hour of six, when the foreign club was visited. Foreigners of every nationality were at the club, drinking as only Europeans in the Orient drink—foreigners, that is, except Germans; not a German was present. But the Canton branch of that immense German company, Carlowitz & Co., then occupied the building next to the club. Every window was lighted up, and when the club was left, a half-hour later, at every window was seen a German clerk in shirt-sleeves, bending over his desk, writing, figuring, casting up accounts, as though that was the last day before judgment. "Seest thou a man diligent in business? he shall stand before kings." This and other such quotations crowded through the mind, and the history-old explanation of failure and success was plain.

"Oh yes, we sell other goods than German goods, of course. We sell any goods of any nationality. We ourselves are the agents in China for Armstrong & Co. (the great English manufacturers); we are the agents of many English firms. We are agents for some American lines of goods. If we cannot sell German goods, as we prefer to do, we will sell any goods we can. Ultimately it is good for Germany to have American goods or English goods or any other kind of goods pass through German hands. With us individual trade and individual profit are the main thing. The trade of the German Empire is a secondary thing. But we do not neglect it, mind you. A difference between us and the English and French, and also the American, is that they are each merely looking out for their own individual, selfish interests, without the slightest thought of whether or no the trade of America or England or France is adversely affected. Well, we are not. Though we are here for individual gain and individual profit, the extension of German commerce and the trade of the empire is a real and living consideration with us also. The government helps us and we help the government." So spoke a German Oriental merchant.

And the government is helping. The German steamship lines to the Orient are subsidized heavily. It is said, and upon sufficient authority to warrant belief, that even the German coastwise and river lines in China receive government aid. A line is maintained between Shanghai and Tien-Tsin by the help of the German government. All ships of this line stop at Kiaochou, and a weekly round-trip service is maintained between that German colony and Shanghai. These ships are quite as good as any engaged in Oriental coastwise trade.

Again, the feeling has been created in the Orient that the official authorities of Germany may be relied on, by personal effort and every other possible means, to aid German merchants in any piece of business they may have on hand. Every German merchant, contractor, or promoter feels free to call for the active and energetic assistance of all German consuls; and the energy and eagerness of the German consular force compel the admiration of all observers. It is as aggressive as the American consular service, with the additional advantage of special training.

Germany, too, is ingenious and insistent in creating an impression on the Oriental mind that she is the world's superior power. Wherever there is an excuse for the display of military force, German soldiery is seen. The writer never visited, on two trips to China, a single Chinese port in which one or more German war-ships were not found. The German military element was so predominant in Shanghai, in the summer of 1901, that a casual and uninstructed traveller might have been excused for thinking it a German colony. No one who knows the peculiar practical quality of the German mind will believe for an instant that all of this is for mere show. It is the working out of a carefully evolved theory about China and its inhabitants, and Orientals in general.

For, with the same patience with which their scientists have evolved working theories in German industry, with the same stolid patience with which they have developed and put into practice theories of navigation, the German has developed his theories of the Oriental mind and character, and upon them bases his treatment of Oriental peoples and conditions. In a word, that theory is that the only two things which the Oriental mind understands are a plain demand and overwhelming force. The German does not believe that the Chinaman is grateful for special favors shown him. The German theory is that the strong hand is the only thing an Asiatic respects. Therefore, everywhere the German bayonet, everywhere the German uniform, and everywhere German ships of war; and now there is the beginning of another "everywhere," and that "everywhere" is German barracks.

How does all this affect German trade? (The writer

expressly disclaims the expression of opinion here as to the soundness or otherwise of the German theory. This is a mere record of facts.) Alongside of the military omnipresence just noticed is a growth of German trade in the East quite unequalled in its rapidity. In Hong-Kong the most active and, with one exception, the largest commercial houses are German. German clocks are found in Chinamen's shops, German buttons, German knives. In Shanghai there are thirty-one German firms, some of which, like Arnold, Karberg & Co., and Carlowitz & Co., are immense establishments, with branches at every treaty port in the empire.

Though the report and returns of trade issued by the China Imperial Maritime Customs show the great bulk of trade at this central port to be still English, there is, nevertheless, a falling off of English and a rapid advance of German importations. And it is claimed that the reports are not accurate. An estimate was examined from a supposedly reliable source, which had been secretly made, and which showed eighty per cent. in value of the foreign goods actually carried on all boats upon the Yang-tse River to be German. Reliable as the source of information was, however, this estimate is undoubtedly a magnified exaggeration. But the striking increase of German commerce on every hand is admitted.

"But does not this constant military menace of Germany interfere with her trade? Does it not anger the Chinaman? Is it not natural that this people should buy of those they like rather than of those they hate?" were questions asked of a leading American merchant in China, and one of the best-informed men in the empire.

"Naturally one would think so," he replied, "but it is not true. Chinamen come to us and abuse the German with words, but go to him and buy his goods. So far from decreasing German trade, this military reputation, which they are working so hard for, is the best advertisement they could have with Chinese customers."

And this is what another American said in Tien-Tsin: "The patting of the Chinaman on the back does not win his favor. The Chinaman likes to trade with the 'big man,' whoever he is. And to him the 'big man' is the man who has the most power. Whether this is correct or not, you can observe for yourself the progress Germany is making."

A German commercial authority in Shanghai, speaking on this very point, said: "The German flag is coming to be a commercial asset to every one of us Germans who does business in the Orient." (Precisely what Cecil Rhodes said about the British flag in South Africa.) "Look at that water-front and tell me what flag is most numerous. The German. What soldiers do you see most of on the streets? German. What officers the most conspicuous on the bund last evening? The German. Well, I am a merchant, and look at this thing purely from the point of view of dollars and cents; but all of that is so valuable to me that I should be willing to pay my proportionate share to have it continue and increase. We are respected now; formerly we were not. Twelve years ago the word German was a term of reproach; to-day it is a term of respect. Every place you hear the word German, German, German. We have created the peculiar condition of mind which your great American department stores succeed in creating when everybody gets to talking about them, everybody gets to going to them. However wrong our views may be in the abstract, you see for yourself that they work very well."

Another commercial German of substance and information, located at a certain treaty port, made a statement of German intention concerning the rich trading district of the Yang-tse Valley which confirmed a general and growing suspicion that, until now, has hardly been breathed louder than in a whisper. "So you think China will be partitioned?" was asked.

"Will be! Why, it is being partitioned. The division

is actually going on. When tens of millions of dollars are being expended in railroad properties, and the right to work mining resources as an incident thereto, is conceded—as is universally the case—the power creating these improvements becomes a dominant influence in that province. It is immaterial whether boundaries are actually staked out or not, or that the little flag of the controlling power is stuck to each surveying stake. It is of no consequence what terms are employed. The fact is the thing."

"I suppose, then, that you mean that Russia will ultimately have Manchuria?"

"Yes."

"That Germany will have Shan-Tung?"

"Yes."

"That perhaps Russia and Germany will divide Chihli?" (Pekin and Tien-Tsin are located in this province.)

"Yes."

"That England will have the Yang-tse Valley?"

With flashing eyes, shoulders suddenly thrown back, he smote his desk with his clinched fist, and almost shouted: "Never! Never! German interests in the Yang-tse are already too great for it ever to fall within the sphere of any other nation's exclusive influence. No, the Yang-tse Valley is as much the sphere of Germany as it is of England."

References are frequently made by German merchants in the Orient to the presence of German soldiers in China, and especially German ships of war in Chinese waters. They are worth noting merely to show the prevailing thought and feeling of German business men in the Orient as to the commercial value of military and naval activities. Indeed, no one can breathe the atmosphere of the Far East very long without becoming impressed with German aggressiveness everywhere, even in the Yang-tse Valley. And yet the Yang-tse Valley has been thought to be securely English. England and Russia have actually agreed, the first not to interfere with any present or future Russian railway enterprise north of the Great Wall, and the latter, in like manner, not to interfere with any present or future English railway enterprise in the Yang-tse Valley.[1] But it is thought that Germany will never permit this vast and commercially opulent region to become exclusively English for purposes of commerce; and the activities of the Russian in Hankow, on the Yang-tse River, eight hundred miles from the ocean directly into the heart of China, suggests the belief that Russia will not either.

These two circumstances have their bright side, because they are substantial, militant, fighting guarantees, for the present at least, that the open door in China is to be kept open. That is to say, the door is kept ajar by the jealousies and conflicting interests of the partitioning powers, and not by their agreement. Could this be overcome, the partition, which appears to be already proceeding, might culminate at a comparatively early day. It might even be accomplished in twenty-five years—yes, in ten years, or even less. Manchuria is already Russian, if the Czar wishes it. Shan-Tung is already Germany's "sphere of influence," and is coming more and more each day under the physical control of the Kaiser. That portion of China opposite the Japanese island of Formosa has been "staked out" as the territory of Japanese predominant influence. If the Yang-tse Valley were conceded to England, little more would be left to do in accomplishing the partition of China.

Freedom of trade of other nations with German, Russian, Japanese, or English provinces would then become matters of separate agreement with the respective controlling powers. It may be that Germany, having spent millions of dollars to create conditions of commerce in a populous territory, may refuse to throw that commerce open equally to other nations, which have not expended a

[1] This Russian and English agreement is given in full in the appendix.

cent, upon the same terms as herself. There is nothing in the history of Russia to show that, after the expenditure of hundreds of millions of dollars in creating the possibilities of modern commerce, she will then yield that commerce to competitors who are better equipped commercially. Their present declarations in favor of the "open door" are borne in mind; but we are now considering ultimate possibilities.

The motives and purposes of nations are to be observed from conditions and not from traditions. Therefore, those who expect England to continue her colonial policy of the free and equal access of all the world to those regions which her energy, money, and valor have opened to the world's commerce are hardly warranted in such opinion. Why was it that England said, "Where my flag is planted trade is free"? Why was it that she insisted upon all the treaty ports of China being open to every other nation on the same terms as herself? What was the reason for that generous, but also statesman-like policy? Admitting that many English statesmen championing this noble proposition were inspired by humanitarian reasons, the real reason must be found in very practical commercial considerations.

For a long time—indeed, up to twenty years ago—England was the workshop of the world. She made the world's goods. There was no other nation which could compete with her. Therefore, it was to her interest to champion free ports and open doors, because in such ports and upon such apparently equal terms with the rest of the world she was, in effect, beyond competition. Nobody could make goods as cheaply as she could. Indeed, comparatively speaking, nobody could make goods at all for export except herself. On the other hand, her one need was raw material; and so, from the two elements—of unsurpassed facility for manufacturing, rendering her unrivalled in the field of commercial progress, and her want of and necessity for raw materials—was compounded her policy of the open door and free ports.

But now these elements have disappeared. Conditions have changed. The inventive genius of Americans, which produce every day miracles of mechanism; the intense nervous activity of the American working-man; his acute and comprehensive intelligence; the marvellous combining and organizing ability of American capitalists; the vast resources of American farms and mines and mills, compared with which those of England are very moderate indeed—all these, and many other considerations familiar to every man, have enabled America to compete with England, not only in the markets of the world, but in the heart of London itself.

On the other hand, the polytechnic schools of Germany, the patient endurance of the German working-man, the persistent and intelligent efforts of German capital, and the driving and directing power of the German Emperor—all focused upon a policy of foreign trade—have made Germany a successful competitor of England, even in England's own crown colonies. So that the reasons why England was for open doors and free ports a quarter of a century ago have now disappeared. And if she continues in favor of them, she does so for other reasons than those which caused her to adopt that policy in the first place. So it is not believed that England will long insist on an open door in China, provided she can have the exclusive trade of the Yang-tse Valley.

It is noted, with keen interest and sincere regret, that English commerce and English policy in China seem to be going to pieces. It is expressive of the sturdy honesty of the English character (and the "bottom" and intrinsic worth of English character will save England at the last) that no one is so ready to recognize this fact, or even tell of it, as are the Englishmen themselves who live in China. Four years ago the writer, untravelled and uninformed at first hand on conditions in the East, and, therefore, believing that the only vigorous power in China was England, observed, with surprise and almost consternation, the too-evident decline of British commercial and political influence in the Celestial Empire. The increase in this decline, upon a reinvestigation of Chinese conditions two years later, was startling.[1]

It is very hard to define it, but you will know it the moment you land. There is an atmosphere of drugged and cocained English inactivity. There is a loss of heart, which some attempt to conceal by boastful words; but time and again the writer has, upon more intimate acquaintance with the most outspoken boaster, found him frankly admitting the strange torpor which seems to have come over English policy and British activity in the Far East. One of the very highest military authorities said: "I confess I don't know what our policy is out here. I do not believe anybody knows."

It has been noted before that English ship-owners are selling out their lines. The Peninsular and Oriental Company must soon renew its fleets or be so out-distanced by the German and French lines that it cannot afford to remain in the contest. The sale of English ship-lines causes a sort of commercial paralysis, visible not only to the heads of great commercial houses, but to the humblest clerks. Said the first officer of a Japanese merchant vessel (he was an Englishman, born in New Zealand, and more "imperial" than a Londoner): "I do not know what is the matter with our people. They do not seem to see when they sell out a ship-line and the German buys it that he has not only got the ships of that line, but has secured the carrying trade that goes with it. And it then becomes just as hard for the former English owner to introduce a new line as it would have been for the German to begin competition against the established English line. When our people sell out their ship-lines, they cannot replace them. They have lost not only their ships; they have lost the trade which goes with those

[1] Lord Beresford reports the same thing.

ships, and, not only that, but the prestige, too. They seem to be blind. I actually think of taking a trip to England just to see with my own eyes what is the matter with the English people." This was the shrewd, practical observation of a thoroughly up-to-date English sailor.

Whatever is done as to a world policy with reference to the future of China will not be done upon the initiative of Great Britain, unless a change in British policy takes place, and any one who leans on that expectation will find himself reclining on a broken reed, unless a metamorphosis occurs soon in the British government's spirit and purpose. The most earnest of England's friends can only hope for this change. But Germany and Russia have in recent years been given such right of way, and they have come so thoroughly to believe themselves the only powers that "do things" in the Celestial Empire, that the most friendly observer becomes cautious in even hoping for a permanent revival of the old-time British clear-headedness, courage, and fighting forcefulness in the Orient.

The recent offensive and defensive treaty between England and Japan is the first manifestation of diplomatic virility by England in the Far East for the last decade or more. Before hazarding anything as to its results, it might be well to wait and ascertain just how far it is a real alliance of blood and iron, and ships and guns, and life and death, on the one hand, and just how far it is a paper alliance, on the other hand—just how far, in a word, England means it.[1]

If it be true that England proposes to back this alliance with force, it probably means, when reduced to concrete terms, that she is convinced that, as the old German merchant said in the conversation above quoted, "Germany and other aggressive powers will never permit

[1] The Anglo-Japanese treaty of alliance is given in full in the appendix.

England to occupy the Yang-tse Valley as her exclusive sphere of influence."

How she proposes to get the fruits of an open door in Manchuria or Shan-Tung, where the Germans and Russians control the railroads and can exclude her goods by the simple process of differential railway rates, is not clear. An alliance to keep the open door in China does not go far enough to accomplish much. As will be pointed out in a subsequent chapter, it is just as important to open the interior, so that merchandise taken through the open door can penetrate inward, as it is to keep the door itself open.

So far as paper statements and agreements are concerned, Russia, Germany, and all other powers have declared their intention to keep the door open. But diplomatic declarations and "paper intentions" amount to little in the face of railroads actually built and building, and the concrete and tangible power that necessarily attends them. The maintenance of the open door is only the first step to the entire reorganization of China.

A comprehensive but not impossibly difficult policy might be agreed upon by three or four of the leading nations of the world, for the reorganization of China. It would be done, of course, through the machinery of the Chinese administrative system. It would have the effect of opening the interior to foreign travel, foreign merchandise, and foreign communication generally, just as the treaty ports are now open to the world; of safeguarding life and property throughout this immense country, and, in general, would result in the accomplishment of many of the ends which the Japanese feel it is their destiny in the Far East to accomplish under Japanese suzerainty. The only thing to prevent this, the greatest reform of modern or perhaps of ancient times, would be the jealousies and ambitions of the powers. Of course, the United States would not take the initiative. For one thing, we are not yet educated up to the point of material and tangible interference in the affairs of other countries, no matter how much our interests may be affected. As has been pointed out, Japan would gladly join with England and the United States in such a programme; but England appears to be too undecided about everything to undertake any further definite work. Germany would probably not hesitate could she be assured that German suzerainty of her portion of the empire would not be disturbed, but even be encouraged; but as the integrity of the empire would be one of the ends sought by such an agreement of the powers, it is likely that Germany would not feel very enthusiastic about it. If it be true that the Czar is secretly the suzerain of the Manchu Emperor, as so many believe, or if it is the ultimate Russian intention to extend Russian power over the whole of China, Russia would probably not favor such an enterprise; and, of course, France would co-operate with Russia. This brief analysis of the agencies which must accomplish this work seems very discouraging. And yet the work is there to be done, and history shows that just such impossible situations have time and again crystallized with startling rapidity.

The open door in China is important to us, but open roads which lead from the open door into the interior among the people are equally important. When we reflect that with the "likin" tax really abolished (it is now supposed to be superseded by a customs arrangement, but in reality it is not) and the interior of China freely open to foreign goods (which it never has been), the trade of the world with China would increase at once to a thousand million dollars a year (and later on to much more), and that the great bulk of this trade would be ours, if we would only take it, the tremendous importance of this subject in regard to the future of American mills, mines, and farms is apparent.

But the questions naturally arise: Why is it that a people so numerous, so ancient, so industrious, so vital as the Chinese, will permit their country to be carved up by the great commercial nations of the world? Why should Americans not keep their hands off, cultivate China's good-will, and increase their trade by force of friendship won by kindness? These are questions of first-class importance, and the next chapter will be devoted to them.

XIII

A CHAPTER OF DIGRESSION: AMERICAN NEEDS IN THE ORIENT

THE Germans have carefully evolved their theory of Chinese trade and Oriental character, and the Russians have done the like. America, however, has paid little attention to this immeasurable and near-by market and to this uncounted and interesting people. We have applied the philosophy of happy-go-luckiness, and such trade as we have in the Orient is the result of our superior position geographically, of our incomparable resources, of the excellence of our goods, and of the diligent, patient endeavors of a few American merchants.

"But is not our trade growing with astonishing rapidity throughout China and the Far East?" is the answer made to the plainest suggestions of our national commercial necessities with reference to this market. Yes, our trade is growing, and rapidly; but its growth is slow contrasted with our advantages. We are only a little more than four thousand miles away from that market, and our competitors are practically twice as far away by sea. We have resources which defy description in their volume and richness; while the resources of our competitors are, comparatively speaking, limited and lean. Germany is an example. Compared with us, her resources are not considerable; she is far away from this market; and yet, by the simple application of system, by the processes of carefully thought-out theory based upon patient investigations, Germany is forging ahead to the position of the first commercial power in the Far East. This fact has been noted before in a previous chapter, but its importance requires its repetition many times.

That the partition of China is imminent, if not actually going on, has been shown; that the growth of German and Russian influence is startlingly rapid and permanently substantial has also been shown; that the decline of English power is apparent all students of the question admit; and that this market is naturally American is demonstrated by the simple logic of geography. But, to make it American, to prevent our great European competitors from taking what is naturally ours, it is necessary that we, too, shall understand the people with whom we deal. It is necessary that we, too, shall study Oriental character with something of the same painstaking care adopted by our rivals; for knowledge of a people's character is a practical element in the problem of trade. Let us consider Chinese character, then.

Singular, is it not, that a nation of four hundred million people permit the occupation of various portions of its territory? Singular, is it not, that a nation which numbers one-fourth of the population of all the world opens its coastwise trade to other nations—the only instance of the kind on earth? Singular that it permits the manifest division of its territory? Yes, singular, indeed, if this aggregation of four hundred million human beings is a nation in the sense that the United States or Germany or France or Russia is a nation.

It has been said by a few acute observers that China is a conglomeration of states, that each province is itself a kingdom, whose governor is, for all practical purposes, an independent monarch, with an independent military force, independent taxation, and accountable to the central Manchu head of the system, the Emperor, only for a remittance of imperial revenues.

This is true, but it is not all the truth. Even these provincial governments are not definite and effective organizations like our States. They are a curious form of administration, founded upon an understanding of the singular selfishness of the individual, and permitting him, therefore, an immense measure of individual freedom, combined with ruthless interference and punishment of the individual when deemed necessary for the security of this government. Careful investigation and reinvestigation will convince any one who goes to the subject without a preconceived opinion that the two elements at the bottom of Chinese national incapacity are, on the one hand, individual selfishness, so profound that we cannot fathom it; and, on the other hand, a singular respect for power and force, which is the common characteristic of all Oriental peoples.

The streets of Pekin are not to be described. The writer was visiting, for the second time, the world-renowned Li Hung Chang, and while there one of the sudden downpours of heavy rain occurred. On leaving, the streets were found to be running rivers of water, which concealed holes and ruts of two or three feet in depth, and gulleys rooted out by time and usage as by the snout of some monster. A naked coolie, attempting to cross from house to house, plunged up to his neck into a hole in the middle of the street. A mule and its rider fell into another, and were not extricated in the course of an hour.

"Why do you not pave the streets in front of your house?" was asked of a Chinaman of superior intellience and education. "Why should I go to that expense? It is not my street."

Mr. Smith, in his excellent book, *Chinese Characteristics* (every one who wants to understand the Chinese from a kindly but just point of view should read that book), explains the philosophy of roads, or the lack of them, in China. These passageways wind in, around, and about, and are worn, by countless feet and the eroding influences of numerous rainfalls, into little ravines. Nobody repairs them. "It is not my business," said a Chinese farmer. The Grand Canal, one of the monumental works of human hands, has become so choked with sand and weeds as to be impassable at one or two points. The government will not repair it, because (as it is said) the government sees no way of making anything out of it for itself and its favorites. And the people will not repair it, "because it is none of their business."

"How do you manage to interest your people in military affairs?" asked one of the first business men of China, and a millionaire (a pure Chinaman). "How do you get your militia companies formed? How do you interest men enough to induce them to enlist?" The whole inquiry of this great man was not of business, but military, military, military. When it was explained to him that, with us, every man feels that the government is his own, that the condition of the roads is his personal concern, that the defence of the country is of the highest individual consequence, that the element of personal selfishness is almost eliminated from the public mind of the citizen, he shook his head sadly and said: "Ah, yes! that is our trouble. How shall the people be lifted out of each one's individual self?"

It was not always so with China. There was a day, some hundreds of years ago, when "I and my house" were not the sacred formulas which every Chinaman repeats to himself to-day. There was a time when China was heroic, masterful, consolidated, militant, devotional. But centuries have passed since then. It is not within the province of this chapter to explain the reasons for the change. What we are noting is the change. We are noting it in order that we may try to understand, feebly at least, these four hundred million people with whom we wish to trade, and whose trade relations with us will more quickly rescue them from their strange decline than would anything else — feebly understand them, for no foreigner may hope ever to understand them entirely.

"The trouble with China," said a penetrating observer, "is arrested development. China is like a man who starts out with brilliant promise and continues to a certain point, and then apparently undergoes an atrophy of all his powers."

It is each man for himself among these four hundred millions, or, at most, each man for his family or his clan. Wealth, power, are the things he chiefly respects. He understands them. If you quote the maxims of Mencius and Confucius, you must remember that they were pronounced when China was great. You must remember the remark of the young Chinese merchant of Shanghai, quoted in a previous chapter, that Chinese merchants care nothing about who governs them, their only interest being an opportunity to make money. Any administration which would secure that supreme end would be welcomed and supported by the commercial men of the empire, if they were sure such a government would stand. It is commonplace that China invented printing; yes, but she prints no books now—at least, none of modern interest; that she invented gunpowder; true, and yet she is practically without arms with which gunpowder is used—only just now she is making them; that she developed the science of astronomy; true again, and yet her instruments are rust. "Arrested development," said the life-long student of China and the Chinese.

It must not be inferred that the individual Chinaman is not a man of intelligence. Decidedly the contrary is the truth. Some of the compradors of China rival, if they do not surpass, the chiefs of the foreign houses that employ them. There are not better business-men in any country than hundreds of the business-men of China. Their bankers and money-changers are keen to the last degree. An educated Chinaman will entertain you with talk as fertile and informing as that of any man turned out of our own universities. The industry, frugality, patience of the Chinese as a people are proverbial; and yet, with all of these good qualities, interest in their government and nationality appears to be wanting. It cannot be said that they are without the instinct of cohesion; and yet that instinct does not manifest itself in government. They are not without patriotism. Everybody is familiar with the passionate desire of the Chinaman to be buried in his native soil; and yet their patriotism does not make them a consolidated, masterful nation such as their individual virtues, above enumerated, would seem to justify. All these things make the peculiar atrophy of Chinese power, as expressed through forms of government, all the more remarkable. And all this emphasizes the explanation which most students of Chinese character give—namely, the selfishness of the individual, his lack of interest in the government of his country, and his appreciation of power, no matter in what form it appears.

These brief outlines, which are the basis of the German and Russian theory of China and the Chinese, will explain why it is that the exhibition of power is considered by these European powers a positive trade asset in the Orient. It explains why it is that Germany, instead of losing, believes that she actually gains by her barracks, her soldiers, her ships, and even by her seizure of Chinese territory. It is power, force—visible, tangible predominance. And the Europeans believe that the Chinese respect it, however much the officials may hate it.

A recommendation that our government should follow the Russian, French, and German example of the seizure of territory in the empire is distinctly disavowed. But it is asserted that America must very soon become an influential external power in Oriental affairs, so that further changes of the map of China will be made only after consultation with us. A great duty—perhaps the greatest of history—is gradually evolving out of the chaos of human conditions in the Orient. Nobody will deny that if China's millions could be kept in China and yet be brought into commercial contact with the civilization of the rest of the world, it would be good for them and good for the world.

It is established that China cannot do this, or rather will not do it, if left to herself. The centuries are unanswerable arguments to sustain this proposition. What she was five hundred years ago China is to-day, save only where the trade aggressions of European nations have forced foreign commerce and western civilization upon her. Leroy-Beaulieu points out that every trade concession of moment, every advance of modern civilization, has been forced upon China with the cannon. An uprising and conflict; Chinese defeat; and, as the fruit of this defeat, treaty concessions, opening of ports, the safeguarding of foreigners and foreign commerce—such, he declares, is the record.

The whole world has profited by each of these "aggressions," which opened up new ports. First of all, and most of all, China herself has profited. Next to China, and, properly, the nation which took a ruling hand in bringing about the new conditions has profited; and, lastly, the rest of the world has profited, too. If the beds of coal, which exceed in richness the deposits of any other portion of the earth, were opened; if the products of China's wonderfully fertile soil could be freely and easily exchanged for the output of other nations; if the wants of these myriads of people could be increased twofold (and wherever modern commerce and civilization have touched Chinamen their wants have been increased not two but many fold); if these wants could be partly supplied by the other nations of the earth, while the Chinese people themselves were supplying those other nations with the products for which nature has particularly equipped them and their country, and which other nations are not prepared to produce, the benefit to the world and to China as a people would be beyond all estimate.

And the supply of most of the wants of China's four

hundred millions should be made by the American people, for the simple reason of location.

What this would mean to us in the immediate present, without further extension of China's foreign commerce, is clear when we reflect that we have scarcely ten per cent. of the foreign trade of China, though we are entitled to fifty per cent. at least. I repeat for the third time that the removal of the "likin," or transportation tax on goods carried into the interior of China would alone and unaided increase China's foreign trade to a thousand million dollars a year. Think of what fifty per cent. of that would mean to us! Employment for America's working-men is the problem that will constantly grow more serious; and no solution is possible except markets for what America produces. And so the question of Oriental export trade becomes insistently important.

But whatever may be done in the way of tax and other reforms in China, all will agree that American trade and American prestige in the Orient must be pushed steadily and by the minuter methods.

Every American merchant in China will tell you that first of all we need American ships. When American trade held the first place in the Orient, the American flag was seen in every port. It was a great advertisement then. A brilliant writer tells of an old Chinese merchant who, in inquiring about the absence of American trade, said: "We used to have it. This port was once filled with your flowery starry banner. Where has your flowery starry banner gone?"

Oriental ship-lines are a prime necessity for an increase in America's trade with the Orient. There is absolutely no difference of opinion among Americans in the Far East upon this point. Here, again, is seen the effect upon the Oriental mind of something which the Chinaman can see, something whose magnitude and power he can behold. The German merchant of Shanghai who pointed to the

German flag in the water-front declared it to be his greatest commercial asset. There is no commercial agent to compare with the patriotic officer of a steamship company, proud of his line, his flag, and his nation. It is not enough for the captain and officers of a ship that they carry their cargo safely—the word upon their tongue at every port they touch is the commerce, the power, the progress of the nation to which they belong.

Then, too, when any nation has ship-lines established, they must have freight to carry, and so the company to which they belong devises new methods of securing this freight—that is, they create new trade. Again, as the trade grows the rates of freight decrease. This is plain reason, and it is plainer history. So that the first great requirement in the substantial and permanent increase of American Oriental trade is American ship-lines. If American capital could be interested in this vast enterprise, which combines patriotism and business, it would be good for the capital invested, good for the merchandise carried, and, best of all, for the increase of American trade.

It is so curious that the historian of a hundred years from now, reviewing this subject, which then will be the great question (indeed, in two or three years it will be the great question), will find it hard to credit the fact he records, that, being nearer to China than any other competing nation, needing her market, having resources to supply it unequalled in all the world, and being, too, the keenest financial nation of modern times, the United States had no banking facilities in the Orient. It is the second necessity for the permanent increase of American commerce with China that a great American banking establishment be planted in every port of the Far East. The Chinaman understands money just as he understands power in any other form.

It is not necessary to explain the intimate connection between trade, on the one hand, and banks of deposit and exchange on the other hand. Every grocery-man in every country village in America understands that from personal experience. England has two immense financial organizations in the Orient—the Chartered Bank of India, China, and Australia, and the Hong-Kong and Shanghai Banking Corporation, and their branches exist everywhere. They have been the chief agencies in conserving England's predominant commercial power, but even they have not been able to check her decline. Germany has established within a few years a large financial institution, whose branches have now spread to most, if not all, the treaty ports of the empire. It has been pointed out that Russia, through her financial agency, the Russo-Chinese Bank, is shooting the filaments of her power throughout the Pacific Far East.

At present American trade must be conducted through these foreign financial institutions. It should not be so. We ought to have in the Orient an American financial institution of magnitude to match the power of the American nation, and which shall be equal to the commanding commercial position to which the American people aspire in the Far East.

The methods of banking in the East are peculiar. A bank discounts its own notes between two ports, estimating the amount of the discount by the cost required in transporting that exact amount of specie, separately and by itself, between them—that is, if you present a note issued by a banking corporation at Hong-Kong to its branch at Tien-Tsin, it will not be redeemed at its face value, but at a rate measured by the cost of transferring that particular amount of silver between those two points. The system of issuing notes of exchange is unscientific, and at every point the bank cuts a profit for itself.

Like Russian banks in Russia, foreign banks in the Orient go into every conceivable transaction, shaving always and everywhere. They are, therefore, not conducted on the broad lines of modern scientific methods, as bankers here and in Europe understand banking. An American bank equal to the task should be established, which would put American inventiveness at work upon the great task of establishing a uniform currency, at least among the treaty ports. Experience would soon show the Chinese merchant and dealer everywhere the unquestioned value of its notes, and a common circulating medium would thus be established, whose influence in facilitating trade would be as great as it would be beneficial. A great American bank, then, is the second need for the permanent increase of American trade in the Orient.

It is said that our consular service should be improved. But whatever fault may have been found in the past with the quality and personal character of the government's commercial representatives in China, it is admitted that our present staff of consuls in the Orient measures quite up to the standard of foreign countries, with the possible exception of Germany. This is a subject (consular reform) in which personal investigation compels more changes of view than any similar problem. On the one hand it is pointed out, and with apparent unanswerableness, that it is quite impossible for the consul without special training and without practical knowledge of his duties, and of the people among whom he goes, to represent properly the commercial interests of his country.

On the face of the paper argument, it seems clear that the longer a consul continues to reside among the people to whom he is accredited, the better acquainted he becomes with their needs and the better equipped for the discharge of his important duties and the extension of American trade. But the fact must be recorded that American consuls in China are, with an occasional and conspicuous exception, quite the most efficient commercial representatives which any government (excepting always

Germany) has on that difficult ground. This will become more and more the truth as our trade with China increases. It will become truer, too, as care comes increasingly to be exercised in the selection of those important officials. Natural conditions and the steadily rising quality of our national administration with respect to foreign countries insure this.

Twenty years ago so little attention was given to our foreign commerce that our consular posts abroad were, with some creditable exceptions, considered exclusively as the proper reward of local political work, without any regard whatever to the tasks the consul was expected to perform at his post. The change wrought by the natural causes above pointed out has been greater and the improvement more marked than in the consular service of any other country. But whatever the cause, it is admitted on all hands that the American consuls in China have a greater keenness of insight into the real nature of commercial conditions where they are sent; they have a better mastery of the practical situation, a higher comprehension in the discharge of their duties, a fresher and more unworn interest in the extension of our commerce than have the consuls of any other country (please note, always, and for the last time, except Germany).

One of the first business-men of China (a pure Chinaman), and an Englishman, whose great reputation is justified by his work and abilities, united in this sentiment concerning the American consul at a certain Chinese port: "He is the most efficient man on the ground. It is the consensus of opinion that his tact, firmness, ready resource, and unwearying energy prevented a spread of the Boxer troubles in the melancholy year of 1900."

"Yes," said another foreign merchant, "the American consuls seem to be unhappy unless they are making some record for themselves or their country."

Certain it is that the reports from at least one consular office in China are the most exhaustive, most trustworthy, and best analyzed commercial statements that come from the Far East. "One point of superiority of your consuls over ours," said an English shipping man, "is their accessibility. Anybody can see the American consul at any time, but," he sourly continued, "to see the British consul is almost an affair of state."[1]

It is freely admitted that consuls of other countries surpass ours in the points of small society duties. They are quite accomplished in all the engaging devices of social intercourse. American tourists travelling around the world for pleasure, and therefore looking for social entertainment, usually come away from the treaty ports of China deeply impressed with the equipment of the consuls of rival countries, particularly those of Great Britain, and with bad opinions of our own men. But our men are the quintessence of the practical. They have been reared in the American school of the practical, and they have acquired the habit of resourceful inventiveness, which is so distinctive a characteristic of our business and industrial civilization. They see the point to things, and, seeing the point, they act.

The thought is repeatedly forced upon one who may have been originally hostile to what a witty observer calls our present "consular chaos," that, after all, it may be that the education which comes to a man from successful and active participation in American politics, the alertness and vitality of mind fostered by the rich soil of American business effort, are of notable value in preparing a man for the practical duties of his country's service. It is certainly true that the adaptability of the American commercial representative is something quite unmatched. He goes to a place fresh from the electric atmosphere of America, filled with the wonder and curiosity aroused by

[1] Lord Charles Beresford, on his return from his extended visit to China, reported the numerous complaints of British merchants against British consuls; and he fearlessly pointed out the decline of British prestige in the Far East.

the new land, the new people, and the strange conditions among which he finds himself. He sees the great points of difference between such conditions and our own, and it is an understanding of these points of difference which is of greater importance than is a dulled comprehension of the people themselves.

XIV

A SECOND CHAPTER OF DIGRESSION: AMERICAN PROGRESS IN THE FAR EAST

IT has grown into a truism that no one who has resided for a long time among a foreign people can write intelligently about them. The reason is that these very points of difference which constitute the essential matters of interest become commonplace after a surprisingly short residence, and the very things which a new-comer notes with greatest interest, and which are, in fact, of greatest interest, soon become obscured by familiarity.

"I have been here in Nagasaki three weeks," said a young American woman, "and, whereas the first week I could not write letters enough of these strange people, now I can write nothing at all except that the *China* arrived yesterday or that one of the *Empress* boats is expected in to-morrow. All of the things which were so novel to me when I landed have now become matters of course."

The same thing is true of everybody else, and, of course, of the American consul, excepting that, in his case, he has duties which keep him discovering new and fresh subjects of interest for a long season. The keenness of his new experiences is a practical asset which statesmanship would do poorly to overlook. Then, too, he goes to the work with determination to make a "record" for himself and for his government. He is a fresh charge of Americanism for the particular point to which he is sent. He is always at the beck and call of the American merchants. He is anxious to make a little better report to the State Department than anybody else makes to any other government. "That man," said an American Oriental merchant, naming an American Oriental consul of almost sixty, "is positively unhappy if he goes to bed at night without having accomplished some specific thing for American trade."

What to do to improve our consular service is, therefore, not so clear. If some method could be devised by which we could continue our consuls for a long period of service—indeed, make them practically life officers, and at the same time keep up their energy and interest, which the experience of other governments has shown is gradually destroyed by long residence in a country—then the problem would be simplified, if not solved.

The German Emperor has accomplished this by his personal interest and activity. Every man is made to feel that the Emperor William's eye is on him, that every German merchant's eye is on him, and that he will be reported, or reprimanded, or promoted, according to the neglect or discharge of his duty. But the consuls of other countries holding life tenures soon become atrophied in interest; their activities undergo a stupefying and relaxing process by reason of the certainty of their tenure and their long familiarity with conditions, a familiarity which, in the end, makes everything commonplace and as a matter of course to them.

This is a perplexing subject. Our consular service must be improved; but the difficulty is to avoid, in the improving, the paring away of that vigorous quality which now makes our consuls, unequipped though they may be, superior to those of any other nation. Dr. Vosberg-Rekow, head of the German Bureau of Commercial Treaties, says that "the United States has covered Europe with a net-work of consulates, and makes its consuls at the same time inspectors of our exports, and vigilant sentinels who, spying out our trade openings, make them their advantage and report them."

This is a tribute to the intelligence and vigilance of our consular service from our most watchful and most increasingly active commercial rival. If to these advantages of practical resourcefulness we can add knowledge of the language of the country to which the consul is accredited, a long tenure of service, and the appointment of none but trustworthy and approved men, and if we can at the same time evolve some method to keep their interest and energy constantly fresh, we shall have solved the problem.

The building of railroads in China will be the one great industrial development of the twentieth century, so far as foreign investment in Asia is concerned. There are probably thirty thousand miles of line projected and actually surveyed, but the extent of the rails laid upon which trains are running in the Chinese Empire, exclusive of Manchuria, is less than four hundred miles. This is not one mile of railroad in China for every million people. That great trunk-lines in every direction will be built, and that speedily, speaking in the historical sense, is as certain as the progress of civilization itself; and wherever a line of railroad goes, trade goes, and where a line of railroad goes the trade of the nation which built it is chiefly carried.

Germany's concession in Shan-Tung has been set out in full in another chapter. Very little goods will be carried along those lines except such as bear the trade-mark, "made in Germany." It has been pointed out that judicial and police privileges accompany these grants, and that, however it may be disguised, and however the machinery of Chinese administration may be employed, the hand of German law and order will in reality be over all. And by this plan, it has been noted, the practical partition of China is moving forward.

The far-sightedness of the Russians in pushing their railway lines through this mighty area of future human development, the associated activities of French and

Belgian syndicates, as is believed in connection and co-operation with Russia, have been observed. In this particular the English themselves have exhibited a flash of their old energy and daring resourcefulness in projecting a line into China, connecting its principal cities with the great British railway system of India.

It is unfortunate that American syndicates have not looked into this matter. One, indeed, did so and was convinced of the profitable nature of the enterprise, and a railway concession was secured from the Chinese government. But it is said that, since the death of its principal promoter, the American interest has been largely abandoned. It is hard to believe that American capital, which is now looking abroad for opportunities of investment and exploitation worthy of its magnitude, energy, resourcefulness, and power, will long overlook these opportunities. Two or three lines of road, built by our citizens and backed by our government with its indorsement (not necessarily financial, of course) and diplomatic aid, could be built in China, and a firm foothold could thus be secured, from which the future of American commerce in the Orient might be safeguarded and satisfactorily and practically increased.

The fear which thoughtful Americans who go over the ground are forced to entertain is that our great aggregations of capital will overlook this most inviting field until the choice routes have been pre-empted by the capitalists of other nations, and until the joint action of rival powers will compel the Chinese government to refuse further railway concessions, or at least further concessions to us. Should this unfortunate development occur, it will, indeed, be a sorry circumstance. Moralizing is of little use in practical affairs, but occasionally a dash of it is needed to give spirit and meaning to material enterprise. And the thought is here interjected that perhaps Americans are taking too much for granted as to our future, that it may turn out in the course of a few decades that we have not been far-seeing enough, that our eyes are fixed so immovably upon the steady stream of gold pouring into our coffers at this particular moment that we look not to the sources which must continue that stream in the future.

Another thing which the government might do, and which would have a beneficial effect upon American trade in China, is to keep in Chinese waters all but one or two ships of our Pacific squadron. Moreover, the heaviest part of our navy should be kept in Asiatic waters. It is there that the conflicts of the future will occur, and it is there where our visible power should be manifest to all beholders. German trade increases, say German merchants, with every German war-ship that appears in Chinese ports. It is a circumstance worth noting that British trade has decreased coincidently with the decrease in the number of British flags appearing in Chinese waters. It is unprofitable to take too much space in tracing out the psychological causes of this; but, briefly, it may be said again, as it has been said before, that the Chinese, like all Orientals, are impressed, in a way quite impossible for our race to understand, by evidences of power which they can behold with the physical eye.

No difference of opinion was found in the pride which European or American residents in China took in the visit of their respective nation's war vessels. Strange as it may appear to those not on the ground, such physical manifestations of a foreign nation's might certainly creates an "atmosphere" distinctly favorable to that nation. "It makes me feel that I am not entirely in another world when I see the flag floating from one of our war-ships," said an American lady living in the Orient. "It is almost funny to see what an impression the frequent visits of the vessels of the German navy make on these people. But the mass of the business people we deal with here think that our country certainly cannot amount to very much, for they never see our war-ships and seldom behold our flag," said an American Oriental merchant.

It is not suggested that our Asiatic squadron should frequently visit Chinese treaty ports for the purpose of awing or intimidating the people. On the contrary, the exact reverse is stated. The point made is that the effect of familiarity with our flag, and that the impression of our national consequence resulting from the frequent presence of our squadron in Chinese treaty ports, is beneficial in creating an American atmosphere helpful to American commerce. It is unpleasant to put it in the following form, but in the end that is what it amounts to —it is an admirable advertisement of our importance, commercial as well as naval.

However reasonable or unreasonable this explanation may be, there is little doubt of the influence upon the Oriental mind of ships, flags, and the material expression of masterfulness in the world. It is quite as cheap for the American government to keep its ships cruising from Chinese port to Chinese port as it is to keep them anywhere else. They would thus be on the seas of the great world movement of the future — even of the present. They would be familiarizing themselves with the conditions with which America must deal; and, by mere contact, would each moment be increasing Chinese respect for our power and Chinese confidence in our ability to do things. Besides, if there is to be a fight between the nations, it is likely to begin in these waters. The Pacific will not only be the theatre of the great commerce of the future, but of the wars of the future, too. And while we want no war, and no part in any war, we must be able to protect our own, and increase it.

Li Hung Chang has been heralded to the world as a great statesman. He was not such. The writer could wish that the scope of this chapter permitted a review of this remarkable personality. But this much may be said, that Li Hung Chang was a very great *business*-man.

In a conversation with him, held more than four years ago, he suggested (after going through his customary talk to Americans about the admission of Chinese into the United States), upon being requested to give his honest views as to some practical and definite method of increasing American trade, that the two corner-stones of American commercial influence in China would be a great banking establishment and two or three, or even one, powerful American trading house. "The English," said he, "have the great firms of Jardin, Metheson & Co. and Butterfield & Swire. They have the Hong-Kong and Shanghai Banking Corporation and the Chartered Bank. Their great commercial firms own their own lines of ships; they have their own commercial buildings at every port; they have their system of compradors reduced to a science. It is these agencies that have helped England in China more than all her diplomatic negotiations, which have been neither clever nor brilliant.

"The German understands this a good deal better than do the English to-day. In fact, the English seem to be forgetting all they ever learned. If there could be an American trading company with ten, twenty, or even fifty million dollars of capital, owning its own ships, flying the American flag, and capable of immense purchases, you would see American trade grow in a way that would astonish you. Then, too, no diplomatic demand of the American government is ever backed up by any cash proposition, whereas England has her banking corporations, and so have Germany and Russia, immediately on the spot.

"If you Americans expect to get a large share of Chinese trade, you can't get it by talk; you have got to go after it."

Thus Li Hung Chang had grasped with clearness the commercial advantages to a nation which flow from great aggregations of capital. Indeed, one cannot see clearly how we are to keep pace with the growing influence of

Germany, with her commercial methods, heavily backed by capital and brilliantly supported by her government, unless there shall be two or three enormous American concerns engaged in competition. All the trade we have in China we owe to location, to the better quality and cheaper prices of our goods, and to the unsupported enterprise of our plucky American merchants in the Orient. But this will not suffice. Our goods must be pushed; Chinamen must know about them; they must wear our cottons, taste our flour, smoke our tobacco. This is a matter of extraordinary expense.

Very practical methods, indeed, must be resorted to in selling foreign goods in China. The Chinaman's demand for nearly all our products is from an acquired taste, like our desire for tomatoes. You must get him used to eating American flour. When you have accomplished this you have created a constant and increasing demand for that staple food product. A few years ago no American flour was sold in China. Gradually, however, flour bread began to be eaten by some of the richer merchants who had travelled abroad. Then the compradors took it up. Then it occurred to some mill-owners in America that if these Chinamen liked their flour the people themselves would like it, and two intelligent agents took the matter up.

The result is that the trade in American flour has now reached such a volume in Hong-Kong that it requires shipload after shipload each year to satisfy it, and this demand is spreading steadily and rapidly, but with a snail's pace compared with the progress it might make if pushed by great capital and comprehensive organizing ability and by broad and far-seeing business methods. After many conversations with commercial men, and after mature thought, it is believed that in ten years Chinese demand for American flour alone could be made to reach the total of thirty million dollars, or more than double the amount of our entire exportation to China proper at present (not including Hong-Kong and Manchuria). It will not reach ten millions probably, but if we should engage in Chinese trade earnestly it could be driven to the limit named.

An American tobacco company has illustrated the rapidity with which an Oriental demand may be created and the success with which the supply of that demand may be monopolized. This corporation decided to enter the Oriental field. It put in charge a general representative in love with his work. Samples of the company's goods were judiciously distributed. One whiff by a Chinaman was enough; he became familiar with that company's brand ("chop" he called it), purchased it almost exclusively, told his friends about it, and they repeated the process until one of the flourishing branches of the company's foreign trade is its Chinese trade.

There is also a growing demand for American condensed milk, and thereby hangs a tale illustrative of Chinese character. The Chinaman becomes accustomed to a certain brand. He knows the can or package by the picture on it, and the characters painted there—its "chop." When he acquires a taste for a brand, that is the brand he wants. A certain American firm had fostered Chinese trade in condensed milk until a considerable demand was created in the district of which a certain treaty port is the centre. A new management came into control of the business. At its head was a young man who did not admire the artistic proportions and the general get-up of the label. "We must have something neater, more modest," said he, and a very becoming label was substituted for the old one. In a single month the Chinese demand for that article fell away more than fifty per cent., and in three months it was practically non-existent. The old label was replaced, and again the demand sprang up. The point is that the Chinaman did not understand that the new label represented the same milk which he had become used to. The firm would have been compelled to go through the original process of creating a new demand for the same brand on account of the new label.

Chinese character is full of these idiosyncrasies, and they must be noted and studied by those who expect to sell goods to the Chinese. And the study is very well worth while. People may talk about Chinese frugality and self-denial all they please, but the Chinaman indulges himself more unrestrainedly than is generally believed. He has seen so many centuries pass; he knows that so many uncountable myriads of millions have died; he realizes, to borrow a phrase, "that we are going through life for the last time"; and so he ministers to his physical senses. Therefore, when you capture his desire you have captured his pocket-book. The Chinaman is bent on satisfying his appetite, and he likes good things. American meats, American milk, American tobacco, most of all American flour, please his palate. But he is not going to learn about our products by intuition, or visions, or dreams. He has got to learn about them by his physical senses. Therefore, they must be brought to his door and placed on his table. The Chinaman is a fish that jumps at no metal fly. The only bait he seizes is the real thing.

Therefore, American merchants ought to have reliable, energetic, tactful agents in China introducing their goods in a practical way. There is one medical firm whose patent preparations are known all over the United States. It has built up a considerable demand for its medicines in the limited area connected with a certain port; but the agent who has created the demand is a man of capacity, patience, resource, tirelessness.

In default of an American trading company of the capital and size which the Chinese commercial field demands, it might be well for American merchants to form a pool and pay very liberally for the introduction of one another's goods throughout the Orient, by giving away samples until the demand is created, and then they should be prepared to fill that demand on the spot. It would be the cheapest form of advertising, and the result would be more permanent than advertising is in America. Indeed, a combination of American manufacturers already uses this plan, but in a hard-and-fast, stiff, unelastic, and unpractical way. There is at Shanghai an American warehouse, and, in the best quarter of the town, a large American show-room for the display of American manufactured articles like machinery, glass, tools, and tiles.

This is the beginning of a movement in the right direction. If it could be supplemented by selling departments, competent to fill any reasonably large orders *on the spot*, and in charge of thoroughly trustworthy selling agents, whose exclusive business would be the introduction and sale of goods without any other connection whatever, the warehouse and show-room would show some returns. Very little result can be expected from the present awkward arrangement, however. Chinamen are too busily sought out by Germans, and even by the English, and most of all by the gallant little company of American merchants on the spot, to spend their time going around to the store-room to look admiringly on wares and then order on their own initiative.

The necessity is emphasized for reliable men, because experience has developed the fact that there are commercial adventurers in the Far East, men of real ability, of singular glibness of tongue and plausibility of manner, who, when given these commercial agencies, do nothing but draw the salary and finally decamp with the proceeds of the investment. On the other hand, there are in the Far East numbers of competent, trustworthy, devoted men, thoroughly in love with their work, and that number is increasing.

It would pay the associated producers of the United States to send three or four bright young men into the Far East for the purpose of studying commercial methods. These men should be chosen with care. The German government sent an industrial and commercial commission to study Oriental commercial conditions. Our government might well do likewise; but, independently of that, the manufacturers and producers should send their own men. The government commission should have to do with making the government and people of the United States familiar with the people and conditions of the Far East so that a steady national policy might be evolved. The business-men's commission should have sole reference to the sheer question of selling. It should learn how the Chinese desire their goods prepared. It should seek new sources of demand and trade.

China is a better field for this than Europe, because Europe's market is pretty well congested now, and its own producers are straining every nerve to supply, exclusively, its own demands. Nothing but our enormous aggregations of producing capital enable us to keep the sale of American goods in that market from rapidly decreasing. But China is a virgin market. Its exploitation has not even yet been begun, and an intelligent, practical, patient (let me repeat, patient, patient, patient) commission sent to China by the producers of manufactures; another one, of like character, sent by our combined producers of bread-stuffs; and, third, one sent by the combined producers of cotton goods, would discover fields for the sale of our merchandise which would surprise Americans and surprise the Chinamen, too. As has been pointed out, the Chinaman individually is a very intelligent man. Even his critics say that in character he is a victim of but two degenerating things—individual selfishness and a sort of paralysis which comes from his worship of precedent.

Mr. Parsons gives an instance in his admirable little book which illustrates this latter quality with surprising distinctness. He tells of a bridge, high and round, which was erected some hundreds of years ago over what was then a stream. But long since, hundreds of years perhaps, that stream ceased to flow. Time has filled in its bed, which is now on the level with the surrounding country, and vegetation grows upon it. But the road still runs over the bridge, and Chinamen, carrying heavy burdens on their backs, instead of walking past the bridge, continue to toil up and down it simply because their fathers did the same thing. Such peculiarities of Chinese character must be studied, and we must act accordingly.

One reason for the decline of British sales to the Chinese, which the inquirer hears repeated over and over again, is that the British put up their goods the way the British want them, and not the way the Chinaman wants them; that the English merchant says in effect to the Chinaman: "This is the way I like to put up goods. Take them or leave them." The German doesn't do anything of the kind. He caters to Chinese desires, therefore he gets Chinese trade. So does the Japanese merchant. A present example is in point. Large bales are difficult to transport into the mountainous interior of Korea The British put up in large bales certain goods sold there. Nevertheless, the British have until quite recently supplied most of the Korean demand, for the reason that no one else competed with them, and that, trade once established, its very inertia helps to continue it. But the Japanese saw their advantage, put up Japanese goods in smaller bales, and are therefore taking the trade of Korea away from England. Such examples should be lessons to American enterprise.

Again, the simpler items of Chinese commerce must receive serious and painstaking attention. A certain high British official in the Far East was talking about the growth of German trade. "Oh," said he, "it is 'muck-and-tuck' trade." By "muck-and-tuck trade" he meant clocks, pins, buttons—the minutiæ of commerce. When it was pointed out to him that this was the seed of all commerce; that from such little germs of trade greater trade is bound to grow; that these small articles make the

Chinese familiar with German goods, German trade, and the German name, he appeared unable to appreciate that commercial point. At an official dinner given that very evening another British functionary, in talking over this same thing, said:

"Oh, well, England has got along very well in the past, and she will get along very well in the future. It is England, you know. Nothing can down England!"

It was the spirit of self-satisfaction, which is the root of all unprogressiveness. No new methods for England; no change of conditions for English merchants; no progress, in short, for England. She had captured the trade in the manner pointed out in the chapter on Germany's activities in China, and she seems to have forgotten that the conditions which gave her that trade have passed away. To-day is not yesterday, even if the same sun does shine. The world moves. On an excursion among the Chinese shops at Hong-Kong it was found that, though most of the cloths were English, the buttons were German, the needles were German, the pins were German, the clocks were German, and so on. All of them ought to be American.

By the same token, all of them ought to be cheap. Peoples of the Far East are not looking for high-grade money. They insist on silver. They insist upon the copper "cash," a money made of hollow disks of copper, of which it takes hundreds, and in one or two provinces almost a thousand, to equal a dollar. Similarly, they insist on cheap goods. They will continue to insist on them until they are raised to a commercial and industrial civilization approaching American and European conditions.

After such commissions (and it is insisted that there should be one for each great industry—each commission would find its hands full and its time entirely occupied) there ought to be a pooling of each great group of American industries, and then the very best representative that that industry can find should be sent permanently to China and paid enough to justify him in exiling himself to the Orient in the interest of his employers and American commerce. But if we have not yet advanced so far in co-operative civilization that our manufacturers of tools, machinery, implements, and the like in one group, our manufacturers of cotton goods in another group, our manufacturers of food products in another group, cannot see their way clear to the pooling arrangement, let each great house that sees the advantages of this market send at its own expense a highly paid representative to China to exploit its own products. I repeat that expression—a highly paid representative. You had better send nobody at all than send some person who has not been successful here, or a picked-up, untried, untested, and unknown, or too well-known, individual who is already in the Far East. You have got to send the very best man you can find, the most comprehensive and alert intellect, the most tactful in disposition, the most engaging in personality, and, above all, the most patient, painstaking, and industrious. Such a person will prove an investment which will pay increasing dividends.

With the increase of trade and the growth of general knowledge and enlightenment as to Oriental conditions, which would come from following this course, new and improved methods would constantly suggest themselves as new branches of wheat stool out from the original grain; and it would not be a great many years before America would be the largest supplier of Chinese trade, and America the first power in Oriental waters. It is the neglected peoples and the neglected markets to which we must look in the future. When you reflect that Germany, including Alsace and Lorraine, has upward of fifty millions of people, and that we sell her nearly one hundred and ninety million dollars' worth of goods every year; that the United Kingdom has only forty millions of people, and that we sell it over five hundred and thirty million dollars' worth of goods every year; that France has less than forty millions of people, and that we sell her nearly eighty-five million dollars' worth of goods every year, and then reflect that China has four hundred million people, and that we sell her not more than twenty-five million dollars' worth of goods, upon the face of the returns (although by counting American goods which go to China by way of London and Japan, and by other indirect routes, we probably sell her forty millions), a child can see the possibilities of American trade expansion in China.

It has been repeated so many times that it is accepted as a truism that the first and last requisite for the increase of American trade in China is the maintenance of the open door. The open door means only that the goods of all nations shall have free access to the treaty ports of China upon the same terms. It must be remembered, however, that treaty ports did not always exist, and that, as M. Leroy-Beaulieu points out, they have all or nearly all been secured by armed conflict; in short, that, so far as China's door is open, it has been forced open by bayonets.

It is quite possible that any further opening of the door (that is, a multiplying of treaty ports, or any aggressive trade concessions to the world) will be secured by the same method, or by the fear of it. Of course, there is a possibility that a new order of things will develop itself in China, that when the new Emperor takes in his hands the reins of government he will grant these concessions to the rest of the world, upon considerations of wise policy and enlightened statesmanship. It is a beautiful hope, and every student of the world prays for its realization. But the practical man must deal with facts.

As important as is the maintenance of the open door, the extension of the avenues to which that door leads is, at least, equally important. If the door is open ever so wide, but you can only just get your goods inside of it, what does that avail you? That is the condition of China now. The tax on goods taken into the interior, an attempt to abolish which has proved a practical failure, prevents goods from going very far from the treaty ports. It is not forgotten that this has been repeated many times in this volume, but it is a fact so essential and so little known that it will have to be repeated a number of times more, and from many different sources, in order to be thoroughly appreciated.

It is agreed, and is now a law (so far as such an agreement can be called a law) that one-half of the customs tariff on foreign goods entering China shall be employed in lieu of and to replace all internal transportation tax. But this has not worked as a practical matter. To get the goods into the interior is still a thing of difficulty. By the interior is meant long distances into the interior. Of course, treaty ports include not only coast cities, but many on the rivers as well; for instance, Hankow, eight hundred miles up the Yang-tse-Kiang, is a treaty port. But foreign goods circulate in appreciable quantities only a short distance, comparatively speaking, from these treaty ports.

With the privilege of free and unvexed transportation of foreign goods into the interior would come another practical difficulty, that of finding a method of transportation. Merchandise must now be borne on the backs of coolies, in wheelbarrows, and on horses, or in some places by carts. This will not do; that is plain. Modern commerce will never be satisfied with such antique methods. Roads will have to be built—first railroads, and then, branching out from these, lines of highways for wagons. This is a practical problem worth while—quite as important as the open door. So far as the open door is concerned, the world may as well understand that it is not to be kept open by talk nor by communications. It has already been pointed out that it is being kept open now more by the jealousies of the aggressive powers than by any agreement.

When these jealousies are removed, or when a common

agreement of the aggressive powers is reached, or when the physical preponderance of Russia, Germany, or France becomes so great that the dominant country can do what it wishes within its sphere, the door cannot be kept open, no matter how much statesmen "communicate." The writer has talked with large numbers of residents of the Far East and with many students of the Far Eastern question, and all are agreed that if the partition of China is to be prevented something must be done of a definite, tangible, visible, material nature. This is a task for constructive, practical statesmanship, such as the present century does not present in any other direction.

It is a good thing for the American people to know this, because, as has been pointed out, we cannot have a national policy except as the people make it. England ought to take the initiative in this matter; but she may not. This is the opinion of Englishmen in the Orient. Mere scoffing at Russia and Germany will not do. Mere excited utterances at a dinner-table or at the social gathering or in the newspaper will not do.

It may be well, in closing these chapters of digression, to note something of the exact statistics of our trade with China at present and in the immediate past. In 1898 we exported to China $9,992,894 worth of merchandise, of which the principal items were cotton goods, oil, and flour; in 1900 we exported (in spite of the Boxer trouble) $15,-259,167 worth, of which the principal items were the same. In 1898 we exported to Hong-Kong (all of which was consumed in China) $6,265,200 worth of merchandise, and in 1900 $8,485,978 worth, so that in 1898 the United States sold to China directly (not including Hong-Kong) some sixteen million dollars' worth of merchandise, whereas in 1900 we sold to China directly nearly twenty-four million dollars' worth. But, perhaps, a third as much again as this was sent to the empire by way of London and Liverpool, and perhaps a similar percentage was exported by way of Japan. The exact amount sent through these last two channels cannot definitely be computed. Only an estimate can be made. It is a safe estimate that our exports to China, all told, now aggregate $40,000,000 annually.

This surprising increase of our export trade is exhibited also throughout Oceania and the entire Far East. No explanation of this sudden increase is given such as has been offered for the growth of German commerce. It is fair to say that something of it is due to the greater familiarity with the American flag and the American people, throughout the Orient, which followed close upon the Spanish war. Countries are very little different from towns in their commercial characteristics, and a country merchant knows that, if you get the people talking about his store and his goods, his trade at once increases. It is a practical point of which the smallest as well as the largest merchant in this and every country takes account. It must not be forgotten in our larger dealings with peoples. If our trade were pushed in an aggressive, material, and visible way, its increase would surprise the most sanguine. The writer has feared to make statements as strong as the facts themselves warrant. Because of our unfamiliarity with the whole question it has been feared that a conservative public would regard them as overstatements, so that the statements here made have been measured with care, and even reduced from their just and proper proportions.

A great American manufacturer recently said: "Our firm is going to invade the Asiatic field. Some of our directors pointed out what seemed to be the folly of this, because our recent trade with that region of the earth is so inconsiderable, compared with our trade with Europe, for example. Therefore, these objecting directors said, 'Why waste time on this little market, when a great market is at our hands?' But I answered them that the Asiatic market is comparatively a new one—virgin soil, as it were—and that what we must look for is not old markets, but new markets."

That was common-sense, was it not? When we have occupied a market, or get under good headway in it, the progressive and sensible thing to do is to look into the next and nearest market, and set out to exploit that. It is observed that the large mine-owners of our Western States were never content with the ownership of one mine. When the successful mine-owner had that under his control and in thorough working order, he sent his prospectors in every direction to search out new ones. He simply applied common-sense and energy to a practical situation.

Consider Russia, for example. We sell her between twenty and twenty-five million dollars' worth of merchandise every year. We might as well sell her eighty or one hundred million dollars' worth annually. The trade is ours for the asking and the going after. Our competitors are asking for it and going after it. They will get it, too, unless we act with skill and address. Germany, for example, sells Russia considerably more than one hundred million dollars' worth of merchandise every year. Even England sells Russia nearly seventy million dollars' worth of merchandise annually. Russia would prefer to buy from us, because we are not in her way anywhere, and because she has political animosities of an historic and permanent character against every one of our competitors. Then there is Asiatic Russia, chiefly Siberia. Our sales to her are inconsiderable. Yet all eastern Siberia, as far as Irkutsk, is our natural market. The Russian occupation of Manchuria (if Russia continues to let our goods in free and does not differentiate against us on her railroad rates) will double our trade there.

Here, then, are virgin markets. Why not have them? The writer calls the particular attention of every manufacturer and of every producer of bread-stuffs in the United States to these markets. Everybody who gives thought to our industrial situation knows that we are in danger of congestion of products at no distant date. What our producers must look for and what American statesmen must give attention to is an outlet to prevent this congestion. Here are markets which constitute such outlets. Let us occupy them. But be it remembered that they are not to be occupied by polite notes or banquet speeches. They have got to be occupied by ships, commercial agents, modern methods, the expenditure of money, and the resourceful vigilance of a firm and comprehensive business policy.

Whether we want it that way or not, we are thrust out upon the waters and into the midst of the peoples of the world. Let us address ourselves to the situation and acquit ourselves accordingly; and that means to adapt ourselves to growing and changing conditions. American traditions and American characteristics are repeatedly referred to; and it is said that "self-government" and "non-interference" and many other excellent things are American characteristics; and so they are. But *the* American characteristic is adaptability. We ought to adapt ourselves, and will, to the world's geography, and to our trade as influenced by that.

XV

SIBERIA: THE HIGHWAY OF RUSSIAN ADVANCE

THE Russian is on the Asiatic shores of the Pacific then, indeed. His banks, his railways, and his shops, his business houses, his vessels of war, his sotnias of Cossacks, and his parks of artillery, his fortifications built for enduring purposes, his civil administrators, his military commanders, his schools and universities for teaching Oriental tongues, all these in a visible way have left the world no longer any doubt of his tangible, substantial, permanent presence. All the world is talking about him therefore. And now that we have glanced at the index of the volume of his activities and achievements in his most recent fields of operation, let us, with judicial vision, pass through Siberia, that other land which the Slav is fashioning for the home of his future millions. And as our interest increases, let us go further back to the original fountain whence this flood of human power and purpose pours forth steadily and in ever-swelling streams. And, that what we see and hear may be the truth as it is, let us go without prejudice on the one hand or prepossession on the other. Let us go with the determination to neither laud nor vilify, neither to praise nor blame unjustly. Let us, in short, proceed as we have through Manchuria and China, holding no brief for nor against the Muscovite, and influenced by no spirit of advocacy favorable or adverse to any phase of his character or civilization, but merely as earnest searchers for the truth, whatever the truth may prove to be.

Let no traveller who is merely going about the world

for sight-seeing or pleasure go through Siberia. Comparatively, there is nothing for him to see. Only two classes of persons should make the trans-Siberian trip: first, men and women engaged in business, and to whom a quick journey from Europe to Asia is highly desirable; and, second, serious, careful students who are trying to get some idea of that increasing force in contemporary affairs, the Russian people. All others had better depend upon the faithful record by other travellers of what may be seen in Siberia and Manchuria, and their interpretation thereof, than to go through what must in any event be a dull monotony, and what, if they mean to learn anything, must be downright hard work.

Two influences operate to deflect the judgment of the American, the English, and the German traveller through Siberia. The first is that all of us have had it fixed upon our minds that Siberia is the land of terror, the region of exile, the domain of doom. We have been told that it was a snowy desert where wander the men and women whom Russian oppressors drove from their homes. It has been pictured to us as a country of prisons, a waste peopled by destroying wolves and sentinelled by grim and savage Cossacks, the agents of a secret, ruthless, and terrible power. For years popular plays have pictured the infamy of this barren world of outcasts; and at the present moment more than one melodrama, played at theatres patronized by the masses of the people, portrays the awful tyranny of the Czar and the bitter lot of his unfortunate subjects who people that dreadful land called Siberia.

Even the best-informed traveller enters Siberia with the above impression constituting his subconscious viewpoint. Fortify ourselves as we will with the tolerance of the scientist and the impartiality of the judicial mind, we find the feelings formed in our childhood days by shuddering tales of this Slav inferno asserting themselves. We have crossed the Urals, and Siberia proper is before us. Now, therefore, for the chain-gang, now for the knout, now for the stench, degradation, and death of those pens of incarceration where Russia herds her rejected till they go mad or expire.

On the other hand, the American, German, or Englishman comes suddenly into this territory from his own land. And his land is thickly settled, highly developed, and organized up to the ideals of modern civilization. He comes from countries of quick despatch, of frequent towns, of mammoth cities, of a perfected commerce, whose complexity has eliminated non-essentials, and is still eliminating them. He comes from a land of comforts, a place where the luxuries of a century ago are the common necessities of to-day.

On the one hand, therefore, Siberia is, in contrast to the first of these influences, a surprise and delight; on the other hand, and in contrast to the conditions surrounding him in his own home, he will declare Siberia to be undeveloped, her people without enterprise, her commerce trivial, the processes of progress within her scarcely distinguishable, and her future hopeless.

Against both of these influences the fair-minded man who visits Siberia must contend. He must take into account that Siberian development has only just begun. He must remember the racial characteristics of the Slav. He must bear in mind the serious conditions of climate and distance with which the government has had to contend. Above all, he must remember the Russian ideal of preserving for the Russian people themselves every foot of territory which Russian blood, Russian diplomacy, and Russian enterprise have won for the empire of the Czar.

"We are going to a new land, but it is still Russia," said the head of a family of emigrants at one of the registration towns along the Siberian railway.

"But why not emigrate to America? There are better chances there," he was asked.

"So there may be, but we do not care for great chances.

We want to live among our own kind of people," was the answer.

There spoke the Slav instinct: he must live in his own communities. He mingles with the natives of Siberia, and even of Manchuria, with familiarity and ease. Finally he absorbs them. And, without thinking about it, the instinct in him would never permit the Slav to go where he could not assimilate the people among whom he lives; for the Russian is the greatest absorber of other peoples which the contemporary world contains. He not only rules them, he appropriates them. They become a part of himself. A century hence will see Finland as much Russian as though it were originally Muscovite.

More than a score of different peoples are now under the colors of the Czar; and, say what we will from our western point of view, they appear to be as highly contented as the people of the more advanced countries, such as Germany or Italy, and far more satisfied with their conditions than are the English. This is due, no doubt, to the peculiar absorbing powers of the Slav. There are about him a somnolence of character and ease and laxity of life which suit the Asiatic native, towards whom his progress tends, and over whom his dominion is extending, far more than the precise and blunt methods of the Anglo-Saxon.

Of course, the answer of the emigrant just quoted did not give the practical reasons for his emigration to Siberia rather than to America. It might even be possible that he never heard of such a place as America; and, besides, he was going to Siberia because the agents of the government held out to him pleasant prospects of life and living there. Also, his home in European Russia was crowded, and, more likely, he had friends and neighbors in Siberia. But, above all, he had actual help from the government itself. His transportation was furnished him, a small sum of money was given him, land had been assigned to the community to which he belongs; for as the Russian in Russia lives in communities, owns land by communities, labors not as an individual, but in companies, so, as a usual thing, he emigrates to Siberia in communities.[1]

Besides all this, the Russian emigrant was following the lines of least resistance. He was going over land travelled by hundreds of thousands of his brothers before him. He was proceeding by the modern railway, to be sure; and yet it was a beaten path. For decades before a single sod had been turned on any Siberian railway, or indeed on any Russian railway, the Russian peasant, obeying his instinct towards Asia, has been travelling on foot towards this young Russian dominion, and there making his home. But far more important than all of these was the answer of this Russian father of an emigrant family; for it revealed in a flash one of the crowning characteristics of the Slav—namely, the cohesiveness and solidarity of his race.

Siberia we find to be physically a continuation of the Russian Empire. The Ural Mountains, which divide it from Russia proper, are, as we Americans understand mountains, no mountains at all. In comparison with our Sierras, or Canada's Selkirks, or Switzerland's Alps, they are hardly more than tree-clad foot-hills. From these mountains to Lake Baikal, Siberia is one vast plain of rich monotony. Locate on your map the Siberian railway, and you have the central artery of productive Siberia. The land on either side for perhaps two hundred miles, both north and south, is excellent for agriculture and grazing; beyond this, on the south, begin the sandy deserts of Central Asia; to the north, eight hundred to one thousand miles, are the great gold-fields; but, speaking of per-

[1] The government gives land to the peasant emigrant at the rate of forty acres for the head of each family. Also, it loans each family thirty rubles without interest, and, if needed, one hundred rubles. And the peasant is never pressed for payment.

manent soil for civilization and empire, Siberia may be said to be confined to a strip not over four hundred miles wide, extending from Russia to Lake Baikal, a distance of about three thousand miles; and, too, there are immense districts good for agriculture in Trans-Baikal Siberia.

This estimate of the productive area of Siberia is, to say the least, generous, if not exaggerated. Bohol, the highest authority, estimates that the really valuable agricultural portion of Siberia is not over five hundred thousand square miles in extent. Such an area, however, is equal almost to the entire Mississippi Valley. It is thus seen that, eliminating the unproductive land of Siberia, there still remains nothing short of an agricultural empire awaiting the plough, the reaper, and the thresher. Cultivated and populated as Indiana, Illinois, and Iowa are populated and cultivated, this minimum agriculturally rich portion of Siberia is capable of maintaining a population of over thirty-eight millions. Cultivated and populated as France and Germany are, it will support more than one hundred and fourteen millions.

And yet the population of all Siberia does not to-day exceed eight millions.[1] Russian emigration, however, is pouring in by the hundred thousand every year. The agricultural products consist of everything that we raise here in the United States. Wheat, millet, oats, barley, corn, and all the cereals of the north temperate zone are produced in abundance. The agricultural products of Siberia are beyond the capacity of the Siberian railway to transport. Immense warehouses, or, rather, sheds, have been erected along the line to shelter the piles of sacks of grain awaiting despatch. You may even see, at certain seasons of the year, great cords of sacks of grain piles on the ground, without cover or protection, except canvas thrown over them; for the capacity of the railway

[1] This is merely an estimate. Exact figures to date are not obtainable.

is already distanced by the agricultural productiveness of thinly populated and poorly cultivated Siberia.

An idea of what agricultural Siberia is doing at the present time is given in the following figures, which are significant when we remember the negligent and decidedly inferior methods of Russian agriculture:

CEREAL PRODUCTION IN SIBERIA FOR 1902

Grain	Quantity	Grain	Quantity
Wheat	30,796,000 bushels	Oats	34,078,000 bushels
Rye	23,080,000 "	Barley	2,628,000 "

The railway itself is not well built. But such is the care taken with the Siberian express, on which you are sure to travel, that, unless you carefully observe and seek reliable information to verify it, you would never know that you were not on an excellently constructed road-bed. It is the opinion of able Russian engineers that the whole line will have to be rebuilt. Certainly the track will have to be relaid, to say the very least. The rails are absurdly light. The reason why heavier rails were not laid in the beginning was, first, that the Russians themselves did not foresee the development of traffic the rails would be called upon to bear; and, second, towards the end of the enterprise a desire for retrenchment and economy developed quite inconsistent with the generosity of the original plan and the lavish outlay of the early stages of construction.

Sidings are being constructed all along the line. These sidings are, in many instances, so long that the observer cannot fail to conclude that they are the beginnings of a system of double tracks. That the Siberian road will have to have double tracks within the next two decades seems to be a matter of no further doubt. The increase in grain shipments alone would require this. A single track could be fairly well employed by the shipment of emigrants, soldiers, and other passengers. So congested is the traffic that emigrant trains are often side-tracked for a week, or even more, at a time.

This was the condition in 1901, when the road extended no further than Stretensk, and when all the Far Eastern traffic carried over the line had to be brought up the Amur by boat or by caravan across the Mongolian desert. Now, however, the road is completed through to Port Arthur and Dalni on the China Sea; the whole trade of Manchuria is transported over it, and you may go without change of cars from either of these Pacific ports to Moscow itself. This means ultimately an immense addition to Russia's Far Eastern commerce. It means, too, the gradual opening of the trade of Manchuria.

Another road is contemplated right across the Mongolian desert to the very gates of Pekin itself. There can be no question that this will be built. It is said that it will be built as a matter of military necessity. But there are more reasons why it should be built as a commercial enterprise.

Consider now the increased commerce that the main line must carry across Siberia when the contributions of these thousands of miles of feeders to the main line have been realized. Thus it may be taken as a settled fact that a double track for the Siberian railway is a certainty of the future. How soon this double track will be laid is, of course, a mere matter of speculation. If it were any other country than Russia which controlled the enterprise a reasonable guess could be made. It will be made when the Czar is convinced that the thing is needed, and that the condition of the Russian exchequer will permit its building. Then an imperial order will come forth, and the double track will be constructed and the old track relaid.

It is not profitable to speculate too far into the future, and yet, at the risk of injecting imagination into a narrative, it may be said that a quarter of a century will witness not only double tracks along the Siberian line itself, but extensive branches running both north and south, and even perhaps parallel lines east and west, one hundred miles or more, both north and south of the original road.

The paralleling of the Union Pacific by the Northern Pacific, and paralleling of the Northern Pacific by the Great Northern in our own country, must be reproduced when Siberia is as thickly populated as the present volume of emigrants to that country and the capacities of its soil make it certain that it will be.

In this connection it is interesting to know that all of the Russian imperial railways (and the Czar's government owns and operates the large majority of all the railway mileage of the empire) are paying investments, excepting the Manchurian line and portions of the Siberian line. Indeed, it is said on authority that the net income of the Russian government from its railways is over one hundred million dollars a year. When you consider the low rate of freight and railway fare in Russia, this fact is as important as it is interesting. Over the Siberian line, especially, the passenger fare is trivial.

The towns along this continental strip of territory are similar and uninteresting. Universally they are built from a mile to five miles away from the railway. Also in every instance they are constructed of wood. And again, uniformly, they are agricultural centres. They are just such towns as the transcontinental traveller saw upon our Western plains a score of years ago, only the Russian towns of Siberia are more populous, and law and order in them are more carefully enforced than in our similar towns at a like period of our development.

Some of these towns are the centres for emigrant distribution. Such towns are equipped with great buildings for the temporary comfort of the emigrant peasantry. Indeed, along the whole road, at every station, large and small, the government has not neglected helpful and indeed necessary devices to aid the peasant on his long journey to his new home. For example, no station is without large ovens where hot water awaits the emigrant, with which he makes his necessary tea. As has been stated, these emigrants are pouring into Siberia at the rate of between two hundred thousand and three hundred thousand each year. Many long trains of cars literally packed with Russian emigrants were inspected. Almost always these peasants, men, women, and children, appeared to be very healthy and highly vital creatures, indeed. Not often was sickness observed. Where sickness occurs at any town which is the centre of emigrant distribution, competent physicians are said to be stationed to relieve the suffering, though no personal investigation of this statement was made.

In but one instance were these peasant emigrants found to be dissatisfied. That instance occurred near a railway station, midway between Khabaroff and Vladivostock, in the Pacific regions. Here the inhabitants of an entire village from the congested districts of southern Russia were found, camped in the open, with no shelter save that afforded by the wagons they had brought with them, and such semi-tent, semi-hut structures as they had been able to hurriedly construct. There were perhaps twenty families in this group.

The elder (or starosta, as the Russians call him) was loud and bitter in his complaints. They had been there in sun and rain for three weeks, he said. Four babes had already died and two more were at that moment seriously ill. The emigration officer had not allotted them their lands or shown them where to go, and nobody knew when he would do so. Indeed, nobody knew where the emigrant officer was. The other peasants crowded around and eagerly and mournfully confirmed the melancholy plaint of their chief. If they had known what they were coming to they never would have left Russia, they complained. The women were strident in their demands that the whole colony should immediately return to Russia.

It was precisely the situation which the writer observed, in 1885, on the plains of western Kansas, when "settlers" from other States were disappointed at not finding the unbroken prairie fields in full flower, and when the women of the household forced the entire abandonment of the enterprise. But in the case of these Russian peasants it was not so easy to return. Indeed, in the case ot these particular ones it was impossible for them to get back to the fatherland at that time.

Not that the Russian peasant emigrant to Siberia is not permitted to return to Russia; on the contrary, two separate and considerable trains were observed on the Siberian line taking back to their homes emigrants who had grown tired or dissatisfied with their new surroundings, and who were unwilling longer to continue in Siberia. But in the hundreds of thousands of those who go to Siberia from Russia only a few thousand, comparatively speaking, go back to the place of their birth. And those who return are, of course, the least stanch and aggressive in character of the entire emigrant population.

So that not only are the hard conditions of nature in Siberia eliminating the physically weak from the new people there being compounded, but the weaker characters are also being rejected by their own lack of steadiness and spirit. From an ethnological point of view these two circumstances are of value in understanding the character of the Russian in Asia, which, in the end, is bound to be an improvement on the character of the Russian in Europe.

It is said that Russian officials whom the government places in charge of the distribution of emigrant lands are notably inefficient. There is no way, short of several years of weary investigation, to determine whether this is generally true or not. Certainly it was not true in one instance which fell under the writer's personal observation. A young Russian civil officer was among a company who floated down the long and hard journey on the boats of the Shilka and Amur rivers. This young man, it was learned, was to take charge of the distribution of emigrant lands at a newly opened post. He was highly educated, belonged to the ultra-Slavophile party of Russia, and appeared to be devoted to his work with almost missionary enthusiasm. Nor was this the fervor born ot anticipation of the untried delights of unfamiliar occupation. This officer had already had experience in similar work, and had been selected because of his efficiency. Of course, this information was not derived from him; but there was abundance of time to inquire into its truth, and careful verification was therefore made.

He took the greatest possible interest in the peasants on board, who seemed to return his attention with affectionate gratitude. A sufficient stop was made at the point where he disembarked to observe how he went about his business; and he entered upon the discharge of his duties with the same trained calmness and energy which you might expect an American to exhibit who is equipped for his work and in love with it. It is true that this example may not be typical, and it is further true that the praise of this officer by his fellow-Russians might have been exaggerated, and his own apparent eagerness for and concern in his employment superficial, But as one of the minor incidents of Slav colonization, this example is believed to be worth recalling.

The raft transportation down the Shilka and Amur rivers is worthy of repeated notice. In the summer of 1901, scores, hundreds of these rafts were observed lazily floating down those Siberian streams. Each of them contains at least one Russian family. On some of them several Russian families were being carried by the slow current to their remote destination. Nor were human beings the only inhabitants of these rafts. The peasant's wives and children were there; but so were his horses, his cattle, and all of the transportable things which the family possessed.

Over and over again the analogy of these Slav frontiersmen with their American counterparts in the period of the early settlement of our own country suggested itself. Here were the same fearlessness, the same daring of the unknown, the same severance from the place of their birth, the same intention to plant in the wilderness the institutions which they had left. With the American pioneer it was Anglo-Saxon individualism and the institutions of a representative government; with the Russian emigrant it is Slav communism and the institutions of autocracy. But here the parallel ends, for with the Russian emigrant all is patience, leisureliness, lethargy. Their slow course towards the ends of the earth, their utter want of hurry or impatience, was suggestive of the progress of their nation through history.

Indeed, the Russian peasant, on his cumbersome raft on the Amur, is the Russian nation floating towards the sea. The progress of the Amur currents is quite fast enough for him, and, besides, it is nature's method of transportation. And the Russian peasant is a very natural human being. He does not see any use of getting very far away from nature. It is believed from what was observed on the crowded emigrant boats that, had not the peasants packed upon these vessels been directed to travel in that manner, they would have been quite as content to have travelled by raft as by the more speedy agency of steam, if, indeed, they would not actually have preferred it.

It is not worth while to waste any lines in the description of these towns, and no traveller should squander a single day in remaining at any of them, excepting only the cities hereafter described. No one but the most studious minded, in search of particular information, should visit them; and even such a student will not find it of advantage to remain long; and having visited one of these towns he has visited all of them, for each is a type of a class, all are representatives of the same model. Broad streets, wooden buildings, fairly good stores, large market-places, many churches—some of them strangely magnificent in comparison with the architectural poverty of the town itself—a centre for local distribution and trade, a focus-point for the Russian fairs to which the peasants of whole districts converge—such, and only such, is the ordinary town of considerable size along the Siberian railway.

A notable thing about both Russia and Japan is the myriads of children. In a street leading out of the beautiful little port of Kobé, Japan, twenty-three children were counted in the arms of mothers or sisters in the course of exactly five minutes of a jinrikisha ride. The same evidence of fecundity may be observed anywhere in Russia; and in Siberia reproductiveness seems to be accelerated. It would be impossible for any traveller to look out of a car-window at any station on the trans-Siberian road, during the season when women can be out-of-doors, without observing children at every age, from a few months to a dozen years.

And if you will leave the train and go into the interior, you will find that the sight at the station was only a suggestion of the universal reality. Children, children, and again children, and still children. Everywhere the Russian is productive, but in Siberia the birth rate is the highest in the world. Next to Siberia the birth rate of Russia is the highest in the world. And the death rate of Siberia is lower than that of Russia proper. When one reflects that the hard conditions of Siberian life exterminates all but the ruggedest infants, one begins to comprehend the physical hardihood of this pioneer race which is growing up in this new land.

"How strong these people look!" observed an impartial traveller. "How ruddy their faces! how broad their shoulders! how deep their chests! how sturdy their arms and legs! They do not at all look the unhappy and down-trodden people they have been pictured, do they?"

"Well," responded an Englishman, "and what are they? They are nothing but so many human cattle deprived of their rights."

It was an illuminative conversation. With much care,

and through an interpreter who was not distrusted by them (and this is one precaution you must look to carefully), conversations were had with many of these, the common people of Russia in Asia. "Did they want to vote?" Why, they did that now. Did not all of them, even the women who were widows, have a free voice in their communes, etc.? "But did they not want to vote as Americans and Englishmen vote?" They were dumfounded; they did not know what it meant. "Did they not want to take part in the government?" Again, they did that in every village which exists in Siberia after the parent Russian form. "But did they not want something to say about what laws should govern them?" No, indeed! They cared nothing for that. That was the business of the government. The government was bad, but they would not make it any better. And if the Czar only knew where the government of his peasants is bad, he would make it right; and the Czar would know some day. In Siberia, as in Russia, with the peasant it is always the Czar. He is the peasant's friend, their father, who is loving and caring for them the best he can, and who, some day, "when he knows," will make everything all right. The devotion of the Russian peasant to the Czar is touching and pathetic, and, by the same token, a circumstance of import to every nation whose fate it is to reckon with Russia.

So it appeared that, as yet, these people have had none of the rights, which the American or Englishman means when he uses that word, of which they could be deprived. So again it appeared that they were in perfect ignorance of these rights, and on the whole it further appeared that they are without the initiative as a mass to inaugurate any movement to secure them, even if they comprehended them. And, as a matter of fact, the Russian peasant, at least the Russian agricultural peasant, does not care the least bit about those rights; and where local self-government has been attempted in

Russia, beyond the ancient self-government of the village community, the authorities have had serious difficulty in getting the peasant to take part in the innovation. Also, it must be said that apparently they are as well satisfied with their government as perhaps any other people are with their government. If the crops fail here in America, do we not lay the ensuing hard times to the fault of the administration?

XVI

HIGH AND LOW WATER MARKS OF SIBERIAN PROGRESS

THREE samples of Siberian towns will serve as illustrations of the highest point of Siberian development. Irkutsk is in the heart of that enormous region. On the one hand, it is thousands of miles from Moscow; on the other hand, it is thousands of miles from Pekin. Well, then, what of Irkutsk?

"I think you will find our museum interesting," said a pleasant Russian business-man of Irkutsk. Museum! The sciences studied here! For this was the very heart of Siberia. It seemed a curious invitation. Down the broad street, therefore, we strolled.

"And what is that fine building?" the stranger asked.

"Oh, that is our opera-house."

"And do you have operas here?"

"Why, certainly; and why should we not? and plays, too. Very good companies, indeed, come here from Moscow. Don't think that we are without amusements. We cannot rival St. Petersburg, of course, but we are far ahead of anything in Russia outside of half a dozen of the mother-country's leading cities."

"And who built this opera-house?"

"It was built by subscription. A number of our rich merchants raised the money, and they raised it, too, in less than a week."

So that here in the very centre of the Russian's Asiatic empire, and on the way to a museum, was found an opera-house as large in dimension and as excellent in appointment as will be found in any of the third-rate cities of the United States. If you consider it in comparison with the places of amusement of our frontier towns of twenty years ago, you will have only words of contrast to describe the two. Indeed, not a dozen New York playhouses surpass it. So it appeared that the Slav is enjoying himself in Siberia with plays and operas presented in a first-class theatre. We are not among barbarians, that is clear, nor even rude and uncultured people, if we are in the Czar's land of exile.

And the museum! Here were skulls and skeletons of races inhabiting Siberia long before the time of Yermack. Here were iron stirrups, lances, and all the accoutrements of warfare of by-gone centuries. Here was a sample of the simple craft with which the aborigines navigated the rivers. And anthropology and ethnology had not alone occupied the attention of these local scientists. Fishes, animals, plants, samples of all the flora and fauna of this unfamiliar region of the earth were carefully arranged, attractively exhibited, and scientifically classified.

"That looks like a church, and not a Russian church," observed the stranger.

"Why, a church it is, and not a Russian church either," said the citizen of Irkutsk. "Yonder is another, too."

And very pleasant—even handsome, in a modest way—were these religious edifices. There are church buildings, then, for several different denominations in Irkutsk, Siberia. Of course, as everywhere, the Russian Greek Orthodox Cathedral, magnificent, picturesque, imposing, dominates all else. But here was a visible exhibition of religious tolerance as surprising as it is pleasing to the Western traveller, who had been taught to look upon all the empire of the Czar's as dominions of oppressive religious intolerance. In short, in Irkutsk, as elsewhere in Russia, a man may worship God in his own way, or not worship Him at all, just as he pleases, provided only that he does not attempt to lead away members of the Russian National Church, or, if he is a member, does not try to leave it himself. Protestants build their churches and hold their services as in America. Mohammedans do likewise, as in Turkey; and a mosque, built by the faithful followers of the prophet, lifts its assertive domes almost within sight of the city.

"You will find the railway from Irkutsk to Stretensk without dinner or buffet, so you had better provide yourself here with food for at least two days' travel," said the friendly Russian of Irkutsk. (From Moscow to Irkutsk, but not beyond, there was, in 1901, well-furnished through trains with excellent buffet and dining cars, and sleeping-car accommodations quite equal to those found anywhere in Europe, or even America. But this service has since been extended over the Manchurian line to Dalni and Port Arthur on the Chinese waters.)

So the stores of Irkutsk were visited. They are numerous, some of them large, all well provisioned. In a single store you can buy things to eat and things to wear: rubber coats and cloaks for the precarious journey on the Amur; canned cherries, peaches, raspberries—all manner of preserves—in short, anything which you can buy in a department store in the United States, and at prices about the same. Most of these goods are Russian; for be it remembered that it is the policy of the present administration of the Czar not only to preserve the lands of the empire for Russian subjects but their trade and commerce as well. Russia proposes in time to become independent of the world. She is in no hurry about it, as she is in no hurry about anything. Are not the centuries hers? Why exploit everything in an hour and get through with life in a year? That is the Russian thought. There is something about the lethargic patience of the Russian which reminds you of the slow leisureliness of the processes of nature itself. Their very inertia has something in it elemental.

There are two additional explanations for the preponderance of Russian goods in Siberian stores west of Lake Baikal. One is that the distance is not so great from Moscow but that a Russian merchant may ship his goods at a profit even to Irkutsk. Also this portion of Siberia is so far from the Pacific, and until recently the methods of shipment were so crude and expensive that it did not pay to put American goods into this portion of Siberia by way of the Pacific, and, of course, not by rail through Russia itself. Even here, nevertheless, most of the mining machinery and things of that kind are American made.

"These Russians," said a young German electrical engineer establishing himself in Irkutsk, "are not to be feared in our lifetime, nor in that of our children, as commercial competitors, but I am full of fear of them for the distant future. I will not be here then, it is true, but Germany will still be here. I do not know whether it is because they are dull, or whether it is because they are far-sighted, but they are going about things in a way which, it appears to me, will make their power irresistible in the long course of time."

Germans in Irkutsk! Certainly. A large German colony thrives in this capital of Russia in Asia. Indeed, the German is everywhere; likewise he prospers everywhere. His activity within the Russian dominions has been noted before and will be noted again. The German agricultural settlements in European Russia are conspicuous for their prosperity. In every city you will find large numbers of German merchants. It appears that at one time foreigners were invited to establish industries in Russia, and to this call the enterprising, watchful German responded promptly and numerously. This is said to be the reason why the German language is so manifest within the Czar's dominions. Certain it is that if you speak German you may travel from St. Petersburg to Port Arthur without an interpreter. You will be sure to find on every train, in every city, and at every possible point of enterprise some one who can speak German. The young German above quoted was returning to Irkutsk from Berlin, with his young German wife, and their residence in Irkutsk was to be permanent. He had already taken the business away from the English electrical engineer located at that point. It is a notable circumstance that German energy, intelligence, and industry is weaving a web of German influence all around the world.

Let us now take Blagovestchensk, in Trans-Baikal Siberia. This remarkable town, thousands of miles from nowhere at all, midway and nearly two thousand miles from Irkutsk on the west, and almost the same distance from Vladivostock on the east, standing on the banks of the Amur, with the inhospitable and, until recently, hostile and menacing Manchurian frontier within rifle-shot across the river, is surprisingly beautiful, astonishingly progressive.

Like every Russian town, its streets are American in breadth. In Blagovestchensk the houses bordering on these streets are almost, without exception, comfortable and attractive. Many of them are commodious; some are positively handsome. Almost everywhere these Russians have made gardens and planted trees. The "hominess" of the residences strikes one with singular force when one remembers that this is not Europe, not Colorado, not Dakota, not even Siberia proper, but a far-off, segregated portion of the earth's surface, on the very edge of what was, until yesterday, Asia's dark and bloody ground.

There are department stores here which are not surpassed by any American city of one hundred and fifty thousand inhabitants. These stores are nothing less than magnificent in their proportions. In them you may buy any conceivable thing you may want, from towels to fire-arms, from mackintoshes to toys, from sugar to paint. And although Blagovestchensk is essentially a "mining town," the prices are about the same as in the United States and not so very much greater than in Russia itself; indeed, not surprisingly higher than in Germany or England.

Of course the greatest of these mercantile establishments is German, although a large Russian house almost rivals its German competitor. The American commercial plant which thrived here for some years looked to be on the point of extinction. American threshing-machines, manufactured by a firm in Ohio, American ploughs, American agricultural implements of all kinds were examined and priced in the German store.

"Do you have sale for agricultural implements?"

"Indeed we do, and the demand is growing. You observe yourself our present heavy stock. We have other consignments coming, and still we cannot supply the demand."

"But I thought that this was a mining town?" was the inquiry.

"So it is, or, rather, has been," replied the German merchant; "or, rather, it is the depot of the products of mines located hundreds of miles away from here. But the future of this country is in its agriculture and grazing, and this is daily becoming more apparent to us merchants. The country around here is settled for scores of miles. Also the farmers seem to thrive—at least they are able to buy and pay for these implements."

"Why does not some capitalist start a factory here?" was asked.

"They have already done so. A German firm has a considerable establishment not far from town."

So the German factory of agricultural implements was visited. The plant was quite respectable and in process of enlargement. It turned out threshing-machines and various things of the sort.

"I suppose you will soon monopolize this market," was asked of the manager.

"Unfortunately, no," he answered. "Material is hard to get; labor is high priced; its efficiency is only a fraction of that of American labor in the same line."

The heads of departments, the highly skilled artisans, were, to a man, German, but all the rest of the labor was Russian. And these laborers live very well indeed. As in Russia, so here, the company had built living quarters for the men and their families. But here in Blagovestchensk the laborers' homes are not, as in European Russia, vast dormitories. They live in attractive little cottages, around which trees had lately been planted, and they have most of the accommodations and creature comforts which it is supposed the American laborer alone enjoys.

Here in Blagovestchensk, too, are three or four flouring mills, and others are projected. They do not hold their own as yet with American flour, for American flour looks better, tastes better, is better than that produced in Blagovestchensk. Therefore, the people like it better, and the people buy it more readily. Given an equal footing, American products will compete successfully even with local enterprises in Siberia itself. Were it possible for America and Russia to enter into some commercial agreement by which American goods could have free access to Russia's markets, it is clear to the thoughtful observer that, almost to the exclusion of all the rest of the world, America and Russia combined would soon feed, clothe, and supply all the wants of the scores of millions who people the world's greatest empire.

Irkutsk and Blagovestchensk are Siberia at their best. Now for Siberia at her worst.

The curious American sauntered down a side street in Misovaia. Misovaia, you must know, is on the east shore of Lake Baikal, where the steamer lands you from the Siberian road on the west side to again take up the rail journey on the east side.

"Don't go there!" came the panting voice of the watchful interpreter as, running and white-faced, he caught up with his employer. "Come back, I beg of you! You will get your throat slit or be mauled in the head or killed some other way if you wander recklessly about this place." Purple evening was quickly falling, and the dark shadows, everywhere around the earth the partners of crime, were already enveloping the little town with indistinguishableness.

"I see no danger, and everything looks peaceful enough," said the American.

"But this is the worst place in Siberia. Last week two men were found garroted [strangled] and stripped of everything right on the streets. Since we arrived I have been told that there was a murder here yesterday. To-day a man was stabbed at noon right in the open streets. And you are unarmed and an American. If you wander around here at night nothing but a miracle can save your life."

Such was the report of this little Russian town not half a day by rail from gay, prosperous, busy, civilized Irkutsk. And yet nothing more harmless than the appearance of its inhabitants could be imagined. Kindly faced, sleepy-eyed moujiks, scores, hundreds of inoffensive peasant emigrants from Russia (for here, as everywhere, are emigrant headquarters), two or three dozen railroad working-men, all very busy with the jam of cars; station-master, telegraph-operator, and a few passengers—and yet this the abode of open assassination and skulking robbery. Everybody confirms the bad reputation of Misovaia. But the uninformed foreign observer could discern nothing that bore the appearance of disorder and crime. On the surface it looked no more dangerous than any American country village—not a hundredth part so formidable and forbidding as certain well-known streets of Chicago and New York. Hence one's inclination is to believe that the stories of Siberian cord and knife and bludgeon are seriously overstated.

Move on now for three days' journey by rail to Stretensk. This town until two years ago was the actual terminus of the Siberian railway. It is practically midway between Irkutsk on the west and Blagovestchensk on the east. It is the head of "navigation" on the Shilka River. Here start the steamers that go down the Shilka River into the Amur, and down the Amur to Blagovestchensk, and then for many hundreds of miles to Khabaroff, the political capital of Trans-Baikal Siberia.

The railroad, with its delta of switches, ends on one side of the river, and on the hill above enormous emigration barracks, provision houses, store-rooms, etc., are visible. Stretensk itself is on the other side of the river. But let us waste no time with local geography.

Stretensk is a typical Cossack settlement. By some early decree or other (and seek not to follow Russian decrees, you never can unravel them) this land and all the adjacent town belong to the Cossacks and their children. Its government is exclusively in the hands of the Cossacks, and is a military—Cossack—oligarchy. Neither the merchant, the banker, the trader—in short, nobody but the Cossack proprietor—has any voice in the administration of municipal affairs.

Whether this or something else is the reason, the fact remains that Stretensk shows absolutely no progress. The houses are wooden and filthy. The yards are pigsties, the streets unpaved, miserable stretches of desolation. A gray-haired woman lay in the mud on the bank of the river in a coma of vodka intoxication. The men are sturdy, broad-shouldered, thick-necked, and bull-headed; the women are creatures of immense physical capacity. Children, pigs, and chickens throng each doorway. Yet Stretensk has not a particularly evil reputation for crime, but it is just the spot of which you would be prepared to believe any tale of horror told you. And, indeed, you are warned to stay in-doors at night, and occasionally rumors of assault and robbery float in the atmosphere.

"Seek for the beautiful even amid squalor," says some writer. So even Stretensk has its oasis. Here is one of the branches of the many tentacled Russo-Chinese

Bank. Connected with the bank itself is the home of the manager. The whole stands in a neat and (compared with the rest of Stretensk) not unattractive enclosure. In this home pleasing rooms are found. The notes of the piano, well played, sound strangely at night, among surroundings so intellectually dense that you can almost feel its oppressive influence.

At the board presides the manager's wife, a Russian girl, Siberian born, and never nearer Europe than Irkutsk, and yet as well groomed and in costume as perfect as her sisters in St. Petersburg. She is Siberian educated, too. There is the grandmother also—you would take the quiet, dignified, white-haired Siberian mother for an American woman of similar condition—and the children, quiet, well bred, clean, modestly attired. The talk is of everything. The great world without, of course, first of all. Here is keen but reserved curiosity as to foreign thinking and doing. Yes, but here also is information of the world surprisingly accurate, when you consider that you are in Siberia's very heart of darkness.

The manager of this bank, like every manager of every branch of this amazing financial institution of the Russian government, was found to be a man of real capacity, of independent views, of fearless expression, well posted on the world's development, and informed to the minutest particular on local trade and financial conditions. The banking-rooms themselves are in charge of the manager and two under-officers, both Russians, the other assistants being, as is universally the case, Chinese; for you must know that the Chinaman has an aptitude for sharp finance not equalled by any other money-changer in the world. Also your Chinaman is the world's most careful and persistent small merchant—and large merchant, too, for that matter, as you will soon learn if you take the pains to investigate into the heavier commercial operations of China. In short, the inhabitant of the Flowery Kingdom, who is disgracefully negligent of government and of all civil affairs, is the most industrious and careful toiler, the most ingenious and persistent merchant, and the most alert and advantageous dealer in money now on the face of the globe.

"Oh yes," said a financial gentleman of Trans-Baikal Siberia, "we must have the Chinese in our counting-houses. Really, they are quite indispensable. We find them accurate and honest; but, mark you, their honesty is not a matter of morals. It is purely a matter of wisdom. With the Chinaman honesty is the best policy, and therefore he is honest. The moment he perceives that honesty is not the best policy he is dishonest." From this it appears that the Chinaman in Siberia, as in China and elsewhere in the world, has the scrupulousness of wisdom but not of righteousness.

On the banks of the Amur you will find other Cossack settlements smaller but still similar to Stretensk. None, however, are so squalid as this Cossack town. Occasionally you may find a Cossack village which is really attractive. Usually there is but a single street stretching along the bluff. Sometimes the homes are neat. In every one of these Cossack villages are well-stocked stores; and whatever else a Russian or Siberian store will deal in, you will find an abundance of two articles — perfumery, candy and sweetmeats, in their various forms. Time and again Russian officers were observed to buy great quantities of these sweets. At one place the entire stock of saccharine goods was purchased.

"We Russians, from the youngest child to the eldest man, love sugar in its various forms," explained a general on his way to inspect the marksmanship of the troops around Vladivostock.

"Oh yes," observed a noble tchnovnick, who was heading one of the innumerable Russian "commissions," "the Russian has a sweet tooth."

Attention was called to the extraordinary stock of perfumes found at the stores in a Russian city where such articles were for sale.

"Well," said the storekeeper, "you see, the Russian adores sweet odors. This passion for perfumes is not confined to our women either; it is common to men and women alike."

Precisely the same explanation was made to a like inquiry when a whole case of shelves was observed to be filled with various perfumes and a large, ornamental pile of the same kind of bottles was heaped upon the cases in the store at Irkutsk. And in a Cossack village, on the frontier borders of civilization itself, the same provision for this national taste was found.

Few world-travellers will ever again take the journey by boat down the Shilka and Amur rivers. Most if not all of them will run right through from Moscow to Dalni or Port Arthur, for the line is finished now. But in all Siberia, in all Russia, no such opportunity offers itself to observe Russian character as on one of the hard trips down the Shilka and Amur, for a thousand miles or so, when the water is low, for both of these rivers are filled with sand-bars on which every few hours the boat is grounded. If the water is falling, no inducement can persuade the captain to proceed at nightfall, but at every sunset the vessel ties up to the shore until morning.

Remember that every boat is as crowded with emigrants as a box is with sardines, so much so that they sleep on the floor and the roof of the vessel, very much as sardines are arranged in their packages. It is an even chance that you will run into forest-fires. In summer the heat will melt you. If the fires are raging within a few miles, the heavy, acrid smoke smarts the eye and irritates the nostril. On the boat are sure to be one or two Russian soldiers in uniform and from ten to a score of others in peasant's garb, on their way to join the already vast military Russian host massing on the Pacific for the expected conflict with Japan. Every month or two a party of generals, a "commission" of officials, perhaps even a highly educated and cultivated Russian lady will constitute a party, which gives to the best-read and most widely travelled foreigner all the mental society he can possibly digest.

For days and weeks, sometimes even stretching into months, this monotonous progress continues. There are all the conditions of vexation. Frequently all the passengers, except the high officials, are ordered to travel over some mountain, while the boat, thus lightened, attempts to glide over some particularly shallow stretches of riverway. Protests? Not one. Complaints? Not one. Grumblings? Not a murmur. Everything is laugh and jest and good-humor. Where a similar crowd of Americans or Englishmen would hold indignation meetings, these Russians accept the situation almost with gayety. Children may be born on the journey; nobody thinks of the discomfort caused by the new arrival. The little fellow is quite welcome. It is an occasion of rejoicing. Congratulations pour in upon the fortunate mother.

"I should think you would object to this crowding and hardship," was remarked to a vigorous young fellow, already the head of a considerable family.

"Object? Why?" he answered. "It is all in a lifetime. We are enjoying ourselves very well."

At one place the peasants crowded about a little pile of stones above which rose a rough wooden cross. Here had died and was buried one of the peasant immigrants who preceded them. In the wilderness, thousands of miles from anybody or any place, reposed his bones. The peasants gathered reverently around the grave of their unknown fellow-journeyer to a far home.

"Very sad, very pathetic, is it not?" remarked the interpreter, on a suggestion from his employer, to some of the peasants with whom he had been told to fraternize and with whom he had fraternized successfully.

"Why, no," came the answer. "All is as God wills."

And thus again on the banks of the Amur spoke the fatalism of the Slav—his acceptance of the universal and the inevitable, his attribution to the great Father above, whom he worships with instinctive devotion, if not with intelligent understanding, of all that befalls the individual and the race.

"God gave me three little mushrooms this morning," said a peasant woman in south Russia, as she sat milking her cow by the side of a pleasant stream. She had found three mushrooms, but "God gave me three little mushrooms this morning," quoth she.

"How many children have you?" was asked of the wife of a working-man in one of St. Petersburg's factories.

"God has given me five," she answered. "And whether I am blessed with more is as God wills."

"As God wills," "God gave," etc. In the capital of the Czar, in the peasant village of the country, on the emigrant boat on the Amur, around the grave of one of the swelling host of Slav emigration in the Siberian wilderness, everywhere and always this is the common speech and thought of the Russian people.

The hardihood of the Russian man and woman has already several times been noted. Here is another instance: On top of the broad, flat roof of the boat on the Amur you may see peasant women fast asleep in the blazing sun, without the slightest protection from its rays. They do not appear to notice it. Transport yourself now back to central Russia. Go again into the country districts. You will see women at work in the fields, as you will, indeed, all over Europe or, for that matter, in some places in our own country. But in Russia it is not uncommon to see a woman, weary with her labor, lie down and go fast asleep by the road-side. That it is a cloudless sky and a fiery day make no difference to her.

And true as this is of the women, it is, of course, much truer of the men. It would seem that the Russian has such nerves that he can sleep anywhere or under any conditions. On a passenger train from Tien-Tsin to Pekin, operated by military authority (the conduct of the railway having not yet been handed back after the Boxer troubles to its accustomed operators), were several officers of different nationalities. There was nothing for them to do. Nevertheless, all were alert, nervously alive, full of complaints—all but one. That one was a Russian colonel. He came in and, rolling his coat into a pillow, stretched himself on a bench and was almost instantly in profound slumber. Perhaps he was trying to overhear the general conversation? Put a bridle upon your instinctive suspicion of the Russian; the colonel was doing nothing of the kind. He was merely sleeping the sleep of the Slav.

And the sleep of the Slav is not the sleep of the just or the unjust, but the slumber of a thoroughly healthy physical organization with untroubled nerves. Every peasant home throughout all the Russias has one characteristic necessity—it is a great stove built of brick. Its top is flat and far broader than necessary for any purposes to which we put stoves in this country. But the Russian peasant family has a different use for it. They sleep on it in the bitter nights of the Russian and Siberian winter. At the same time every possible crack or crevice which will admit the outside air is carefully sealed. Yet in this vitiated atmosphere, where an American would find it hard to breathe, the Russian peasant, his wife, and children sleep refreshingly. No other lungs or nerves but those of a Russian could stand it.

These instances will give you some idea of the physical vigor of these people and of their capacity to resist those influences which would be unbearable to an American. But it again calls to mind the fact that the unhygienic conditions prevailing throughout Russia and Siberia kill off all but the very hardiest of infants, and thus leave only the steel-wire constitutions surviving. Perhaps it is this weeding out of the naturally weak and decrepit which has made and is making of the Russian people a nation of amazing physical vigor. But whatever the cause, the vitality and strength exist and is national.

In trying to form an opinion of the quality of people which are being reared by Russia on the Siberian plains, the criminal or exile element has been overestimated. Conceding the truth of the worst pictures drawn of this unhappy phase of this new empire of the Czar (and the picture has been painted to us in blacker colors than all the facts justify), still the exile element will be literally submerged by the peasant inundation now pouring over Siberia. Indeed, it has been overwhelmed even now, and exiles to Siberia are, numerically speaking, a comparatively small portion of the people of this new land.

Nor are the conditions of the prisoners who are expelled from Russia so bad as one expects to find them. For example, the student who deliberately murdered the Minister of Public Instruction in St. Petersburg about three years ago was found on one of the prison-boats of the Amur. These prison-boats are, doubtless, very uncomfortable, but they are by no means impossible; at least it must have so appeared to the prisoners themselves, for behind their bars they were laughing and joking in quite a good-natured way.

The student murderer of one of the Czar's ministers seemed to be in particularly high spirits.

"I expect to be out in a year or, at the most, two years," said he.

If you are astonished at finding a murderer and a slayer of one of the highest officials of the empire in a prison-boat instead of on a gallows, you are brought startlingly face to face with a fact peculiar to Russian jurisprudence (a fact all of us might well have known had we taken time to read, but which hardly any of us do know), and that fact is that there is no capital punishment in Russia. At least, this is so generally true that it may be stated to be universal.

If the condition of the exiles on prison-boats is fairly good, so much cannot be said for the prisoners in the prison-cars which the railway transports. The condition of the prisoners in these cars would be very hard, indeed, for an American. But that does not mean that they are hard for a Russian, for, as has been pointed out, the Russian can endure in every condition of life things which to the American would be unbearable. So it is not necessary to say more of the prison-cars observed on the Siberian line than that they would be thought in America to be very bad, although from a casual inspection of the prisoners being transported in them they do not appear to be highly objectionable to their Russian inmates.

It must be stated, however, that no careful examination of this subject was made, but the comparison by Professor Wright, in his two admirable and scientific volumes, *Asiatic Russia*, of conditions in Russian prisons with the reports of prison officers in the United States of the condition of prisons here, shows that, relatively speaking, American prison conditions and Russian prison conditions are not so widely different after all. And upon such slight and surface observations as the writer made this view appeared to be confirmed.

Furthermore, it must be remembered that not all of the exiles to Siberia are sent there by the Russian government on its own initiative. Many—indeed, the majority—are expelled by their own villages in Russia. It is a sort of "rogue elephant" process by which the peasant communities eject their bad and impossible members. Furthermore, when the ban of banishment is over and the exile returns to his home, his village has the right to say whether it will receive him again or not, and this is true whether he has been sent to Siberia under a judgment of the court or by direct order of the Czar or by the village community itself.

If upon his return his village community refuses to receive him again, that fact settles that man's case with the government, which, without further investigation, immediately orders his return to Siberia. In this way large numbers of exiles are sent to Siberia by what is called the "administrative process"—that is, by direct order of the government, and yet without the government having anything more to do with it than to ratify the decision of the commune to which the exile belongs. But even taking all this into account, the total exile element, both past and present, is inconsiderable among the increasing millions of the sturdier and more upright men and women who are voluntarily going to Siberia to erect homes, cultivate fields, rear children, plant communities, and build empires.

XVII

THE RED DAY OF BLAGOVESTCHENSK

NOW for the crowning "infamy" of recent Russian history in the Far East. You will know at once that the massacre of the Chinese at Blagovestchensk in 1900 is referred to. The writer sifted this "crime" from every point of view and by means of every source of information he was able to approach. The accounts were received of attorneys from the courts, hands in factories, clerks in banks and mercantile houses, who formed part of the volunteer company of citizens quickly organized, just as citizens would organize here in America under like circumstances. A Russian colonel of almost Anglo-Saxon independence and enterprise gave his account of the event. A Cossack officer told all he had seen. A voluminous recital was listened to from a well-informed lawyer. In Blagovestchensk pamphlets had been written on this circumstance which "shocked civilization," for you must know that this event is quite the most important and dramatic in the history of this thriving and modern commercial Siberian city. There were many differences of detail, but all accounts agreed upon the main facts. And here they are:

The town of Blagovestchensk is unprotected by fortifications. While there are considerable barracks there, there was at the time of the outbreak but five hundred Russian soldiers stationed near the city. Within the city itself were several thousand Chinese. Immediately across the river was Chinese territory—Manchuria. A Chinese town stood directly over the river from Blagovestchensk. So much for locations. Now for the event.

First of all, Russian boats were fired on from the Chinese shores when approaching the Russian town from the east. Before this, for days, rumors of Chinese uprising, somehow or other, were in the air. The Chinese in Blagovestchensk were observed to neglect their work and gather in groups. As the days passed they were seen to be laboring under some unexplained excitement. Then threats and hootings came from the Chinese side. The business community of Blagovestchensk began to be seized with vague fears. The great Boxer disturbance, involving many millions of the yellow men, had been preparing for months and was on the verge of being ignited. These Russians in Blagovestchensk were right up against the fuse of this awful Oriental bomb, whose explosion, when it came, reverberated around the world. That psychic intelligence which somehow conveys the purpose of a great mass of human beings to other imperilled human beings fairly saturated this community, comparatively trivial in numbers. Then came the firing of artillery from the Chinese town across the river directly into Blagovestchensk. About this there is absolute agreement on all hands. This was accompanied by the firing of musketry and with it wild demonstrations on the Chinese side.

Then with the culmination of the fears of the people of Blagovestchensk came, almost simultaneously, reports that Chinese had landed both below and above the town. The fears of the Russian business-men and working-men, and all the citizens of Blagovestchensk, rose to a panic. What to do was the question. Their homes, their wives, their children—how could they be saved? Was another Chinese butchery such as had more than once before horrified the world to again occur in this unprotected spot, with thousands of unprotected citizens and their families as the victims? And these fears were far more to those who lived shoulder to shoulder and face to face and breath to breath with the danger than they appear to us between whom and the terror an ocean rolled.

"Intelligence," which may have been only a rumor, was received that the Chinese governor had marched large bodies of troops to the frontier immediately opposite the Russian town. If the Chinese in Blagovestchensk combined with those on the opposite shore, and a juncture was made with the Chinese forces reported to have been landed on the Russian side, the destruction of the little Russian city appeared to its citizens to be inevitable. At least that is the way they reasoned. Immediately everybody flew to arms. The shops were closed, business suspended. Merchants, bankers, clerks, artisans formed a military company. Any kind of weapon that would shoot any kind of a ball was utilized. The Chinese in the city itself were driven by the few Cossacks down to the river's edge below the town and forced into the river. Three or four thousand of them perished.

For weeks the bombardment of Blagovestchensk from the Chinese city continued. You may now see the bullet-marks made in the walls of the home of the local governor. Many houses of Blagovestchensk still show these signs of actual peril. Finally reinforcements arrived, the Russians crossed the river, and literally wiped the Chinese town off the face of the earth. You may visit its site now, but you will see nothing but waving grass and here and there the demolished remains of the crumbling wall of a house. Such, stripped of its many variations, is the story of the great "massacre" of the Chinese by the Russians of Blagovestchensk in 1900 which made the world "shudder." Highly colored anti-Russian accounts of this atrocity were published broadcast among mankind; but the narrative as here given is as nearly accurate as anybody can get it. Not only Russian sources of information but sources distinctly anti-Russian were availed of, and cross-examination in the form of peasant conversation in every instance confirmed in large substance the above general description. And none but eye-witnesses were interviewed.

So much space has been given to this incident because of the tremendous publicity given to it and the distortion of all of its features, and because, too, it is a very fair illustration of the manner in which any incident of Russian advance is painted to the American and European world. When we hear of Russian outrages we must always bear in mind that while it may well be that all of their bloody details are entirely true, yet the chances are that the forbidding aspects of each affair are magnified.

There are plenty of things for which the Russians as individuals and as a nation may be criticised without stretching the truth about them. The plain facts, as far as they can be obtained, are always best. Misrepresentation, no matter what may be its momentary effect, is sure to be exposed by that great revealer of all things, events, and therefore is sure to react in favor of its victim.

In this connection it is useful to know that the Boxer uprising had its first physical manifestation in Manchuria. As has been detailed in another chapter, the Russians had secured a concession to build the Manchurian railway. Work had begun, the whole survey had been made, much grading had been done, many scores, perhaps hundreds, of miles of rail had been laid. Immediately before the Chinese attack on Blagovestchensk signs of an uprising became unmistakable throughout all Manchuria. Finally the uprising occurred, beginning at Blagovestchensk; but it was almost simultaneous everywhere throughout the provinces which make up Manchuria.

The railroad was destroyed, homes and buildings were demolished by the infuriated and fanatical Boxers, and horrible outrages were committed upon every Russian who fell into the yellow fanatics' hands. Whatever may be said of the cruelty of the five hundred Cossacks who drove three or four thousand Chinamen into the river at Blagovestchensk, the other side must be stated, that everywhere throughout Manchuria the Russian railway laborers, officers and troops guarding them, retired in good order, protecting and bringing with them, at their own imminent peril, considerable numbers of Chinese converts whom the Russians refused to abandon to the mercy of the military mobs of their fellow-countrymen.

Indeed, it is worth repeating that not a Christian Chinaman in Manchuria whose life it was possble to save was deserted by their fellow-Christians the Russians.

That certain Chinese high officials participated in this anti-foreign outbreak the whole world is, of course, now thoroughly informed. The Boxer uprising is the origin of the military occupation of Manchuria by the Russians, which continues to this day and probably will continue until both China and the world concede that Manchuria is Russian territory. From this military occupation, whose purpose was to restore order and to begin again the work of building the railroad, followed the necessity of exterminating the robber bands, the story of which has already been told in earlier chapters.

The sale of ploughs, reapers, and threshers at Blagovestchensk and other Siberian towns means two things of importance. The first is that the Russian farmer in Siberia is emancipating himself from the old methods of agriculture, which has been and is such a drawback to Russian farming on the one hand; and on the other hand, that he is little by little breaking away from the system of farming in common which immemorially has prevailed among the Slavs. This last emancipation, however, is very, very slow—hardly perceptible, indeed—and may not continue. It must be here again repeated that in Russia, and even in Siberia, the land heretofore has been held by a community in common, each head of a house having so much soil apportioned to his family as his share; and so important is this fact that attention will be called to it many times hereafter.

Accompanying this system of agriculture is crudity of method, ancient and necessarily inferior implements, and rapid exhaustion of soil. In Siberia, with its vast extent of land and its paucity of population, natural conditions are beginning to change this, and so there is more room for the American plough, reaper, thresher, cultivator. How far this process will continue when Siberia shall become more thickly populated is a subject for speculation, and therefore each reader may form his own conclusions. Of course, the modern ploughs, reapers, and threshers are used, and increasingly, by the Russian agricultural commune as such, the only difference being that the machines are bought by the community and used and owned in common.

From Blagovestchensk to Khabaroff is, by river, an interesting journey of many hundreds of miles. Khabaroff itself is of no commercial importance; it is the political and military capital of Trans-Baikal Siberia. Here are immense barracks for troops who are stationed at this point in large numbers at all times. Here is the headquarters of Governor-General Grodekoff, in 1901 the autocrat of Pacific Russia. As a description of this remarkable man has been given elsewhere, and as he alone is worthy of note in Khabaroff, excepting only the immense numbers of Russian troops there, let us rather give a paragraph to the much-talked-of Ussuri littoral.

For many miles north of Vladivostock this extensive strip of coast territory is the Russian granary of the Far East. In comparison with Siberia it appears to be well settled. My observation was that the Russian peasant is here fairly prosperous and well content. A curious phenomenon has occurred in this region. On the advent of the Russian it was occupied by Chinese agriculturists. These were driven out, not by force, but as an inferior race naturally disappears before a superior people. And yet within the last few years the Chinese farmer has been reinvading the Ussuri littoral—very humbly, modestly, inconspicuously, it is true. He takes up a small piece of ground, cultivates it with the intensive method prevailing in China, and is successfully content and well-to-do so far as could be observed or learned. He is unmolested and happy under the equal protection which the government extends to him as well as the Russian settler; and this, too, notwithstanding the well-grounded fear that he will in turn, by his thrift and more intelligent industry, oust the Russian farmer. However, he is there in such very small numbers at present, and so unobtrusively, that perhaps that peculiar Russian lethargy which encases Russian apprehension has not yet been broken.

Nikolsk, not far to the north of Vladivostock, is the centre of this notable grain district. Here was found Tugovitch, chief engineer of the Manchurian railway, the illuminating conversation with whom has already been recited. The description of this town, by even fair-minded Englishmen in serious publications, is hardly judicial. Its temporary character, its straggling nature, etc., are extensively dwelt upon. It is forgotten that this is decidedly a frontier community. Just opinion can be obtained only by comparison with a like place in America under like conditions. Such comparisons will reveal the fact that the development is about the same. Here again, as has been noted, American agricultural implements were found on sale, and the merchants said that the demand was steadily increasing.

Did not the Irkutsk merchant say that a circus would be found some place in Siberia? Well, why not in Nikolsk?

The stranger within the walls was "put up" at the home and store of some vigorous young German merchants. The chief of the establishments was absent early in the evening. Where was he?

"Why, at the circus, I think."

"Circus! Have you a circus here in Nikolsk?"

"Why, certainly, about a block down, across the street."

A stroll in that direction revealed the great white tents for horses and all the other familiar sights connected with this itinerant and encamped form of amusement seen in our own country. The acrobats were the same, the horses the same, everything the same. But for the foreign speech you might well have imagined yourself in the suburb of one of our American cities on a summer night when "the circus comes to town."

But the ordinary traveller never stops at Nikolsk. The man who is going to write a book stops here; but even he, so far as observed, never penetrates the secrets of this really remarkable place. Go some distance out of town in a certain direction and mighty buildings come upon your view. They are the barracks already described, capable of quartering thousands of soldiers. Go farther and you come into a delightful little town, all to itself, hidden, until you are within its gates, by some ancient Chinese mud wall not yet demolished. This is the military settlement, the homes of the officers and their families, and in the centre the residence of the commander of the post. Personal observation of some of our military "forts" and "outposts" on the plains, some twenty years ago, compels the statement that these Russian officers in Nikolsk are far more comfortably housed and cared for than our American officers under like circumstances were in the early eighties.

And now for Vladivostock. We are used to think of it as a barren, ice-bound Russian military post; but in summer time, at least, it is a place of surpassing loveliness. The Russians claim (and the careful observer who critically visits all its surroundings is compelled to admit the probability of the claim) that from a naval and military point of view it is the most impregnable spot on the shores of any sea. It is the naval headquarters of the Asiatic fleet. Until now it has been Russia's single outlet on the Pacific, and, conversely, the one *entrepôt* from the ocean to Russia from the east. The Russo-Chinese Bank has here a very handsome establishment; and the manager in charge of this bank in 1901 was a person of conspicuous keenness, highly equipped for his work. Large stores are present in numbers, which suggests a much heavier purchasing population than exists in the city or in the surrounding country. The streets are well paved, the docks are well built, and the dry-dock at Vladivostock is one of the largest and finest in the world. Rising swiftly from the water's edge, the view from a war-ship in the bay is one of gratifying loveliness.

"Will you not go to the opera?" was the courteous invitation of a Vladivostock gentleman. And the opera! It was midsummer, and yet here in Vladivostock, the city of snows, a very competent company were presenting a light opera of the same character that you will see in Berlin, Moscow, or Chicago. In no respect was the opera-house different in interior arrangements from the common type seen in America. Only the auditors were different, for everywhere were the white coats of Russian officials. In a stage box sat the uniformed Governor, heartily applauding. He is a Cossack whose liberal ideas and advanced methods surprise an American. His distinction of manner, the genuine kindliness of his nature, his sincere courtesy, and, above all, his accomplished tactfulness, render him particularly useful to the government as the first high Russian representative whom foreigners meet on entering the empire from the west, and the last high Russian representative he leaves on departing from the empire towards the east; for he "makes a good impression," and that is a thing not to be despised. He is heartily, openly, aggressively American. Heartily American, yes; but more heartily Russian, of course. And be it noted that every Russian, gentleman or soldier, noble, peasant, or merchant, officer or civilian, is Russian, and again Russian, and always Russian. They have no foreign sympathies; but, keeping this in mind, their heart friendship is universally American. It is never English. It is distinctly anti-English.

"Why are no English sympathizers ever found among the educated classes of Russia?" was asked of a gentleman of a certain non-Russian nationality, who himself had a score of years of familiarity with all classes in the empire, and who was decidedly "against the government."

"Why, it is plain enough," said he. "The English have been Russia's enemies for centuries. Everywhere it has been England who has blocked Russians in the Far East. And her Far Eastern progress Russia deems an inevitable movement and her divine right. Then, again, the Russians claim that the English have persistently misrepresented them. The Russian attributes to the English the bad opinion which the world holds of him. I myself am a great admirer of the British Empire. Undoubtedly it is the greatest government in the world. Also, you know that I do not have any too much sympathy with the Russians; but I must admit that the grievance of the Russians against England is justified. I have seen reports in English newspapers of terrible things that occurred in Russia at a time and place where I myself happened to be present. And these reports were just pure imagination. Of course," he continued, "the truth is bad enough, but the English seem to consider it a religious duty to prejudice the world against Russia by the same kind of stories with which peasant women frighten their children when they do not want them to go out of the house."

This expression is given neither as an endorsement nor denial of its statement. It was the frank comment of a credible man of substance and probity, and is given for what it is worth.

Neither is the Russian friendly at heart to the German.

The reason is clear enough. Germany is the greatest military organization in the world, and night and day menaces Russia's western frontier. The possibility of war with Germany is constantly before both the Russian military authorities and the German cabinet. It is not forgotten, in saying this, that their interests in the Far East at the present time are identical; and if war should be declared between Russia and Japan, that Germany would be decidedly friendly to Russia. But Russia and Germany have so long looked upon conflict of interests as possible, and even probable, that deep and sincere friendship does not exist, notwithstanding their present unity of policy in China.

America and Russia, on the contrary, have always been friendly. The American people are a young people, and the Russian regards himself as quite as young a man as the American. The American has "go-ahead" in his make-up. The American "gets things done." That is what the Russian admires, and he likes to think that he is doing the same thing. So there is a natural friendship on the part of Russians for Americans. Such is the Russian view.

"Oh, you Americans are greatly beloved by the Russians!" said a young English officer in Pekin. "That is, you are greatly beloved at present. But there is no real brotherhood between you, and cannot be. Language and race divide you, whereas language and race unite the English and the Americans. Who was the American naval officer that said, 'Blood is thicker than water'? However, Russia's present kindly feeling for you is good for the next fifty years, anyhow; and I do not much blame you for taking national advantage of it."

"What is that building?" was asked of the Russian admiral standing on the deck of a flag-ship of the Russian Asiatic fleet stationed at Vladivostock.

"That is our University of Oriental Languages."

So the "university" was visited. It was closed at that

particular period of the year, but it was by far the most important item of interest in Vladivostock. It is a large structure of brick, just such as you will see in the principal buildings of any of the State universities of our various American commonwealths. It was founded by Grodekoff. Here the Russian and Siberian youth intended for consular, diplomatic, or even commercial pursuits are instructed in Oriental languages; and, as has been noted, such is the Russian facility of acquiring foreign tongues that the "university" has apt students.

Comment has been made of the strange circumstance of Russian common soldiers carrying on intelligible speech with Chinese or other natives in less than a month from the time of their arrival. Pokotiloff, general manager of the Russo-Chinese Bank in Asia, and the right hand of Witte in the Far East, speaks English, French, German, Chinese, Buriat, and all the various dialects of north-central Asia. He speaks them, too, with the facility of the native himself. The writer can testify that his English is as good as can be found in New York or Boston—not an accent, not the mispronunciation or the slurring of a single letter. All of this he has learned without instructors. He "picked it up," as the saying is. This illustration might be extended for a whole page of instances. Enough has been said to show that within a decade Russia will have in the Far East men as familiar with the languages of the peoples with whom she deals, and as carefully instructed in Asiatic politics and intrigue, as they are profoundly loyal to the central government of the Czar.

XVIII

RUSSIAN CAPITAL AND LABOR

SO it seems that Siberia is not all prison, Manchuria not all slaughter. Constructive industry appears to be a conspicuous method of Russian activity in the latest fields of Slav occupation. Agricultural productiveness the processes of commerce, and even some of the politer elements of civilization appear to be predominant in what the world has understood to be Russia's Botany Bay. With all her forts and fleets, with all her soldiers, barracks, bayonets, it is the agriculturist, the artisan, the merchant, and the banker who already seem to be the principal agencies of Russia's energy in her continental advance on the Pacific.

These various manifestations of labor and capital, so noticeable where you had expected to find nothing but the movement of troops and the various forms of military occupation, suggest that, now that we are to go back to our starting-point of Russia in Europe, the industrial features of this at once old and young people are fuller of meaning and interest for us than Russian government or Russian art, Russian monuments or Russian history, Russian administrative efficiency or the reverse. The Russian capitalist and what he is doing is of more concern to us than the spendthrift noble. The Russian peasant, his condition and progress, his home and his habits, mean more to us than the lives of men and women in the brilliant society of St. Petersburg.

Let us, then, take up modern industrialism in Russia proper. Let us consider her manufacturing progress, the condition of the working-men and women of the empire, and in general the economic forces in Russia herself, whose operations we have noted for many thousands of miles eastward along the whole extent of the Asiatic shores of the Pacific.

Within the last twenty years Russian industrial enterprise has rapidly progressed. Within the last four years its growth has been so marked that the calm observer cannot but regard it as forced, and therefore unhealthful. Indeed, some years ago Finance Minister Witte frankly and openly stated that industrial progress in Russia was too quick and sudden to be sound; and the serious depression which followed soon after demonstrated the correctness of his view. But, the panic past, industrial development in Russia is again proceeding with celerity. Factories have sprung up all over the empire. Foreign capital has invested in industrial establishments generously, almost wildly.

Some years ago a peculiar financial enthusiasm seemed to seize upon European capital for Russian manufacturing exploitation. Everybody said to everybody else that here was a great empire requiring clothing, machinery, food, and compelled largely to import all but the latter. Surely, it was reasoned, here was virgin soil for profitable manufacturing plants of almost every kind. Then, again, the present policy of Russian protection was adopted, which is as complete and high-walled as that of the United States. And when a tariff fortification is built around one hundred and forty millions of people it seemed to the European investor only reasonable that the manufacturer who was inside of it must necessarily reap rich rewards.

And so many of them have. Especially the Russian capitalists who have built factories have profited heavily. Many of the foreign enterprises, also, have realized the dreams of their promoters. On the contrary, within the last five years, a large number of the establishments built by foreign capital have proven unprofitable, and, indeed, many of them have been forced into liquidation. The reasons for these conflicting industrial phenomena are too complex to admit of their intelligent analysis within the limits of a single chapter, or indeed a single volume. The unfamiliarity of foreign manufacturers with Russian labor was undoubtedly one cause. Another was their failure to take into account the large number of holidays, which in Russia are an institution, and which, up to the present time, have been increasing. Still another was the foreign operator's ignorance of the methods of Russian administration. Again, they failed to understand how to get their goods properly on the market. Very largely also, while the market is practically inexhaustible if gradually invaded, it is nevertheless a market which must be cultivated; so that there was the economic contradiction of a great potential market unsupplied and an actual and realized market glutted and congested. Later on some account of the growth and profitableness of various Russian industries will be given, but meanwhile let us observe the instrument of all this industry, the Russian laborer, as he is to-day.

Lodz, in Poland, is the chief centre of cotton industry, though Moscow itself is a very formidable competitor. In less than twenty years the Polish cotton centre has grown from a town of fifteen thousand people to a city of over four hundred thousand souls. Tula, near which is the country-home of Tolstoï, is the place where government arms are made, and perhaps the most notable seat of steel and iron manufacture of small articles in the empire. Ekaterinoslav and Usofka, in southern Russia, are steel-producing centres, although important rolling-mills are in operation in St. Petersburg and Moscow. Just beyond the border of Russia proper, and over the line in Siberia, are splendid deposits of ore and coal, and there, too, material for coke abounds in unlimited profusion. Here, indeed, is the natural seat of the steel industry of the empire. But at the present time antiquated methods are employed, and the Siberian steel industry is so inconsiderable as not to be taken into account; and yet, in the Urals alone, impartial engineers have demonstrated that there is enough iron ore to supply the wants of the whole world for decades, and of Russia alone for centuries.

As the scientist examines specimens of a class, and not every individual of the entire class, it will be most profitable to the reader to observe laboring conditions in two or three of these greatest centres.

"Our chief difficulty," said the head of a large English steel mill in one of these places, "is a curious and almost absurd circumstance. The number of Russian holidays, including Sundays, on which the working-men actually quit work, now number well towards one hundred. You see, then, that we are deprived of labor on those days. On those days, too, a majority of our men get drunk. Therefore, on the day immediately succeeding the holiday they either do not return to work, or, if they do, they are good for nothing. Thus we are actually without labor on the holiday itself, and short-handed and poorly equipped on the day succeeding. It is a difficulty with which no other country has to contend, and cripples us severely."

Add to this the comparatively low efficiency of the Russian working-man, who has not yet become skilled nor methodical in the American or western European sense of that term, and it is easy to see that in industry Russia could not hold her own at all, except by an almost prohibitive protective tariff. Should Russia abolish her tariff barriers, it is the judgment of the most thoughtful business-men of the empire that there is not a factory which could survive that catastrophe for five years.

And yet there is a party in Russia which bitterly resents these practical methods of modern industrialism. At the head of these is Tolstoï. "These chimneys irritate me," said the great challenger of modern civilization. The iron mills to which Tolstoï refers, in his renowned article in the *North American Review* of April, 1901, are directly on the road from Tula to his country estate. This class, however, are pure idealists. They are not against the spread of factories in Russia any more than they are against the same development ("decadence" they call it) any place in the world; and yet they number among them several of the highest-class nobility, and a few of the literary and scientific men; but, taken all in all, they have no appreciable effect on Russian thought and purpose.

Of course, to these must be added those business-men who are importers, and generally the great traders with foreign countries. This is the same class of men and firms engaged in similar enterprises found in our own country, and they use the same arguments. Then, of course, there are the landed proprietors engaged in agricultural pursuits, who think they have to pay more for what they buy than they would if there were no tariff-protected factories, and who have not yet learned that these home factories give them better home markets; and these "agrarians" also resent the rising walls and the clouded smoke-stacks of the encroaching and, to them, oppressive mills. Their reasons, too, are exactly those which formerly were used in the United States by those who opposed protection upon the ground that it made the farmer pay more for what he had to buy.

Nevertheless, all of them put together are not influential. Strong men of the empire, at whose head stands Witte, have convinced the Czar, as they did his father before him, that, to use the language of Pobyedonostseff, elsewhere quoted, "Russia is a world" of itself; that it must, in the long run, become self-supporting; that its industries must be variegated and multiplied; that it must manufacture what it wears and uses, as well as raise what it eats. And so protection may, for many decades to come, be regarded as the settled economic policy of all the Russias. Therefore, factories will multiply and enlarge, and the evolution of the Russian peasant into the modern working-man will continue.

And yet the other manufacturing nations have little to fear from Russia as a competitor in the markets of the world outside of Russia itself for certainly a generation or perhaps even a century. Industrially, Russia has only begun the process of "finding herself"; and it will be decades before the process is completed. Her labor is unskilled and inefficient, and in comparison with American labor greatly inferior. On the other hand, her population is so immense that her factories cannot supply her own wants. And the wants of her people are increasing more rapidly than the number of the establishments with which her capitalists and foreign investors try to supply them.

"Let me illustrate this by a very simple fact," said a cotton manufacturer of Moscow. "The masses of Russia wear comparatively little underclothing. If they could be made to adopt the practice of wearing more undergarments, the demand for our cheap fabrics would increase manyfold. Now that practice is beginning. Its effect on the trade is as yet hardly appreciable, and still the most careful of us have noted it."

This is a very simple and yet a very important fact. Its truth was inquired of from the English manager of a great Russian estate of some hundred thousand acres, who had spent thirty years in the empire.

"Oh yes," said he, quite off-hand, "certainly, that is true."

But the Russian peasants are beginning to go to the great manufacturing cities, especially during the winter, to work in the mills. For the first time in their lives they see the great stores of Moscow, St. Petersburg, Warsaw. For the first time they learn that different food is eaten, different apparel worn by those in the cities. They return to their communes (their villages are communes) in the spring and summer with strange tales. Peasant women do the like, and they go home with their feminine heads filled with new ideas of dress and adornment. And so, slowly, very slowly, weaving backward and forward among the people, moves the shuttle of changing methods of dress and living. All of it has its effect upon the manufacturing industries of the empire; and, what is far more important, all of it has its effect upon the ideas of the people.

Some seventy-five miles south of Moscow there is a certain little peasant village. You may travel Russia from the Arctic to the Caspian and not find a better illustration of the slow evolution of peasant life that is going on in this empire than in this little village, many miles from any railroad; for here is the peasant's cottage, as it used to be, a mere hut, thatched with grass, with earthen floor, and horses, pigs, and cows occupying the tiny court or yard attached to it. Here, too, are modern homes of the typical Russian agricultural peasant, built perhaps ten or fifteen years ago. In these an improvement is noted. There is still the earthen floor, but there is also a sort of tidiness not observed in the older dwellings. Then there are later cottages,very well built and covered with a kind of tin or sheet-iron roofing.

But, now, to connect all this with the village peasant who goes to Moscow. Here is a cottage the little yard of which has trees and vines. It is painted, too, and inside you will find wooden floors. On the walls hang pictures—prints, it is true, but attractive copies of good paintings. In short, this dwelling has begun to take on the appearance of what is expected in an American working-man's home. There is not everything in the abode of this Russian laborer that is found in the home of his American working brother, for we must not forget that the American working-man, in comparison with the foreign working-man, lives in luxury. But there are the beginnings. And, when it is remembered that Russian industrial progress commenced at a period still within the memory of young men, these items are significant and important. This cottage is the home of a working-man in a Moscow cotton-mill.

"What are your wages?" was asked of a skilled artisan, who operated one of the printing machines by which flowers and other figures were stamped upon calico in one of the most extensive of Russia's textile factories.

"One hundred and fifty rubles a month," said he. That is seventy-five dollars of American money; and very heavy wages, indeed, in Russia—quite as heavy, I believe, as is paid in England or Germany. This expert was a Frenchman, as was the active manager of manufacturing of the whole plant. This latter man received three hundred rubles, or one hundred and fifty dollars, per month. On the contrary, a Russian common working-man in the same factory received only eighteen rubles per month. This is nine dollars of our money. Women and girls engaged at the machines get less than this. But, low as these wages appear, yet in comparison with the same American labor these common working men and women of Russia may truthfully be said to be overpaid. If their wages are less than the wages of American working-men, their working ability is still smaller. One cannot believe, either, that the Russian working man or woman will, for a long time, be as efficient as the American working man or woman. Their slowness is racial. But, on the other hand, they display a patience which, perhaps, may counteract their stolidity.

This factory, like many Russian factories, in addition to paying its working-people the wages described, furnished them shelter and food. The working men and women live in enormous brick buildings or dormitories, built for them by the company they work for. The rooms are moderate in size, and in each room there are from three to five sleeping-booths, divided from one another by curtains. These are for the working-people who are married, and a man and wife occupy each of these rude, limited, and uncomfortable apartments. The unmarried men and women occupy different portions of the building, and their quarters are not so inviting even as the hard and unattractive surroundings just described for the married people. And yet, in comparison with the crowded squalor of the hut or cottage of the Russian village in which these people were brought up, and in which they have lived until recent times, when the improvements just noted in the description of the peasant village began, these factory quarters are an improvement.

The food is simple, but substantial and abundant. Back of the dormitories are heavy, well-built log structures, in the cellar of which ice is kept for these working-people, and in the body of which their various belongings and things which they themselves buy are stored and cared for.

"Of course, you are not troubled in this country with damage lawsuits by injured working-men, which is the common thing in America," was observed to the general superintendent of this cotton plant.

"Yes, indeed, we are. We have no means of indemnifying ourselves as your manufacturers have. The government interferes even in our contracts; and when it comes to personal injuries, if a man gets his finger hurt a government inspector of labor makes us pay the injured person a certain amount, and if we do not do so, files suit against us in the name of the person supposed to be injured, whether that person desires it or not."

While this statement was, perhaps, exaggerated, there was in it a general and substantial truth. Every factory in Russia has its labor inspector, whose business it is to care for the work-people of that establishment, and to exact as much as possible from their employers. And he does that with the alertness which the agent of a paternal government always shows to people who, he feels in his heart, think themselves quite above him in every other respect, and also with that vigor which the non-rich, armed with official authority, usually display towards men of capital within their power. This single factory had to pay considerable money in 1900 because of accidents which even the government inspector himself admitted were caused by the negligence of the persons injured. Several manufacturers stated that the law of contributory negligence was unknown in Russia, and that such a thing as attempting to escape liability for injury caused by a fellow-servant was unheard of. These statements were not verified, but are given simply as information culled from several different sources, and from apparently reputable people.

The world-wide conflict between labor and capital, in the form we Americans know it, has not yet appeared in Russia, nor will it appear as long as the present form of Russian government endures. Before the "labor question," as that enigma of the ages is understood in England and America, will appear in Russia, a distinct workingman's class, in the modern sense of that term, must be created there. The ever-increasing volume of agricultural peasants, who work in the factories of the cities during a portion of the year and then return to their country villages to cultivate their fields during the other portion of the year, must develop into a permanent class of city laborers, severed completely from the country and the soil to which they are now tied. The village industries, or "kustar trades," as they are called, of which a brief description will hereafter be given, must be eliminated by the modern factory, equipped with machines, which will do all of the work now done by the fingers of the artisan peasant beneath his own roof-tree. The government must radically change its whole theory and practice with reference to the maintenance of order.

More important even than this, the customs of centuries, which are so deeply embedded in the lives of the people that many of the best-informed students declare that those customs are racial, must be replaced by popular practices distinctly and characteristically non-Russian. And, most important of all, the very spirit of the Slav itself must undergo a transformation so complete that he will be changed from what he is now and what history tells us he always has been. Yet so lightning-like are the revolutions being wrought in every field of human endeavor at the present time that no thoughtful man will dogmatically assert that the fundamental alterations above indicated will not take place among the Russian people.

What, then, of the present? Perhaps it will be most useful, first of all, to glance at the attitude of the government towards both capital and labor, as we understand those terms in America; for the attitude of the government on this particular question represents, at the present moment, at least, the thought and will of the Russian people.

On the one hand, whatever may be said of the influence of money corruptly to purchase privileges in Russia, it must be admitted that the capitalist, as such, has no more influence in Russian legislation or administration than has the laborer; and neither one of them, as such, has any influence. Awkward as it is complex, burdensome and unscientific as it may be, the impartial observer must admit that from the large and long view-point, Russian legislation and administration appear to intend the common good of the Russian people. We all hear of the influence of classes with the Russian autocracy, and all of us go to that country with an almost ineradicable impression that the insistence of this class or that class for a desired end has undue weight.

Especially are stories numerous of corrupt purchases of personal privileges, comforts, etc. In small affairs and in individual conveniences this may be true, and some business-men say that it is even true in the matter of municipal franchises and the like. No opinion is expressed on this; but in the sum of Russian administrative thought it is not true. The only thing dominant, imperial, all-compelling in the mind of the Russian statesman is the nation. With Witte in the Finance Ministry, it is the Russian nation; with Pobyedonostseff in the Holy Synod, it is the Russian nation; with Grodekoff in Trans-Baikal Siberia, it is the Russian nation; with Alexieff on the seas, it is the Russian nation.

This, too, is the thought of the Russian people. The Russian peasant has a slumberous intellect and thinks very little about anything, but yet there is, saturating his very being, the thought of Russian nationality, inherited from generation to generation, until it has become with him an instinct. Even the most aggressive opponent of the government and of the present methods (and such were many of the most enlightened of those who freely gave their views) have in their minds in all their schemes for reform the principal object of solidifying the Russian people and advancing the power of the Slav nationality.

So the government does not regard the capitalist as a partner in affairs of state; it regards him as a subject of the state. It does not regard the laborer as a partner in the affairs of state; it regards him as a subject of the state. Both capital and labor are, in the thought of the Russian, merely factors in the common development of the people, like lands, mines, etc. So we find that the Russian government does not understand the philosophy of strikes, as it is understood here in America. It regards a labor strike, if it passes the point where the inspector can settle it, as the captain of a vessel would regard mutiny among the crew. It looks upon labor disturbances, where violence occurs, as a lawless interference with the orderly on-going of the nation. Therefore it interferes instantly, ruthlessly, and with the "iron hand."[1]

[1] See chapter on Labor Laws.

"It is denied that the Cossacks shot and killed working-men in the labor riots of St. Petersburg three or four years ago. They may say what they please," said a young working-man, half English and half Russian, who acted as interpreter, "but the fact is that the Cossacks did not fire blank cartridges. They fired ball cartridges and they shot to kill." But this is only gossip. You cannot get at the real truth of any of these rumors, which the correspondents uncage from every point in Russia. Undoubtedly there is overstatement on both sides.

As yet no considerable labor riots have occurred. The world has not yet learned the extent and causes of the recent commotions in southern Russia.. It is possible that they may have been exaggerated; but whether their seriousness was under or over stated, it appears that they have speedily subsided. If some of the disturbances which we in America have experienced were to occur in Russia, they would be made the subject in the newspapers of other nations of columns of lurid description, with red and black paint lavishly used in the picture. Should such an uprising as the famous disturbance at Chicago several years ago, or such as the serious troubles in Colorado in the days of Governor Waite, or any other of our notable instances of the uprising put down by the militia, occur in Russia, the statement would be positively made to the civilized world and accepted as true that actual revolution was in progress in the empire of the Czar.

On the other hand, as has been noted, the excesses of vested capital are as sternly handled as any labor agitation would be. More than once the appropriate department of the government has peremptorily compelled employers "to do the right thing," as we would put it here, by their work-people, and there are recent instances where Witte has corrected attempted frauds of business-men with all the sternness with which we are accustomed to look upon the processes of autocracy. In one case he absolutely broke up a corner in wheat, which had been skilfully manipulated by some crafty capitalists. In another instance cargoes of grain were confiscated by the order of this same minister, because of proof of unquestioned fraud in its shipment.

The weakness of this whole system, of course, is that no matter how good the intentions of the government may be, it is impossible for it to interfere in even a small number of instances among all the enterprises of a people and an empire larger and more numerous than any on the globe. Nevertheless, the Department of Finance does assume direct supervision, for example, over every manufacturing enterprise of any consequence in the whole empire. While there are general laws conferring as regular and definite rights, duties, etc., on corporations of every kind as we have here in America, the Ministry of Finance actually undertakes to examine into the soundness and responsibility of every one of them before they are permitted to begin business, and exercises visitorial powers over them afterwards.

The reason assigned for this is plausible in theory, and the Russians, also, claim that experience proves that it works well in practice. This reason is that if haphazard investments are permitted in Russia, any kind of an enterprise may be started without the sanction of the government and its supervision, and therefore capitalists, especially those from other countries not understanding Russian conditions, may make investments ruinous to themselves, and so become propagandists of aggressive slander against the Russian government and the Russian people throughout the world; and, conversely, that mere adventurers, exploiters, and promoters may get into the empire, blow financial bubbles, which, on bursting, will work mischief in financial conditions; and so forth and so on. Therefore, the paternal hand of the Russian government interferes alike in the business of the capitalist and the affairs of his employé.

In support of this, it is the undoubted fact that only a few years ago Russia was fairly overrun with unscrupulous promoters, mostly foreigners, and the investors of other European nations, particularly France and Belgium, were cheated right and left. "Here is an example of the financial trouble which led to our policy of examining every enterprise that now enters Russia," explained a certain Russian official. "There was a set of exploiters," he continued, "who got up a great manufacturing concern on paper. The plant was to be established here in Russia. They had secured a Russian 'charter,' and all that sort of thing. They got up the most alluring kind of a prospectus. Their stocks were subscribed for generously. They assured the investors that they 'had behind them the Russian government.' They actually did begin a little work, but in a short time this was abandoned. They pocketed the proceeds of their robbery, and left to exploit some other portion of the world. So the investors lost every cent they put in the 'enterprise.'

"Then you should have heard the Russians denounced. Every man who had put a ruble into this bubble was a walking denunciation of the Russian government and everything Russian. We could not stand that, you see. There was nothing for us to do but to adopt our careful policy of examining into the responsibility and good faith of every proposed enterprise which capitalists intend to establish in our country. We make sure that they are real capitalists, and not promoters. We require guarantees. They have got to convince us that they really mean to do bona-fide work and erect factories on real earth and of real brick and mortar, instead of on paper and with ink."

For another failure and consequent loss to investors, the Russian government was severely assailed by the press of a certain other European nation. You can find instances of this by the score. At the present, however, it is not the government's fault if a concern gets into the empire which is not substantial and sufficiently responsible to meet all of its engagements, and which does not mean business, and permanent business at that. And after the enterprise is actually under way, the government continues its careful watchfulness and frequent interference with its work, but always, as is claimed, for the real good of the enterprise itself, and to make sure that its methods and purposes are solid and honest.

All this leads to more dissatisfaction on the part of capitalists, manufacturers, and other business-men than it does on the part of laboring-men. Nor are these commercial elements slow in expressing their views. You will have no more difficulty in hearing dissent from any economic policy by business-men in Russia than you will hear of complaints of an unsatisfactory policy in America when it does not suit the complaining interest. This suggests the fact, elsewhere noted, of the surprise which the ordinary foreigner has at the liberty of speech prevailing in Russia. Compared with the ordinary American conception that the Russian business-man submits to everything without protest, the dissent of Russian importers, for example, to certain schedules of the Russian tariff is illuminating. A conspicuous example of this freedom of opinion was afforded by the outcry of certain financial and commercial interests at some of Witte's early reforms. This is not true, of course, of the common people. The peasants, who are really the Russian nation, always speak of the Czar with profound and devotional reverence, and, if they object to their hard conditions, are, nevertheless, quite sure that if the Czar could learn about their misfortunes he would adjust them. But while the business-men of the empire also regard the Emperor with reverent and sincere respect, they look upon the policies of the government as the plans of responsible ministers whom the Czar appoints; and with these business-men those policies stand on their merits, just as the plans of American statesmen are subjected to the same merit analysis by American business-men. The ministry of the Russian Czar is by no means immune from criticism from the lips of important Russians. Indeed, it is not free from open attack by certain fearless minds.

"Did you really send the letter to the Czar and his ministers, as published in the London *Times?*" was asked of Tolstoï, who, by-the-way, was not found in banishment at all, but exercising all the liberty an American farmer exercises on his own land.

"Why, certainly I did," was the reply. "Why not?"

And this famous letter begins, "More assassinations, more murders," etc., and goes on to denounce, in the boldest terms, certain recent measures taken by the government in some trouble or other, and proceeds to suggest measures as radical as most of those advanced by dissenters from the present order of things here in America. Read *Anna Karenina*, and you will find that the conversations in Russian society in St. Petersburg are, apparently, as unrestrained as they are in Washington. It must not be inferred that any of these adverse opinions are directed towards the government itself; for the ordinary Russian, whether business-man, banker, or what not, appears to be devoted to his Czar and to Russian institutions.

The Russian government maintains that Russia is at present the best place in the world for the investment of capital in manufacturing enterprises, if those enterprises are conducted with great conservatism; and it certainly is true that the dividends frequently paid are astonishing, even to an American accustomed to the large profits of our own young republic. More than two hundred per cent. annual dividends have been paid within the last twenty years by foreign manufacturing corporations in Russia, and one hundred per cent. has more than once been paid. The Russian manufacturer himself feels that his business is going to ruin if its yearly dividends sink as low as fifteen per cent. Twenty, even thirty, per cent. are more common. Even in the great industrial depression which swept over Russia about three years ago the annual dividends of well-established and well-conducted commercial enterprises seldom sank lower than ten per cent. On the other hand, as has been noted, large numbers of industrial concerns barely pay expenses, and many of them failed entirely. The number of these enterprises that were forced into liquidation present a strange paradox to the heavy dividends paid by the prosperous ones, but that liquidation is, as has been noted, explained upon the ground of over-capitalization, negligent attention to business, unfamiliarity with Russian conditions, etc., and is used as an argument by the government to justify its paternal supervision over industrial ventures, both foreign and domestic.

XIX

THE RUSSIAN WORKING-MAN

WHATEVER the truth may be as to the profitableness of wisely invested capital in Russia, and as to the beneficial effects on business itself, which the government so sturdily maintains is the result of its paternal methods with capital, the visible facts seem to justify the government's contention that its progress in the regardful care of the rights and happiness of its laboring-people is greater than that of most other countries. For example, you may find in St. Petersburg an institution which, it is believed, is without an exact counterpart anywhere. It is a large and even handsome iron structure, devoted to the recreation, comfort, and amusement of the laboring-people of the Russian capital. When visited, in 1901, it was barely completed. Tea and other refreshments were served at actual cost. Free performances were given by fairly good theatrical companies.

In one section of a great building was a beautiful auditorium, well equipped with comfortable seats, an excellent and well-appointed stage, where a superior class of theatrical entertainment was on at a price below that charged by our cheapest popular theatres in America. The culinary department of this "Labor Palace," as it is called, was carefully inspected, and was found to be, in contrast with like arrangements in Russian hotels, surprisingly clean and attractive; and it was well managed. I believe that this great building was the government building at the National Exposition at Nijni-Novgorod, removed from the latter place to St. Petersburg when the national fair was over, and made into the "Labor Palace" of the capital, as above described.

Again, in Moscow there is a free amusement park, given over to the entertainment of the working-people. It may be visited freely by any one—noble, priest, peasant, foreigner, native—but its purpose is to give to the working-people of the factories a good time, and especially to wed them away from habits of intemperance, for this park is a temperance affair. You are informed that it is maintained by a philanthropic society in St. Petersburg devoted to the practical work of stamping out intemperance among the common people and generally bettering their conditions.

This place was visited many times, and on each occasion was found to be well attended, and on Sundays positively crowded. Here acrobats give their performances and singers render their songs, all without price to the hearer. Everywhere quass, the non-alcoholic Russian drink, and all other kinds of "temperance drinks" are served at the most trivial prices. There are all sorts of popular amusements, most of which charge a nominal fee for admission, but so small as to be within the reach of the very poorest laborer present.

And these thousands of work-people of Moscow apparently enjoy themselves in this temperance playground. Groups of boys and young men will stroll up and down, with the accordion in the hands of one of them, playing some Russian air; and it is as well to note here as elsewhere the singular fact that the accordion is the national Russian musical instrument—a strange circumstance, since it is a foreign instrument, and the Slav ordinarily sticks to the methods and instruments of his fathers. But the accordion has captured the Russian common people. You will hear its muffled and throaty notes in the darkness of an agricultural village, where bands of boys and girls in the early hours of the evening stroll up and down, singing their weird folk songs to its accompaniment. You will hear it on the banks of the Amur. You will hear it in St. Petersburg. In Manchuria a soldier was observed rifle slung across his back and accordion in his hands. Wherever the Russian peasant is, there is the accordion.

Not a shabbily dressed working man or woman was observed in this temperance park of Moscow. Their clothing was plain, of course, but good and serviceable. So far as the eye of the observer could determine, they were healthful, too; and certainly they looked happy. Here laugh and jest and badinage; yonder a Russian boy, wrought up by some strain of music, suddenly begins the national dance of the people, very picturesque, and increasing in vigor until it ends in a whirl of action, amid the loud applause of the crowd of on-lookers. Then another one takes it up to see whether he cannot win more praise than his fellow. And so the day is spent in innocent amusement and good-fellowship.

So much has been heard of the habitual drunkenness of the Russian that careful search was made for it.

"It is likely that you will find this unfortunate thing most conspicuously in the 'human market,'" said a young Russian, to whose kind offices the writer was indebted for many valuable directions.

The "human market," as it is called, is really a place where laboring-people, who come into Moscow from the country districts, assemble to sell their services. It is an open square in the congested part of the city. On one side of it are vodka shops; on another side of it a big sort of iron shed has been erected, like the sheds into which our trains enter at any American railway-station. But, although it was Sunday and although those of the lower class of unskilled labor were there assembled, only three drunken men were observed.

Several were lying out on the ground, with bundles under their heads, in the open glare of the hot sun, apparently in a state of bestial intoxication. But investigation discovered the fact that they were merely rugged young peasants taking a nap. For it is worth repeating again that the Russian peasant, man or woman, can sleep right out in the open sun on the hottest day, whether it be on the top of a boat on the Amur River, under the blazing sun of a Siberian summer, or in the fields in the country, or on the hard, stone court of the "human market" in Moscow.

"That is very bad," the American remarked to his Russian friend.

"Why bad?" said the Russian.

"Why, all those men and women so frightfully drunk," answered the American.

"Yes, but they are not drunk," answered the Russian; "they are just taking a nap."

Observing the American's incredulity, the Russian gentleman called a policeman, explained the situation, and asked the policeman if he would not kindly show the American that these people were not drunk at all. Good-humoredly, the officer laughed, and said, "Certainly." Whereupon, very kindly, he woke several of them, apparently explained the situation, and, without the slightest ill-humor at being aroused, the awakened one, when he comprehended the situation, would laugh as though it was the best joke in the world, get up, and walk off, clearly in possession of every faculty, unclouded by alcohol.

At this particular spot you may observe the Russian laborer and the Russian peasant at his worst, however; and you must expect very rude speech and very shocking words, indeed, if you have your interpreter faithfully translate what is said. For the purpose of such a visit the professional interpreter and guide is practically worthless. He will tell you as much as he pleases and no more. The best thing—indeed, the only way—is to be accompanied by a Russian friend, with whom you are sufficiently well acquainted, and whose character is such that you know you can trust him.

The most conspicuous building in Moscow, except the Cathedral of the Kremlin, is an immense white structure near the banks of the river. It is the foundling asylum, maintained partly by the municipal and partly by the national government. One informant said that it was maintained entirely by the imperial government. However it is maintained, it is a public institution where new-born children are taken and cared for. Not all of these— nor, as is claimed, even the majority of them — are irregular.

The majority of the infants received are said to be the regular offspring of married working-people, who cannot attend to their infants themselves, and who leave them there for a period and pay a small price for their maintenance. Such investigation as was possible leads the observer to believe that this is true; and yet a large number o them are certainly not so happily circumstanced. Indeed, many well-informed men declare that nearly all are foundlings.

A drunken man in a Russian town, whether it be in Moscow or in the heart of Manchuria, is treated very kindly by the police. Indeed, no trivial disturber of the peace is handled roughly. At one of the better-class places of amusement in Moscow, business-men and their wives, and generally well-to-do people, gather for entertainment and refreshment. You may hear French opera in an admirable little theatre; witness a balloon ascension; have any kind of refreshment you want; but, best of all, you can witness a strange entertainment confined exclusively to a representation of things peculiarly Slav. Before this stage, which, unlike the theatre, opens on the grounds and does not require an additional fee, gather, of course, the greatest throngs. Very enthusiastic is their appreciation of a particularly good thing. But when a company of young Russians, fresh from the country, but very carefully drilled by a Russian master in Russian songs and dances, appear and arrange themselves in a semicircle, and sing old Slav songs, weird and thrilling, the spectators' enthusiasm increases in vigor; and when, finally, one after another, these young fellows, all dressed in the national Russian costume of the old time, advance to the centre of the stage and whirl in a frantic maze of some dance of the Russian people, the crowd grows fairly frenzied with delight.

In this crowd was a man with his wife and two children. Evidently he was a Russian small shop-keeper or a Russian well-paid laborer. He was very drunk, indeed, and as demonstrative as he was intoxicated. He not only applauded but interrupted the entertainment with cries and suggestions. There were plenty of policemen, too; but everybody took him quite good-humoredly except the wife, who, like a wife any place under similar circumstances, appeared to be covered with embarrassment. Finally his noise became unbearable, and some one connected with the playgrounds came to him and very courteously asked him to subside, smiling while he asked him.

The man, happy with the show and happy with his vodka and happy with everything, consented; but in less than a minute forgot it again. Then a policeman came forward and took him in charge. At first the man resisted, but, with laughter and good-humor and with all possible kindliness, the officer led him away. There was no display of force, no club drawn (the Russian policeman, however, does not carry a club, but a revolver), nor any brutality of any kind. Surprise being manifested at this, a Russian friend observed: "What is the use of hurting him; he is enjoying a holiday; he means no harm; he does not hurt anybody, and the policeman feels that he is a brother Russian, and so he is."

In Trans-Baikal Siberia a young Russian priest had consumed so much vodka that he was crazed with it. Unlike most Russians, who when drunk are exceedingly good-natured, this young Russian priest, apparently, had all the combative and selfish animal instincts uncaged by the liquor. He insisted on occupying a first-class carriage when his ticket called for a third-class carriage, where his wife and children were quietly sitting. The railway officials argued with him with the utmost patience. Time and again they would induce him to go to his proper place, and time and again he would return to the place from which he had been led. Finally he would not move at all. Force had to be used, but it was employed with just as little roughness as was possible. In the end, it became necessary to take him to the baggage-car; but the officers, who appeared to be as pained and humiliated as the poor fellow's wife herself, firmly but kindly held his hands, lifted him to their shoulders, and put him into the baggage-car, locking the door after him. Perhaps a dozen such interferences with drunken Russians were observed, either in European Russia or in Siberia, and in not a single instance was any brutality or signs thereof exhibited by the police.

Not only is Russian drinking undoubtedly on the decrease, but the quality of liquor has within the last few years been improved. Indeed, there is said to be no comparison between the quality of vodka now consumed by the people and the villanous concoction formerly sold to them. The reason of this is that the manufacture and sale of vodka are now conducted by the government, whereas it was formerly made and sold by private interests; also it can now be purchased only under careful regulations, which are rigidly enforced. So much only may be purchased at a time. Public vodka-shops, as they were formerly conducted, are now becoming extinct. In addition to this, the central government is distributing all over the empire plain and simple little temperance pamphlets. At the capital of one zemstvo (that is, the town where the offices of this peculiar district government are located) large quantities of these were seen, and a Russian friend translated them.

Let us now visit a typical Russian steel and iron mill. The greatest of these are in the coal and iron districts of southern Russia, and perhaps the next greatest in St. Petersburg itself; but, for purposes which the description will reveal, selection is made of a certain plant operated by foreign capital and under foreign management in Moscow, a characteristically Russian city. It is a large affair, although unimportant compared with the mammoth works to which we Americans are accustomed in such places as Pittsburg and Bethlehem. It was noted, too, that the furnaces were not of the latest type; on the contrary, the machinery for fashioning the manufactured steel was entirely up to date. This concern turned out great quantities of wire, locomotive and car wheels, engines, and several other varieties of steel and iron machinery. The wages paid were much better than those paid the employés of the cotton factories. The working-men in the machine department, where the lathes and various other mechanical devices common to all such establishments were located, appeared to be active, energetic, and intelligent.

These, of course, were the highest grade of skilled labor in the whole place. Many of them were foreigners, mostly Frenchmen. The common laborer, as elsewhere, was exclusively Russian, and was slow, and, compared to our American working-men, stupid, although willing, strong, and industrious. Then, too, in comparison with a similar American mill, with our precision of organization and our carefully and sharply maintained discipline, the state of affairs in the Russian establishment was very inferior. Indeed, contrasted with the accurate adjustment of service to service which prevails in our American mills, the work in the same kind of a Russian establishment seemed confused. And then, too, where the corporation itself is a French corporation, most of its skilled employés are French artisans.

But here was a development well worth attention. Immediately across the street from the mill itself is located a private school for the children of the working-people. This school is built and maintained by the company. It is much superior to the ordinary Russian country school; and while it does not, of course, approach the common school in our American cities, it was, nevertheless, a very creditable establishment. The children of the work-people are furnished with instruction here free of charge to the parents.

This is only an item, however, of the labor development here noted. On the same street with the school-house is a considerable establishment, owned by a joint-stock company, whose stockholders are made up exclusively of the working-men of the factory. It is also run by other working-men employed by this working-men's stock company. This establishment supplies groceries and all table provisions to the employés of this mill at cost—that is, without any middleman's profit. There is even a bakery connected with it, where bread is baked for the families of this mill's work-people. The employés of this working-men's establishment sleep and live in the place itself. Their sleeping-rooms were visited, and were found to be clean, comfortable, and, in comparison with the sleeping accommodations in the dormitories above described, where the work-people of the cotton factories are housed, commodious and almost luxurious. Iron bedsteads, comfortable mattresses, clean bed-clothing make these quarters almost as good as those found in middle-class Amerian hotels.

Inference must not be made that all of the working-men of the mills and factories come from the country districts. A large part of the operatives are permanently located in the cities themselves. Nor must it be understood that all manufacturing establishments house and feed their employés. On the contrary, many factories do not maintain their work-people, but supply them lodging at low rental, the laborers themselves providing their own food.

Many work-people live in rooms or flats rented from their employers. Some of these quarters were visited in various cities. Certain ones in St. Petersburg are a fair illustration of the rest.

Uncomfortable board buildings these structures are found to be. What prevents frequent and destroying fires is not clear. The stairways are narrow and winding, the corridors are the same. Usually two rooms, or at most three, suffice for a family consisting of husband and wife and an ever-increasing number of children. No place in the immediate neighborhood where these children could play was observed, although inquiry was made for it. And yet the children's "sand heap" and children's "playground" are things on which Russians particularly pride themselves. There are sections of some of the cities which appear to be without them. But fairness compels the statement that open spaces convenient for children's play are frequent in Russian cities.

To return to the living conditions of some of the most poorly circumstanced of Russian city working-men, squalid as they are, as bad and even worse can be found in London or New York. About these Russian workingmen's families, however, there is a submission to existing things not found anywhere else in civilized countries. It is a mistake to assume that this is on account of the repressive measures of the government.

"At least these people seem to be fairly well content," was suggested to a fellow-English observer.

"Content! They have got to be. Most anybody would be content with a bayonet at his breast," answered the Englishman.

"Oh, come now," suggested a Russian gentleman, who by no means approved of some of the sterner methods of repression said to be sometimes practised by the police and soldiery to prevent labor demonstrations, but who insisted that reports of such disturbances published in other countries are absurdly exaggerated—"oh, come now," said this friend of the Russian laborer and the Russian peasant, "the government's repression is not the reason for these people's contentment with their wretchedness. It is a great deal deeper than that. It is racial. Do not forget that we are Slavs. In a measure, we are fatalists. Our people take things as they come, and live the lives to which they feel that they are ordained." A good deal of talk here and there with the Russian working-men and the wives of Russian working-men lends plausibility to this theory.

"Do not you find it cold here in winter?" was asked of one of these Russian women, the wife of a working-man in a manufacturing shop near by. She was still young, though the mother of five children.

"Oh yes; sometimes, of course, it is cold," she answered; "but God made the winter."

"But it is hot enough here now," was remarked to her. (It was one of those blazing days that St. Petersburg occasionally has in the summer-time.)

"Yes, it is hot; but God sent the summer."

"And do you look for better conditions—I mean larger rooms and more things to live on and live with?"

"Ah, that is as God wills."

And pages could be consumed by examples of the same kind. It is not said that these are true representations of the Russian working-people's mind. They may have been mere evasions. They may have been the easiest answer which unthinking minds made to questions which they did not understand. The statements alone are noted, and their value and the proper inferences to be drawn from them are left to the reader. But sure it is that they bear out the Russian theory that the racial characteristics of the Slav are a fatalistic indolence, a stolid lack of initiative, an acceptance of conditions as they are, or of directions received from superior sources. It recalls the remark of a Russian nobleman on the Amur boat, when hundreds of peasants, with great labor, dragged heavy chains a quarter of a mile in order to fasten them to a tree, none being nearer, so that there might be a leverage with which to wrench the boat from a sand-bar on which it had unluckily run. The stupidity of the whole thing was remarked by an American traveller.

"Ah, well," said the Russian count, "you have been abusing the bureaucracy of Russia for a week now. Look at those people. You have a good example before your eyes of exactly why it was that Peter the Great, our ideal reformer, founded the present bureaucratic system in Russia. Peter the Great knew his people. He ordered all of their beards cut off because they never would have cut them off themselves. He autocratically destroyed the ancient garb of the boyar, which was also, in varying degrees, the national costume. He had their coats cut short and their trousers made sensible and serviceable simply because the people would have continued that custom to this very day if they had not been ordered to alter it."

In short, there are many reasons to believe that the lethargy of the Russian people as a mass is due to racial causes. These reasons are to be found all through Russian history and are before the eyes of the contemporary observer throughout the whole country. The writer's observation has been too rapid and perhaps too superficial to afford an independent and mature opinion on this subject, important though the subject may be. The mere facts are stated as far as they could be obtained.

A Russian common laborer in a steel mill at St. Petersburg came running after the English manager and his visitor during the course of a fairly thorough inspection of the works. The working-man called to the manager, who excused himself and went to his employé. Presently he returned laughing.

"Now there is an interesting incident," he said, "and it is thoroughly characteristic. What do you suppose that fellow wanted with me? "Why, he said: 'Master, look out for that man who is with you. I think he is trying to discover some of the secrets of our works.'" (Recent inventions had been placed in this mill, and the new process, the proprietors hoped, would make it superior to any other then existing in northern Russia.) "You see, he saw you looking around very carefully, and when I was over on the other side of the mill he saw you closely examining everything you came across. His suspicions were aroused instantly, and that little incident, which you might not have seen in many days of travel in Russia, shows you a peculiarity of all classes. That characteristic is their suspicion. They suspect everything and everybody. But you see he was perfectly true to me. That same man would cheat me if he could, but he would not let anybody else cheat me. Our own employés might rob us right and left, but they would risk their lives to prevent anybody else from robbing us. They get drunk on holidays themselves, but they will be very hot about the same offence of working-men in Mr. So-and-so's factory."

XX

THE LABOR LAWS OF RUSSIA

THE labor question is the universal question. As the world's civilization grows more complex, the labor question must steadily grow more delicate. In estimating the quality of other nations, the treatment of their laborers is an element of prime importance, for, after all, at bottom it is the labor and capital of sister nations with which we Americans must compete. For this reason much space has already been given in these pages to this subject, and for this reason much space is still deemed necessary; for we want to ascertain—do we not?—what kind of a force it is which the world beholds along the Asiatic shores of the Pacific Ocean. We have looked upon the Russian laboring-man in the great, modern factories and mills of Russia; we have seen how he works, how he lives, what he eats, how he is amused; have noted his inefficiency as a working-man, have observed his strong points of patience and endurance, and, in general, have hastily surveyed those qualities of human interest which go to make up the real man and woman. We have seen something, too, of the general spirit of the Russian state as it affects the laboring people of the empire. But the laws which govern laboring conditions in Russia have not been set forth, and it is believed that these are of sufficient interest and importance to justify a chapter of general examination. It is felt, too, that the provisions of Russian legislation which govern and safeguard the factory workers of the empire will give a fair idea of the statesmen who devise and the government which enacts them.

Perhaps the most striking manifestation of the humanitarian movement in the field of labor legislation in all countries was that relating to the employment of children in factories and other industrial works. The history of such legislation in England, France, Germany, and the United States is of most absorbing interest, and of highest possible contemporary and historical importance. Of course, the same is true of Russia also. In 1882 a law was placed upon the statute books of Russia upon this important subject. This law prohibited the employment of children under twelve years of age in all kinds of manufacturing industries except the "kustar trades," hereafter described. This law requires that children over twelve and under fifteen years of age shall not be employed to exceed eight hours a day. These eight hours do not include the time spent at school and in resting. It further provides that children shall not be required to work continuously longer than four hours, at the expiration of which time the employers are obliged to give the children a stated period of rest. Employers are prohibited from requiring children to work at night, on Sundays or on holidays; and no work is permitted to be done by any child which is deemed by the factory inspectors to be injurious or fatiguing. The employer is compelled to allow the children to attend the necessary schools in the vicinity of the factory; and factories are given the right to erect schools at their own expense, which the children of the factory may attend. A description of one of these schools has been given elsewhere. Many such were visited by the writer, and were found to be fairly well conducted.[1]

[1] The law concerning child labor gives the Minister of Finance the right to allow the employment of children of from ten to twelve years of age during the day, and children between twelve and fifteen years during the night, where the nature of the industry requires this, and where it cannot do the children any harm. Such investigation as could be made showed that this power has been exercised by the Minister of Finance very sparingly indeed, and usually with more careful consideration than might be expected.

To insure the enforcement of this child-labor law, an inspectorship of factories was created and a staff of factory inspectors appointed for the empire. It was believed at the time the law was passed that the supervision of these inspectors, and the fear of the displeasure of the government, would prevent the employers from infringing it, and so no penalty for its violation was provided. It was found, however, that the factory owners violated the law in several instances, and two years later it was amended by fixing a fine of one hundred rubles ($50) for the infraction of any part of the child-labor act; and this penalty amendment provided that if the owner or manager of the establishment could prove that the infraction took place without his knowledge, but through the fault of the person directly superintending the work, the latter person should be liable to the penalty.

A year later a law was enacted prohibiting the employment of all young persons under seventeen years of age and of all women in cotton mills at night, and this was afterwards extended to other textile industries. The government inspectors present in every factory are said to enforce this law rigidly, but that there is evasion of it in many instances is, nevertheless, undoubtedly true. Very careful provisions are made for the enforcement of the law by the inspectors. For example, if a manufacturer intends to employ children, he must first declare that intention and make a statement of the number of hours he expects them to work. When he employs these children their names must be registered in a special book. This book sets out various details descriptive of the child's capacity for work, and a column is left at the end of the page in which the inspector must write his conclusions or remarks.

If the inspector deems any child to be either too young or too weak for the work required of him, the child must be examined by a physician. After an examination, if the physician thinks that the child is either too young or too weak for the work, the employer must immediately discharge the child. Any resistance on the part of the employer is promptly remedied by the police. That all may know their rights, a list descriptive of the work that must be performed by children is required to be posted in the workshops. If any adult working-man or working-woman violates the law in his or her treatment of any children who are at work, the manager of the factory is responsible therefor.

It is interesting to note that, in the matter of the fine of one hundred rubles ($50) for the infraction of the child-labor law, the schooling of the child is especially mentioned. If the employer violates the law by overworking the child, or employing a child under age, or requiring a child to work an illegal number of hours, he may not only be fined, but also be imprisoned for one month.

The child-labor law may be said to have been the first step in modern Russian legislation on the labor question. It is, however, claimed by enthusiastic Russians that Russia led the world in legislation on the labor question. They cite the fact that in the eighteenth century imperial decrees began concerning labor inspection, requiring working-men to be paid in full, forbidding ill-treatment of employés, preventing over-working, and restricting hours of labor to twelve hours in the twenty-four; and that such ukases were issued is undeniable. Indeed, for the last two centuries, in spite of the serfdom under which the great masses of the Russian people were held in bondage, many regulations were enacted by the Russian government for the care of laborers in manufacturing industries.

However fascinating the study of the development of Russian labor laws, space forbids more than mention of present statutes; but it may be said that distinctly modern labor legislation in Russia began with the child-labor law, of which an abstract is given above. All human legislation obeys the law of growth as much as does the development of animals or plants. So, when the Russian government began modern legislation by the child-labor statute, it was inevitable that that act should set in operation natural forces requiring further labor legislation. Sure enough, not four years passed until a general law was enacted concerning the hiring of working-men, defining the relations of employer and employé, perfecting factory inspection, and extending it generally to adult labor as well as to child labor. This law was very general in its application. It has since been amended several times, as experience showed the original law to be defective and inadequate.

In general, this law sets out regulations singularly minute concerning every feature of the contract between the employer and employed. It also provides special regulations concerning the maintenance of order in factories and mills. Some of these provisions are of sufficient general interest to be set out. For example, the manufacturer must either make a written contract with the working-man, or give him a book which contains the terms of the agreement. In no case can a working-man be employed for more than five years.[1]

The employer is required to pay the employé his wages in cash. He cannot pay him in food, clothing, materials, and the like. In this way the evil known in America as the "pluck-me stores" was anticipated and prevented. The penalty for paying the working-man in anything but cash is a fine not less than twenty-five nor more than one hundred and fifty dollars. If the laborer is hired for several months, he must be paid his wages at least once each month; if for an indefinite period, at least twice a month. If he is hired, not by the time but by the piece of labor to be performed, he is to be paid on the completion of the job.

[1] As a matter of practice, many, perhaps most, of the working-men are employed in groups, and a book is issued to the elder or leader whom these laborers elect, for the whole group, instead of to each man singly.

The employer is required to take hygienic care for the protection of his laborers, and to supply them, free of charge, with medical attendance.

In addition to the contract-book, which must be issued to the operative who is employed for a period of time, instead of by the job, the employer must issue him a pay-book, and in the book the money received by the laborer must be set down, as must the fines imposed upon him. If the employer does not keep these books of his laboring-men properly, he may be fined for each offence not less than five rubles ($2.50) and not more than twenty-five rubles ($12.50).

On the other hand, the employer may fine his working-man for any one of three causes—first, for defective work; secondly, for absence without sufficient cause; and, thirdly, for any infraction of the shop regulations.

In determining what is defective work the employer is not the sole judge. The government factory inspector may be appealed to. Moreover, the law prescribes minutely what shall constitute defective work for which the employé may be fined. For example, defective work is defined to be such as causes damage to raw material or machinery, and fines for this are calculated by the nature of the defect, and not by the loss sustained by the employer. It was feared by the government that these fines might be used by the employers to their own profit. To prevent this, it was provided that the fines should not go to the employer, but should be collected into a special fund to be used for the benefit of the employés. Fines for absence without sufficient cause may not be imposed unless the absence is for at least half a day; nor can the laborer be fined for absence because of such unavoidable circumstances as fire or flood, illness of the working-man, or of his wife or parents, or of the death of either. Of course, wherever fines may be imposed for absence without sufficient cause, the wages of the laborer may also be deducted for the time missed.

Fines may not be imposed for disobedience to shop regulations arbitrarily. They apply only to unreasonable infractions, such as leaving the premises without permission, disobedience to rules for protection against fire and cleanliness, quarrelling in the factory, or for insubordination and the like. For these the fines must not exceed more than one ruble for each offence. If the laborer is dissatisfied with the fines, he may complain to the government inspector of the factory. If the inspector, on investigation, decides that the fine has been unjustly imposed, he may bring an action against the manager of the factory in the law courts. That the working-men may know their rights, a list of all possible fines must be posted in the shops.

Moreover, the total amount of all fines imposed on a working-man must not exceed one-third of his wages. When that sum is reached the laborer may be discharged, but if he feels himself aggrieved, he may, within a month, bring an action in a court of law for damages against the manager who discharged him.

It will be noted that these fines do not go to the employer, but form a special fund for the benefit of the working-man. The law does not leave the disposition of this fund to the employer, but prescribes what the "fines fund" shall be used for. For example, it may be used to help sick or injured workmen, or working-women who are near the period of confinement, or to relieve the financial distress of a laborer, caused by fire, flood, and the like, or for funerals of working-men, etc. When the fund exceeds one hundred rubles ($50) in amount it can no longer be kept by the employer, but must be deposited at the state savings-bank, and can only be drawn out on an order signed by the manager of the factory and the factory inspector.

When a working-man has been employed under this law, both the employer and the employé must give fifteen days' notice. Furthermore, the law prevents the reduction of wages during the time for which the laborer is employed, on the one hand, or the reduction of the number of working-days, on the other. Conversely, the employé cannot demand an increase of wages or any other alteration of the contract. If either employer or employé violates the law, severe punishments are provided; for example, three hundred rubles ($150) fine for the employer, and a month's imprisonment for the employé.

It is interesting to note with how firm a hand the government deals with employers of labor in its effort to prevent labor disturbances. For example, if the manager of a factory breaks three times any of the regulations provided for in the law, or if he causes a disturbance among his laboring people, making necessary the assistance of the police, the head of the factory may be imprisoned for three months and prohibited from managing a factory for two years.

On the other hand, any fight or strike on the part of the laboring-men is punishable by imprisonment for not less than one week nor more than five months; and if the strike is actually made the strikers may be imprisoned for not less than two nor more than eight months. But if the strikers do any damage or attempt to intimidate a fellow working-man, the individual may be imprisoned for the maximum term of sixteen months.

The provisions by which the contract may be terminated are interesting, but the one most curious and illustrative of industrial conditions in Russia is that by which the laborer is released from the contract if his village community refuses to extend his leave of absence —that is, extend his passport. The reader is referred to the explanation of the passport system in another chapter.

The attempt to balance delicately the respective rights and obligations of the employer and working-man, which is manifest throughout the whole labor legislation of Russia is, perhaps, best illustrated by the reasons for which the employer may discharge his working-men, on the one hand, thus terminating the contract, and the reasons for which the working-man may terminate his contract, on the other. For example, if the working-man is absent for three consecutive days without a sufficient reason, or if he is absent for six days in the course of a month, whether consecutive or not, or if he absents himself for fifteen consecutive days, even if he has a sufficient reason for such absence, his employer may discharge him, thus terminating the contract. On the other hand, the employé may leave his employer instantly if he is assaulted or beaten. He may also terminate his contract and quit his employment if the food and shelter supplied him have been bad, or if the work required of him is unhealthy. He may also leave if the bread-winner of the family to which he belongs should die, thus leaving the famiily without its laborer in the village community to which he belongs.

In 1897 the law was amended, fixing twelve hours as the time beyond which adult working-men might not be required to labor, and the factory was permitted to run night-shifts and day-shifts of twelve hours each. In government work the working-men were given Sundays and official holidays, amounting to forty in the year, exclusive of Sundays. While the law makes it optional whether the private establishments shall observe these holidays, as a matter of practice it is said that the working-men observe the holidays anyway. It was impossible to verify this from actual observation; but the information upon which the statement is based is credible.

The existing law on the subject of hours of labor is confused, but the following is believed to be a fairly accurate statement.

Eleven and one-half hours may be required for day-work. This applies to both men and women. The working-day begins at 6 A.M. and ends at 7 P.M. An hour and a half is allowed for the noon meal and rest. This applies to only one shift. If two shifts are employed, the day's work may be eighteen hours, beginning at 4 A.M. and ending at 10 P.M. It will be seen that this in reality requires but nine hours for each shift.

As before stated, eight hours out of the twenty-four constitute a full day's labor for a child under fifteen.

A curious provision of the law is that overtime work, which is carefully prescribed in the statute, must not exceed, for the entire year, one hundred and twenty hours. It should be noted also that the provisions of the law may be suspended as to overtime and other items when there is a fire in the factory or breakage of machinery, or some other cause which interferes with the operation of the plant and which needs immediate remedying.

The effect of religion on the labor situation in Russia is shown by a single provision to the effect that working-men belonging to the Greek Orthodox Church must be given the holidays of their Church, and also Sundays, while for the working-men who are not members of that Church these holidays may be omitted. If the working-men happen to be followers of another faith—for example, Mohammedans—they are given the holidays prescribed by that religion, instead of Sundays, as prescribed for the Christian religion.

If a factory has a thousand employés, it must maintain an infirmary or hospital, with at least ten beds; if there are more than a thousand working-people (men, women, and children) employed, the factory hospital must have fifteen beds. This hospital and the medical treatment and attendance of the working-men are all paid for by the factory.

Perhaps the most characteristic feature of Russian labor legislation is the voluminous laws on the subject of factory inspection. It was found after the enactment of the first law for factory inspection that the inspection was not perfectly performed. Sometimes the inspectors were oppressive to the factory owners; sometimes they were unjust to the operatives; sometimes they were undoubtedly corrupt. To remedy these many defects, a factory and mining board was established in 1889, and was made one of the sub-bureaus of the Ministry of Finance.

The powers of this board are very broad. It may make, from time to time, such rules and regulations concerning factory inspection as experience shows to be desirable. It may over-rule any action of any factory inspector; and, finally, it acts as a sort of court of appeal from the decision of local factory boards.

These local factory boards exist in every manufacturing province. They consist of the governor of the province, the prosecuting attorney, the chief of police, the chief factory inspector for the province, and the two representatives of the manufacturers. These boards may provide rules and regulations particularly applicable to the industry within their jurisdiction. Especially do they look to the preservation of health, life, and morality among the work-people.

From these local boards we come down to the factory inspectors themselves. The latest law of a general character, defining their powers and duties, was enacted in 1900, though so constant are the amendment and alteration of all Russian laws that it has been changed many times since, but not in important particulars. The following is believed to be a fair statement of its more important provisions.

To these inspectors all disagreements between the laboring people and the factory managers are carried. The inspector is then supposed to investigate the complaints, to explain the causes of them to the aggrieved party, and generally to act as peace-maker between the employer and the employé. If the inspector cannot make an amicable arrangement between the hostile parties, he must refer the whole matter to the courts.

The inspector fixes certain days, not fewer than one a week, on which he will receive any person having a complaint, whether manager or employé, and make verbal explanation as to rights and duties, etc. In addition to this, it is the duty of the inspector to ascertain for himself whether the factory manager is observing all the provisions of the law. In doing this, he may question all of the working-people whenever he thinks it desirable. Should he think it necessary, he may summon the owners of the factory themselves. Indeed, this is often done.

In determining the observance of the law by the factory managers, the inspector may, upon presenting a permit from the Department of Trades and Manufactures, go through any and every part of the mill or factory at any hour of the day or night, and through all of the dormitories, hospitals, schools, and other buildings attached to the factory.

When one of the work-people is injured, the factory inspector immediately investigates the cause. If he finds that the accident resulted from the non-observance of the law by the factory-owners, the inspector draws up a sort of complaint. There are many sections of the law under which this complaint or statement may be drawn up. Sometimes it is under a provision of the criminal code; sometimes under what is called the industrial code. It may be made either by the factory inspector alone or by him in conjunction with the officers of the police. When so drawn, it is transmitted to the authorities for inquiry and trial.

It is also a part of the duty of the factory inspector to superintend generally the schools which the factory is required to keep for the children of operatives, and to see that the children attend the schools, and that instruction is given according to the provisions of the law.

Where strikes or other labor troubles are threatened or under way, the inspector goes instantly to the spot. First he attempts to bring the employers and the employés to a friendly understanding. Failing in this, any measures may be taken, carefully provided for by law, which the justice and necessity of the case seem to require. It is said that in such cases the local inspectors of the factories keep in continuous communication with the chief inspector of the city or district by telegraph and telephone, and the police are carefully in touch with the entire situation.

Finally, the inspectors pass upon the opening of factory shops, the issuance of pay-books, the payments to sick or injured operatives from the funds collected from fines, the charges which the factory makes on their workingmen for lodgings, bath, etc., the prices of articles sold to the co-operative stores, the rules which the factory managers desire to make on their own motion, in addition to the regulations fixed by the general law or by the regulations of the factory boards. Also, he must certify general scales of wages and countersign different kinds of records which the law requires the factory to keep, such as books for boilers, for children employed, for fines, etc.

The entire laws, rules, and regulations concerning factory inspection in Russia are voluminous in extent, minute in the specification of duties and powers. No attempt will be made, of course, to set them out in their entirety, or even to give a complete general analysis of them. It has been thought worth the space to detail the above provisions, that the reader may have some general idea of this most important branch of Russian legislation.

The law is still unsatisfactory on the question of accidents. Nevertheless, Finance Minister Witte, some four years ago, prepared and presented to the Council of State a bill on the civil liability of employers which pretty effectually covered the situation from a Russian point of view. The Council of State approved the bill at its first reading; but when it came to the second reading, the manufacturers of Moscow and St. Petersburg presented a petition to the Finance Minister, asking for the postponement of the proposed measure, for the reason that they were about to form mutual insurance societies for their employés, and if the proposed bill became a law before this reform was perfected, it would cause many factories and mills serious financial difficulty. Indeed, it was demonstrated that in some instances it would threaten them with insolvency. It is understood that for these reasons the bill has not yet been passed. This proposed law defines the liability of the employer for all accidents to his employés. A limit of the amount of damages which may be recovered in each case is fixed. The law of contributory negligence is introduced by a provision reducing the amount of damages in proportion to the contributory negligence. Our law, placing the burden of proof on the plaintiff, is by this proposed Russian act directly reversed and the burden of proof is placed on the employer. He can only release himself from this burden of proof by showing three things — first, that the accident was inevitable; second, that it occurred by reason of the fault or intention of a third party for whom the employer was not responsible; third, the fault or malicious intention of the injured working-man.

There are provisions in this law concerning the settlement of all such disputes by amicable arrangements between the employer and the injured employé. This, of course, is to prevent lawsuits; but, fearing that it might in some instances lead to fraud on the part of the employer and injustice to the employé, it is provided that such amicable agreement shall be made before a magistrate, who is required to see that no injustice is done to the injured working-man. If both parties desire it, they may leave the settlement of the amount of damages to a court of arbitration or to the factory inspector himself. There are no appeals from such decisions.

If the case is not settled in some such way the action for damages must be brought by the injured working-man, or, if he dies, by his wife or relatives. To prevent damage-suit lawyers working up unjust cases, the bill provides that the case shall be conducted on the part of the injured party by lawyers appointed for this purpose by the Council of Barristers; and the fee of such lawyers is fixed in the law. There is a queer provision, very illustrative of the temper of Russian legislation, in this proposed employers' liability bill—damages for the death of a working-man must be paid to those members of his family who need it, and not to some one who happens to be his nearest relative or who was living with him at the time of his death.

For fear that employés would take advantage of this liability law and live on the damages recovered, which were not in all cases to be paid in a lump sum but in the form of periodical allowances, it is provided that the amount of such instalments might, after five years, be reconsidered and refixed according to the capacity of the working-man to labor at that time.

The salient features of this law have been given thus fully because, if not already enacted, it is only a question of time when the above will substantially be the labor law of Russia. When this bill is passed, the labor laws of Russia will be fairly complete.

But it must be said that in the labor legislation of Russia we behold again that paradox which is so striking a feature of every department of Russian life—permanency of policy inextricably intertwined with perpetual change of method. The general laws of Russia, not only in labor legislation but in the statutes relating to agriculture, to commerce, to every conceivable subject, undergo almost continuous modification. The theory is that as experience shows that a certain law or regulation does not work well, it is immediately modified to suit conditions.

While it is not possible within the limits of this volume to devote an entire chapter to the methods of Russian legislation, which is a subject of most absorbing interest, a paragraph may serve to enlighten the American reader upon the general idea upon which Russian legislation is drafted and enacted.

First of all, then, it may be said that, so far as her written laws are concerned, Russia is governed by commissions. If the labor situation does not seem to be satisfactory, a commission is appointed, with careful instructions to study the causes by original investigation and to report recommendations. If there is agricultural depression, the same thing is done. If the subject of forestry needs attention, again there is a commission to study, report, recommend.

When the report is made to the ministry to which the commission is attached, the assistant ministers and the presiding minister are supposed to go over it carefully. The result is the drafting of a law. This law is submitted first to the Council of Ministers and then to the Council of State, which, in theory, thoroughly debates every provision of it. In practice, it is said that this is seldom done; but it must in fairness be stated that it is undoubtedly true that in many important laws the Council of State does very thoroughly discuss the proposed statute. Finally it is submitted to the Czar, who approves or disapproves of it.

Again, the Russian law may be for the entire empire, or for only a province, or even for one city. If it is for the entire empire, it is, as a general thing, not immediately put into effect among the Czar's one hundred and forty million subjects. It is usually tried in one province first. If it works well there, it is gradually extended to others until the whole empire is covered. If it does not work well in the first province, the reasons for its defective operation are remedied by amendment before it is applied to other provinces, and, as its application spreads, modifications are made as experience requires. The theory is that in this way Russian legislation is not so much the product of some statesman's brain as it is the reflection of actual conditions. It is also said that in this way Russian legislation more carefully answers the needs of the people than the legislation of any other country. While, of course, an American would not for a moment concede the correctness of this view, it is worth noting as the belief earnestly entertained by those who hold to the existing order of things in Russia. Indeed, it is claimed by these advocates of autocratic methods that the processes of Russian legislation, as above briefly defined, are far superior to the parliamentary methods existing in countries like England and America.

XXI

THE INDEPENDENT PEASANT ARTISAN

WITH all of Russia's development of her manufacturing industry during the last fifteen years, her mills do not in any line supply her own market. There are really very large concerns in Russia devoted to the manufacture of railway locomotives, of which the establishment at Kolomna is the best example; also, there are mills for the manufacture of steel rails and all other items of railway equipment. Yet Russia must yearly import considerable numbers of locomotives and large quantities of everything else necessary for her rapidly growing railway system. Most of these ought to be supplied by the United States. In 1901, most of the importations of railway equipment and general machinery, up to July at least, were German. Before that time most of them had been American; and certainly the bulk of imported agricultural implements were American. But the tariff war precipitated by our controversy with Russia over her sugar rebates, which our government construed to be a bounty on sugar exports from Russia, seriously interfered with our growing sales of American manufactured products throughout the whole Russian Empire. Other European nations were quick to take advantage of this, and of these Germany was the most aggressive and successful. But, in spite of this, American engines were still the rule in the Russias of the Far East.

"What is that?" was asked of the traveller's Russian friend during a cross-country journey in the troika, through the lanes and over the fields of his estates. What was, apparently, in the near distance, a mound of grass-grown earth rising in a field, and perhaps a mile from a small village of a dozen or fifteen houses, was pointed out. A thin column of smoke was rising from it—a strange thing in the centre of fields of ripening wheat.

"I do not know from here," was the answer, "but I think it is a country blacksmith-shop. If it is you will find it very interesting. It illustrates a vastly important branch of Russian manufacturing industry, and one peculiarly and exclusively Russian."

The narrow lane, wheat-bordered, took the troika directly in front of this mound of earth, which was found to be in reality a sort of dug-out, not unlike those which the first settlers upon our Western prairies twenty years ago rudely constructed as a temporary shelter. It was partly excavated from a natural rise in the ground at that particular point. The walls above had been constructed of sod; wooden rafters or poles, placed tent-wise on top of this and covered with a thick layer of earth, on which grass was waving, constituted the roof. The whole space inside made a room not exceeding twelve by fourteen feet. Yet within this space, three men and five boys were at work. As the troika stopped, all came out smiling; and sure enough it was a blacksmith-shop, and more than a blacksmith-shop.

"Oh yes," said the father of this little industrial ant-heap, "we do more than blacksmithing—we make bolts," and at a word one of the boys ran in and brought out a double handful of hand-made bolts. "We also make nuts for bolts, of course, and many other things like that."

These nuts and bolts and other things which these peasant artisans fashioned in their rude earth-shop were marketed in the nearest city. "Oh yes, there is a demand for more than we can supply," answered the father to a pertinent question. "We get very good prices for them, too." The prices, however, were absurdly low in comparison with American prices for similar articles — absurdly low, too, when we consider the number which each man could make in a day. Nevertheless, three families, numbering many souls, live very well indeed, according to the Russian notions of living, on the proceeds of these country laborers' toil, together with the produce of their fields; and, so far as you can see, all appear happy and content. But the significant point was that the factories of Russia are not making as many iron things of this kind as are required for the daily uses of the country.

"If this work pays so well, why don't all the farmer-peasants engage in it?"

"Why," said the Russian artisan, with plain surprise pictured on his face, "other farmers do work at it, and many other things, too."

This answer revealed what investigation showed to be one of the most extraordinary phases of Russian industrialism. This is that class of Russian peasant manufacturing industry known as the "kustar trades." All over this most extensive of empires, and among all of these most numerous of peoples, the agricultural peasants in their country villages form little associations for the manufacture of almost every article used throughout the Czar's dominions. Not only this, but surprising quantities of manufactured goods wrought by these peasant hands in their villages are for export trade. The little group of workmen busily engaged in the earth-constructed shop just described was one of the poorest and humblest of these communities of peasant artisans. They were working at their "kustar trade" in that short period between the cultivation of their fields and the harvest of the grain which was not yet ripe. Thus their time and labor were turned into productive industry.

In tens of thousands of the little country villages larger associations of these peasant working-men employ every moment of their time during the long winter months in some kind of manufacture. Not only the men, but the women and children work at these trades. Silk is woven by them. They produce cotton fabrics. All kinds of woodwork are done by them, and the wooden utensils turned out are surprisingly well finished. In many lines a fair degree of art has been developed. For example, the writer was shown wooden spoons, shaped and richly enamelled by peasant villagers, and a village of considerable size was visited where the entire population fashioned various forms of jewelry. It is said on excellent authority that the Russian peasant product of jewelry annually runs up into millions of articles. Also, all kinds of leather work are done. Without consuming space to enumerate, it is said that there is nothing that these peasant manufacturers of Russia do not create, from horse-shoes to clothing, from icons to ink-stands. Indeed, the immense majority of all the painted saints and virgins and other pictured sacred representations are the work of peasant hands; and very reverent work it is. No amount of money, for example, could induce a peasant artist to paint or carve a sacred image or picture in different colors, attire, or attitude than those familiar ones which immemorial custom has sanctioned.

While most of the products of peasant's work is consumed in Russia itself, a very respectable quantity of it is exported. Most of these peasant exports, however, go to Asia. And a curious and significant thing must here be noted: the prejudices, likes, susceptibilities, and tastes of the people to whom these export goods are sent are carefully respected in the manufacture of the articles intended for them. In this the imperial government helps the peasant artisan by instructing him upon these points. And instruction once received and understood by the Russian peasant becomes a fixture in his mentality, and is handed down unchanged throughout succeeding generations.

Indeed, it is in this way that the "kustar trades" were first established among the Slav millions, and that of itself is a curious tale. In the days of serfdom, the nobles who owned these peasant slaves were required to maintain them during the entire year; and yet the mass of them was self-supporting during only the summer months; in the winter months much labor was necessarily wasted. A certain noble, possessing the commercial instinct, hit upon a plan of sending the brightest of his peasants to the great cities of the empire, there to learn some craft, and then, returning, teach it to his fellows, so that the labor of the serfs might be employed to some useful and profitable end during the long months of the Russian winter.

The idea was a distinct success. Other nobles immediately imitated it, and the practice grew until the best minds among all the millions of Russian serfs were sent not only to the great cities of Russia itself, but to the most advanced industrial centres of Germany, Austria, France, and, it is said, even to England. When these peasants were called back they were the masters of numerous crafts, which they at once taught their fellow-slaves in their remote and isolated Russian village homes. And so it was that the serfs became able, not only to till the land of their lord, but to make, with as high degree of skill as the artisans of the most advanced countries of Europe, every article required in the domestic establishment of their noble owners.

The emancipation, of which some account will hereafter be given, did not extinguish these peasant industries, which were as widely spread as the empire itself and as variegated as the wants of the Russian people. And so it is that to-day the peasant manufacturer constitutes the most formidable rival of the great factories, which it is the present and future policy of the Russian government to foster by a protective tariff and by every possible device.

And here occurs a strange paradox of statesmanship. As has been stated, it is the fixed and settled policy of the

Russian government to build up great, centralized factories, such as exist in other European countries and in America. It would appear that this policy, if successful, would destroy the peasant artisan industry called the "kustar trades." Nevertheless, the imperial government carefully fosters these popular industries, as it does the greater and centralized manufacturing industries.

"Why, certainly we encourage the 'kustar trades,'" said a Russian official. "For example, teachers are sent at the expense of the imperial government to instruct these peasant manufacturing communities in more careful and exact workmanship, and even to teach them new methods."

Investigation proved this to be the fact; and not only so, but colored prints are distributed among these village shops to guide the peasant in the most remunerative forms of workmanship. When this is considered, and when it is remembered that the peasant artisan employs himself at these trades during months when his labor is otherwise absolutely wasted and worthless, that the women and children also work alongside of the men, that the labor thus furnished costs practically nothing, that they live in their own homes and consume the food which they themselves, in other portions of the year, have produced, that raw material is practically at hand, it will be seen that the Russian peasant manufacturer in his little village shop is no mean antagonist for the great manufacturer of the cities. Indeed, many Russians ascribe the failure of numbers of foreign manufacturing enterprises to the competition of these Russian peasant manufacturers, and there is, no doubt, a reasonable amount of truth in this explanation.

Another industrial and economic paradox is afforded by the growth of great factories in Russia on the one hand, and the persistence of the "kustar trade" on the other. With the racial characteristics of the Slav to community of effort, it has been thought by many economists that the modern tendency to industrially organize, which is so marked in our own country, notwithstanding our individualism, would be repeated in greater magnitude and by more solidly knit organizations in the Russian Empire. But, on the other hand, these peasant village manufacturing shops are also maintained by this very instinct of the Slav to organize, for every one of these peasant trades is communistic. There is no working of individuals as individuals and for themselves alone. There is no separate work done even by single families. It is all done by industrial communities, who work in common and have in common. The building where they themselves labor, and which you may see in almost every Russian village, is built in common and owned in common. Even the division of their industry is on the communistic principle. For example, many of the articles produced by these "kustar trades" are so elaborate that one community of peasants does not undertake to do it all. It does part of the work, and then passes the unfinished article on to another community, which does another part of the work, and so on until their joint labor is completed, and the proceeds are divided among all these communities, and then subdivided by the heads of each among the various families in proportion to the work done by each.

And so it is that industrially the great mass of Russian people may be said to be self-supporting. Indeed, the boast is made that, if every factory in Russia were suddenly destroyed, and no imports of foreign goods allowed, it would not greatly inconvenience the larger part of the Russian millions. They would go right on, says the enthusiastic Russian, making their rude wagons in the villages, making what iron implements they needed, spinning and weaving and putting together every item of their clothing, and, in short, constructing, from the poorest necessity up to the most dispensable luxury, everything required, regardless of all the world. When one visits the peasant artisans in the villages of Russia, hundreds of miles from any railway, and thinks of what is going on in this line among this most numerous of Christian people, the words of Pobyedonostseff, Procurator of the Holy Synod, again flash with dazzling brilliancy before the eye of the inquiring and reflecting mind. "Russia," said Pobyedonostseff, "is no state; Russia is a world."

In short, industrially, the Russian people are still an elemental people. The great masses of the Russian people, with their own hands, on their own fields, and in their own homes, still make what they wear and use.

Returning from the peculiarly Russian phenomenon of the "kustar trades" to the conditions of the great factories, and the laboring-men whom they are attracting within their walls, and to sum up this very inadequate series of observations on Russian industrial conditions, it may be fairly said that the lot of the Russian laborer in mills and factories is steadily improving. Compared with what it was less than a score of years ago, the progress has been very considerable indeed. Also, the manufacturing development is steadily influencing the agricultural population. More and more a thin stream of Russian agricultural working-men are going to the cities in winter to work in the factories, and returning to their homes in the spring and summer, bringing with them new ideas, a broader mental horizon generally (though still mean and limited from our view-point), and, what is more important, actual creature comforts, and even some of the more refined things of civilized life.

In comparison with the millions of Russian peasants, this thin stream of itinerant workmen is perhaps scarcely appreciable. But it flows, nevertheless, and the volume swells. It is unprofitable to speculate as to the future, but the forecast may be hazarded that this process will continue until, as elsewhere, Russian industries will become both more diversified and yet more centralized, the number of laboring-men who work in factories will increase; their skill with machinery will, year by year, become greater, and, finally, in the distant future the steam-driven mechanisms of modern inventive genius will take from the fingers of the peasant artisan the work which he and his fathers have for centuries performed. When this time comes, Russia's industrial conditions will approach those of Germany, England, and France.

But one thing appears probable: progress or no progress, improvement or no improvement, industrial classes or not, Russia is not to be feared as an exporting competitor, so far as manufacturing products are concerned, for perhaps a generation to come, or maybe longer.

It may be that Russia's statesmen prefer to depend upon the ability of the Russian peasant to make his own clothing and implements, in gradually lessening quantities, until the centralized manufacturing industry of Russia itself can catch up with the Russian demand, and so keep the Russian market exclusively for the Russian factories and mills. If so, it will be a long process. This theory is occasionally suggested, and has a substantial basis of reason. Certainly appearances seem to support it, and, in addition, the one sovereign thought always in the mind of the Russian public man — namely, the solidarity of the nation, would support this view. Indeed, arguments much heard now in Russia, in support of keeping the markets of the empire for the labor and capital of Russia itself, are very similar to those familiar to Americans.

In the statement that Russia need not be feared by the other commercial nations as an exporting competitor of manufactured articles in the markets of the world, the export trade of Russia is borne in mind. Let us look at a table (see p. 311) of Russian exports during the last three years, showing what kind of merchandise it is that Russia is selling abroad. In 1902 Russia sold more than four hundred and ten million dollars' worth of merchandise to other countries. On their face, and at first blush, these figures appear formidable; but when we consider that they represent the total exports of Russia, and then

PRINCIPAL ARTICLES EXPORTED FROM RUSSIA DURING THE LAST THREE YEARS

Articles	1900	1901	1902
Horses	No. 58,990	No. 71,900	No. 91,900
	R. 5,252,000	R. 6,556,000	R 8,827,000
Fowls and Game	R. 8,658,000	R. 9,547,000	R. 9,017,000
Cattle, Sheep, and Pigs	No. 130,184	No. 156,000	No. 90,000
	R. 3,743,000	R. 3,748,000	R. 3,367,000
Brandy and Corn Spirit	R. 575,000	R. 591,000	R. 1,049,000
Bran	P. 30,684,000	P. 32,403,000	P. 29,906,000
	R. 14,867,000	R. 16,406,000	R. 14,926,000
Bristles	P. 133,000	P. 129,000	P. 143,000
	R. 5,508,000	R. 5,425,000	R. 5,854,000
Butter	P. 1,190,000	P. 1,968,000	P. 2,309,000
	R. 13,476,000	R. 26,432,000	R. 28,415,000
Caviare	P. 191,000	P. 129,000	P. 189,000
	R. 2,549,000	R. 1,852,000	R. 2,420,000
Clothing, Ready-made	R. 1,182,000	R. 547,000	R. 398,000
Corn, Flour, and Meal, Total of	P. 420,194,000	P. 466,011,000	P. 578,914,000
	R. 306,402,000	R. 344,166,000	R. 432,226,000
Corn, Wheat	P. 116,876,000	P. 138,513,000	P. 185,807,000
	R. 104,280,000	R. 122,681,000	R 162,216,000
Rye	P. 93,227,000	P. 82,732,000	P. 98,220,000
	R. 65,017,000	R. 56,009,000	R. 69,907,000
Barley	P. 53,676,000	P. 77,580,000	P. 104,120,000
	R. 33,675,000	R. 47,930,000	R. 64,135,000
Oats	P. 80,047,000	P. 80,307,000	P. 63,313,000
	R. 49,726,000	R. 58,507,000	R. 49,706,000
Maize	P. 19,057,000	P. 29,706,000	P. 68,445,000
	R. 10,574,000	R. 17,209,000	R. 41,937,000
Pease	P. 4,596,000	P. 5,122,000	P. 6,170,000
	R. 4,153,000	R. 4,654,000	R. 5,415,000
Flour of Wheat	P. 4,577,000	P. 3,683,000	P. 3,157,000
	R. 7,287,000	R. 5,090,000	R. 5,177,000
" " Rye	P. 9,752,000	P. 8,956,000	P. 10,033,000
	R. 9,200,000	R. 8,171,000	R. 9,526,000
Cotton, Manufactures of,	R. 11,719,000	R. 16,924,000	R. 16,616,000
Eggs (thousands)	1,777,000	1,997,000	2,230,000
	R. 31,313,000	R. 35,392,000	R. 38,617,000
Flax, Raw	P. 10,571,000	P. 8,519,000	P. 10,753,000
	R. 43,829,000	R. 44,438,000	R. 51,460,000
" Tow	P. 1,967,000	P. 1,975,000	P. 1,675,000
	R. 5,257,000	R. 5,554,000	R. 5,249,000
Fur and Sheep Skins	R. 6,440,000	R. 6,107,000	R. 6,453,000
Hemp, Raw	P. 2,422,000	P. 2,564,000	P. 2,124,000
	R. 8,147,000	R. 9,864,000	R. 7,709,000
Leather and Hides, Untanned	P. 840,000	P. 701,000	P. 851,000
	R. 7,746,000	R. 6,578,000	R. 7,941,000
Oil-cake	P. 22,302,000	P. 23,559,000	P. 23,530,000
	R. 15,530,000	R. 16,743,000	R. 17,122,000
Oil, Illuminating, Petroleum, etc.	P. 87,963,000	P. 93,372,000	P. 92,357,000
	R. 46,506,000	R. 52,289,000	R. 42,143,000
Seeds, Oleaginous, Linseed	P. 16,941,000	P. 4,565,000	P. 6,178,000
	R. 28,677,000	R. 8,794,000	R. 9,705,000
Rope and Koptrabi Seed	P. 3,961,000	P. 1,301,000	P. 1,940,000
	R. 3,984,000	R. 1,232,000	R. 1,839,000
Sugar	25,274,000	17,630,000	17,354,000
Wool of all sorts	R. 58,435,000	R. 57,122,000	R. 55,122,000
Wool, Raw, Unspun	P. 852 000	P. 650,000	P. 809,000
	R. 5,924,000	R. 5,580,000	R. 5,120,000
Total value of principal and other articles	R. 716,418,000	R. 729,815,000	R. 825,277,000

NOTE.—Figures for 1901 and 1902 relate in most cases only to trade over the European frontier. 1 Pood=36.1 lbs.—1 Ruble=$.515

remember that they are more than a hundred million dollars less than the merchandise sold by the United States to the United Kingdom alone, their real importance begins to assume its proper proportions. Their relative significance will be disclosed by the consideration of just what these exports consist.

This table speaks for itself, and discloses the fact that, with the exception of refined sugar and illuminating oil, practically all of Russia's exports are of raw material. Substantially none of them are of manufactured goods in the popular meaning of that term. It will be noted that the value of corn, flour, and meal exported from Russia in 1902 was something over two hundred and fifteen million dollars, while the exports of manufactures of cotton were only a little over eight million dollars; and cotton manufacturing is the industry which Russians have most carefully fostered in recent years.

It may be interesting to know where these Russian exports go. This is shown in the following table of exports for the last three years for which figures are available.

TOTAL VALUE OF EXPORTS OF DOMESTIC PRODUCE (MERCHANDISE ONLY) FROM THE RUSSIAN EMPIRE DURING 1898, 1899, AND 1900

Countries	1898	1899	1900
	Rubles	Rubles	Rubles
Finland	33,264,000	35,116,000	41,034,000
Norway	4,470,000	4,948,000	6,419,000
Sweden	8,316,000	9,295,000	12,742,000
Denmark	9,857,000	12,341,000	18,278,000
Germany	179,436,000	163,564,000	187,635,000
Holland	72,257,000	48,821,000	69,304,000
Belgium	28,788,000	23,532,000	23,353,000
United Kingdom	139,906,000	129,162,000	145,576,000
France	68,594,000	59,869,000	57,450,000
Spain	2,798,000	7,429,000	4,271,000
Italy	54,608,000	27,755,000	36,790,000
Austria-Hungary	42,416,000	26,637,000	26,260,000
Greece	9,653,000	9,794,000	8,733,000
Roumania	12,675,000	6,588,000	5,277,000
Turkey	14,478,000	12,682,000	18,517,000
Persia	17,034,000	17,859,000	20,649,000
Egypt	6,727,000	5,588,000	9,195,000
United States	3,014,000	4,388,000	3,419,000
China	6,257,000	7,526,000	6,702,000
Other countries	18,125,000	14,080,000	14,814,000
Total	732,673,000	626,983,000	716,418,000

NOTE.—Figures for 1901 and 1902 not available.

Now compare these Russian exports with Russian imports from the same countries during the same period:

Countries	1898	1899	1900
	Rubles	Rubles	Rubles
Finland	19,112,000	18,439,000	20,016,000
Norway	5,394,000	5,620,000	5,848,000
Sweden	4,121,000	6,030,000	5,172,000
Denmark	5,249,000	3,061,000	5,900,000
Germany	202,198,000	230,871,000	216,853,000
Holland	9,777,000	11,414,000	8,822,000
Belgium	23,608,000	17,976,000	9,086,000
United Kingdom	115,295,000	129,644,000	127,144,000
France	27,110,000	28,481,000	31,445,000
Switzerland	5,851,000	7,034,000	6,199,000
Portugal	1,451,000	1,648,000	1,451,000
Spain	3,250,000	3,115,000	4,876,000
Italy	10,171,000	9,259,000	8,935,000
Austria-Hungary	23,925,000	30,617,000	26,083,000
Greece	723,000	916,000	761,000
Roumania	1,874,000	2,061,000	1,590,000
Turkey	6,867,000	7,184,000	7,705,000
Egypt	22,636,000	12,998,000	11,963,000
United States	50,059,000	43,772,000	44,170,000
Brazil	1,278,000	561,000	256,000
China	40,293,000	43,515,000	45,945,000
Persia	21,551,000	21,686,000	20,413,000
Other countries	15,666,000	14,583,000	14,842,000
Total	617,459,000	650,485,000	626,375,000

It will be noted that, while we buy of Russia between one and two million dollars' worth of merchandise each year, Russia purchases from us between twenty and twenty-five million dollars' worth of merchandise every year.

The comparative sales of Russian merchandise to other countries, and Russian purchases of merchandise from these same countries, can best be brought to mind by a balance table (see p. 314) showing just how much each country buys from and sells to Russia.

Much has been said in these two chapters descriptive of the iron and steel industry of Russia as revealed by an actual inspection of factories and mills, the condition and efficiency of the labor there, etc. It has been noted that the growth of this industry has been considerable. That the total present product of iron and steel in Russia is not overwhelming is shown by the actual number of tons of

IMPORTS INTO AND EXPORTS FROM RUSSIA OVER THE EUROPEAN FRONTIER DURING THE YEARS 1900, 1901, AND 1902 BY COUNTRIES

Countries	Imports (in Rubles)			Exports (in Rubles)		
	1900	1901	1902	1900	1901	1902
Finland	20,016,000	22,032,000	22,681,000	41,034,000	38,699,000	38,030,000
Norway	5,848,000	6,158,000	5,112,000	6,419,000	4,967,000	6,250,000
Sweden	5,171,000	3,373,000	3,476,000	12,742,000	8,809,000	10,731,000
Denmark	5,900,000	4,561,000	4,268,000	18,278,000	25,893,000	27,836,000
Germany	216,727,000	208,823,000	202,886,000	187,635,000	178,856,000	203,596,000
Holland	8,822,000	8,545,000	11,337,000	69,304,000	84,689,000	103,013,000
Belgium	9,086,000	8,878,000	6,963,000	23,353,000	21,188,000	28,434,000
United Kingdom	127,088,000	102,913,000	99,307,000	145,576,000	156,751,000	188,775,000
France	31,273,000	27,566,000	26,284,000	57,450,000	61,222,000	55,158,000
Switzerland	6,175,000	5,781,000	6,688,000	....	....	....
Portugal	....	....	....	....	....	....
Spain	....	....	....	....	....	....
Italy	8,928,000	10,224,000	9,213,000	36,790,000	37,751,000	48,885,000
Austria-Hungary	26,964,000	24,858,000	23,506,000	26,260,000	30,217,000	35,701,000
Greece	....	....	....	....	....	....
Roumania	1,590,000	2,158,000	1,541,000	5,277,000	10,375,000	14,782,000
Turkey	7,234,000	7,198,000	6,510,000	18,261,000	21,329,000	15,338,000
Egypt	11,963,000	18,299,000	15,082,000	9,195,000	9,816,000	6,792,000
United States	44,154,000	34,111,000	39,150,000	3,419,000	4,009,000	4,413,000
Brazil	....	....	....	....	....	....
China	16,193,000	21,440,000	19,446,000	1,145,000	3,635,000	944,000
Persia	....	....	....	....	....	....
East Indies	4,774,000	6,590,000	10,190,000	3,777,000	9,072,000	5,618,000
All other countries	14,158,000	9,436,000	13,455,000	22,520,000	22,537,000	30,981,000
Total	572,064,000	532,944,000	527,095,000	688,435,000	729,815,000	825,277,000

pig iron, wrought iron, and wrought steel produced during the last twenty years. But these figures also show astonishing growth in Russia in that infant industry—indeed, it may be said, an industry actually created within the last quarter of a century. So excellent a standard of industrial progress is the production of pig iron, wrought iron, and wrought steel that it is felt that space can very well be spared at this point to present a table showing the growth of this industry:

COMPARATIVE STATEMENT SHOWING THE PRODUCTION OF PIG IRON, WROUGHT IRON, AND WROUGHT STEEL IN THE RUSSIAN EMPIRE IN EACH OF THE UNDERMENTIONED YEARS

Year	Pig Iron	Iron (Wrought)	Steel (Wrought)
	Tons*	Tons*	Tons*
1881	469,000	292,000	No data
1882	463,000	297,000	
1883	482,000	323,000	222,000
1884	510,000	362,000	207,000
1885	528,000	362,000	193,000
1886	532,000	363,000	242,000
1887	612,000	369,000	225,000
1888	667,000	374,000	222,000
1889	740,000	428,000	259,000
1890	926,000	433,000	378,000
1891	1,005,000	448,000	433,000
1892	1,072,000	497,000	515,000
1893	1,149,000	499,000	631,000
1894	1,332,000	502,000	726,000
1895	1,452,000	440,000	879,000
1896	1,612,000	500,000	718,000
1897	1,869,000	500,000	868,000
1898	2,224,000	499,000	1,146,000
1899	2,675,000	566,000	1,322,000
1900	2,898,000	565,000	1,464,000
1901	2,784,000	....	....

NOTE.—The above particulars include the production in Finland.
* Metric tons of 2204 pounds.

Although not necessary for the purposes of this chapter, it may be interesting to set out the associated facts as to imports of merchandise into Russia during the last three years. Again, this can best be done by a table, which shall not only state the total amount of merchandise which Russia buys from the rest of the world, but also the articles purchased:

PRINCIPAL ARTICLES IMPORTED INTO RUSSIA

Articles	1900	1901	1902
Agricultural Machinery	R. 13,962,000	R. 15,867,000	R. 18,255,000
Books, Maps, etc.	R. 2,295,000	R. 2,093,000	R. 1,751,000
Cement and Earths	P. 11,875,000	P. 10,884,000	P. 9,847,000
	R. 1,908,000	R. 1,584,000	R. 1,544,000
Chemicals and Drugs	P. 6,036,000	P. 6,780,000	P. 5,999,000
	R. 12,642,000	R. 13,131, 000	R. 13,543,000
Coal and Coke	P. 274,570,000	P. 223,633,000	P. 201,032,000
	R. 42,298,000	R. 21,431,000	R. 21,907,000
Coffee, Raw	P. 503,000	P. 562,000	P. 588,000
	R. 5,424,000	R. 3,717,000	R. 4,852,000
Copper, Unwrought	P. 784,000	P. 683,000	P. 1,084,000
	R. 9,038,000	R. 7,583,000	R. 9,263,000
Cotton, Raw	P. 10,289,000	P. 10,375,000	P. 10,866,000
	R. 68,036,000	R. 63,795,000	R. 68,083,000
" Yarn	P. 145,000	P. 137,000	P. 147,000
	R. 4,502,000	R. 4,796,000	R. 4,695,000
" Manufactured	R. 6,488,000	....	....
Dyes, Coal, Tar, etc.	P. 62,000	P. 70,000	P. 69,000
	R. 3,314,000	R. 3,385,000	R. 3,579,000
Engines, Machinery, and Parts	P. 7,182,000	P. 4,463,000	P. 3,866,000
	R. 62,759,000	R. 40,658,000	R. 33,104,000
Fish, Salted or Dried	P. 8,338,000	P. 9,621,000	P. 9,623,000
	R. 14,542,000	R. 13,635,000	R. 13,323,000
Fruit: Oranges and Lemons	R. 4,648,000	R. 5,748,000	R. 3,578,000
Fruits, Dried: Figs, etc	R. 5,398,000	R. 5,821,000	R. 5,642,000
Glass and Glassware	R. 2,226,000	R. 1,933,000	R. 1,843,000
Hides and Skins, Raw	R. 8,496,000	....	....
India-Rubber and Gutta Percha	P. 479,000	P. 581,000	P. 552,000
	R. 21,508,000	R. 19,098,000	R. 18,409,000
Indigo	P. 43,000	P. 48,000	P. 50,000
	R. 2,750,000	R. 2,817,000	R. 2,914,000
Pig Iron	P. 3,165,000	P. 1,847,000	P. 1,114,000
	R. 1,903,000	R. 857,000	R. 5,537,000
Iron Bars, etc.	P. 2,782,000	P. 2,290,000	P. 1,154,000
	R. 4,538,000	R. 2,305,000	R. 1,234,000
Iron: Sheets and Plates	P. 3,017,000	P. 3,105,000	P. 2,584,000
	R. 4,600,000	R. 4,032,000	R. 3,456,000
Lead, in Pigs, Rolls, etc.	P. 3,232,000	P. 2,587,000	P. 2,702,000
Litharge	R. 5,911,000	R. 5,009,000	R. 4,833,000
Metal Wares, Iron	R. 30,864,000	R. 28,164,000	R. 25,974,000
Oils, other than mineral	P. 845,000	P. 905,000	P. 1,081,000
	R. 5,778,000	R. 5,553,000	R. 5,743,000
Plants and Seeds	P. 4,785,000	P. 5,625,000	P. 6,047,000
	R. 9,845,000	R. 11,815,000	R. 13,085,000
Rice	P. 2,951,000	P. 4,174,000	P. 3,625,000
	R. 3,674,000	R. 5,119,000	R. 4,371,000
Silk, Raw	P. 83,000	P. 98,000	P. 108,000
	R. 13,344,000	R. 11,130,000	R. 15,524,000
Silk, Yarn or twist	P. 2,000	P. 3,000	P. 4,000
	R. 568,000	R. 860,000	R. 1,046,000
Manufactures, Silk	R. 4,400,000	R. 3,346,000	R. 3,264,000
Tea	P. 3,493,000	P. 2,887,000	P. 4,368,000
	R. 47,223,000	R.	R. ....
Tobacco, Manufactured and Unmanufactured	P. 57,000	P. 45,000	P. 44,000
	R. 2,266,000	R. 2,512,000	R. 2,504,000
Watches and Clocks	R. 3,227,000	R. 3,289,000	R. 2,483,000

PRINCIPAL ARTICLES IMPORTED INTO RUSSIA.—*Cont.*

Articles	1900	1901	1902
Wine in Casks	P. 569,000 R. 7,485,000	P. 502,000 R. 6,992,000	P. 485,000 R. 7,435,000
Wine in the bottles, sparkling and other	P. 2,028,000 R. 5,439,000	P. 2,007,000 R. 5,643,000	P. 2,069,000 R. 6,019,000
Wool, Raw	P. 927,000 R. 12,556,000	P. 1,067,000 R. 16,461,000	P. 1,280,000 R. 19,094,000
Woollen Yarns	P. 322,000 R. 10,734,000	P. 501,000 R. 17,707,000	P. 509,000 R. 15,762,000
Woollen Manufactures	R. 7,084,000	R. 6,242,000	R. 6,639,000
Total value of principal and other articles	R. 626,375,000	R. 532,944,000	R. 527,095,000

NOTE.—Figures for 1901 and 1902 relate in most cases to trade over the European frontier only.
R.—Ruble ($.515). P.—Pood (36.1 lbs.). B.—Bottle.

Again, this table is its own best commentator. Two or three items of particular interest to American manufacturers may, however, be profitably pointed out. It is noted that the sale of agricultural machinery to Russia in 1902 is over $9,000,000 It will also be observed that these sales of agricultural implements are steadily, though not rapidly, increasing. The annual increase of Russian purchases of agricultural machinery from abroad is suggestive. For example, from 1897 to 1902 Russia bought agricultural implements abroad as follows:

1897	5,590,000	Rubles	1900	13,962,000	Rubles
1898	9,594,000	"	1901	15,867,000	"
1899	12,399,000	"	1902	18,255,000	"

It is thus seen that Russian purchases of agricultural implements from other nations show a steady increase of not far from one million to two million dollars a year. This is not a great deal, it is true. But when it is remembered that Russian agricultural progress is only in its beginning, that agricultural implements of a modern kind are still very sparingly used in the Czar's dominions, and that once their use is well established and the peasantry familiarized with them, their sales to the Russian agricultural millions will be out of all proportion to these small beginnings; that this hour is near at hand, if, indeed it has not already struck; and that, more than all other nations combined, the United States has the advantage in the agricultural implement trade, the importance of this market can be understood.

These remarks are also true of engines and machinery. The very significant fact is, however, to be noted that during the last three years the purchases of foreign engines and machinery by Russia have steadily fallen off, whereas, before 1900, the growth of Russian purchases of engines and machinery were extremely rapid. For example, from 1897 to 1902 Russia bought engines and machinery abroad as follows:

Year	Amount		Year	Amount	
1897	49,204,000	Rubles	1900	62,759,000	Rubles
1898	70,301,000	"	1901	40,658,000	"
1899	98,000,000	"	1902	33,104,000	"

Many causes are given for this decline, but the two principal causes are, first, the growth of Russian factories for the construction of engines and machinery, and, secondly, the tariff wars which Russia has felt compelled to wage with other countries. Particularly is this latter true of Russian purchases from America. The decline in the sales in Russia of American manufactured articles, and especially of machinery and engines, etc., was undoubtedly influenced by the tariff retaliations of Russia to the action of our government in the matter of the export of Russian sugar. Whatever the cause, the fact itself is important, because the field is new and practically unexploited.

XXII

FEBRUARY 19, 1861, THE BIRTHDAY OF RUSSIAN INDUSTRIAL FREEDOM

THE Russian peasant is the Russian nation. The nobility, the clergy, the merchant form important classes, it is true; but the peasant so overwhelmingly outnumbers all other classes combined that when we speak of the Russian people we necessarily mean the Russian peasantry. He it is who tills the soil and fills the factories; he who consumes the tea, drinks the vodka, pays the taxes; he who equips the army and fights the empire's battles; he who mans the ships of Russia's growing fleets; he on whom the whole government rests; he who holds in his breast the destiny of the Slav race.

On the other hand, all institutions of Russia are his; the Greek Orthodox Church is the peasant's Church; in a way not to be comprehended by us, his, in the end, is the Russian government itself. Indeed, most of the great strokes of Russian statesmanship have been brought about by peasant conditions and influences; while, on the other hand, the Autocrat has dealt mercilessly with the nobles. From the days of Ivan the Terrible down to the time of Peter the Great, the Czar of the Russian people smote the nobles with mailed hand; and so, within the memory of living man, the ruler of the Russian people again struck down the nobility and exalted the peasantry in a fashion which in other lands might have caused bloody resistance.

Indeed, in all of its legislation the prejudices, customs, and conditions of the peasant are powerful circumstances influencing the laws formulated by Russian statesmen and issued under the hand of the Czar.

The Autocrat of all the Russias may do what he likes with noble or with merchant; but if he dared trifle with the Russian Church he would find himself confronted with furious millions of peasantry, from one end of his empire to the other. For example, the whole religious world knows how the mere change of one letter in spelling of the word "Jesus" almost caused a revolution and split the ancient Church of Russia into fragments that two centuries have not sufficed to unite. Again, if the Czar should attempt suddenly to destroy the communal system, by which the peasantry live and work in common, all his bayonets could not enforce it.

To understand Russia, then, it is clear we must have some conception of that shaggy, undeveloped, but also unexhausted giant, the Russian peasant. Of course, we cannot even then hope to understand Russia entirely; for, as has been said, no man, Russian or foreigner, can comprehend this strange human mosaic, which is even yet in the process of formation, so contradictory are its various elements and yet so homogeneous; from such different sources, racial and historical, spring the influences which control and form it. Indeed, no attempt will be made to comprehensively describe the peasant himself. But a few fundamental facts may be given which will be helpful in understanding this unfamiliar being of whose work and future this volume so largely deals.

The greatest fact in connection with the Russian peasantry is the emancipation of Russian serfs, proclaimed February 19, 1861. Most other facts lead up to this; all subsequent facts lead down from it. And in addition to this stupendous feat of autocratic statesmanship in the interest of human liberty, affording the view-point from which both the past and the future of the Russian people must be surveyed, it is also the most amazing circumstance of its kind in the history of the world. Indeed, it is the only circumstance of its kind. At first it was thought by some students that the emancipation of the peasant in Prussia and Austria were similar, although on a comparatively small scale. But students now understand that these incidents, while bearing some resemblance to the Russia achievement, were not at all the same thing; while the emancipation of the American slaves by Abraham Lincoln bears only surface resemblance to the emancipation of the Slav bondman. What, then, of this astonishing exercise of autocratic power in the liberation of the humble millions, for whose oppression the autocracy was supposed to exist?

The study of the processes by which the Russian peasant degenerated into slavery is interesting, but neither the purpose nor limits of this volume admit of historical references except where absolutely necessary. At this particular point it is enough to say that in the middle of the nineteenth century the overwhelming majority of the Russian people were serfs. The Russian peasant was a slave. He labored for an absolute master. His toil was the subject of barter like that of cattle or mules. Men and women were bought and sold. This slavery of a nation was attended by most of the degrading effects characteristic of human bondage everywhere.

This was the situation when Alexander the Liberator determined at a single stroke to free the scores of millions of Russian serfs. Nor was this a mere whim of autocratic leniency. The emancipation of the Russian serfs was the result of a national movement. It was dictated by public opinion. The Czar expressed in concrete form the thought of the Russian nation. He merely gave practical effect to the purposes of Russian progress. The elements of the whole mighty question were discussed in Russian novels, much as negro slavery in the United States was brought to the mind and conscience of the American people by similar means. Every phase of the proposed reform was debated in the Russian press. Even

Nicholas, in 1848, had appointed a commission for the study of this tremendous subject; and so it was that the Czar Alexander, in becoming "the Liberator," merely reflected the soul of Russia.

The Russian slave was to be given not only his personal liberty, by which is meant his right to work, and himself enjoy the fruits thereof, instead of being compelled to labor for another without reward; the Russian statesman's thought went farther and declared that this serf should be endowed with land. Not only were his chains to be broken, but he was to be given the implements of livelihood; not only was he to be made as free in his personal relations as the merchant or nobleman who owned him, but he was also to be made the owner of the soil to which he had been chained.

Nor was this all to be done recklessly, thoughtlessly. The details of it were maturely thought out by the commission of experts appointed by the Czar. The vast movement had its own particular statesman in the person of Nicholas Malutin, one of the notable constructive reformers of history. This practical dreamer and his associates, all men of extraordinary ability, singleness of purpose, and martyr-like devotion to high ideals, gave the best work of their lives to solving this complicated problem of progress.

Finally, on February 19, 1861, their work was given practical effect by the proclamation of emancipation pronounced on that day to the assembled peasants in every church of Russia, and from that day until the present time the work of carrying out this vast plan has been in progress. Remembering now that, before this date, the great body of the Russian nation were serfs; remembering that their labor and persons were bought and sold; remembering that they owned not a single foot of land, nor even the miserable huts in which they dwelt; remembering the brutalities to which for ages they had been subjected (though inconsiderable in severity compared to the treatment of serfs or slaves in other countries); remembering these things, let us consider what, by a single act, the Czar of Russia accomplished for these, the real Russian people.

First of all, the serf was given his personal property as his very own. He was given the dwelling in which he lived and the ground on which it stood as his absolute possession. He was endowed with the liberty to labor for himself and use the proceeds of his toil as he might see fit; and, lastly, he was given, under provisions for its payment, land which now amounts to upward of four hundred million acres. This was done in order to make the people of Russia a land-owning people. It was done to give them a permanent and inalienable "stake in the country." The Czar desired that an empire of land-owning nobles should be transformed into an empire of land-owning people. And this rule was applied impartially to the serfs and lands belonging to the Czar himself (to "the Crown," as the technical expression is), as well as to the lands and slaves belonging to the nobles.

It was as if the United States, when it freed the negro slaves from their Southern masters, had at the same time given them, under provisions for payment, the lands of their late owners. Nor is this comparison sufficiently radical. If at the time of our civil war four-fifths of the people of the United States had been slaves, we should have had, comparatively speaking, the situation which confronted Russian reformers when Alexander issued his ukase of freedom. Nor does this adequately state the relative situations. If, in addition to this overwhelming majority of slave population, the land of the United States had been held by a very small fraction of the already small number who were not slaves, we should have had precisely the agrarian conditions which existed in Russia on February 19, 1861. And if, with these conditions existing in the United States at the time of our civil war, this immense majority of our population, being slaves, had suddenly been made free, and hundreds of millions of acres of land had been taken from the private owners thereof and placed in the possession of the newly freed slaves, we should have had exactly the social and industrial revolution which the Russian Czar effected by his autocratic signature.

In thus taking from the nobles the land which belonged to them, and giving it to the slaves, it made no difference that the noble objected. A maximum and minimum amount of land, belonging to the nobles, was fixed by the government, and with this he was compelled to part, whether he wanted to or not. On the other hand, the peasants were compelled to take at least the minimum amount of land, whether they wanted to or not. This minimum of land was calculated to be sufficient to serve the needs of the community which was compelled to take it, for the land went to the communities and not to the individual peasants. Any attempt to force the land on individual peasants would have been fruitless. Accustomed as he is to living and working in common, the Russian peasant was incapable of taking and cultivating the land individually, as an American farmer does, if, indeed, the Russian is not incapable of doing this as a matter of nature.

Within certain limits the peasant and the proprietor were permitted to make their own terms, and to these terms, once made, both parties were compelled to adhere. For example, one provision of the law permitted the noble proprietor to give absolutely, and without payment, one-fourth of the maximum of the land designated by the government to the peasant; and if the peasant accepted it, the noble proprietor was released from the necessity of parting with any more of his land. In many instances the peasant availed himself of this provision, being influenced by the universal human desire to get something for nothing, with the result that such peasants soon found themselves comparatively impoverished.

As in every undertaking of large dimensions, even when most carefully thought out, it was found that this great reform did not work as well as had been expected. For example, where arrangements had been made between the noble and the peasant for payment for the land thus taken from the noble and sold to the peasant, the peasant was still to be under "temporary obligations" until the payment was made. It was found that these "temporary obligations" were rapidly degenerating into the conditions of serfdom from which the whole movement was designed to lift him. On the other hand, the noble was seriously crippled in the operation of his estate by a reform which changed everything and yet left old conditions. It can be truthfully said that a few years after the emancipation, agriculturally and economically, Russia was in a state of chaos.

The government promptly came to the aid of both peasant and noble. It was arranged that the government itself should pay the noble for the land, and that the peasant should be responsible for his payment to the government, instead of to the noble. This involved an immediate expenditure on the part of the Russian government so immense that no treasury could stand the drain; and, therefore, government scrip or bonds of two classes was issued to the nobles in payment of the lands of which they had thus been deprived. Both of these classes of government securities were negotiable, one of them easily and the other with difficulty. The nobles, finding themselves in sore financial need, immediately disposed of their securities, which, of course, depreciated; and it is still the wonder of students of the science of money that Russia escaped a financial catastrophe from which she could not recover. But, while experiencing embarrassments, the empire passed through the crisis without serious difficulty.

The consequences to the nobles were desperate and permanent. Large numbers of them, following the profligate habits of their former lives, squandered their cash and mortgaged the remainder of their holdings. In this way many splendid estates have passed from noble into capitalist hands. Others of the nobility embarked in commercial and manufacturing pursuits, with varying degrees of success. Through the change wrought by the emancipation, it may be said that the Russian nobility, as a class, were all but ruined. Vast estates in Russia are still held in noble hands, but they are insignificant compared with the holdings of half a century ago, and thousands of Russian nobles have become both moneyless and landless.

On the other hand, the peasants, of course, could not immediately pay for the lands which the great majority of them had been forced to take. This was true even where the peasantry availed themselves of the provisions of the emancipation and voluntarily took over the lands of the nobles. So the government arranged that the peasant might repay the government in instalments. These instalments were to continue for a period of forty-nine years, capitalized at six per cent. on the value of the lands estimated in dues. This annual payment of six per cent. was to extinguish, in that period of time, the peasant's entire indebtedness, both principal and interest. To facilitate this process, as well as to aid the nobility with its scrip, land banks were established all over the empire. Even this was not enough. The peasants were continually falling into arrears, and more than once the government has extended the time of the peasant's payments, and it is said that remittances of arrears have more than once been made. Indeed, it is proposed to remit the entire remaining indebtedness of the peasantry for the land which it now owns.

The effect of this unparalleled act of statesmanship has been complex, far-reaching, and contradictory. In Russia you can get no two opinions about it that entirely agree. Any view expressed will be contradicted by some one.

It was not entirely satisfactory to anybody. The nobles bitterly complained after they had, by reckless expenditure or bad investments, been seriously injured or absolutely ruined. The peasants complained because it was inconvenient to make the payments for the land with which they had been endowed. Indeed, they objected to making any payments at all. They had heard of the emancipation which was coming, and they had looked upon it as an event which would not only give them their personal liberty, but also bestow upon them, without money and without price, the lands of the nobles.

You will be informed by authority whose disinterestedness and accuracy you cannot possibly doubt, that there are peasants in Russia who still look for a second emancipation, giving them new additions of land absolutely and without any cost whatever to themselves. They soon forgot the severities of serfdom, and remembered only the comparatively trivial inconveniences of the present. Also, as their families increased and the lands owned by entire communes had to be subdivided into smaller lots, the amount given them by the original emancipation has gradually and rapidly become insufficient, although it was sufficient at the time of the emancipation. This difficulty is partly overcome by emigration to Siberia and by the increased manufacturing industries which take numbers of the commune, through a portion of the year at least, to the great factory centres.

Again, a curious set of conditions arose which has given all parties concerned endless trouble, but which, of course, cannot be said to be insurmountable. For example, when the Russian peasant was the slave of his owner he felt perfectly free to use all his master's tools, implements, and other property; indeed, it was his duty. He has not yet been able to get it through his head that although he is released from the obligation of working for nothing for his master, he is not correspondingly obliged to refrain from using everything belonging to his master, as in the old days. Again, in the days of bondage he was at liberty to cut from the forests on his master's domains the timber necessary to build himself a house, or for any other purposes; and even to the present day he is not able to understand why, when there happens to be no forests on the lands belonging to his commune, he may not cut timber from the lands of the man who was formerly his master, exactly as he used to do.

The most curious situations are even yet arising, growing out of this inability of the peasant to comprehend the obligation as well as the benefits of his emancipation. Liberties are taken by the Russian peasant with the property of a Russian proprietor which would not be tolerated for an instant by an American in the same situation. In all of this there is not the slightest impertinence, not the least intention to wrong the landed proprietor, nor the faintest conception on the part of the peasant that there is anything immoral in what he does. He or his fathers did the like before, and he just continues to do the same as a matter of course. Nevertheless, this inability to distinguish property rights is gradually fading away. When the peasant is remonstrated with he is all humility and repentance, and this humility is real and this repentance is very genuinely felt.

Another curious effect of emancipation upon the Russian peasant was the occurrence of the exact reverse of what Americans would expect to happen under like circumstances. It would be urged by the theorists here, or indeed anywhere, that for people formerly slaves to be given their liberty, and formerly landless to be presented with farms, would necessarily induce them to greater individual effort and to improved methods of agriculture. Indeed, this very argument was asserted with vehemence and iteration in Russia itself, as one of the expected beneficent results of liberation; but nothing of the kind immediately occurred. Indeed, nothing of the kind became manifest for several decades. On the contrary, the first effects were the exact reverse; and this might have been expected had the Russian reformers looked through the spectacles of the practical instead of gazing into the mists of fancy. For the Russian slave who found himself thus suddenly freed and equipped with independent land holdings actually retrograded agriculturally. This is true, notwithstanding the fact that it is hard to think that agriculture could retrograde in Russia, so bad was it at that time, so bad is it even now.

But the Russian peasant lacks initiative. As has been pointed out, this appears to be a racial peculiarity of the Slav. Also, an influence common to all countries worked within the breast of the newly liberated serf—he had yielded simple obedience to simple command in the old days. He was merely ordered about and did precisely what he was directed to do; so when he was left, in a measure, to shift for himself, he did not know what to do. Before the emancipation many of the nobles were beginning to introduce new methods of agriculture; indeed, large numbers of them were doing this, but even with the aid of their authority, intelligent direction, and abundance of ready money with which to buy implements, improved methods of agriculture were introduced with the greatest possible difficulty. Even these progressive nobles found it hard to get the peasant to abandon the methods of his forefathers, so deeply steeped was he in custom. The Russian peasant is saturated with precedent.

Nevertheless, of course, under the old conditions thus briefly described, perceptible progress was making. But with the new order of things established by the emancipation the authority of the noble over the peasant was abolished, his financial ability paralyzed, and, worst of all, his personal interest, which influenced him to improve Russian agricultural methods, was suddenly extinguished. So one of the first effects of emancipation was a positive reaction in agricultural progress. No new farm implements for the freed slave; he refused to use them when he was a serf except upon the insistent orders of his lord; very well, he certainly would not use them now. No iron or steel ploughs for him; he found them heavy and difficult in the days of bondage; now in the days of liberty he would return to or continue the wooden plough of his youth. No reaper for him; the few of his brothers whom certain advanced nobles had compelled to work those awkward machines never understood them; and, now that he was free, his hands and his sickle were quite good enough. And, besides, all of these innovations of the evil one were expensive. And did not the good Czar require him even to pay for the land that he had been compelled to take?

This agricultural retrogression furnished multitudes of instances with which pessimists in and out of Russia fortified their arguments against the possibility of any real material advancement in the conditions of the Russian people; but to the man who looked beyond the hour a more hopeful horizon appeared. It was inevitable that in time the Russian peasant, having grown accustomed to his new industrial independence, would himself perceive the advantage of better m thods of farming. It was clear, too, that it would be not only the interest but the actual necessity of the government to instruct him to use the modern inventions in the tilling of his land and to aid agricultural industry by every possible means.

And of course, just these plainly inevitable things are beginning to arrive—have even now arrived to a degree astonishing when we consider the condition of the Russian peasant within the memory of living men and take into account also his racial lethargy. Everywhere throughout the empire the latest agricultural implements are being introduced. You may now find the most improved threshing-machines at work in more than one-quarter of the Czar's domain. American reapers may actually be said to be numerous, and if the use of steel ploughs continues to grow as it has recently grown they will be in practically universal employment among the scores of millions of Russian farmers before two decades have passed away. A single illustration will show how the Russian peasant, whose father was a slave and whose ancestors for generations have known nothing but the wooden plough, is now taking to the steel implement instead, and how the government is encouraging him.

After a long day's journey in the agricultural districts of the "black belt" (the black-soil district of Russia), we came to a country town which was the seat of local government for that particular section. In this town is a large store for the supply of the simple needs of that agricultural neighborhood, and here great numbers of steel ploughs of different sizes and prices were found. They were of Russian manufacture, and sold to the peasant at very little above the cost of the making and the transportation.

"Oh yes," said a young man who had charge of this department, himself a peasant, "we sell great numbers of these ploughs and the demand is rapidly increasing."

"Yes," said my Russian friend, "the worst pessimist now admits that our common people are at last making tangible progress in agricultural industry, and I must admit that the government seems to be waking up in this vital department of our national life. It is doing all it can to encourage every agricultural improvement among the people. And that the people on their side are taking kindly to it is evidenced not only by the sales of these ploughs, but by the more important circumstance that this is a co-operative store. The whole enterprise is a mutual undertaking. There is no profit in it for any one, and the prices of the various things there sold are only enough above their actual cost to pay the expenses of running the establishment."

It is said that these little communistic establishments are forming all over the empire. They are very much like the granger store with which the American public became familiar in the great farmer movement of the seventies. Their bottom idea is similar to that of those American socialistic enterprises which with us flourished for a few brief months and then died at the hands of that individualism which appears to be an ineradicable part of the Anglo-Saxon nature. But it is by no means certain that a like fate awaits the Russian granger store. Indeed, it is more probable that it will endure; for it has back of it the racial tendency of the Russian to do business on the communistic principle. Where like undertakings by Americans or Englishmen, or even Germans, would first be interrupted by contentions and then distracted by quarrels, and finally break down by the inability of the various members of the association to agree among themselves, the same number of Russians get along very well together, and practically without antagonism. In addition to this it must be remembered that the influence of the government is always favorable to every form of communistic industry. Indeed, the Russian state may be said to be at the bottom communistic. The government's policy in this particular is not so much the plan of cunning statecraft as it is obedience to the tendencies, conditions, and natural aptitudes of the Russian people.

Again, instead of increasing the independence, alertness, and energy of the Russian peasant, the first effect of the emancipation was the contrary. The shiftlessness of the slave became the lethargy of the freedman. In bondage the serf worked only as much as he was forced to; in liberty the freedman would work just as little as he possibly could. But this effect also was, historically speaking, temporary, although it has taken decades to work a change. Indeed, the unsympathetic foreign observer who usually contents himself with a little country journey of a day or two out of Moscow or some other large Russian city, where he spends most of his time in witnessing cathedrals and admiring pictures, will declare that the Russian agricultural laborer is hopeless as respects his personal industry, his methods of farming, and his character as a man. And such an observer will cite scores of instances to establish the truth of this generalization.

For example, the writer observed within easy sight of Moscow itself a peasant ploughing land with the same kind of wooden implements with which his ancestors tilled the same soil in the days of the Tartar subjugation. Bare-headed, his profuse mane of hair loose to the winds, his cotton blouse belted around him, his one poor horse hitched to the ancient plough which his own hands had hewed from some tree cut down by himself—this peasant looked like the fifteenth century personified at work in the early dawn of the twentieth century.

But these are only the remains of the ancient conditions that are passing away even more rapidly than any rational thinker might have expected; for it is not good sense to expect that the conditions of ages are to be transformed in a day, a year, or a generation. Nature works slowly in all of her processes; and she works just as leisurely in transforming the soul of man as in modifying vegetation. So many people expect things to occur instantly. Time, which is the great factor in all human development, is so seldom taken into account. And when you do take time into account, and also take into account that past out of which present conditions grew, the sane observer of the Russian industrial situation in the country districts must admit that real, substantial, and, historically speaking, even rapid progress is being made.

"No one need talk to me about Russian popular progress," said a young American gentleman who last year made a journey through the empire from the German frontier to the shores of the Yellow Sea.

"The Russian peasant," continued he, "has not the faintest conception of what manhood means. For example, we were going along a country-road in our carriage, which was not at all ostentatious. We passed some moujiks. Off went every cap, and bowed in shameful obsequiousness was every head. It was both disgusting and pitiful."

This young American gentleman, a graduate of Yale, a man of wide travel and exceptional culture, was unable to see anything in this but the slavishness of soul of the Russian peasant; and this was to him a confirmation of his preconceived belief that the oppressions of the government have extinguished every spark of self-respect in the Russian people, and carefully kept it from being rekindled. Yet his interpretation of what he saw, and on which he based his reasoning, was wide of the mark; for this apparent humility was in large measure the Russian peasant's method of being polite. The obsequiousness of it was due to the custom established when these peasants or their fathers were slaves, and when that method of salute had for generations been a custom; and once a custom among the Russians, always a custom.

Formerly anybody who rode in a carriage was certainly a landed proprietor, and, therefore, a noble and an owner of serfs. So now he who rides in a carriage must certainly be a person of consequence, to whom deference is due merely as a matter of politeness. Also, the Oriental strain in the Russian blood must be taken into account. And every one knows that the Oriental will go through profound prostrations and a magnificent eloquence of gladness on greeting a superior, which do not mean anything more than the casual nod of the head, shake of the hand, or our "how do you do?" means among ourselves. So the exaggerated deference which the

Russian peasant pays to any one who seems to be a person of consequence must not be mistaken for any lack of personal independence.

Of this independence, a story which you will hear over and over again in Russia is an excellent illustration. It is said that, at the exact hour when the peasants understood that their emancipation would be proclaimed, a certain noble was travelling in his carriage with coachman, footman, and other servants. Also, he was a man particularly beloved by his serfs. At midnight of the day of emancipation his vehicle was in the thick of a forest through which the road passed. When the serfs were quite sure that it was an hour past the time of their promised liberation, the horses were stopped and the coachman, footman, and all the rest of them came courteously to the door, cap in hand, and, profoundly bowing, wished their former master good-night; and, in spite of his expostulations, threats, and pleadings, they left him. They did this, so it is said, to show him that he no longer owned them. They meant to demonstrate that they were freemen.

Of course this story, which is so well embedded in current Russian anecdote that it is almost folk-lore now, is entirely untrue; for the kindliness and consideration of the Russian nature would never permit the peasants to do such a thing. But there is absolutely no doubt that many thousands of incidents showing the peasants' personal independence did occur.

With all of the immediate apparent ill effects of the emancipation (which are here recited to correct any misapprehension of the character of the Russian peasant), the permanent and hopeful results are even now beginning to appear. In comparison with the American farmer, the intelligence of the Russian farmer is very low; but in comparison with what you are told of the density of the Russian serf of less than half a century ago, the intelligence of the Russian farmer of to-day is credible. In comparison with the wide-awakeness of the American, the alertness of the Russian is somnolent; but, in comparison with his former blindness as a serf, his eyes are now fairly opened.

Slowly but surely he is coming to an understanding of the meaning of his independence, the rights of property, the commercial value of truth, the good effects of personal industry, the happy consequences of applying new methods in his work, the sure results of economy—in short, all of the lessons which personal industrial liberty teaches human nature anywhere are being learned by the Russian peasant. And so it is that the common man is appearing in the modern Russian; the serf is developing into self-mastery; the Russian peasant, who is the Russian nation, is gradually evolving into a knowledge of his own powers through the exercise of his own industrial liberty given him by the Czar at the expense of the Russian nobility.

And while this Russian peasant, who was but yesterday a slave, is thus slowly becoming a man, with all that manhood means, his loyalty to his Czar is taking deeper and deeper root. But while this evolution is in progress, his racial instinct to dwell and labor in socialistic communities has not perceptibly abated. He still continues to.be the social being as opposed to the individual being. He is willing to undertake any enterprise, perform any labor, brave any danger in company with his fellows; but he is not yet willing to go it alone. And no student or observer of Russian character with whom the writer ever talked believes that the time will ever come when the Russian people will ever proceed upon anything but communistic lines either in their social living or in their industrial efforts.

Here, then, is the Russian man, the Russian nation, with whom the world must deal. Here is the man who is planting replicas of the ancient Muscovite community over the agricultural portions of Siberia and making of that imperial domain another Russia. Here is the man who, floating down the Amur on his raft, or toiling eastward with his impossible wagon, or even travelling towards the rising sun on foot, or going by companies of hundreds and thousands on his world railway, is indolently launching himself on Manchuria and the Far East.

This is the man who has arrived at the Pacific and looks with dreamy eyes upon the world's waters towards which he has instinctively been pushing for hundreds of years. And, finally, here is the man whom we Americans must study and consider, if we expect our foreign statesmanship, wherever it touches Russia, to be intelligent and therefore wise. And remember, too, that he is yet a man in the making. The Great Moulder of all human agencies is not yet done with his fashioning of this Russian man of the future. But we may even now see some of the outlines of His large handiwork. We behold this human being, about whom all the world is talking, humorous, patient, obedient, with brain and nerves and heart stored with the sleepy energies of centuries of stolid living; for Russian energy is a field long fallow, in which, nevertheless, the first furrow has already been turned.

XXIII

HOLY RUSSIA, THE ORTHODOX NATION

YOU may know all about the industrial and social life of the Russian peasant—you may know how he works and how he lives; but you know nothing about him, after all, unless you know the religious side of him, and the religious side of him is all sides of him. It has been noted that he is a social being, as distinguished from an individual being. And he is even more of a religious being than he is a communistic being. "Faith," said a Russian friend, "is as necessary to the Russian peasant as food or air." That we may make a little more definite what must at best be our vague understanding of this human force which is now taking the attention of the world, and with whom all nations must deal in the future, let us observe the Russian people from the religious point of view.

The icon is a little picture or image of the Saviour, the Virgin, or of some Russian saint.

In the telegraph-office on the Amur hangs the icon; in the private office of the Minister of Finance at St. Petersburg hangs the icon; in the peasant cottage, far out on the plains of Russia, hangs the icon; in the saloon and in almost every room in the passenger-boat on the Volga hangs the icon; in the head offices of the great manufacturing establishments you will find the icon; in the palatial homes of lordly wealth, the icon; in vodka shops again the icon; in the basest places of sin, still the icon.

Always and everywhere in Russia is this holy presentment. It is the outward and visible emblem of a religious feeling instinctive, profound, racial—a religious *feeling*, more than the intelligent idea of any concrete faith. And be sure that it is a feeling really religious, and not, as almost every traveller will at first assert, merely superstitious. Not that the Slav is not superstitious. He is superstitious, but he is genuinely religious too. These sacred images, in one form or another, are frequent in the streets of the great cities. It is profitable to stroll quietly down any thoroughfare of the Russian capital. Devote several of these strolls exclusively to observation of the people's manifestations of adoration. To be sure that the practices you will observe are habitual, take a week-day instead of a Sunday.

There is an icon on the other side of the street. Observe the poor and humble moujik as he passes it. Off goes his cap; his body reverentially bows; his lips move, apparently in the recitation of a brief formula of prayer; meanwhile he makes with his hand the Russian sign of the cross. This sign of the cross is unlike the briefer Roman Catholic observance. The forehead is touched where rested the crown of thorns, the side is touched where entered the cruel spear, and other motions make it a condensed reproduction of the Saviour's crucifixion on Calvary, quickly done and yet comprehensive. On goes the moujik. Here now comes a merchant. Clearly, this man is well-to-do. His comparatively rich clothing indicates that. He will pass it. He has been "emancipated" from the custom which the moujik's "ignorance" and "superstition" and all that compel him yet to perform. But off goes the merchant's cap, too, and he does exactly as did the moujik. A woman of good condition comes along. Her reverence is even deeper. The clatter of horses' hoofs is heard. A carriage comes, bearing an officer. He is a man of high rank, too. You have learned that from the uniform. He must be going to an audience of some kind or other, for he wears certain orders, which his unbuttoned great military overcoat, flying back, reveals on his breast. Surely this military commander of the forces of that autocrat who is also the head of the Church (not theoretically, but in the people's mind) will not observe this "nonsense." Besides, he is going too fast. But with hardly slackening speed the officer and his coachman alike perform precisely the poor moujik's obeisance, mutter apparently the same reverent words, make precisely the same holy sign. Clearly, this observance is mortised very firmly into the external habits of the Russian people.

Go to Moscow now. There you will find the same practice, if anything intensified. Now travel into the country districts. Here is not the slightest difference between what you observed upon the street in St. Petersburg, unless, indeed, you feel as you watch that there is a deeper fervor on the part of the adorers of Him of the thorn-crowned head, who, after all, is, in the hearts and minds of the Russian people, the real prince and lord of them all; for in the Russian mind the Saviour is their real ruler and protector; and in the common thought, the popular belief, the people's conviction (however, not, of course, in the theory of the Church itself), the Czar is His personal representative on earth. To this may be traced a large part (and many versed in Russian life assert by far the larger part) of the profound hold which the Czar has on the loyalty of the Russian millions—a loyalty not understood, and perhaps not to be understood, by Americans or non-Russian Europeans.

"I-con," said a successful and typical American business man of large affairs, with whom the writer spent several days, "it is a good name. This whole thing is a big confidence game. These priests rob the people. Look at the treasures of jewels and gold heaped up in their churches, and all that. They take it from the people. Do not tell me that these priests do not know better. Do not tell me that this government is not simply playing on the superstitions of the masses. I tell you, the whole thing, the Church and the government, too, is the greatest confidence game ever played upon a people."

"Is it not unbearable," said a cultivated English lady, who, however, herself was a High Church woman—"is it not unbearable," said she, "all of this miserable superstition?"

These two views fairly well represent the common opinion of the American, English, German, or French traveller through Russia. The writer is compelled to believe that such views are widely inaccurate. Superstition there undoubtedly is in Russia, perhaps more so than in any other Christian country, but religion there is, too; and there is more of the genuinely religious aspiration, of the pure Christian spirit, of worship, in short, in what to some travellers is "mummery," in the habitual religious practices of the Russian people than there is of superstition.

In a magnificent cathedral of St. Petersburg two Americans stood uncovered, observing the beauty of the pictured works of art, uplifted by the majesty of the architecture, humbled, as every sensitive mind must be, by that strange feeling of reverence that comes into the consciousness of every one of us when standing under the arches of any noble religious edifice or in the presence of the sublime lift of a mighty mountain, or on shipboard in the middle of the ocean at starry and moonless midnight. An occasional worshipper entered. Here was only a poorly dressed child of the people. Straightway she went to the life-size sacred picture, and, kneeling, kissed its feet. After a while came another, apparently a woman of wealth and rank, for she was richly and daintily attired, and bore in her demeanor evidence of training and culture. And she also did the like.

"Do these people really believe and feel anything of a religious nature when they do all these things?" asked the visitor of a Russian gentleman, educated out of Russia, and of learning and travel not surpassed by any president or professor of any American college or university. He was himself a dissenter from the Russian Greek Orthodox Church on its religious side, but a stanch adherent of it on its national side (for you must know, as will be pointed out later, that the Russian Church is first a religious institution, and, second, a patriotic organization; and the paradox is quite common of a man or of a woman who will tell you they reject the Church on its religious side, and yet who are hot adherents of the Church because it represents the nation more even than the government does, and is by far the most powerful influence in unifying the Russian people). And precisely this question is the first one asked by any American or non-Russian European when told of these devotional exercises habitually in use among all of the people throughout all the dominions of the Czar.

"Yes, indeed," answered this cosmopolitan Russian; "I know what you are thinking. You are thinking that this is mere form on the part of these people. You are thinking that at the very moment when they are apparently mentally and spiritually prostrating themselves before an icon, their minds are, in reality, intent on their business or their work or their intrigues. You could make no greater mistake. I, who, as you know, am not impressed at all by this sort of thing, tell you that nine hundred and ninety-nine out of every one thousand of our people are really, truly, deeply, reverently religious. They mean every item and particular of what their action implies. They believe fervently, unquestionably, devoutly. It is not a matter of mental process with them at all. They make no argument about it. With them God is a fact—the greatest fact in the universe. To them the Saviour is His only begotten Son. There is some superstition in it, of course; but, taking all that into account, there is more genuine religion in it than there is among any people whom, in all my travels around the world, I have observed."

This information was tested in many ways—by similar

questions to men of different opinions, occupations, and stations in life; by careful scrutiny of these customs in their various forms, in points of the empire thousands of miles apart—and the conclusion was forced, by these various lines of inquiry, that the interpretation given in the conversation above quoted is far nearer the truth than the bitter sarcasm of the American business-man and the English lady of culture above quoted.

That there is superstition mingled in all this reverence is believed to be undoubtedly true. Not only are the obeisance, the murmur of prayer, the sign of the cross physical manifestations of the religious feeling of the men and women who perform them; with most of them they are also a sort of incantation, a kind of formula of motion and words directed against the evil eye and the unseen powers of darkness, which, to the Russian mind, are in the air about us. The average Russian would probably ascribe any ill-luck which might chance upon him to his failure to observe these reverential practices.

"Yes," said a highly educated Russian, "the truth is that even the best of us feel that there are unseen powers to be propitiated; but, speaking for myself and what I feel to be an intimate knowledge of our own people, I beg you to believe that most of this is serious, earnest worship."

Friends were driving in the national Russian vehicle, the troika (a carriage with three horses, with which everybody who has seen any picture of any kind representing Russian life is familiar), across the seemingly limitless plains of agricultural Russia. It was not one hundred miles from Moscow. It was ancient land therefore.

"This column of trees," said the Russian gentleman, "was planted by the great Catharine." He referred to an avenue of fine elms enclosing the roadway on either side for many versts. "I have forgotten," said he, "what caprice was in her mind when she did this, but we are much obliged to her for it. You see what a beautiful variation it makes in the monotony of this journey."

"But what can this be?" said the American, pointing ahead. Up the road, half a mile away, a banner was seen advancing, followed by what, at a distance, appeared to be a column of people.

"You are in luck," responded the Russian friend. "We will drive to the side of the road and wait. This particular thing is a ceremony that you might have stayed a year in Russia and not witnessed. If I am not mistaken, it is a religious procession of the common people, praying for rain."

Sure enough, he was right. As the strange company approached, you could see peasant men and women running from the fields to join it. At its head marched a blond, broad-shouldered peasant, perhaps thirty years of age. Bare-headed, blue-eyed, ruddy of countenance, fair of brow, with long, yellow hair, trousers in boots, he was for all the world the ideal Russian we all have in our imaginations. He bore above him a banner, hanging from a cross-piece attached to the staff which he held in his hand. This banner, to the uninstructed observer, was very much like any one that you may see in the procession of some secret order in this country. On it was the pictured form and features of some Russian saint. The standard-bearer's eyes and face were lifted towards the skies. His lips moved in appeal, and behind him came perhaps seventy-five or one hundred peasant men and women, their whole souls apparently intent on fervent prayer.

"Yes, I was right," said the Russian gentleman; "they are asking the heavens for rain. They believe they will get it, too, if they are earnest enough in asking for it, and sincere enough in repenting for their sins or the sins of somebody or other who brought the catastrophe of this drought upon us in this part of Russia."

"I am glad you saw that," remarked a Russian interested in Church affairs. "It illustrates the character of our people, and the great task the Church has on hand, after all—a task which you Americans do not understand, and, perhaps, cannot understand. The ancestors of all of our people were pagan, as you, of course, know. Only a few years ago the great majority of them were serfs. Then, too, please remember, we are all Slavs. It is in our blood to believe in something. So you will find that a great many of the Russian superstitions, centuries old, and having their roots far back yonder in pagan times, still exist, only Christianized in form, if you will permit the expression. It is no easy thing to stamp them out. They must be taken into serious account.

"So you will observe that from a religious point of view the great duty, the vast work of the Russian Church is to instruct these people in the simple tenets of right and wrong—in the fundamentals of faith in God and Christ and personal immortality. Thus, slowly, very slowly, paganism's superstitions, imparted from remote antiquity, are being extinguished; but to violently try to cast them out suddenly would be worse than useless, for such a process, even if successful, would tear growing Christian faith as well as declining pagan superstition out together at the same time. It would be a realization of the injunction against too violently pulling up the tares —'Nay, lest while ye gather up the tares, ye root up also the wheat with them.'"

And the more you look into this side of Russian character, the more you will see in this comment. The Russian people believe, without any qualification, in a personal God. The Russian peasants have no more question about that than they have about the existence of the soil they till, of the air they breathe, or any material form with which they come in contact. As has been said, they also believe in Christ as His only begotten Son, and in immortality, and in the power of heaven saints. Indeed, Christianity made conquest of the Russian people with greater ease than it overcame the paganism of Germany,

Scandinavia, or any other country. There was something about the sweetness, charity, and humility of the Christian faith that instinctively appealed to the Slav; for, whatever may be said to the contrary, the truth is that the Slav is, by nature, humble, sweet-hearted, charitable.[1]

But, nevertheless, the very ease with which Christianity established its dominion over the Russian nature left remaining many of the old pagan observances, and so you see, side by side with what your eyes and ears

[1] A Danish gentleman of some twenty years experience with the Russians was asked what he considered their chief characteristic. He quickly answered, "Oh, undoubtedly the principal element of Russian character is kindliness." The same question was put to a German of large affairs, very great familiarity with the Russian people, and of undoubted probity of character. After thinking for some time he replied, "It is hard to say that one characteristic is more pronounced than another; and yet if the most prominent trait of the Russian had to be selected I am sure that all who know him would say that it is his desire to please others." Again, the French consul at a certain port, who has lived in Russia many years, was requested to give his opinion. He responded, as promptly as the Dane, that, "Certainly the distinguishing feature of Russian character is the wish not to offend —the pleasure the Russian takes in obliging others."

These are samples from notes of several score of like expressions from men whose intercourse with and knowledge of the Russian people qualify them to speak with authority. Even the young American Russophobist elsewhere quoted said in the same conversation, "I will admit that the Russian has charm. Much as I hate the Russians, that quality of their character is undeniable."

No contrary view was heard in numerous conversations in many different parts of the empire and in several different countries.

Yet this estimate of Russian character sharply conflicts with those violent outbursts of peasant ferocity of which the world hears occasional accounts. The writer's personal observations confirm the judgment of the competent witnesses above quoted; and this, too, is the conclusion of the most careful students. Still the instances of popular frenzies of cruelty are authentic. Again, therefore, we face that familiar thing in Russia, elsewhere noted, the paradox.

compel you to believe to be genuine devotion to the highest religious ideals and a pure and lofty faith, very simple, childlike, absurd superstition.

Let him who doubts the intense devotion of the Russian mind attend the services of the Orthodox Greek Church. Any church will do, and any service will do, but preferably take some notable cathedral beloved of and frequented by the people. If possible, let him attend upon the day of some Christian celebration. Of all the churches of the empire, let the traveller, if he can, choose the cathedral in the Kremlin at Moscow. Before the altar all people, in the opinion of the Russians, are one. The noble, the peasant, the millionaire, the pauper, the native, the foreigner—there is no distinction on account of any human conditions. All are human souls, all worshippers of the one and only most high God.

So you have difficulty in entrance only because the great audience-chamber is already packed with worshippers. There are no seats. No grave usher directs you to a decent pew. You must stand. And here the people stood—the Russian people in miniature—a tiny atom, but reproducing, in every detail, the vast empire made up of millions of similar atoms. Here are working-men and working-women. Here are richly dressed, highly educated ladies, leaders of society. Here are small tradesmen and by their side great manufacturers. Here are officers, and beside them, or perhaps in front of them, for that matter, common soldiers. There stands a Russian nobleman who still holds vast estates and bears one of the ancient names of the empire, and by his side stands a cab-driver.

And this historic chamber, too, is the spot where, for hundreds of years, the Czars of Russia have been crowned. A little back of the centre is a small, raised dais, or platform, perhaps a foot in height, where the Czar and Czarina take their places during the coronation ceremonies. Yet the people stood on it, too. The writer found himself crowded, by the movement of the throng, close to this spot. Immediately before him stood a young workingman from the country. He might have been the twin brother of the peasant who bore the banner in the procession praying for rain, above described. As the service proceeded, time and again he would sink to his knees and bend his forehead to the floor. Instinctively the crowd made room for these fervent prostrations which here and there all over the church were taking place. Otherwise, they excited no curiosity. Evidently the mind of every auditor was doing the same thing. Everywhere all eyes were intent on the altar and the priest. From their faces shone the fervor of a faith which you may see nowhere in America, except at our occasional revivals. All heads frequently bowed, and all hands as often made the sign of the holy cross. The most hardened infidel, the most *blasé* man of the world, the most blasphemous scoffer cannot, on one of these occasions, fail to feel an atmosphere of religious exaltation. Prayer, devotion, adoration are in the air.

Prayer, devotion, adoration, exaltation are in the service, too. The singing especially is rich and sweet.

"You must not fail," said an American friend in Paris, "to hear the singing on some notable occasion in one of the great Russian cathedrals. Until you have heard that, you have never heard religious music." And in that he was quite right. Whatever else you miss in Russia, do not fail to hear the vocal music of religious Russia. It is futile to attempt to describe it, except, perhaps, to note the luxuriant wealth of the bass voices.

"You know," said a Russian lady, "that we are so vain and provincial as to think that there is no bass-singing in the world except in our cathedrals."

The statement is made that the priests who conduct the services in Russian cathedrals are selected always with a view to the depth and richness of their voices. One would be compelled to believe it from the service here poorly described. Deep, sonorous, mellow, without effort, the voice of the priest was the sound of virile, unexhausted, elemental vocalinity itself, suppressed, purified, beautified by devotion and lofty spiritual feeling.

You may go when you like, but do not go until, after a brief space, the doors behind the altar open and you look into a distant room, golden with holy religious emblems (which, of course, you will not understand), and mysterious with gray-haired priests and swinging censers, and the rising smoke of incense. Indeed, stay through it all, from beginning to end. It is something you will never forget, and something which will interpret "Holy Russia" to you as nothing else can possibly do. And when you go away, you go enriched with a consciousness that, granting all that is said of their superstition, there is a depth and breadth of religious life in Russia as pure and lofty as the world has seen since the Master lived and taught, and, for the sins of mankind, on Calvary died. You may try to reason yourself out of it; you may debate with this one or that one, but you will come into possession of an internal and personal knowledge of that subject which no debating or arguing or reasoning can shake, much less overthrow.

Indeed, all the writers who have with intelligent and sympathetic insight looked into Russian character have admitted in the last analysis that it is saturated with a pure religion and uplifted by a sincere faith. No analysis of the growth of Christianity in Russia is here attempted, of course, nor is any account of the doctrines and constitution of the Greek Orthodox Church assumed to be set forth. All that is here attempted is to give a faithful statement of things observed, and discriminating conversations throwing light upon them. It is sought simply to place a picture as accurate as may be of the various things which an impartial traveller is compelled to note in this interesting land, with some of the more obvious reasons of things seen and heard.

Nothing written about Russia is worth while which leaves out of account the Greek Orthodox Church. You may describe the American Republic, and give a very fair idea of the life of the people, without reference to any particular Church. England may be pictured, and not a word written concerning even her established religious organization, and yet you can get a very good understanding of English character. So with other nations. But Russia is the only state where nothing can be understood without some comprehensive outline of the part religion plays in the life of the people and the affairs of the government; for in Russia the Church is, on the one hand, a definite part of the government itself; on the other hand it is the chief factor in the life of the people. On the one side a state institution, on the other side it is a popular institution.

You could make no greater mistake than to assume, as the casual traveller always does, that Russia is priest-ridden. It is nothing of the kind. The Russian priest is people-ridden. The Russian Church is the people's Church. Very emphatically, the priesthood is the servant of the masses. There is astonishing reverence for the Church itself and for all that it stands for: there is an intellectual and spiritual regard for the holy icons, amounting almost to idolatry—certainly to worship. As has been pointed out, there is the most utter, abandoned, and unquestioning faith in God and Christ and the Czar (for the Czar is always included in the minds of the peasant, and the peasantry are the Russian people, with the All Father and with the Son of Man).

But the priest exercises no such sovereignty over the minds of his parishioners. In the opinion of the people, the Church is theirs, the icons are theirs, Christ is theirs, Jehovah is their Father, etc., and the priest is their servant, who is supposed to attend to certain necessary formulas to keep the great spiritual machine in motion. There are two things which even the Czar cannot do, and one of these is to disestablish the Church. Even if the Czar had the legal power to do so, he has not the real power. He might as well attempt to disestablish the Russian people themselves. Indeed, the Czar himself must avow his "orthodoxy" as a preliminary to his crowning.

Nothing would start a revolution in Russia more quickly than an attempt to confiscate the holy treasures, for the accumulation of gold and precious stones, etc., is the property of the icons, the holy images, whose residence is in the respective monasteries; and these icons, in turn, are the spiritual property of the Russian people. No matter how wretchedly poor the moujik is, he derives extreme satisfaction from contemplating the wealth of his pictured saints. Indeed, it is probable that the monasteries of Russia would become extinct through starvation were it not for the support they receive from the people themselves. All of the famous ones are the centres of enormous pilgrimages.

In July of the present year (1903) the Associated Press sent out a statement, printed in all English and American papers to the effect that "the Czar, the Czarina, and their suite" had left St. Petersburg "to join the great orthodox pilgrimage to Saroff, province of Tamboff, where the Orthodox Church is to celebrate the canonization of the hermit, Pekhor Moshnin, under the name of St. Seraphin. Six thousand bishops and clergy of European Russia will participate in the ceremonies."

This despatch of the Associated Press illustrates the Russian passion for religious pilgrimages. It is estimated that the ancient monastery at Kief is annually visited by over one million Russians. This million comes from all over the empire. The same is true of other ancient and famous sacred establishments. Some of these derive an income mounting into tens of millions of rubles a year from the voluntary contributions of these pilgrims. Bear in mind, too, that the pilgrims come to them voluntarily.

It is quite a spontaneous affair. There is no encouragement to do this on the part of the government. Emphatically it is not worked up by the priests themselves. It is a purely popular movement, and apparently as permanent as it is popular, for the Russian must worship something. His mind is chiefly concerned with only two things — the first one is his physical livelihood, his food, and his clothing; the second one is his spiritual welfare.

And this latter with him is not so much a matter of good deeds as it is a question of sheer faith, of childlike belief. His mind must attach itself to something tangible. It is not true that he has no mental conception of the Saviour, of the saints, and of their heavenly offices, for he has; but it is just as true that it is necessary for the Slav to have some physical representation of these holy images which dwells in the mind. And it is also true that to these figures and paintings the Russian attaches something of the feeling of reverence that he has for the divine personages and the heavenly ideals they are designed to represent.

Even this does not put it strong enough. Some of them are, to the mind of the Russian peasant, actual, living beings, endowed with miraculous powers. Even the hurried traveller who visits Moscow for only a day is sure to hear of the miracle-working Virgin. This ancient and sacred image has a chapel of her own near one of the historic gates of Moscow. The sick visit her for healing, and where the afflicted are too ill to come to her she is taken to them. Her revenues are very great. Nevertheless, let it again be called to mind, for it cannot be repeated too many times, that this peculiar veneration of icons is not something trumped up by the clergy; the clergy themselves, as has been stated, do not exercise any particular awe or even reverence in the Russian mind. Indeed, it may be said that, while the Church is the most popular institution in Russia, the priest is the most unpopular person in the empire. And this again brings us face to face with another of those paradoxes of Russian character and practice, which confront you on every hand, in industry, in religion, in statesmanship—everywhere excepting only in foreign policy, which is a uniform plan of advance.

XXIV

PRIEST, PEOPLE, AND CHURCH

THE priesthood of the Russian Church is divided into what are popularly called the white clergy and the black clergy. The black clergy are monks who are unmarried. The white clergy, who are the real officiating priests in Russia, are all married, and must be. They cannot be priests otherwise. If the Russian has any reverence for any priest it is for a brother of the black clergy. And yet in all Russia, with her one hundred and forty millions of people, there are not twelve thousand monks all told, including the novitiates or applicants for this sombre branch of the Church. Also, it is true that the black clergy is slowly dying out; its members have, for scores of years, been diminishing, and are decreasing now. On the other hand, few as they are in number, they are by far the most important factor in the administration of this great national church organization. But, in spite of their power, in spite of the hold they have on the popular imagination, as keepers of the holy images, in spite of the prestige which is theirs as the inheritors of an illustrious ecclesiastical past, it appears that ultimately they are doomed to extinction merely by lack of recruits. It is futile to attempt to explain this paradox; the facts alone are given.

On the other hand, the white clergy are themselves fewer in number, in proportion to the people they serve, than the number of Christian ministers of various denominations who have made the service of the Church their life business in America. Also these Russian married priests, in comparison with the servants of any other Church in any other country in the world, lead lives of poverty, and, in many instances, of actual want. Pitiful tales, and true, are told of how, in order to keep their families alive, they are reduced to direst extremities. By the Russian people —meaning the Russian peasant—they are treated with an indifference and even a contempt which an American Protestant minister or Catholic priest would not tolerate for an instant.

This has been thought by some careless observers to mean that religion has very little hold on the people, and that they chafe under the rule of their Church. In reality it indicates the reverse; for, even at the risk of repetition, it must be stated that the Russian people do not regard the Church as belonging to the priests by any manner of means, but exactly the contrary. The Russian people regard the Church as *their* institution and the priests as *their* servants.

So hard are the conditions of the Russian married priesthood, whose exclusive business it is to conduct Church services, that one wonders why any young man ever goes into the priesthood. Indeed, it is believed that few would do so were it not for the fact that the white clergy of Russia is an hereditary institution—that is, the sons of priests themselves become priests. And here is a curious thing worthy of note, although its final results defy intelligent speculation: If a Russian priest dies, another Russian priest, probably the son of some neighboring priest, takes charge of his church and marries one of the members of the dead priest's family. Thus he is provided with a sort of combined spiritual and earthly dowry.

The question of keeping full the ranks even of the white clergy has been a matter of serious thought on the part of the imperial government. At one time it was proposed to better the conditions of this oppressed priesthood by decreasing their numbers; but this did not work, because the extent of territory assigned to each priest and the number of souls in each district were already so great as to tax his utmost endeavors. So this device was abandoned. Of course, as everybody knows, the partial support of the Church—that is, of the priesthood—is a part of the business of the imperial government, as you will read in the annual budget of appropriations for this purpose. It is probable that these appropriations will be increased in the future, for the Church is one of the most powerful, if, indeed, not the most powerful arm of the Russian government. The reason of this is that the Church is the one influence which has a greater hold upon the mind and heart of the Russian people than all other influences in the Russian Empire combined; for, again let it be stated that the Church is distinctly a popular institution. Its common faith, common forms, etc., hold the Russian people together. There is nothing like it in all Russia, unless, indeed, it be the hold which the popular conception of the Czar has on the mind of the Russian myriads.

So the Russian Church is a state affair, although the state, of course, did not create it. It existed before the Russian autocracy, as at present organized. Peter the Great seized upon it purely as a measure of statecraft. He had two reasons for this: On the one hand, he feared that it might become more powerful even than the Czar; on the other hand he saw here, with the instinct of the statesman, a method of solidifying the affections and loyalty of the Russian people in the autocrat himself. And so that mighty personality, one of the greatest reformers that the world has seen in a thousand years, and of course, the most powerful Czar who ever reigned over all the Russias, changed the administrative constitution of the Russian Greek Orthodox Church. He took its government away from itself and placed it in a council of state, called the Holy Synod, which in his day was, and still is, principally an arm of the sovereign secular authority.

In this Holy Synod, which consists of dignitaries of the Church, appointed at will by the Czar, the Great Peter placed the personal representative of the Czar. This representative he called the Procurator of the Holy Synod. Theoretically this man was not, and is not, himself a churchman. He was designed to be, and is, the eyes, ears, brain, and will of the Czar in this council of Church administration. It immediately resulted as Peter had calculated. The Holy Synod soon became an administrative bureau, a department of state, whose minister, the Procurator, was the Czar's representative. This was, and is, no fiction, and Peter the Great did not intend that it should be; for the Procurator of the Holy Synod was made, and is now, a member of the Czar's ministry, quite as much as the Minister of Finance, the Minister of Foreign Affairs, or the Minister of the Interior. Indeed, the two dominant minds of the Russian cabinet at the present time are Witte, Minister of Finance and now President of the Committee of Ministers, and Pobyedonostseff, Procurator of the Holy Synod.

Thus again we see how elemental in its simplicity, after all, the Russian government is; for if on the one side a government has absolute control of the finances of the nation, and on the other side absolute control of the religious administration of the Church, to which the people are passionately devoted, all other elements of power follow obediently in the wake of these. As leading a part as the army plays for the empire, either as a threatening power in the hands of Russian diplomats or as actual force in Russian physical advance, it is weak compared with the strength perpetually derived by the government from the reverent souls of the Russian people through the administration of their beloved Church.

In short, Peter the Great grasped all the chords of devotion and reverence and worship extending from every Russian hamlet to the great religious capitals, and centred them all in his own royal palace. Before this time the Russian Czars had worn the temporal crown and sat upon the real throne of tangible power; but he saw that if that crown remained and that throne continued unshaken, he must grasp also the sceptre of spiritual power and make himself and his successor, in the minds of the numerous and widely scattered population, their spiritual father as well as their temporal lord. And with Peter the Great, to see a thing was to do it; and so he did it. The result is that to-day the Russian peasant regards the Czar, whom a Russian business-man will refer to as a "modest little officer," as the direct representative of Heaven on earth, the anointed of Jehovah, a being all but sacred, and entitled to the moujiks' reverence in much the same way as is the Master Himself.

Thus we begin to comprehend the profound reasons of state underlying the policy of the Russian government towards the Russian Greek Orthodox Church. Loud has been the cry made through Christendom that the Russian Church permits no proselyting. But to the Russian statesman there are sound reasons of state for this. In an empire stretching over such inconceivably vast dominions, ruling so many scores of millions, embracing so many different peoples, and in the process of absorbing so many separate and distinct nationalities, a common faith, a common spiritual life, a common church membership, are far and away the greatest cohesive power existing or that can exist.

"Putting aside the purely religious side of the question, what instrument of unity could we invent equal in its efficiency to the solidifying power of the Church? As an intelligent observer, you must grant that no other element of solidarity compares with it." So spoke a Russian public man.

And so the Russian statesman argues that if the Russian people were split up into the scores of creeds prevailing in other countries, the element of solidarity which the Church affords would be lost, and nothing could be found to take its place.

"Besides," said, in substance, Pobyedonostseff, in a recent thoughtful article, "the Orthodox Church is doing its real work. It is teaching our one hundred and forty millions the few fundamental beliefs that are important, and instructing them in the simple differences between right and wrong."

On this point of Church unity it is asserted that the Slav is quite unlike the Teuton, especially unlike the Anglo-Saxon. For example, with us here in America the sufficient reason for sects and denominations is, that in this way we appeal to all classes, and thus bring to the Cross by different routes various groups of personalities which one great central organization could not reach. But with the Slav it is said to be different. Also, it is said that the other peoples and nationalities over whom he has extended his dominion are, after all, very much like him; and, besides, that the peculiar absorbing and assimilating powers of the Slav, after a few decades, make an alien people, who have been taken into the empire, as much Russian as the citizen of Moscow. And so it is said that the excuse which is given for the existence, say, of Methodists, Presbyterians, Baptists, Episcopalians and the like in England or America does not exist in Russia.

"And besides," said a Russian gentleman, "what is the need of all these denominations, after all? You tell me you are a Methodist. I suppose you have friends who are Presbyterians and Baptists and Episcopalians. Is there any essential difference in your creeds when you reach the bottom? If a stranger were to go into one of your cities, not informed beforehand, could he tell from the service itself or from the preaching he heard or the songs he listened to, whether he was in a Presbyterian, a Baptist, or a Methodist church? After all, every one of you are trying to accomplish the same thing. Every one of you, I take it, believe in God, in Christ His Son, and in the soul's immortality. I also take it that none of you have anything else extremely important. But those are also the things our Russian Church teaches. So what purpose would be served by permitting our Church to be disrupted by foolish proselyting among its membership, except the disruption of the empire, and that would be the greatest calamity of all."

So the Russian imperial government more than rules the Church; and rules it with far more of an "iron hand" than it rules the Russian people. For instance, there was a time when the Russian monasteries and religious associations were extensive land-owners. The Czar remedied that by taking their lands away from them, and the state support to some of these monasteries to this day is excused upon the ground that it is a sort of meagre return for depriving them of their property two or three centuries ago.[1] Indeed, the most strenuous advocates of autocracy (and there are plenty of them, and very sincere ones, too) insist that the autocracy exists exclusively for the people, and that history shows that the Czar's authority brooks no rivalry within Russian domains. In support of this they point to the seizures by the Czar of the lands of the monasteries, on the one hand, and, on the other, to the forced sale by Alexander the Liberator of the landed estates of the nobles to those very nobles' former serfs, whom the emancipator at the same time set free.

"You foreigners," said one of these apologists for autocracy, "can rail at our Russian autocracy all you please, but you rail ignorantly; for, after all, the government of the Czar is first, last, and all the time for the Russian people. The Russian noble is not a power in our land. The

[1] The government might take lands from the monasteries and arouse no popular resentment; but confiscation of the gold, jewels, etc., stored there would be dangerously unpopular, because these treasures belong to the holy icons.

Czar compels him to sell his estates to his former serfs, whether he wants to or not. The priest is not a power in our land. The Czar, the spiritual head of this great people, makes the priest his servant and agent."

Thus we begin to see how it is that a Russian who is in religious belief a dissenter from all the doctrines of the Russian Greek Orthodox Church, or who is even an infidel or an atheist, may nevertheless be a devoted member and adherent of the national religious organization. It is a part of the empire. It is the soul of Russian nationality. He is a loyal Russian, ready and glad to give his life on the battle-fields of his country in defence of its flag. Why should he not, therefore—nay, why must he not, therefore—uphold that institution which, in popular meaning, is the breath of life of Russian solidarity. On the other hand, it again becomes clear why peasant, business-man, or nobleman, who is dissatisfied with the civil administration, or who is a civil reformer and yet a devout believer in the Russian Greek Orthodox Church, is held firm in his loyalty by the latter fact.

Perhaps this is one reason for the solicitude of the Holy Synod as an arm of the government in extending the service of the national Church wherever the colors of the Czar advance. It has already been noted that the Russian village is seldom without its church; that even in considerable towns the number of these sacred edifices appears to be entirely out of proportion to the spiritual needs of the people; and that in the cities ecclesiastical architecture is the dominant and commanding feature. Also it is true that these scores of thousands of Christian temples are constantly attended by the faithful.

But the activity of the Church authorities does not stop with the erection of these stationary edifices of worship. At a certain village of no particular consequence in Trans-Baikal Siberia the familiar sounds of the Russian sacred service were heard before the train stopped. Where could these sounds come from? Certainly in the many towns and cities visited no cathedral had before been observed so near to the railway-track that you could hear the voice of the priest from your car. Yet the rich intoning continued, and the responses rang with a distinctness which showed that they came from a point not many feet away.

"Oh, that is some church-car," explained a Russian fellow-traveller, in answer to the stranger's inquiry. "Yes, there it is on the siding."

And there it was on the siding. This car was a cathedral on wheels. It was fitted up just as a Russian church is equipped. It was attended by priests assigned to this railroad church service. The purpose of this is that the travelling Russian, and particularly the peasant, who is temporarily without a spiritual home, may be afforded the customary, and to him necessary, religious ministrations. Not that the peasant does not go through his devotions whether he has a church and a priest near or not. For he does go through his daily form of worship no matter what else he may omit.

On Siberian trains or Amur boats you may behold this exhibition of fervid faith any morning you may please to bestir yourself in time to see it. No matter that the car or boat is crowded; no matter that curious foreigners are scrutinizing him; no matter what the conditions or who is present, the Russian peasant will stand with his face to the east, murmur his prayer of supplication and of praise to his Maker, and prostrate himself before an invisible throne which only the eyes of his faith behold. And never will you hear from the lips of the most contemptuous traveller a single syllable of criticism, so unmistakably genuine is this Russian peasant's devotions.

Another striking circumstance is that the Russian soldier is, if possible, even more punctual and exact than his peaceful peasant brother. It is a mere commonplace that military life destroys the practice of religious worship, and even uproots religion itself. But certainly this does not appear to be true of the Russian soldier. Observed under numerous and different conditions, he never failed to appear, in outward form at least, reverent, devotional, full of the spirit of worship. Recall the description previously given of the chanted prayer of the company of Cossacks in the rainy night in central Manchuria. And it is said that the Russian soldier's spiritual and mental attitude before or after great battles is even more impressive. The following vivid description of religious services held by the Russian troops before the terrible redoubts of Plevna, during the Turkish war, is taken from the brilliant account of "Army Life in Russia," by F. V. Greene, of the United States Army:

"After the troops had all been visited an open-air mass was held. One division of about ten thousand men was drawn up on the plain west of Plevna, and about two miles from the high range of hills on which the Turkish batteries stood; the division was formed on three sides of a square, with a few squadrons of cavalry on each flank. In the centre stood the Emperor, alone and bareheaded, slightly in advance of his suite; in front of him was the priest, in gorgeous robes, with a golden crucifix and the Bible laid on a pile of drums which answered for an altar; a short distance to one side was a choir consisting of twenty or thirty soldiers with fine musical voices. Every one uncovered his head, and the service began in that slow, sad chant which is peculiar to the Greek Church. At the name of Jesus every one of the vast crowd crossed himself. On the opposite hills, as the service went on, could be seen large numbers of Turks congregating in wonder at the assembly of this large number of men. Finally came the prayer for the repose of those who had died in the battle of a few days before. The Emperor knelt on the ground resting his head on the hilt of his sword; every one followed his example, and the whole division knelt there with their guns in one hand, crossing themselves with the other, and following, in a subdued voice, the words of the chant.

"Nothing could give a clearer perception of the relations between the Czar and his men than this strangely impressive scene; the Gosudar Imperator (our Lord the Emperor) surrounded by his people, with arms in their hands, facing their hereditary enemies in religion and politics, and chanting in slow monotone, whose periods were marked by the booming of distant cannon, the requiem for their dead comrades. The Russians have no fewer daily sins to answer for than other people, but the feeling which binds the lower classes to their Czar is one of purely religious enthusiasm and veneration, which finds no counterpart elsewhere in these latter days."

All of this means something; and that something, no matter what you may call it, is the most vital influence in Russian character, and must be taken into serious account in all estimates of the Russian people, their purposes and their future.

The icon, or sacred image, in every place of business—every store, every vodka-shop, every factory, every dwelling-place, whether the lordly mansion of the noble rich or the hovel of the Siberian emigrant; whether in the enormous palace of the Czar himself or in the vilest abodes of licensed shame in the empire's cities—all this, let it be repeated, means something. Russian life, Russian culture, even Russian business, and, most of all, Russian purpose are not to be even dimly understood, unless this deepest and yet highest, and certainly most universal, phase of the Russian mind is taken into account. It is not for nothing that noble, peasant, prince, criminal, philanthropist, society leader—all classes—make obeisance to the holy images. It is not for nothing that every Russian, utterly without regard to station, condition, or any possible human circumstances, wears about his neck and upon his breast, next to his very heart, the little cross.

Nowhere can you see this latter significant fact better than on a large and crowded boat on the Amur River, at low water, where frequent and long stops are made necessary and where bathing in the river by everybody is practised at each stop. Peasant, emigrant, business-men *en route* to the Far East, army officers on their way to their commands in Manchuria, noblemen bearing special commissions from the Czar, wealthy mine-owners from the great gold-fields far to the north of Irkutsk, men, women, and children — not one of them was observed without the little cross hung around the neck, and never removed, not even for bathing. Around the neck of the millionaire it may be attached to a finely wrought gold chain; around the neck of the moujik it will be suspended by a common stout string; but it is there, and it is the cross, and it means exactly the same thing to both of them.

The Russian soldiers in citizens' garb, surreptitiously advancing by tens and scores towards the militant Russian host massing in the Far East for the impending conflict with Japan, bowing to the rising sun and repeating the same prayers uttered at the same moment by scores of millions of other Russians scattered all over the vast empire; the Cossack company in the heart of Manchuria chanting their nightly petition to the throne of grace; the nobler choir in the Kremlin on Easter Day pouring forth songs of joy that Christ is risen—are all engaged in the same service, which has the same meaning, and which reveals the same profound and universal faith. In the magnificent cathedral of St. Isaac's at St. Petersburg, in the extemporized service at a railway-station, amid encamped battalions of armed Russia in the Ussuri littoral, everywhere and always it is "Holy Russia" which speaks —"Holy Russia" ever singing, ever praying, ever advancing.

And doubt not that it is "Holy Russia" indeed. Granting all their superstition, conceding their ignorance, giving full credit to every unfortunate phase which the Christian religion takes among this peculiar people, he who travels the empire from end to end, with eyes to see and ears to hear, cannot but admit that here is a power in human affairs, blind it may be, cruel ofttimes, no doubt, but still reverent, devotional, and fairly saturated with a faith so deep that it is instinctive, and the like of which may not be witnessed in all the earth. What it will all result in he would be foolish, indeed, who would predict. But that it exists is certain; that it moves forward, slowly perhaps, to the eye of the hour, but rapidly to the eye of history, and, in any case, irresistibly, is merely a fact. "Holy Russia!" There she stands, or, rather, yonder she marches. Make of her what you will; say of her what you will; but do not forget that she exists, and exists increasingly.[1]

[1] Most of the thousands of Russian churches and cathedrals are built with money voluntarily given by the common people.

SPITZBERGEN
A R C T I C
KARA SEA
KARA STRAIT
GULF OF OB
North Cape
Varanger Fiord
Kolguev I.
WHITE SEA
Tornea
ARCHANGEL
Onega
Kotlas
Obdorsk
Bergen
CHRISTIANIA
Abo
STOCKHOLM
ST. PETERSBURG
Perm
Tobolsk
Tomsk
Omsk
Ufa
BALTIC SEA
NORWAY
SWEDEN
FINLAND
URAL MTS.
BRITISH ISLES
LONDON
BERLIN
WARSAW
MOSCOW
Kiev
GERMANY
PARIS
FRANCE
AUSTRIA-HUNGARY
ODESSA
ASTRAKHAN
Sergiopol
Turkestan
BLACK SEA
Batum
CASPIAN SEA
Khiva
Bokhara
EUROPE
MADRID
SPAIN
Rome
ITALY
CONSTANTINOPLE
Baku
MEDITERRANEAN SEA
Athens
TURKEY
PERSIA
AFGHANISTAN
Port Said
ALEXANDRIA
ARABIA
Delhi
Nile R.
RED SEA
AFRICA
ARABIAN SEA
BOMBAY
INDIA
INDIAN OCEAN
GULF OF GUINEA
BORMAY & CO., N.Y.

RUSSIA, AND THE REMAINDER OF EUROPE AND ASIA

XXV

RUSSIAN NATIONAL IDEALS

NO matter how casual his observation, every traveller through Russia will run across evidences of Russian idealism. On the other hand, men who have given their lives to the study of this curious people declare that the Russian is, first of all, an idealist. Again, even we Americans who read Tolstoï, and Turgenieff, and Gorkey have revealed to us in the writings of these first of Russian literary intellects the characteristic of ideality in spite of their realism. Even those who remember the diary of the Russian girl, Maria Bashkirtseff, which, through Mr. Gladstone's enthusiastic endorsement, gained world-wide currency, remember it as a queer conglomeration of idealistic impressions. All testimony from all sources leads to the conclusion that the Slav mind is essentially idealistic.

Remember, now, that even deeper than this idealism in the soul of this strange people is religion; and then call to mind its passion for order, its devotion to mere form; and, with this, recall again that, buffeted for centuries by Asiatics on the east, by other Asiatics on the south, by warlike Europeans on the west, Russia has been compelled to d velop a foreign statesmanship, unnecessary and unknown to any other nation, and a diplomacy skilful and resourceful beyond that of any other people of ancient or modern times. Take all these things into account, and you have the great springs and sources whence flow the two sovereign ideals of the Russian people.

These two ideals are, first, the preservation of religious faith, and, when the rest of the disputing world shall have grown weary of its spiritual conflicts, the restoration of that simple faith to all mankind; and the second is like unto the first—namely, the preservation of order, form, and authority in civil affairs, and when the rest of the world shall have completed its circle of liberty, and then license, and finally anarchy (which is what the Russians believe we are doing), to restore to the confused, hopeless, struggling peoples of the earth those forms of social order and political authority which the Slav thinks are, after all, the foundation-stones of civilization.

Incident to this last is the more immediate Russian idealistic purpose of spreading her dominions over all of Asia. To the Russian mind, China is to be Russian, Persia is to be Russian, India is to be Russian. It is Russian power which is to restore the cross to Jerusalem. It is Holy Russia that is to bring the authority of His faith to the land where the Saviour of mankind walked and taught and was crucified. So thinks the Russian.

The son of one of the greatest of Slavophiles happened to be a travelling companion for several days. Tall, slender, blond, blue-eyed, cultivated to the very last point to which the universities of Europe could finish him, the ardor of this young Russian was as startling as it was engaging.

"Why make a secret of it?" said he. "Did not our great Czar, who made but one fundamental mistake (the mistake of attempting to force western European notions upon Russia), but who was a prophet, point out our destiny with the very finger of inspiration? Oh yes; never permit yourself to doubt it for a moment. India will be Russian just as surely as Manchuria will."

A Russian soldier, not a St. Petersburg carpet knight, nor ladies' warrior either, but a Slav hotspur, a man whose life has been spent on the stricken field, and who at the time of the following conversation was in active service, said:

"You foreigners call us a rapacious military people. Don't deny it, for we know what is said; we know about the slanders published of us. The world, especially England, call us the 'nation of the sword.' There is Mr. Kipling, who refers to Russia as 'the bear who walks like a man.' Our occupation is supposed to be conquest, and yet"—and here this successful soldier grew as animated in gesture as any sensational orator or emotional evangelist in America—" and yet," he continued, "Russia has never waged a war except for an ideal. No other country on earth or in history can say as much, except, perhaps, your own American republic. Look at the lives we lost in our conflict with the Turks. Why did we go into that war? It was purely the act of a Christian nation to protect Christians. There was not and could not be any gain to us. Why do we maintain large numbers of troops near the Balkan states? Because we want those principalities? No sensible person, unless he is crazy with prejudice against us, would say so. What good would they do? Why did Skobeleff strike with the sword of Gideon in central Asia? Look at that land to-day, as peaceful as any section of your own country, as orderly and as safe; and then recall the terrible waste it was before the maligned Russian soldier gave it civilization, and even an Englishman must see the answer." And much more to the same effect.

The strange thing about this was that this Russian officer believed exactly what he said as fervently as any missionary that ever went forth in the world's dark places to give to the benighted the light of the gospel.

"Why do you doubt our zeal and its purity?" said a member of the Slavophile party. "You boast of your high purposes in the Philippines. Other countries have produced men of a faith so passionate that they gladly yielded up the comforts of their native land, and even life itself, in preaching the Word. Take the Jesuit missionaries in the early history of your own country; take the same class and consider their fate some centuries ago in Japan. Well, are we Russians the only people who are without the element that other nations pride themselves upon? I tell you, no. I tell you that, of all peoples of ancient and modern times, the one most devoted to ideals, so high that they are almost mystical and scarcely understood by the people themselves, is the Russian people."

Students of expansion will agree with Russian economic statesmen that Russian advance towards the Persian Gulf, on the one hand, and the Yellow Sea, on the other, is due to the fundamental cause of the absolute necessity that this most numerous of peoples shall reach the open sea. An American newspaper, in a studious and thoughtful editorial on the Manchurian question, recently pointed out the fact that the Russian occupation of Manchuria was permanent, and was caused by natural pressure of the growing Russian people combined with Russia's just rights to ice-free ports on the open sea. These contentions of thoughtful American journalists, of capable and observant travellers, of students of the movements of races, and of Russian economic statesmen themselves are probably correct. They explain Manchuria.

They may even explain central Asia. But they do not explain the presence of Russian agents all through Afghanistan. They do not explain Russian influence in Thibet, and practical Russian sovereignty at Lahassa. They do not explain those silent influences in China, always persuasive, never sleeping, which are gradually making groups of Asiatics all over that most ancient and populous of countries Russian in their sympathies. They do not explain the mysterious moral and mental processes going on in the Far Eastern mind, which no observer who really gets beneath the surface of things has failed to note, and which looks to the future turning of the Asiatic peoples to the standard of the Czar.

But the Russian's conception of his duty and his destiny

in the Far East does explain it. His subconscious thought that it is to be the glory of his race to set up the cross over all of Asia's myriads of millions, and to bring them to the faith of the Crucified One, does explain it. You could not find a Russian business-man, much less a Russian statesman, and least of all a Russian diplomat, who would admit for a single instant this proposition when thus baldly put before him. Indeed, the Russian business-man is pretty generally opposed to expansion.

"Give me no more China wars," said a Russian cotton manufacturer. "That was a ridiculous mistake. It cost hundreds of millions of rubles, and not a kopeck do we get for it. Future trade!" he exclaimed, in answer to a question. "Nonsense; we cannot supply our own market for a generation to come. I should like to know what profit there will be for me to manufacture goods when I consider the price of raw materials, the cost and inefficiency of our labor, and then add to all of that railway freights for thousands and thousands of miles."

"Do not be afraid that we won't give Manchuria back to China," said a Russian nobleman, whose conversation weeks of close companionship had made quite casual. "We have too much territory now. It strains our machinery of government to run what we have. Of course, we must keep Port Arthur and Dalni. But they are leased to us, with a little piece of land around, and have nothing to do with Manchuria, which is nearly as big as the whole of Russia itself. Of course, even I, who am what you call in America an anti-expansionist, do not like to see that great province given back to Chinese barbarism again, and I feel that we must do our part in Christianizing the world; but our load is already almost heavier than we can bear."

Nevertheless, as is elsewhere pointed out, no probability in the world of international politics seems greater than the permanency of Russian occupation of Manchuria. But the great reason underlying the continuous march of

Russia over Asia, from the time when the Russians threw off the Tartar yoke, may be found in a national thought and purpose, a popular ideal so deep and ancient that it may be really called an instinct, which propels the Slav to bear the law and order and authority of the Czar and the religion of the Master over all the East.

Russia's peculiar preparation for this will be pointed out to you by any enthusiastic Russian. The argument runs in this wise: Russia is next to Asia. From time immemorial Russia has been the barrier that has saved western Europe from inundations of Asiatic military hordes during the terrible centuries of the past. For two hundred years the Russian people were under the actual government of the Khan. These two centuries of Tartar subjugation of the Slav race made Russia familiar with Asiatic peoples, methods, habits, and thought as no other people will or can ever be. Also, the rule of Russia by the Tartars for these two centuries added to the Slav blood a perceptible strain of Asiatic blood. (And did not Napoleon say, "Scratch a Russian and you will find a Tartar"?) Indeed, many of the noble houses of Russia bear Tartar names. You may find nobles in the empire who are prouder of their Tartar origin than they are of their title to nobility, etc.

However runs the argument, or whatever the causes, full of charm as they are to the contemplative student, the fact remains that Russia is advancing over Asia, and will continue to advance. The fact remains, too, that she does this against well-reasoned conclusions of her own statesmen; against the almost unanimous conviction of the business interests of the country; against the surface thought and present-hour consideration of her most intelligent minds; against the protests of the exaggerated humanitarianism of her intellectual classes, like Tolstoï. But in spite of the best reasoning of her statesmen, those very statesmen themselves continue to advance. It is a strange phenomenon. Of course, it will not do to say that this is in obedience to the intelligent will of the Russian masses; for the Russian masses, as an actual, tangible proposition, perhaps know nothing about it and think nothing about it. And yet among these very masses there is this instinct towards Asiatic expansion, above noted, which has at the root of it a religious impulse.

These two statements make an exact paradox, and seem unintelligible. Contradictory as they are, they are true. Go into the peasant home of the country districts, and, if you find no other pictures on the walls of the dilapidated dwellings, you will find a cheap and tawdry print purporting to set out various scenes in the suppression of the Boxers in China by the allied troops. In any book-store of Moscow which caters to the work-people (and you will find many of these little booths), there are piles of these prints. All of them represent the white-clad Russian soldiers leading the charge, and in most of them there is some representation of the advancing cross. It is noteworthy that these prints, of which the Russian peasant is so fond, are almost equally divided between religious and military subjects. Pictures of the Saviour, the Virgin, the saints, prints representing scenes from the Bible, others representing Russian soldiers battling for the cross in heathen lands—these comprise the entire and exclusive stock-in-trade, so far as pictures are concerned, of these little stores, patronized exclusively by the moujik.

So, beginning at the bottom, and with the purpose most nearly at hand, control of Asia may be said to be an ideal of the Russian people. Whether the realization of this ideal will be good or bad for civilization, whether American policy should fall in with it or fight it to a finish, whether in the end it will be accomplished or not, it is not the purpose of this study to inquire. Facts are being noted, and this idealistic purpose of Holy Russia to advance on Asia is a fact—a present fact, an aggressive, militant, ever-progressing fact. It is a fact which the

British Foreign Office troubles over more than any other of its imperial world-problems. It is a fact constantly before the Viceroy of India and his cabinet. It is a fact discussed in the counting-houses of Hong-Kong. It is a fact which the English soldier who holds the "thin, red line" on the outpost of English dominion in the Far East encounters in armed and deadly form and force in his unending skirmishes with the hillmen.

Enlarge this ideal now until it spreads around the world. Take as its interpreter the most intense personality, one of the most instructed minds, and certainly as courageous a soul as Russia possesses, Pobyedonostseff, Procurator of the Holy Synod. He is said by some to be the soul of bigotry; he is certainly bitterly hated by many; but he is the personification of orthodox Russia. This man has written a book. It is published in English under the title of *Reflections of a Russian Statesman*. There are probably not a dozen copies in the United States; and yet, if anybody expects to understand the Russian point of view, he must read this book. Nearly all of it is given to an attack upon the democratic form of government and atheistic tendencies in religion. Here are the titles of some of these essays: "The New Democracy," "The Great Falsehood of Our Time," "Trial by Jury," "The Press," "The Malady of Our Time," "Power and Authority," "The Ideals of Unbelief," etc.

The views set out in these remarkable essays are a very fair and, at the same time, powerful statement of the prevailing thought and aspiration of the Russian people.

An intensified summary of them is as follows: Democracy is not natural. It cannot be permanently successful. It is false, too, because it pretends to be a rule of the people, whereas it is only the rule by a few politicians, whose purposes are usually selfish and corrupt. The result of government of this kind is constant diffusion of power, constant increase of license, until all respect for authority is destroyed, and the country so unfortunately circumstanced must choose the alternative of anarchy or the tyranny of some bold, resourceful "man on horseback." Substantially, the same is true of religion. By debating about nonessentials, by quoting this or that unimportant passage of the Scripture, by cultivating a passion for innovation in Biblical study, by endless disputes, by splitting up into unending sects and creeds, Protestantism gradually demoralizes the very foundation of faith itself, until nobody believes very much in anything. Finally, reasons Pobyedonostseff, the non-Russian world will be reduced to atheism in religion and anarchy in government.

And to restore to sanity, faith, order, a world thus demoralized, is the great ideal of the Russian soul.

"Take a long look over the other so-called Christian nations of the world," said a Russian scholar, who is a fervent believer in the ideas above condensed from Pobyedonostseff's book. "Can you help seeing that what you call the free preaching of the Word is nothing but a disorderly and ignorant mutilation of it? Look how many sects there are in England. Even in Germany it is nearly as bad. My own study of religious life in America compels me to believe that your people are not very firmly or deeply grounded in religion. How many of your acquaintances believe, without question, in God, a personal father, in Christ, His only begotten Son, sent for the definite purpose of saving the world; or in the personal, conscious immortality of the soul? I will not ask you to answer, but I will make bold to say that I do not think you can name a hundred. My own observation in England and America has been that religion is, to non-Russian peoples, merely a respectable habit, a method of civil decency. Now, that is not religion at all, and this process is going to go on and on until, no matter how many church buildings you have and how many preachers and all that, you are all going to arrive, certainly at agnosticism, and very probably at atheism itself."

The Russian religionist argues that some place in the

world there must be, not only a Church, but a *people* who preserve faith in its purity, fervor, and exaltation; not only a Church, but a *people* who are really, genuinely religious; and that when the rest of the world, weary to death of the vain disputes about this or that point of doctrine or dogma, and with their faith in God Himself destroyed, shall cry out, like a child in darkness, it will be Russia's sacred and divinely appointed mission to give to her sister nations thus benighted an example of a people still believing, still trustful, still religious; a people in whose temples the sacred fire has never been permitted to die or even languish, and who have borne forward to the blessing of those who have submitted the cross of man's universal Lord.

The Russian of education, travel, and culture, who is still, in spite of these things, fervently attached to the Greek Orthodox Church, believes most earnestly that there is no other Church in the world but his Church; and he thinks, with all possible sincerity, that the religion of the Russian masses, in spite of all of its superstitions, which he freely admits, is far better, fuller of hope for the future of the race, than what he calls that spiritual license, and what we call religious liberty prevailing in other countries. He has sincere respect for the Catholic Church; although he cordially dislikes, he understands its purposes. But for Protestantism he has no respect at all. Without going into detail of his complaint of the Catholic Church, but stating the largest and most important objection he has to it, it is that even the Church of Rome is too changeable, and that it is not the Church of any one organized, united, consolidated *nationality;* not the religious expression of any one single *people as such*, and a part of their physical and civil government as well as of their spiritual life.

Nevertheless, to the Russian, the Catholic Church, with its superb organization, with its permanence in comparison with the ever-changing Protestant creeds, is an intelligent and tolerable institution. Also, the Russian approves of the Catholic Church's method of reaching the soul through art—through painting, sculpture, and music; and he denounces Protestantism for excluding these simple and yet, at the same time, as he thinks, most refined and exalted methods of appealing to the instinctively religious feeling in the soul of man. The bitter antagonism of the Greek Orthodox Church, as such, to the Roman Catholic Church, is said to be political, the Catholic Church being the Church to which the people of Poland belong.

Holy Russia, then, looks to the regeneration of the world as one of her great, if, indeed, not her very greatest historic mission. Of course, even the most fanatical Russian churchman does not consider this a thing of the present day or the present decade or the present century. Indeed, the centuries, to the thought of the Russian churchman (or, for that matter, the Russian statesman), are small matters. "All in God's own time" is the motto of the Russian peasant. "If the mills of the gods grind slowly," to us, they do not grind slowly to the Russian. He sees no particular reason for hurry. Let the processes of evil and good work out their distinct results naturally. Let the world's age-old battle between darkness and light not be waged in the flash of a spark struck from the meeting of swords of single combatants in some portion of the universal field. It is a gigantic struggle in which the decades are but moments and the centuries but hours. In the end, light will conquer darkness, thinks the Russian; and, to his mind, the Christian faith is the all-conquering light and the Greek Orthodox Church the only true bearer of that sacred torch.

Such is the Russian religious ideal. There are strenuous dissenters from this view in Russia itself. The American traveller who makes acquaintances among the better classes will find this Russian ideal ridiculed and the Church itself denounced. It is doubted whether in any place in the world there is more bitter resentment against any institution than there is against the Greek Orthodox Church within Russia itself, and that, too, among men and women of exceptional culture; or, it would be more accurate to say, perhaps, against Russian ecclesiastical policy as practised by Pobyedonostseff. For example: "It is an outrage!" exclaimed a Russian of excellent attainments and abilities—"it is a shame and an outrage, I say, that I, who am a Protestant, must see my children members of the Greek Orthodox Church if I should marry a Russian lady who is a member of that Church, no matter whether she or I or the children themselves wanted to be members of the Greek Orthodox Church or not. How shameful that we have not the liberty of our own consciences!" His bitterness towards the Procurator of the Holy Synod was marked. All he complained of was laid upon this well-hated statesman of the Church. "Your great humanist Lincoln said, quoting the Bible, that 'If a house be divided against itself, that house cannot stand'—did he not?" (You will be surprised to find how widely read some of these Russians are.) "Well, then, how can I found a house? How can I found a family? I do not believe in the Greek Church. Perhaps a Russian whom I might marry, and who was a member of it, because she was baptized in it and because her parents were members of it, might not believe in it either. Perhaps our children would revolt against it. Yet she must continue a member of it, and our children must be members of it. To us Russians that is an awful circumstance, for the worst of us are religious. I am none too good, but I myself am religious. We must worship. It is in our blood. Yet here would be the spectacle of a father in one Church and the mother and children in another, with no possibility of joining them, unless I became an apostate to my Church and went into the Russian Greek Orthodox Church. Is not that intolerable?"

The explanation of this is that in Russia, "once an orthodox, always an orthodox." The children of orthodox parents are orthodox by reason of that circumstance, and cannot be anything else. They may become infidels in belief—atheists even; nevertheless, they are members of the Greek Orthodox Church. They cannot join any other. Moreover, the children even of a father or mother who is a member of the Greek Orthodox Church are, by reason of that circumstance, members of it, are baptized in it, and, most important of all, that fact constitutes a part of their civil status; for, be it remembered, that the Russian Greek Orthodox Church and the Russian autocratic government are woven inextricably into each other. They are, socially, one. The Church membership is a part of the civil life.

The above conversation, which is very faithfully reproduced, might be duplicated by scores, even if you remained for but a brief time in Russia, but during that brief time are so fortunate as to have your associations neither marked out, on the one hand, and confined to the lines marked out, or, on the other, if you get acquainted with more than one class of people.

Nevertheless, and taking all this into account, it is believed that the religious ideal here described, briefly and in rough outline, is the instinctive purpose and distant hope of the Russians *as a people*. Among the educated classes it may be said that there are one hundred thousand, or perhaps two hundred thousand (any estimate is a mere guess and practically worthless), who dissent from and denounce the Russian Greek Church and its members; among the people it might be that there are, roughly speaking, a handful of millions of the same thinking; but there are nearly one hundred million people in Russia proper, and in all his dominions more than one hundred and forty million souls acknowledging the sovereignty of the Czar. And it is such a holy Russia that holds this astonishing ideal, an ideal entertained vaguely, stupidly, and more through instinct than thought by her multiplied millions, but an ideal most vividly held and advocated with astonishing force and plausibility by some of the most highly cultured men and women in the empire.

Now for the second great thought of Russian destiny. This is purely civil. Its key, too, is found in the essays of Pobyedonostseff, whose argument is condensed above. But do not make the mistake of thinking that Pobyedonostseff's is the only tongue that utters this thought—mountainous and cyclic, we must admit, no matter how distasteful it is to us. This ideal, as has been stated, is the belief that it is the manifest destiny of Russia to restore order, form, law, respect for authority to a world whose experiments in democracy will finally land it in a chaos of license and anarchy.

Said a Russian colonel in Manchuria: "We Russians expect some day in the centuries to come to give back to mankind civil order, now disintegrating in all democratic countries and even constitutional monarchies." You may hear this everywhere from the lips of the adherents of autocracy.

"It is strange to us that thinking men in countries like England, France, or the United States, and even, to a lesser extent, in Germany, do not see the disintegrating effects of so-called free institutions," said one of these frank, fervent believers in despotism. "Of course," he continued, "it is a far cry to the end of the process, but the influences are at work very rapidly. No doubt it will take centuries, but 'the Terror' of France is the natural beginning of a democracy, and it will be its natural ending. Can you not see yourself that disorder is constantly increasing and that respect for law is constantly diminishing? Of course, I do not mean to say that this is rapidly growing, but it is growing, nevertheless. It is a natural thing, but it is like other vast natural movements; it is slow, and, I suppose, to you, who are in the midst of it, imperceptible. You are like a man on a raft, who does not look at the landmarks which are passing, but looks only at the floor of the raft and what is going on on board. There are the same dimensions, the same floor of the raft, the same utensils, the same companions; and so, refusing to look any place else except inwardly, as it were, you people in so-called free countries fail to observe whither you are tending. But the rapids are below you just the same, and you are hastening to them. It is only a question of time; it may be centuries, but, nevertheless, only a question of time, when you will be caught in the boiling waters, your raft broken up, and yourself lost."

So it is the ideal of the Russian, of the genuine believer in autocracy (although not of the small but, nevertheless, growing class who are in favor of a constitutional government in Russia itself) that it is Russia's high destiny some day, centuries hence, to be the only nation, the only organized *people*, who can give to the rest of the world an example of system, order, and authority, and all of the repose which the enthusiast of autocracy believes can only come from these.

It will be very difficult for us Americans to grasp this point of view, but it is all the more important to grasp it for that very reason. Otherwise, you shall not understand Russia. Not that any of us will understand Russia, even if we do grasp the meaning of her civil and religious ideals. As has been stated, it is probable that no foreigner, no matter how long there, ever will comprehend the Russian millions or the Russian mind. "There are more than a score of different beliefs and separate nationalities now under the Russian colors," said one of the ablest business-men in the empire. "I have lived here all my life; I am a Russian born; I have studied our people with care, and I do not yet understand them myself, and do not expect to."

In support of this view, and in contradiction of the description of the civil and religious ideals of the Russian people, given in this chapter, is the fact that considerable numbers of Russian subjects are Mohammedans, some few are Buddhists, and still others hold other faiths, not only dissimilar, but antagonistic to Christianity. It must in fairness also be stated that these antagonistic religions meet with no interference from the Russian government. Indeed, the administration does not even appear to disapprove of them; or, if the government does disapprove of them, at least it does not make its disapproval apparent. More than this, it must also be said that large numbers of the subjects of the Czar who are famous for their intense devotion to their imperial master are, spiritually, the followers of the Prophet. This is particularly true of the Caucasian Cossacks

Not only is there no interference by the Russian government with these adherents of anti-Christian religions, but the Russian people—peasant, merchant, and soldier—get along with them very well indeed. Do we ever hear of any bloody fanatical outbreak between Russian Christians and Russian Mohammedans where these elements mingle? It is a significant and interesting spectacle to behold in Russian Asia orthodox Slavs from Russia in Europe and subjects of the Czar from near the Afghan frontier rendering separately, and in one another's presence, their religious devotions without the slightest apparent animosity, and to see the disciples of these hostile faiths mingle like brothers the moment their daily worship is over, and, like brothers, live together day after day.

Mr. Burton Holmes, the American traveller, tells of the ceremonies attending the administration of the oath to two regiments of young Russian soldiers. One was a Jewish regiment; its services were conducted by a Jewish rabbi. The other was a Christian regiment; its services were conducted by a Greek Orthodox Russian priest.

Again, when a Mohammedan regiment or other body of troops is mustered into the service, the necessary religious ceremonies are performed by a priest of their own faith. Indeed, it is said that throughout their entire active duty in the army the spiritual needs of the soldiers of the Czar are administered by priests of their own faith. These examples might be multiplied almost indefinitely, and it must be admitted that they do not tend to sustain the theory of the Russian national religious ideal presented in this chapter.

This contradictory state of affairs affords another paradox of Russian statesmanship; just as, in her economic policy, the active encouragement by the government of centralized factories, and the paternal care and fostering protection given to her "kustar trades," is a paradox of statesmanship in the domain of Russian manufacturing industry. Indeed, all through Russian life, Russian administration, and Russian history, these counter-currents, flowing side by side in opposite directions, are encountered. But, taking them all into account, it is believed that the general direction and flow of the great stream of Russian purpose are along the lines of the large racial ideals of the Slav, which in this chapter we have been dimly following. The word "dimly" is used advisedly. We might even better, perhaps, employ the word "vaguely," for no one, least of all the casual observer, can perceive, even by the most careful scrutiny, anything more than the mountainous proportions of Russian thought and purpose in the twentieth century, nor faithfully determine more than the general tendencies of the glacier-like movements of this lethargic and multitudinous people.

So stupendous, so complex, so various are the elements which make up the Russian Empire; so remote are the springs of those influences which mould and direct Russian thought; so elemental and enormous is the evolution going on at the present time; so indescribable is the whole mighty mass of human beings ruled by the Czar, that their progress might be compared to the building of the earth itself. It is slow; it reaches back through the centuries and forward through the centuries; it defies analysis and will defy analysis until the long process is completed. Certainly no human mind to-day, Russian or non-Russian, can comprehend it. Perhaps when a thousand years have passed and our own part in history has been performed, and Russia, now comparatively resting undeveloped, shall have had her cue, and in turn advanced and played her part in the drama of the centuries, and in turn has gone off the stage—then, it may be, some comprehensive historical analyst may be able to read the riddle of Russian development, work, and purposes in the world, but not until then. Meanwhile, the best that one can do is to note such things of interest as one may in rapidly passing.

XXVI

RUSSIAN POINTS OF VIEW—RUSSIAN OPINIONS OF AMERICAN INSTITUTIONS

NOTHING can be more engaging than the opinion held by frank and intelligent men of other nations concerning ours. Conversely, this is, as every traveller knows, the thing first inquired of by foreigners concerning themselves and their country. After all, human beings are very much alike, it appears. "How do you like our town?" is the familiar question that every one of us puts to the visitor within our gates. Enlarge this question a little bit, and it becomes: "How do you find our country?" "What do you think of our institutions?" "What is your opinion of this or that or the other phase of our national life?" And these, too, are the questions addressed to the serious and earnest foreign visitor to most other countries; and of no spot on the globe is this more true than of Russia.

Driving across the steppes with a Russian not entirely satisfied with the present state of things in his country; conversing with a manufacturer and again with a banker and at another time with a merchant; talking with men highly influential in Russian affairs and shaping the present policy of the Russian people; discussing matters of interest with a Russian administrator in the Far East; talking with a group of civil and military officers, for weeks travelling companions — always and everywhere your opinion of Russia, of the Russian people, Russian institutions, Russian government, and everything else Russian is eagerly asked for.

And, reciprocally, their opinions of America are given with frankness and unreserve.

Of course their opinions are not uniform. But it is the note through all of their talk which is dominant, and may be said to be the major chord of Russian opinion of things American, which this chapter seeks to strike. And while their disapproval of the theory of republican institutions applies to us as well as to France and England and other free countries, while their rejection of the whole practice and doctrine of representative institutions is distinct and emphatic, another paradox of Russian reasoning is presented in their sincere admiration of American character, as they understand it, of the American people as a nation, and of American achievements in every line of human effort. For the apparent friendship which the Russian people feel for the American people, and which has again and again been observed and set down by scores of unprejudiced American travellers, can be seen, heard, and felt by any visitor to any portion of the empire of the Czar. The causes for this seeming Russian predisposition towards the American people have already been presented in the language of an eminent Russian; and many other and minor causes have aided in producing the same result. And no just reason occurs why this apparent friendship is not genuine.

These minor causes cannot, of course, be even enumerated here; but one may be mentioned because of its pleasing nature, and of the light it throws upon the character of the Russian people. The Czar is always passionately beloved by the great body of his subjects, with an adoring affection not accorded any other ruler. Particularly was this true of Alexander the Liberator. When this autocratic breaker of the chains of Russian slavery escaped death at the hands of the assassin in 1866 the American Congress passed resolutions congratulating the Emperor and expressing the friendly feeling of the American people for Russia. This resolution was sent to the Czar by our Assistant Secretary of the Navy. Several war-ships, among which were two of our monitors fresh from their triumphant engagements in our civil war just closed, was sent as an escort of the representative of the republic who bore this friendly message. The heart of Russia was deeply touched. The American people's message was presented to the Russian throne, it is true, but in effect it went to the Russian millions. It is said that news of this act of tender courtesy travelled with lightning-like rapidity from mouth to mouth throughout all Russia, even to the poorest country village, and that in an incredibly short time there was not a cottage in the whole empire whose inmates were not talking of this kindly act of the great American people across the sea. This incident, comparatively insignificant in itself, meant, to the simple Russian peasant mind, that the American people were the friends of the Russian people, and that impression has remained among the common people of Russia although the incident which caused it may have been forgotten. This circumstance shows the peculiar sensitiveness of the Slav nature to kindly sentiment.[1]

[1] An extract from the report of Mr. Fox, who bore to the Czar the resolution of Congress, is worth reproducing:

"All that I have written myself, and all that was written for the press by persons far more capable than I feel myself to be, to describe the manifestations of these feelings, fail to convey any adequate idea of the enthusiasm which pervades the people of Russia towards the United States, and their sincere wishes for the continued prosperity and power of our country. The expression of the sympathy felt by the Emperor for this country in its great struggle for national unity, made by Prince Gortchakoff in 1861, when several of the great powers of Europe were co-operating in the effort to destroy it, and taking measures to profit by its destruction, was gratefully appreciated by the government and people of the United States as a timely and effective demonstration in our behalf. But it was not until I had traversed so great a part of the Russian Empire and witnessed how cordial and wide-spread, among all classes in that powerful country, was the friendship for America, that I appreciated the practical importance of

But no matter what the causes, the friendly feeling of the Russian people for the American people is believed to be both strong and genuine. And that fraternal regard is not in the least impaired by the Russian opinion of the theory and practice of our institutions, presented in this chapter, harsh and intense as those opinions are.

"I do not well see how your bureaucracy can be defended even by its most radical apologists," said the American. By bureaucracy, as everybody knows, is meant the great system of bureaus established by Peter the Great. As a matter of fact, Russia is governed by clerks and officials—hundreds of them, thousands of them, tens of thousands of them. Peter the Great saw that his government must have some system. It could not be mere caprice of the imperial will all the time. The country was too vast, its population was too great, its dominions were growing and must continue to grow in extent, and the number of its people were increasing and destined to increase for centuries to come. So the constructive Peter classified everything.

He established bureaus for this and bureaus for that and bureaus for the other. These bureaus were grouped under

the Emperor's sympathy in its bearings upon the course of our great contest and in its influence upon the conduct of other nations towards us.

"The crowds that gathered around us at every social meeting, singing the plaintive national songs; the flowers presented by the hands of beauty and innocence; the numerous presents offered upon all suitable occasions; the imperial honor granted at Kostroma of casting down their garments for us to walk upon; the deep feeling which the great mass of the people evinced whenever the name of our country was mentioned, and the very many touching incidents which such sympathies evoked, were not produced by curiosity or instigated by officials. The Russians have been familiar with royal embassies from powerful and magnificent courts for many centuries. It was a heart-impulse of the people in favor of our country which occasioned these extraordinary demonstrations towards the messenger of good-will, founded on their instinctive knowledge, that while our countries departments. At the head of each of these departments was a minister; at the head of each of these bureaus was a chief. Under these were sub-chiefs, and so on down to the humblest clerk. The theory was that this whole service was to be a merit service. Officials were to be advanced from the very lowest grades to the very highest grades, by length of service and by efficiency, or, rather, by a combination of the two. This is the system of government which prevails in Russia to-day. It is what we would call a perfect "civil service." The great governmental machine invented by Peter the Great, perfect in theory, has become all-powerful in practice. Everything in Russia must be referred to an official, and this official refers it to the next higher official, and this official in turn refers it to his bureau, and there it runs the gauntlet of still other officials.

It is said that the result is that there is not a department of the Russian government to-day which is not behindhand with its work. The affairs of the Holy Synod, for instance, are reported to be seriously congested. So, on good authority, it is said the business of nearly every other department is too great for the best

were widely separated from each other on the globe and in forms of government, there was yet a community of interest on great points, which identified the friendships of the people with patriotism itself."

The resolution adopted by Congress is as follows:

"Resolved by the Senate and House of Representatives of the United States of America in Congress assembled, that the Congress of the United States of America has learned with deep regret the attempt made upon the life of the Emperor of Russia by an enemy of emancipation. The Congress sends greeting to his Imperial Majesty and to the Russian nation, and congratulates the twenty million serfs upon the providential escape from danger of the sovereign to whose head and heart they owe the blessings of their freedom.

"Section 2. And be it further resolved, that the President of the United States be requested to forward a copy of this resolution to the Emperor of Russia."

attention. In short, the affairs of the empire seem to have grown beyond the capacity of the legion of clerks who attend to its business. It could hardly fail to be so, since most details must be passed on to St. Petersburg. As a result, it is said that thousands of matters are simply "pigeon-holed," as we say here in America. Many thousands more are said to be decided without adequate or perhaps without any knowledge. And to the American observer it appears to be nothing short of marvellous that the government can get along at all. As a matter of fact, the efficiency of the government is amazing when one considers the minute and complex organization of administration.

So, when an American's opinion is asked, these conspicuous facts are frankly pointed out. It was suggested that the simple expedient of even a small degree of local self-government would relieve the centralized power of the immense amount of business which is literally breaking it down, as foreign critics assert, but which the Russian emphatically denies. It was pointed out that this simple and natural process would create initiative on the part of the people; and, further, that the people of each locality, aided, if necessary, or even directed by the local nobility, could better understand their needs than a chain of officials running from the locality clear up to St. Petersburg.

And, indeed, there is a considerable and, it is believed, a growing sentiment in Russia along this line. It is not so many years ago that the zemstvos were inaugurated in Russia by Alexander the Liberator. These were, in a fair degree, machines of local self-government. They were made up of peasants, land-owners, and nobles elected in various ways by their respective classes. At the head of each zemstvo sat as its president the marshal of the nobility of the district, appointed by the Czar. In most of these cases the nobles, and especially the marshals of the nobility, were in hearty sympathy with the people, instead of with the central government at St. Petersburg.

This sudden development of self-government in the

empire of the Czar did not long continue its work of popular legislation. Within recent years there began to be curtailment of its power and privileges. This retrenchment of popular self-government in Russia has gone on with ever-accelerating speed, until at the present time the zemstvo might as well not exist, so far as any real self-government is concerned. The tendency steadily is to place all of this power again in the hands of the Governor of the district, appointed directly by the Czar and responsible directly to him.

At this reaction there are loud and indignant protests. Russian noblemen, who want local and popular self-government, are very outspoken in their indignation, far more outspoken than the people themselves, who seem to care very little about it. Indeed, one reason given for curtailing the power of the zemstvo is the difficulty of getting the people to vote or do anything else in connection with it. We in America, who are accustomed to believe that nobody speaks his mind in Russia, will find it hard to understand that the Russian country gentleman will talk with about the same emphasis against the recentralization of governmental power in St. Petersburg as the American politician will here in America against the administration with which he is dissatisfied. And these expressions of dissent and dissatisfaction are by no means concealed.

It must not be inferred from the reaction from the local self-government of the zemstvo towards autocratic recentralization of power that there is no self-government in Russia at all. On the contrary, any Slavophile will assure you that the only real democracy on earth is found in the peculiar Russian village, or, as the Russian word is, "mir." This is the famous Russian commune. As has been stated, all Russian peasants live in villages. These villages are self-governing, so far as their local affairs are concerned, with the one exception of fixing the imperial taxes. As has been noted, the land belonging to the peasants is held by them in common. This land is allotted among the peasants, not by the government but by the peasants themselves, and not at stated intervals but whenever necessary, and not to the individual members of the commune, but to the families. The unit in the Russian village is the family. The unit with which the government deals is the village. The heads of families in these villages get together at a call from the elder. This elder is elected by *viva voce* vote. These meetings thus called divide the land among the various families.

There is for this no hard-and-fast rule. These assemblages simply talk over the matter. They debate among themselves what is right and what is wrong, what is just and what is unjust, and they allot the land accordingly. In these meetings the women who happen to be at the head of the household—as, for instance, the widow of a deceased peasant—participate and do as much talking as the men.

These little village communes also pass upon and settle many of the minor and petty offences committed by their members. The community exercises a power over each member of it more autocratic than that exercised by the Czar himself over his individual subjects. For example, each member is compelled to do his fair part of the work. He must pay the portion of the taxes which the commune or village allots to him. The government itself collects the tax from the commune and not from the individual. The commune says how much of the tax each family shall pay. If the head of any family is in arrears of his taxes the commune will not let him have a passport, and without a passport the government will not let him leave the village. The same is true of the son or daughter of a family, except, we are informed, that in these cases, while the commune itself is supposed to deny or grant the passport, in reality it is the family to which the son or daughter belongs who determines it.

Of course, such a system as this would not work with us at all; but the Russian peasant is a peculiar human being. He is exceedingly good-natured and reasonable. In their meetings, which, weather permitting, are usually in the open, under the trees, and which may last for a few hours or several days, there is merely a crystallization of opinions. Then a vote is taken. The minority fall in with the majority. Everybody "lines up," to use a familiar American political expression. Grumbling there usually is, but it is confined to the person against whom the decision runs; and everybody laughs and jokes the grumbler out of face, and so everything goes along very smoothly. It must be added that the elder (starosta) elected by these villagers does not exercise any influence over the decisions of his fellows. Indeed, he does not attempt to. If he did, he would be put down by the rest. Nobody wants to be elder. There is no pay in it, and a great deal of responsibility; but when anybody is elected, there is no getting out of it as a usual thing. And all this, declares the Slavophile, is the only real self-government in the world.

A number of these villages are combined into a larger kind of a tribunal, which settles more important disputes and adjudges more important crimes. Again, a number of these are combined together in what has already been referred to as the zemstvo, or district legislative assembly.

To return now, after these modifications, to the great burden of bureaucracy which the American traveller, when asked for an opinion, always criticises.

"Of course, our system of bureaus and government by them, or rather through them, has its defects. But what government has not?" answered a Russian civil officer. "Take your own American government, for example," he continued. "To us it appears most irrational. For instance, there is an uprising against some vicious element, as in the case of the Italians some years ago at New

Orleans." (You will find the Russian educated man pretty well up on most of the things going on in the United States and elsewhere in the world.) "It looked absurd to all Europe, and especially us Russians, that, while your national government admitted the offence, it could do nothing, because a State government within your national government alone was responsible. That looks to us Russians like a contradiction in terms. How, we ask, can there be a government which is sovereign over its whole territory and yet not responsible for what is done within that territory?"

"We will have our meals at the following hours," said General Deitrich, on his way to take command of the "Russian railway-guards" (in reality, picked Russian soldiers) in Manchuria. "You see, we do not permit any republic over here, not even on our boats," said he, laughing pleasantly.

Regretful comment on parliamentary institutions is not uncommon. Below is given a Russian's criticism upon our American form of government, which can be heard in Russia from the lips of the highly educated Russians, who also happen to be apologists for and advocates of autocracy. It is useful only as showing the opinions of such Russians of all liberal government and their profound misunderstanding of our republic.

"I am very free to admit almost all of your criticism of our Tchinovnic (clerk) system," said he. "Of course, it is cumbersome, and of course business gets congested. At the same time, I do not think it is much more congested than it is in the English Parliament, where I have myself listened to half a day consumed by a fruitless debate over some trivial local matter affecting some town in Scotland." (Any one who has spent a day in the British House of Commons has witnessed the same thing.) "Then, too, you must take into account the difference in race. We are Slav; do not forget that. We are devoted to form. We are not so much accustomed to take orders as we are under a mental, a moral, and physical—racial—necessity to take orders."

And he referred to the fact that when the Russian people had literally thrown the Czar headlong from the throne, and had the government in their hands to do with it what they liked, they simply crowned another Czar and went about their business as before.

"But now consider your own institutions," he continued. "The educated and instructed Russian always laughs when he hears you Americans boast of your free self-government. As a matter of fact, do you have as much self-government as we do? From the best information I have been able to obtain, both from reading and from travel, the impression received is that you are governed by parties. Your parties nominate your ticket—do they not?—and set forth certain declarations in what you call a platform. Then everybody belonging to that party votes for it, and you call that self-government. It does not look to me very much like self-government; but conceding that there is a measure of self-government in it in theory, is it so in practice?

"We understand that your parties are really ruled by a few powerful politicians, who give up their entire time and energy to that business. The delegates to American political conventions, which are supposed, in theory, to be selected by the people, are usually selected, as we understand it, by a few local politicians who are powerful in their community, and who do the bidding of other powerful politicians higher up. Furthermore, we are informed that these men are not powerful by reason of pre-eminent virtue or culture or patriotism, but by skilful use of corrupt methods. Men who can be depended upon to do the bidding of these politicians are placed on the committees which prepare your platforms of principles. In short, in your so-called democratic government everything is 'cut and dried,' as I heard the expression used in England. Your conventions of delegates, which are supposed to be elected by the people, but which, in reality, are selected, as I have indicated, accept the platform just as it is presented to them by the few who constitute this committee, and this committee receives its instructions from the big politician who runs the whole thing.

"Now, we Russians do not see very much difference between this and an autocratic form of government, except that in the case of the Czar's government the sovereign is above all reward or the hope of it, above all fear of displacement, and is forced by his conscience and the public opinion of the nation, and his own desire to do the best he can for our people, and perhaps, above all, by his wish to appear well in history, and hand his government down to his son in a better condition than it was when he took it up; whereas, with your political czars, they last for but a short time, and are influenced more or less by their own selfish designs.

"Then, again," continued the Russian critic of our institutions, in giving this curious Russian point of view, "suppose your government is run exactly as it is supposed, in theory, to be run. Consider the immense waste of energy it entails. Suppose your public men to be unselfish and patriotic to an ideal degree. Well, after they have proposed certain laws or declared certain principles, they must waste the greater part of their energy going about the country in your campaigns speaking to the people. As a matter of fact, they go about the country speaking not to the people but to their partisans. The point that I am now making is that the very best that is in them is given, not to the study of public questions, not to the grave consideration of laws, but to haranguing crowds.

"After this expenditure of energy, and to no great purpose either, your public men have very little real strength left for the actual work of the nation. So in the nation or the State, or even the city, the result of this is that your laws are not carefully drawn, are almost certain to be repealed, etc. Another result is that your government, take it altogether, is by far and away the most expensive in the world. I mean if you take the expense of your city and other municipal governments, your State government, and your national government, that you Americans spend far more of what your producers create than any other government in the world. As I have said, it all ends in your not governing yourselves at all. To us Russians it appears that your boasted self-government is merely a government by cliques.

"Of course, I admit that you sometimes have great exceptions; sometimes, doubtless, you develop public men of such pre-eminent ability that they command the attention and respect of your people themselves. No doubt, such men, when such exceptions are found, are more powerful than the temporary and corrupt cliques of politicians who usually dominate your public affairs. I am willing to admit that when such a man is encountered in American public life the cliques are unable to overthrow him, and will not try to do so, because so great is the hold of such a man on your masses that the people would turn and destroy your little governing groups of politicians who thus offended them. It seems to us Russians that such men occasionally appearing in American public life are about the only hope you have of being saved from yourselves. Your Washingtons and your Lincolns are, after all, your salvation; and so, in spite of your theories of popular government, you get back, in the end, to the principle of autocracy disguised under the name and character of some popular hero who is worthy of and receives the support and affection of your masses.

"Then, again, take it in diplomacy. It appears to us Russians, and indeed to most Europeans, that there is no such thing as American diplomacy, and cannot be. This year you have one political party in power, and that party pursues a certain foreign policy. The next year, perhaps, the opposing political party gets into power, and that succeeding administration, which may have been elected solely on account of some internal policy and not at all with reference to the foreign policy pursued by the party it succeeded, nevertheless reverses the whole foreign policy of your nation, or tries to do so. It even turns out of office your nation's ambassadors all over the world, no matter how able those ambassadors are and no matter what serious and delicate problems any ambassador may have on his hands. It may be that he is in the very midst of an important and far-reaching negotiation which all the other statesmen of the world regard as highly beneficial to your nation. No matter; out he goes. The reason is that he does not belong to the party that has come into power.

"Now, to us Russians that seems childish. Then, again, your ambassador may only have begun to get acquainted with the country to which he is accredited. In reality, he may only have begun to master the usages and practices which might make him valuable at the court to which he is sent. Again no matter; out he goes; and just because he belongs to the unsuccessful political party which, as I say, may have come into power purely on account of some exclusively internal policy affecting your country and your country alone. This silly practice extends even to your consuls at all important points; and, strangest of all, the only consuls you keep in office, when there is a change of administration, are those at unimportant points. To us Russians this practice of your American Republic seems almost insane; and yet it is a part of what you call your free institutions.

"Or take the question of taxes. Our government is criticised because the people have no part in saying how much taxes they shall pay. As a matter of fact, of course, this is not true in local affairs, although it is true in imperial affairs. But suppose it were true even in municipal affairs? Where is the difference between your democratic form of government as it is practised in your cities and our autocratic form of government as it is practised in Russia? How many men who really pay the taxes of New York have, as a matter of fact, very much to say about it? Some of our statesmen have made a practical study of the American cities as they have of the municipal governments of all other countries, in order to see where we could improve conditions here, and we have been astonished to find that in the matter of at least two of your great cities the whole question of taxes and municipal administration is said to be determined by two or three men, sometimes only one man at the head of some political organization.

"Now, referring again to the exhaustion of your public men in what is really idle harrangue on the stump, compare them with our Russian statesmen. Of course, our statesmen have their failings, too, and very great ones. No Russian claims that his public men are perfect. But, nevertheless, they have all their time and all their energy to devote to the real work of the empire. Your public men, on the contrary, are compelled to dissipate by far the greater part of their time and energy in the work of your almost continuous elections. It is strange to us that you Americans do not awaken to the enormous expenditure of energy in your numerous campaigns. There is always some campaign or other on hand. You are always electing somebody to something. It entails a loss of vital power which, it seems to us, might be better given to the real service of the nation."

When reminded of our miraculous progress in comparison with the snail-like progress of Russia, the Russian critic replied: "All that is conceded, but yet your progress has not been greater than ours since we started to adopt modern methods. And, besides, can anybody say what the end of your apparent 'progress' is going to be? May it not be that you are exhausting yourself and your resources, like a man who gets false energy out of stimulants. I cannot admit," said he, "that our respective experiments have gone far enough for anybody to give a just opinion of the comparative merits or demerits of American and Russian so-called progress."

Many pages of similar opinions might be given here, but the above is typical and fairly illustrative of the autocratic Russian point of view. Of course, it is not said that this is the unanimous Russian conclusion. On the contrary, very able Russians hold to the opposite opinion; but the above is believed to be a fair presentation of the prevailing Russian thought. The best way to learn to appreciate our American institutions is to visit other lands and find how immeasurably better off we Americans are than any other people. Go about the world and you will come to love the United States more than ever.

XXVII

THINGS CASUALLY OBSERVED

ALL Russian stores and shops, of course, have "signs," just as American stores and shops have. But the Russian signs are peculiar. Instead of having the word "dry-goods" or "meat market" or what not on their signs, there are, instead, pictures of what the shop or store has to sell. Here is one that has pictures of fruits—very well, that is a fruit store. Another picture has a quarter of beef, or sausages and the like—that is a meat store. You cannot fail to find a dry-goods establishment, because a picture of its wares is conspicuously placed in front of it. The reason for this you perhaps will be told, is that the people cannot read, but that they do understand the pictures. This is not the exact truth, but it is a suggestion of the truth. It was the original reason for making the pictures rather than written signs, but that reason has to a considerable degree now passed away.

This method of sign-painting is now continued more largely as a matter of custom than of necessity; for be it again repeated, that of all the people in the world, except perhaps the Asiatics, those most devoted to custom are the Russians. No doubt it is true also that large numbers of people, particularly the older members of the poorer classes, cannot yet read and write, and the picture signs may be continued for their convenience. Nevertheless, in cities like St. Petersburg and Moscow the change from picture signs to written signs is rapidly going on; and in the two or three cities of this class the pictures are usually accompanied by the written words. Also, especially in St. Petersburg, the pictures are being dropped from the signs entirely. This indicates a rapid advance of literacy, because it is being done in spite of the fact that much illiteracy remains, and in spite of the more powerful influence of custom.

Do not imagine that you cannot get anything you want in a Russian city as readily as you can in an American city. The fact has already been noted that even in Siberian cities any possible thing you desire may be purchased in their department stores. Of course, the same is true in the larger Russian cities, although it is a singular fact that the idea of the department store has not developed in Russia itself as it has in Siberia. Whereas the tendency in Siberia, and even in Manchuria, is towards the department-store principle, in Russia the shop principle is still dominant.

In Moscow there is an arcade which, it is said, is not surpassed by any similar arrangement in the world. In this arcade are shops which sell every conceivable thing except meats and the like. They are similar to the shops in the arcade in Cleveland, Ohio. Residents of Moscow also boast that this Muscovite metropolis has the greatest and best-equipped apothecary establishment in the world. Careful inspection of this immense drug-store makes the visitor believe that this claim is perhaps not an idle one. The singular circumstance should be noted that in chemistry and the science of medicine Russia (always comparatively speaking) has made more rapid progress within the last half-century than any sister nation. Many reasons are assigned for this, and perhaps the most plausible is that, shut off from political activity, the vigorous and aggressive minds of the empire devote their energies instead to science in its various forms, and especially to medicine. It is said that even Vienna cannot boast of as perfect a medical college as exists in one of the universities of Russia.

The points of similarity between Russian and Chinese

customs are so many that a very entertaining little volume might be written comparing them. It has already been noted that the Russians, like the Chinese, live, as a usual thing, in little clumps of houses—small, rural communities called villages. In the course of an inspection of Chinese agricultural districts, the farmers were always found living with their families in these little villages. The same is universally true in Russia. But since we are speaking of medicine, let us note another strange similarity—the practice concerning the paying for medical services. In China, as everybody knows, the physician is paid as long as the employer is in good health; the doctor's pay ceases when his employer gets sick, and does not begin again until he recovers. Of course, this is not true in Russia, but there is an analogy, nevertheless. For example, if you stay in Russia any length of time, and are too active in your investigations, as the American is sure to be, you will, of course, get sick more or less seriously. You must have a physician. Usually you find him an excellent doctor. He goes about his business without loss of time, and you recover as quickly as you would under the care of his American professional brother. Then you ask what the fee is. But there is no fee. "Nothing at all," the Russian doctor will say to you, or "What you like." But if some Russian friend has recommended this physician to you, he will tell you beforehand that nobody in Russia ever asks a physician for the amount of his bill. There is a sort of universal understanding that a gentleman is to pay his doctor a certain amount, and the physician depends upon his patient's generosity and sense of the proprieties for adequate compensation.

It is a curious custom. The Slavophile will assure you that it is a custom peculiarly Slav, and that it has its origin, like most Russian customs, in humanitarianism on the part of the doctor and graciousness on the part of the patient. The Slavophile's theory is that the custom originated in the desire of the physician to give his healing services freely to the afflicted, and with no thought of pay. "It is repugnant to the Russian mind," said a Russian friend, "that the physician engaged in the almost holy calling of alleviating pain, of curing human ills, of saving human life, should put a price upon his services. You might as well expect a drowning man, in a shipwreck, who is saved by the efforts of life-savers, who risked their own lives in the attempt, to say to his rescuers, 'What is your fee for this?'"

Another explanation was that the practice has its origin, as do so many Russian customs, in the Scripture, and that the healing of the afflicted by the Saviour, without money and without price, was the sacred ideal out of which grew this strange modern custom. "The Good Samaritan is at the bottom of it," said a Russian lady. Of course, nobody knows what the first reason of this practice is, but it exists. Russian doctors seem to get along very well, for the Russian patient who is cured is a very generous man. Indeed, generosity is a Russian trait, especially among themselves. No doubt is here expressed of their sharpness in money matters, of the hard bargains they drive, or even that there may be corruption in business and governmental life, on stories of which the English-speaking world has been for a century fed. But without affirming or denying this, it is, nevertheless, true that the Russian nature is a peculiarly generous one.

The Russian peasant's hospitality, for example, reminds one of the stories which we Americans love to hear of the hospitality of our forefathers when they were settlers in the wilderness. A certain Russian nobleman introduced an American to the father, the head of the family, before whose cottage, or hut, the troika stopped on entering the village. Immediately, of course, the peasant father invited both gentlemen into his very humble home. There the most simple and, because simple, charming manners were found. The coarse fare of the family was laid before their guests. There was no apology about it. The women were very glad to show their guests how they wove the family clothing on the rude loom, etc.

For this courtesy a piece of money was offered the head of the household. He received it without a word, but with a look of grave surprise. When this small Russian home had been left, the Russian nobleman said: "Oh, I forgot to tell you never to give a Russian peasant or any member of his family anything when he *invites* you into his home. He does not expect it, and is very much offended at it. You are his guest. In his opinion he is the lord of that castle. He and all of his family are immediately at your service, and everything they have, simple though it be, is yours."

On the contrary, the servants of every Russian house of any pretensions, and even minor officers on guard at public buildings, etc., all expect gifts of money, and sometimes considerable of it, too. But these are not a part of the Russian people, and this practice, which is common to English, French, and Germans, as well as Russians, is not characteristically Russian.

It is doubted whether there are one hundred thousand out of our eighty million Americans who believe that there is any jury system in Russia. Even few men who have given considerable attention to the rise of Russian power in the modern world understand this fact. The law courts in several cities, both in Russia and Siberia, were visited. In Moscow the writer saw criminals tried by a jury of twelve men, and, except for the language spoken, it would be impossible to tell that that jury was not a very substantial American jury instead of a Russian one. Inquiry as to its membership showed that on that jury there were shopkeepers, clerks, merchants, one nobleman, a banker, etc. The methods employed seemed to be very similar to those you may witness any day in an American criminal court. The only visible exceptions were that there were three judges instead of one and that these judges were uniformed; but when it is remembered that every class of government officials in Russia has its distinct and separate uniform, and that uniforms in Russia do not necessarily mean military service at all, but, on the contrary, may distinguish the civil official from the military official, this fact is not strange. Another exception is that the lawyers all wear evening dress—that is to say, the low-cut vest, the white and stiffly laundried shirt, the standing collar, the white lawn tie, and all of the appointments of the dress of an American gentleman when he goes out to dinner in the evening, are the costume of the Russian lawyer during the sessions of court. At least, this was true in Moscow on the occasions when the courts of that real Muscovite capital were visited.

Visit now another court-room. This time let us take a department answering to our equity court here or in England. Here is the bench for the judge, precisely as in America. Here are seats for anybody who wants to observe the proceedings of the court, exactly as in America. (This is also true in the criminal courts, which are frequently largely attended by interested spectators.) A man and a woman, evidently a Russian farmer and his wife, are sitting expectantly on two of these seats in the body of the room, just as you will see American litigants of the same class awaiting the opening of court. The judge enters, seats himself, opens a book, and then calls the names of these two people. There is no answer, for evidently they are without a lawyer. So the judge looks about, and asks if these people are there. The man gets up and says that they are. The judge tells them to come forward. They go forward, and then there are other proceedings, without the least bit of difference, so far as you can see, in form of procedure, from those of the similar courts in our own country.

Some differences, however, are even visible to the eye and ear of the uninstructed stranger. Over the bench of every court-room hangs the portrait of the Czar. In every court-room, too, and in every judge's office, there is the holy icon. Also, on a pedestal near the bench, is a volume of the Sacred Scriptures.

"What is this room for?" was asked of a Siberian lawyer who was explaining the various rooms of the court-house in a Siberian city. Here was a room for the witnesses who were waiting until they could be examined. Here was a room for the lawyers. Here was the judge's room. Over there was the jury-room, and, of course, the court-room showed in itself what it was, because it was like a court-room any place else. "But what was this room for?" was asked. The answer became apparent almost with the question, for out of it stepped the familiar Russian priest, benevolent of appearance, with long, blond beard and flowing hair, and dark garments reaching to his feet. The priest in Russia, it appears, administers the oath to the witnesses. At least, this was true in two courts visited, one in Russia itself and one in Siberia.

"You see," said a lawyer, with great irreverence, all the more astonishing because irreverence is seldom found in Russia—"you see," said he, "these people would not think they had been sworn unless the priest administered the oath on the Scriptures." Thus, again, cropped out the religious nature of the Russian.

It is rather startling, considering our notions of Russian and Siberian life, to hear the cry of a newsboy on a boat in the Amur River. Yet at certain points the Russian counterpart of the American news-vender boards these far-Siberian craft and sells daily papers, magazines, and other current and transient literature.

A long, low, one-story brick building attracted the traveller's attention in Irkutsk, Siberia. It was the office of one of the daily newspapers of this commercial capital of the Czar's far dominions. It is a two-sheet, four-page publication, filled almost exclusively with news. The more important information from Europe it receives by telegraph. Other news is copied from the news items of the more notable Russian journals. In the few copies inspected there was a fairly free discussion of all subjects of local and provincial interest; no editorial comment, however, was found on any political subject in the sense that we understand political subjects here in America.

To the American stranger within her gates St. Petersburg presents many surprises. But no surprise, perhaps, is greater than the news-stands on her streets, which are not unlike the news-stands in New York, only, of course, smaller and fewer. Numbers of different daily papers are published in the capital, and sold just as we sell them here. In Moscow the same is true. No business man in this industrial capital of old Russia is without his daily paper any more than the American business man is. Upon having random copies of different papers translated, they were found to be surprisingly full of both local and foreign information, and the expression of opinion concerning matters of interest to their readers was astonishingly free—surprising and astonishing only when we consider the prevailing American view as to the suppression of free speech in Russia.

Of course, in comparison with our American newspapers, these Russian newspapers are inferior from every point of view. Indeed, the American newspaper man would not call them newspapers at all, perhaps. Also, there is, of course, nothing but contrast in the freedom of speech and opinion as exemplified by English, French, or American newspapers and the relatively guarded and timid utterances of the Russian press. The point is that Russia is not without her daily newspaper. The people are not without their current literature. Here is a partial list of newspapers and magazines published in Moscow, which will give some idea of their scope: *Architectural Motives*, *Bulletins of the Polytechnic Society*, *The Veterinary Review*, *Round the World*, *Philosophical and Psychological Matters*, *The Sunday*, *Sunday*

Conversations, Medical Communications, The Moscow Metropolitan Police News, Statistics of Prices on Materials and Provisions, The Pedagogical Magazine, The Booksellers' News, The Bicyclist News, The Surgery News, The Friend to Animals, Reading for the Soul, The Children's Magazine, Physics and Geography, Russian Physician's Journal, The Sport Journal, Communications of the Moscow Imperial Technical Society, Geography, The Dentist, The Moscow Townhall News, The Physical Anthropological Review, The Clinical Journal, The Hunting Journal, The Pilot, The Courier, The Commercial and Technical Advertiser, The Lumber Trade News, Little Tales, The Mathematical Review, The Medical Guide, The Medicinal Review, The Miller, The Moscow Newspaper, The Moscow News, The Moscow Messenger, The Moscow Ecclesiastical News, The Ant, The News of the Day, The News of the Season, The Pedagogical News, The Orthodox Messenger, Nature and Hunting and Sport Journal, The Breeding of Birds, The Distraction, The Artisan's Journal, The Native Language, The Russian Thought, The Russian Archives, The Russian Messenger, The Russian Zither-Player, The Russian News, The Russo-English Commercial News, Russian Horticulture, The Russian Speech, Garden and Orchard, The Agricultural Journal, The Family, Judiciary Dramas, Play Bills, Theatrical News, Technical Communications and Industrial News, The Commercial and Industrial News, Communications of the Physical Society, Communications of the Physiological Institute, Moscow University, The Pharmaceutical News, The Pharmaceutist, The Philological Review, The Photographic Review, Lectures at the Imperial Historical and Archæological Society, The Ethnological Review. All told, there are over one hundred periodicals in Moscow alone.

Here is a small number of St. Petersburg periodicals: *The Artillery Journal, Archives for Biology, Archives for Veterinary Sciences, Archives for Psychology, Neurology, and Judicial Psycho-Pathology, The Typical Theatre Play*

Bills, The Bibliographical Newspaper, Bibliographical News, The Bibliographer, The Exchange News, God to Aid, The Hospital Gazette, The Tartar, Care for Your Health, The Russian Telegraphic Agency's Bulletins, The Bicycle, The Veterinary Library, The Veterinary Assistant Surgeon, The Byzantine Messenger, The Violoncellist, The Army Physician's Journal, The Military Magazine, The Revival, The Sunday, Education and Instruction, The Physician, The Homœopathist, The World's Post, The Universal Technical Review, The Metropolitan News, Statistics of Prices, The Vienna Fashion, The Military Clergy's Messenger, The Graphical Art News, The European Messenger, The Physical Sciences Messenger, The Imperial Russian Horticultural Society's Messenger, The Foreign Literature Magazine, Foreign Agriculture, The Engineering Department's Messenger, The Fashion, The Corn Trade Gazette, The Sea Engineer's Society's Messenger, The Military Science Journal, The Technical Society's Gazette, The Veterinary Gazette, The Law Messenger, The Breeding of Birds, The Russian Red Cross Society's Messenger, The Agricultural Journal, The Russian Brewery Journal, Theatrical and Musical Journal, The Sobriety Gazette, The Financial, Industrial, and Commercial Messenger, The Orderly, The Mining Journal, The Advertiser, The Citizen, Graphical Art and Printing Industry, The Freight's List, The Village, Journal for Theatre and Art, The Home Library, Leisure and Work, Leisure for Blind People, The Russian Newspaper, Leisure for Children, The Childhood, The Zoological Museum's Annals, The Imperial Theatre's Annals, The Weekly Report, The Railways, For Women, Old Times, The Picturesque Review, The Life, Life and School, Journal for Feminine Pathology, The Journal for Everybody, Review of Reviews and Encyclopedian Review, The Medical Chemistry and Pharmacy Journal, The Board of Schools Journal, The Justice Department's Journal, Words for the Soul, The Star, The Agricultural Gazette, The Architect, The Dentist's Journal, The Toys, Communica-

tions of the Agricultural Department, Art and Artistic Review, The Historical Review, The Breeding of Horses, The Peasant's Housekeeping, The Horizon, The Deaf Mute's Education, Literature, Literature for the Family, The Ray, The Forest Journal, The Lord's Worlds, The World of Art, The Fashionable Courier, The Naval Magazine, Music and Song, The Observer, The People, The Scientific Review, The Architect's Week, The News and Exchange Gazette, The New Journal for Foreign Literature, Art and Science, The Novelist, The Culture, The St. Petersburg Gazette, Polytechnic Sciences, The Post and Telegraph Journal, The Government's Messenger, The Industrial World, The Explorator, Russia, The Russian School, The Russian Elementary Tutor, The Russian Tourist, The Russian Wealth, The Russian Economist, The Metropolitan Courier, The Insurance Review, The Insurance News, The Northern Courier, The Prison's Messenger, The Church Messenger, The Church News, School and Housekeeping, The Electricity, The Electrician, The Lawyer's Gazette, The Universal History Messenger.

The total number of St. Petersburg periodicals is considerably over three hundred.

Of the publications above mentioned, those which deal with scientific and military subjects are very creditable. Perhaps there are no more thoroughly scientific publications printed in America than there are in Russia. This, of course, however, is a matter of opinion. The military publications, too, are said to be quite equal to those of any other country.

The censorship of foreign newspapers and magazines is still rigid in Russia. However, it is in the process of relaxation; also it is by no means perfect. For example, the letter of Tolstoi to the Czar and his ministers, which went to the limit of our American ideas of free petition, was found blotted out in one copy of the London *Times*, and yet another copy, obtained in Russia, had the whole letter without an erasure. This suggests a languor and indifference on the part of the censors. The method of censoring foreign publications distasteful to the government is simple. It consists merely in obliterating the entire article or paragraph. In the middle of a page you will see, perhaps, a whole column made blank and black. It is as if a roller of printer's ink had been run over the objectionable article. Where the obliteration of an article is attempted, it is, so far as observed, quite thorough. Not a word or a letter can be made out. The whole thing is simply sponged off, as it were, with blackness.

Not all books are permitted in Russian book-stores, yet suppression is not so complete as the uninstructed American visitor imagines. For example, a certain novel by an English author, which the writer was informed would be objectionable if found by the custom officers on crossing the German frontier into Russia, was thrown out of the car window; yet in the English book-store in St. Petersburg this very novel was found on sale. Again, information was had in London that a certain book on Russia was not permitted within the dominions of the Czar, yet this entire work was purchased in a Russian book-store. Still again, a certain writer has published several volumes of great learning and astonishing research upon Russian institutions and practices. Positive information was had that this work also was excluded, yet an excellent English translation of every page of it was procured right in St. Petersburg. Nevertheless, books, papers, magazines, and all literature which tend to discredit Russian institutions and to undermine the people's respect for authority of the government are still carefully excluded.

"We do not understand why we should allow other people to abuse us in our own house," said a Russian apologist for this practice. "With the exception of a very small percentage of us, we Russian people are very well content with our Russian institutions and Russian administration. Yet here comes a volume by some fanatical critic of everything Russian, with ideas and notions subversive of the whole scheme of our Slav civilization. Nine times out of ten the writer is ignorant of the facts which he assumes to set forth. Oftener still his views and arguments based on those facts are plainly the work of some hare-brained person who wants to reform the world. Very frequently people abuse us with the pen who have never been within the borders of our land; but if we admit the work of a thoroughly studious, well-informed writer, whose facts are accurate and whose criticisms are carefully reasoned, we must admit all. We think it better and easier to exclude all. Especially is this so when we fail to see what possible good it could do, anyhow."

Reading among the people is increasing. This is due to the rapid growth of both common and ecclesiastical schools throughout the empire, and it is also due to a peculiar custom prevailing in the Russian army. It is said to be the duty of the officers to instruct the illiterate recruit in reading and writing. No doubt this duty is performed very negligently; yet certain it is that peasants from the agricultural districts of the empire hundreds of miles from any large city, who had been taken into the army and were being sent uninformed to the Far Eastern frontier, were seen day after day absorbed in various little pocket volumes. One of these little books, which a peasant soldier was not only reading but carefully studying, was a simple and elemental work on physiology. Another soldier had a little paper-covered book on the horse, its proper management and care, together with an account of the diseases of the horse, and how they should be treated. Still another one had a paper-covered novel, dealing of adventure and hair-breadth 'scapes. It was the Russian counterpart of our American dime novel.

It is certain that the working-people in the great cities do considerable reading. The country peasants also do some reading. In the book-stores, or stalls, where the military and religious prints to which reference has been made were sold there were perfect stacks of these low-class works of fiction. Mostly they are stories of desperate adventure. Also they have pictures on the back covers representing frightful encounters. One of these novels was found which assumed to tell of the life of the American pioneer and his conflicts with the American Indian. On the back of it was a picture of the American Indian and the trapper engaged in deadly conflict.

"I should judge from your supply of those books that you have a heavy demand for them," was suggested to the bookseller.

"Oh yes, that is quite true," he answered. "The people buy these novelettes constantly, and in great quantities. They buy more of these than they do of any other kind of books we keep. Next to these are Bible stories and religious legends. Indeed, the sale of these religious booklets almost equals the sale of the novels of adventure."

It was found that the sale of this low-priced and low-grade literature was in about the reversed proportion of the sale of the colored prints or pictures; that is, more religious pictures were sold than prints representing war scenes, although the sale of the latter almost equalled the former. Conversely, more stories of adventure and travel are sold than books containing stories of Biblical times, although the sale of the latter almost equalled the former.

At several of the book-stands patronized exclusively by the working-people, some of Tolstoï's stories were found on sale. They are readily purchased and widely read. Time did not permit such careful inquiry as to discover whether or not all of his novels are published and read in Russia, though the information was—and such investigation as could be made confirmed it—that only one or two of Tolstoï's novels are suppressed. Practically all of his religious and sociological essays, however, are probably prohibited. Many of these essays and articles of the great Russian dreamer are fearless, even violent, and most direct attacks upon the Russian national Church, on the one hand, and upon all government, and especially Russian government, on the other hand.

Their suppression is not surprising when one considers the Russian point of view. No one ever attacked any Church organization more unsparingly than does Tolstoï, and this while still a member of the Church organization which he is assailing. His last attack upon the Church was so bitter, and he denounced with such violence not only the Church organization and administration of Russia but the whole modern practice of Christianity, that the Church authorities excluded Tolstoï from membership in the Church. It was the same thing frequently done twenty years ago in every religious community in the United States. The expulsion from a Church society of any of our American denominations years ago because some member of some local Church disagreed with the teachings of his denomination on some Scriptural passage was, in a very mild form, the same punishment for the same offence for which Tolstoï was excommunicated from the Russian Church.

XXVIII

THE RUSSIAN COMMON SCHOOL AND COUNTRY HOSPITAL

"PERHAPS our hospital will interest you," said a resident of a Russian country town, which was the headquarters or seat of the zemstvo of that locality. Hospital in a town of that size! It was surprising; for no such institution would be found in an American town of many times its population. So the hospital was visited. It was located perhaps half a mile from the town itself. It stood in a pleasant field, with shady trees hard by. It was a long, low building of brick, with but a single story. Two young physicians were in charge. Busy about their duties were several women nurses, dressed as the American trained nurse is attired. The rooms, and, indeed, the whole place, were scrupulously clean, and the familiar odor of disinfectants characteristic of all such places filled the air. The few patients appeared to be well attended, and the beds on which they lay were comfortable and spotless. The laboratory equipment of this establishment appeared to be extremely generous, and the surgical instruments especially were numerous and up to date.

"Yes," said the Russian who guided the visitor from the town to this institution of healing, "we are very much pleased with our progress in hospital building and in all departments of the medical profession. Indeed, there seems to be in recent years an epidemic of hospital building, but whether it is permanent or not, of course I cannot say." But whether permanent or not, certain it is that you will run across a surprising number of up-to-date hospitals in certain country districts of the empire. Upon this being called to the attention of a Russian lady of travel and education, she said: "I think it is a very hopeful development. There are four such hospitals within a radius of one hundred versts from this spot. They are all for the common people, too. This does not look like we are such a hard-hearted people as our enemies make us out to be, does it?"

In travelling across the country, from one estate to another, three little red school-houses were noted and examined. One was found in the centre of, perhaps, the most thriving agricultural village visited. It was about the size of an ordinary American country school-house, surrounded by a little yard, fenced in, and full of young trees. In the school-room itself were wooden benches and desks, exactly like those in an American country school some years ago. Every American who was raised in the country and who has reached thirty years of age has gone to school in just such a school-house, and sat on just such benches, and carved just such wooden desks. And these Russian boys and girls apparently do the same things that the American boys and girls in our country schools did twenty years ago.

The school was not in session in any country school-house visited, because it was summer, and the year's term had expired and the fall term had not begun. In the little school-house described, in the peasant village, the teacher was a young woman. She did not live in the village, however, and there was no opportunity of conversation with her. Several peasant mothers of the children who attended the school dropped curiously in, however, and the conversation with these women was engaging in its simplicity and fervor. None of these women could read and write, but they were delighted beyond measure that their children were being taught these wonderful accomplishments.

"Oh yes," said one of these Russian mothers, "we are

so glad that our children will know how to read and write and make figures and do everything else that the high people can do."

"We had no chance ourselves, you see," said another, "and it makes us all happier to think that our boys and girls can have a chance."

With others the expressions were duplicates of those old-time American fathers and mothers who "had no education," but who were willing to deprive themselves even of the necessaries of life to "give our children a chance." With all the racial differences and the improvements of them, how alike, after all, is human nature when you get to the heart of it.

Many copy-books were still in the school-room, and these were inspected. The penmanship of the young learner was very poor. Not in one single instance, in the copy-book of either a boy or girl, were observed neatness and precision of chirography. It was pointed out that this inattention to the details of penmanship was perhaps partly racial, the Russian being universally negligent, despite his passion for form; and that it was partly due to the intellectual languor from which the Russian peasant is just recovering. The contrast between the writing of these Russian children and the penmanship of the children who are beginning to learn to write in American schools in our Pacific possessions is startling.

Scores of copy-books were examined in various towns of Luzon, and the printed copy at the top of the page was reproduced with almost the precision of an engraving. No American copy-book has been seen which presents such perfect, literal, exact reproduction of the copy at the top of the page as those made by the Philippine children in our American schools in the Philippines. This superiority of penmanship on the part of Filipino children over Russian children does not, by any manner of means, indicate greater intelligence of the former; it indicates, first of all, a peculiar adeptness in copying and in all things done by the hand, which is a characteristic of the Filipino and Malay everywhere; it indicates, in the second place, the superiority of our American method of teaching.

At another little red school-house, standing perhaps a quarter of a mile from another Russian country village, the teacher was a man. He was married, and at the time the school was visited husband and wife were living in the school-house itself. It was a duplicate of the school-house above described. This particular teacher seemed to have in his work the enthusiasm of a missionary. And when your Russian is an enthusiast he is the most enthusiastic enthusiast in the world. The mission of this young Russian man was to give his whole life to the instruction of the rising generation of Russians, so far as he could.

"I find my scholars eager to learn," said he. "I do not find teaching hard. I am in love with my work. My pay, of course, is small. I can hardly live on it; but what of that? I do live on it, and that is enough. I am not teaching in order to make money. I am teaching in order to do good. All I expect, all I ask, all I want is enough to keep me comfortable. My wife and myself are very happy in our work."

Also, throughout the country is an occasional ecclesiastical school or seminary. These are usually large brick buildings, very much like similar brick buildings in the smaller American towns. These are established and conducted by the Church authorities. In these institutions everything is taught that is taught in the common schools of the country, and much more besides. Especial stress, however, is laid upon religious instruction.

Indeed, religious instruction permeates every branch of study and every hour of the school-day in the Russian school, just as religion saturates all Russian life, official, commercial, domestic. A set of school-books was purchased in a Siberian town. Here is a translation from one of the elementary readers, which, perhaps, gives a better idea of how religion is the beginning and the end of all Russian instruction than any other description can give. The first paragraph of the first page, after the alphabet and numerals (in Slavic, Arabic, and Roman), is as follows:

> "Now, dear boys, we have finished the spelling, and may, without haste, read words and whole sentences. In all this God has helped us in His love and mercy to us. To Him we consecrate the learning we have gained, and this we fulfil in reading and learning prayers with which it is necessary for us to commence, live, and finish every day. But before we commence to learn to pray to God, let us try to acquire the clearest possible understanding about what praying means and how should we pray. In the prayers we either glorify, that is, praise God, or beg Him satisfy our wants, or thank Him for His mercy to us," etc.

This book, as has been said, is an elementary reader. It is paper-covered, and on the outside is a picture of a child kneeling in prayer, its head lifted to a light which is breaking from heaven through the clouds. The hands are brought together in an attitude of supplication. The second picture in the book is of two of the Scriptural prophets holding between them the Russian cross. Then follow pictures representing the creation of the heavens and the earth; of Adam and Eve in the Garden; of the Tower of Babel; of Abraham about to sacrifice Isaac, and stayed in the act by the angel; of the Egyptians perishing in the waters of the Red Sea.

Then full-page and very fair illustrations of the angel telling Mary of the coming of Christ; of the Saviour in the manger; of the star in the east and the wise men adoring it; of the ascension into heaven, etc., etc. Throughout the book the majority of the illustrations are from the Bible.

That we may get some idea of what is taught in the Russian common schools, let us take from a descriptive geography some quotations. Here is a description of the United States, its people, government, and institutions, taken from a Russian elementary descriptive geography:

"The United States form a federation of thirty-nine (1894) independent republics (States), ten Territories, and one District, Columbia, in which is situated the capital of the empire, Washington.

"The federation is governed by the Congress, which is composed of deputies elected by the inhabitants.

"Congress makes the laws concerning war or peace, dealing with other empires, settles duties and taxes, etc.

"The President watches over the execution of these laws (elected four years).

"In all other affairs of State administration, every State is governed by its Senate, which is composed of deputies elected by the State.

"The executive power in each State belongs to the elected Governor.

"The Territories are administered by the Governors nominated by the President of the United States.

"*In this country there is no difference of class among the people. All inhabitants enjoy the same rights, and only differ in the way of occupations.*

"*There is no state (government) religion. Everybody is at liberty to confess to the faith which he likes best.* The most people belong to the Protestant Church, which here is divided into many sects.

"In no empire is there paid so much attention to the public instruction as in the United States; no other country has such enormous money sums donated for this purpose as the United States, and, therefore, the number of public schools and other educational institutions here is very great. The towns of Boston and Philadelphia especially have numerous institutions for the culture of science.

"The sources of wealth of the inhabitants of the States remind of Russia; just as here agriculture and cattle farming form the principal occupation of the people. But through the warmer climate of the States, both these sources are more productive than in Russia."

The maps in this geography are fairly accurate, but are, of course, enormously inferior to the maps in our American elementary geographies. The pictures, however, representing animal and plant life and native customs in various countries, are equal to and not dissimilar from those of our American geographies of like grade studied by most Americans, who are now grown men and women, when they were boys and girls.

Extracts from still another book, an elementary history, will show what the Russian children are taught concerning the other European countries. Here is one on Germany:

"Thirty-six per cent. of the German population confess to the Catholic and sixty-four per cent. the Protestant faith; the Catholics are in majority in the South, the Protestants in the North.

"Elementary instruction is obligatory all over Germany for all inhabitants. Nowhere in Europe, except in Switzerland, are there so many public schools (sixty thousand) and other places of instruction as here; in Germany are twenty universities, of which many are famous all over the world, gathering scholars not only from Europe but from other parts of the world. Such are the Universities of Berlin, Leipsic, Heidelberg, and others.

"The German Empire is a federation of twenty-six states, each of which has its own government and its own laws; but affairs concerning the defence of the German Empire, its dealings with other states, as also the administration of posts, telegraphs, railways, and the monetary system, are laid in the hands of the German Emperor, whose power in all named matters is limited by the parliament (Reichstag) and Imperial Council, consisting of deputies from all the states of the empire. The Prussian King at the same time is German Emperor."

Here is one on France:

"Nearly eleven-twelfths of all the population belong to the Catholic Church.

"The instruction of the people ranges lower than in other empires of Central Europe, with the exception of Austria, but higher instruction in France has many institutions, and Frenchmen have done much in the field of science and art.

"The form of government is the republican; the law-giving power belongs to the National Assembly, the executive power to the President. In administrative respect the country is divided into eighty-seven parts, called departments. The departments carry the names of the rivers on which they are situated."

Again, here is one on England:

"State religion, Anglican Church, but a great part of the people in Scotland profess the Presbyterian faith, in Ireland the Catholic; besides, there are in England many followers of different sects.

"In England, as in France, the public instruction is not widely expanded; but for higher instruction you find many institutions and twelve universities.

"The form of government is the monarchical, in connection with a parliament. In administrative respect all England is divided into one hundred and seventeen counties."

"That structure there will interest you," said the interpreter, pointing to a very large and fairly attractive brick building in a certain Siberian city. "It is the Girls' Seminary."

To the real extent to which the instruction of women is carried in Russia no guess is hazarded. But it seemed that there was no end of girls' schools and girls' seminaries, and this, that, or the other institution for the instruction of girls. Also technical schools of various sorts are springing up throughout the empire. Frequently you will run upon some special institution of learning such as the University for the Study of Oriental Languages at Vladivostock. In Blagovestchensk, Siberia, a neat little structure was pointed out as a school of riparian navigation. And Russians contend that their military schools, and particularly one institution of this kind, are the most perfect in the world. The common schools are fairly numerous, too. Strange to say, they are more numerous in Siberia, in proportion to the population, than in Russia itself. Here again it is observed, in education, as has before been observed in railway administration, that reforms come from without inward, instead of the reverse.

It must not be inferred from this that education in Russia is universal, or even general, and especially that no great educational wave is sweeping over the empire.

But the truth is that popular education in Russia has a very fair beginning, and that substantial and even notable progress is being made. A good index of this is found in the increasing numbers of peasants who can read and write when taken into the army from their homes. It is said that at the time of the Crimean war but one peasant out of every fifty taken into the service was able to read and write. Only a few years ago this had been reduced to five; and at the present time the information is that one out of every three Russian peasants can read and write when first taken into the army. This shows deplorable illiteracy, it is true, even at the present time; but it also shows extraordinary progress during the past five decades. For if fifty years ago but one peasant out of every fifty could read and write when he went into the army, and to-day one in three can read and write when he is taken into the army, the increase of literacy among the common people of Russia is shown to be astonishingly rapid.

There are, all told, something over eighty thousand schools in Russia, taught by over one hundred and fifteen thousand teachers, and attended by about four million pupils. Compared with the immense school attendance in the United States, the number of children in Russian schools is very small indeed; and when it is remembered that the population of the Russian Empire is approximately sixty millions greater than the population of the United States, the disparity of the school attendance in the two countries becomes all the more striking. The contrast between school attendance in Russia and other European countries, including England, is also considerable; but, of course, by no means so emphatic as the comparison of Russian and American school attendance.

From another view-point, however, these Russian educational statistics are by no means gloomy. Remembering that the overwhelming masses of the people of Russia were slaves within the memory of living men; remembering that Russian educational progress, as Americans understand that term, can hardly be said to have begun a quarter of a century ago; remembering the wilderness of popular ignorance which education had to penetrate throughout the empire, it is the contention of patriotic Russians that education among the common people of the empire has made very respectable progress and that the present outlook is decidedly hopeful. It is certain that, in estimating the quality and weight of this people in the coming affairs of the world, other nations must understand that, speaking in historical terms, they must reckon with Russia as a consolidated nation, whose peasant masses can read and write and think, and whose intellectual advance, while slow, like all the massed movements of the Slav, is steady, continuous, and increasing, and also like the characteristics of Russian advance in every other direction.

XXIX

THREE RUSSIANS OF WORLD FAME

THE subjects of the Czar number one hundred and forty million souls. Out of these one hundred and forty million human beings, three men loom so vastly that they have taken the attention of the entire contemporary world. So true is this that it is no immoderate simile to say that they are three mountain peaks, rising sharp and clear and to far heights out of the steppes and plains made up of the masses of Russia's millions. Two of these three men were the most determined upholders of the theory and practice of autocracy. One of these three men is the most determined opponent now living of the government of the Czar and of all government. Two of these men are the ablest minds to whom the Czar looks for counsel and the strongest wills that guard his throne; one of these three is the incessant protestor against the plans, policies, and purposes of his sovereign.

It is a striking and significant fact that the two of these three men who are the Czar's ablest and most efficient helpers, as well as the most determined believers in autocracy as the only correct theory of government, came from the common people, and rose through a series of lowly stations to the seats of the mighty; while the one of the three who objects, protests, denounces, is one of the great nobles of the empire, belonging to one of Russia's oldest and most illustrious lordly houses. The first two are of the common people in birth, of the common people, too, in toil and struggle; but of the autocracy by virtue of their very natures, by force of their astonishing wills, and by reason of their firm and almost fanatical convictions. The other one of these three men is by birth an aristocrat of the aristocrats, by training and early life, again, an aristocrat of the aristocrats; but by his very nature a socialist, and by conviction more fanatical than the autocratic convictions of the other two, an aggressive disbeliever in every form of human government which maintains itself by force, no matter whether that government be republican or monarchial.

These three men are Leo Tolstoï, Sergius Witte, and Constantine Pobyedonostseff—Tolstoï, the noble, whom nature, conviction, and desire have made a peasant; Witte and Pobyedonostseff, whom nature, conviction, and desire have made the high officers of autocracy.

In considering these three men, we note that, first of all, there are certain similarities. Each is equally dogmatic. Each is equally sure that he is right and that everybody else is wrong. Each is an autocrat of nature's making. Neither is acquainted with the verb "to fail." Neither believes in the word "impossible." And all of them are intensely unpopular.

A charming bit of rural Russia are the gently rolling slopes and woods that lead up to Tolstoï's estates. Almost in sight of them an immense manufacturing establishment has been erected, and it is to this which Count Tolstoï refers in his article in the *North American Review* of April, 1901. It is a splendid road over which your troika dashes until within full view of Count Tolstoï's house—one of the few excellent roads of Russia. Before entering Tolstoï's grounds you turn from this splendid highway onto a dirt road that leads down between modest hills, green with grass or proud with noble forest, and pass through a valley. On the left are fields, and peasants at work. From this valley the ground rises by easy elevation to a knoll, concealed and adorned with great trees. The road leads directly between two massive stone pillars, which, however, support no gate. One of them perceptibly leans out of plumb. A heavy mud-hole, just before you pass between them, has hastily filled in. A little pond or lakelet to the left, with all the possibilities of loveliness, is muddy and unattractive. To the right a smaller pond is covered with patches of green scum. An avenue of trees, cathedral-like, border and bend above the roadway leading from the entrance to the crest of the hill, where the buildings are. The roadway itself has not seen gravel for a long time, and is full of furrows and ruts. The house, painted white, and with vines climbing up the slender pillars of the porch, is modest. There is an open space just before it, then more trees, and then beyond another house, where the son of the great Autocrat of Protest has his residence. Beyond this are the stables. Upon the other side of the house is the great square common to pretentious Russian country homes, surrounded by a broad and generous walk or avenue, which is bordered on either side by splendid trees.

Before the Count has risen you will have time to visit the peasant village across the ravine. There are two or three brick houses, of a single story, of course, in its long, broad street. They seem to be evidence of some spurt of activity many years ago. They are neglected now. Most of the cottages are neglected, too. Poverty, want of care, rebellion at system are visible on every side. The peasants look poor and ill-dressed. A legless beggar cries piteously for alms. Conditions of non-improvement and degeneration are so pronounced that your mind reverts to another peasant village, on the estate of a certain noble, not two hundred miles away—clean, well built, well kept, industrious, with yards and vines and fruit; and, in the midst of all, a little school-house, with desks and benches, for all the world like an American country school-house many years ago.

Some beggars are seated beneath the tree, immediately

in front of Tolstoï's door. They enter while you wait, and then return apparently pleased. Soon Count Tolstoï comes out himself. What a mighty man he must have been in his youth! What a mighty mind still glows through those clear and cold, gray eyes! The front-head is a dome where thought dwells; but the back-head, too, is powerful—a thing so often absent in mere thinkers. This man, you are sure, will never be content merely to think—he must do. And the face—it is the face of determination itself. William Lloyd Garrison had such a face. The spirit of Garrison is there—"I will not equivocate, I will not retreat a single inch, and I will be heard."

The garb of the man fits in well with the picture of his mentality and character. It is a coarse, cool, bluish stuff; trousers thrust, after the Russian manner, into the top-boots; the simple blouse belted; no collar to conceal the shrunken but yet sinewy neck. To be sure, the physical appearance of the man is not remarkable; on the contrary, it is typical. You may see thousands upon thousands of Russian peasants who look like Tolstoï; but let his personality seize upon you and you will see no person who looks like Tolstoï. It is a personality to compel and repel. It is mentality which does not compromise or argue, but announces.

More charming manners cannot be imagined. He has the courtesy of nature—of the trees, the flowers, and the breezes of the spring. Like every great man, he is simple; but there is a touch of the grandeur of the old-time fashion about him, too. And as you walk with him among the stately avenues of trees, and listen to his large conversation on great topics, the vastness of the man looms up—vast in his conceptions, vast in his fanaticism, vast in his dogmatism—above all, vast in his utter fearlessness.

He talks about great things from the very first sentence and without any invitation. No trivialities for him. It is unnecessary, of course, for Americans, who have so thoroughly read Tolstoï to recount his views.

Some passages, from a half-day's listening to his words, may serve to vitalize the printed page, however. The subject of first interest to him is his own land; the subject of next interest to him is America—not that he approves of our institutions, for he does not. He is in as complete revolt against our form of government as against all other forms of government. And for our material development he has nothing but contempt.

"You are given over to material things," said he. "Your forces seem to be spent on mills and railroads and the like. None of your great minds is now engaged in literature. The literary productions of America to-day are trivial—foolish. And in your statesmen there has been a decadence almost appalling. From Lincoln and the men of that time to your present public men has been a dreadful descent.

"Who are your writers now?" he asked. Upon their being named, he recognized two or three, and the rest, he declared, he never heard of. He put the stamp of "trivial" on most he knew of. Henry George he excepted, with enthusiasm. Whittier, he admitted, had a nobility of purpose and felicity of expression that lifted him out of the ordinary. So had Emerson. He mentioned Thomas Paine's *Common Sense*, the *Age of Reason*, the *Rights of Man*—he had read one of these and wanted the others. "He is your greatest mind," said Tolstoï. "Paine was profound and truthful, and dealt with fundamental things. Paine was worth while. So is Henry George. He is dead, is he not? Too bad. Your country and the world lost one of its greatest thinkers when he died. Both of these men had something of a conception of the wrong of governments and society, as now understood."

It was not a far cry from the subject of Paine to the subject of religion in general. Questions are unnecessary. His vivid mind burns steadily and needs not the fuel of interrogation. Of the Saviour he spoke reverently but not worshipfully. "Christ," said he, "the last great superstition." Did he not think Him divine? "Divine? Certainly not, except as all great teachers are divine; not otherwise." Inspired? "Yes, as all great teachers are inspired, and not otherwise." That He is the literal Son of God, that there was immaculate conception, that His agony saves people? "Superstition, superstition!" "The sacraments of the Church, founded upon the doctrine of his body and blood, are disgusting and foolish. But Jesus of Nazareth is the greatest teacher mankind has yet produced." Such was the tenor of the talk.

The failure to apply the teachings of Christ to the concrete activities of every day was an easy transition. "All rulers are usurpers," he said. But did he not think order and law were necessary? "What order or what law does Nature give? Such as she gives is enough, and anything more is irrational and artificial." The courts are points upon which his hostility is especially focused. Did he not think that the introduction of the jury system into Russia was a far step towards the protection of popular rights and liberties? "The jury," he exclaimed—"a jury is worse than a czar.[1] It is just twelve times worse, for it is twelve czars. What right have twelve men to sit in judgment upon another, more than one man?" According to the words of the Scriptures, "Judge not, that ye be not judged," was suggested. "Yes, that is it; but it is even deeper. We are all here in a state of nature. We have been perverted by artificial things. Let us return to a state of nature. Who gave man authority over his fellow-men?"

But would he have no restraint? "No; none at all." No matter what was the cause of violence, would he have no restraint? "No; none whatever."

"The statesmanship of Russian statesmen is stupid. No other word describes it. The maintenance of our great armies is unnecessary and outrageous. All war is

[1] Notwithstanding Tolstoï's antagonism to all government by force, it is said that the Czar is very fond of him, and that Tolstoï is the ardent personal friend of the Czar.

murder. The extension of our power over Manchuria, and the whole Chinese business, are without reason or sense. What good will it do?"

"It is too bad to see our statesmen following in the footsteps of yours in the matter of manufacturing and commercialism in general. Look at the hideous smoke-stacks of the great factories that are now scattered over Russia. They disfigure God's landscape." Count Tolstoï's whole talk here was Ruskinesque. Turning to the economic and political features of the manufacturing advance of Russia, he said: "It is all a mistake. We have more than a hundred million people. Scarcely more than one million of these are engaged in manufacturing." (He did not mean the hand manufacturing done by the "kustar trades"—that he approved of.) "How unjust that the remainder should be burdened for these few! Our country is naturally agricultural. We are an agricultural people. No good can come from turning us away from the natural current of our capabilities and physical condition." Tariffs are his particular abomination. "Tariffs," he said, "are unnatural. They are a pitiable artificiality to secure selfish ends. They keep the people of the world from mingling with one another."

"You are still having trouble in the Philippines, are you not? What is the condition there?"[1] He was extremely curious about our progress in the archipelago. "It is all a mistake," commented he; "so is England's experiment in India, South Africa—every place. So is ours in China. I do not consider that the so-called civilizing effects of the more advanced peoples justify, from any point of view, the government of another. Let them be as nature made them. If they are happier in their nakedness and beneath their palm-trees, let them remain so. It is not important that they do not develop the resources of the countries where nature has placed them. If nature

[1] This conversation occurred in June, 1901.

has placed mineral and wood and other things there, nature also placed them there. They may be better clothed, better fed, understand more under so-called civilized administration, but a bird in a cage is not as happy as one on the wing, no matter how gilded the cage may be."

Referring to the famous letter printed by the London *Times*, which he was represented as having sent to the Czar and his ministers, Count Tolstoï said that it was true that he had written and sent this letter. "Why not?" said he. "Why should I not say what I think and what I please?"

Such were the general tenor, atmosphere, and character of his remarkable conversation. It was protest against everything in the existing order, including religion. Witte he regarded as a foolish surface juggler, and Pobyedonostseff as the intellectual incarnation of tyranny. Any one, by reading certain of Tolstoï's later writings, such as his *North American Review* article of April, 1901, may reproduce for himself the conversation which he would be sure to have with this fearless Russian idealist and greatest of modern literary artists. His mind does not now dwell with any particular pride on his immortal creations of fiction. One gets the impression that he considers them trivial also—trivial, at least, in comparison with what he feels to be the mature thought of his advanced years. And all of his thought now is of fundamental reforms which search out the very heart of things. Of recent years, and at the present time, he has given attention chiefly to the problem of education. He thinks very poorly of our methods of education. Curiously enough, on this point his mind coincides somewhat with that of Pobyedonostseff, his great antagonist. Both of them seem to agree that the important thing is to instruct the people in morals, but when they come to what morals mean and how to teach them their minds instantly fly apart again.

Hasty though this sketch of Tolstoï is, space must be

taken for the mention of one without whom Tolstoï, with all his genius, all his art, all his fanatical will, would not be so well known to the world. That person is Tolstoï's wife. It could be well wished that some person sufficiently familiar might write a volume on the subject of the wife of this greatest literary artist which the nineteenth century has produced. Tolstoï himself is no exception to those weaknesses which genius everywhere, in some form or other, displays—a negligence of his affairs, which, if some person did not attend to them for him, would soon starve him out, and an almost abnormal dissatisfaction with his own work.

For be it known that Tolstoï's great novels, such as *Anna Karanina*, *War and Peace*, and the like, have been rewritten time and time again before they were given to the world. It happens that the great dreamer's handwriting is almost undecipherable. It is current that he has difficulty sometimes in reading it himself. There is only one person in Russia that can read every word that he writes, and that person is his wife. Every piece of literary work that Tolstoï has ever done has been copied, from the first word to the last, by this devoted woman. It is said, on good authority, that she copied over her husband's novel, *War and Peace*, no fewer than six times. *Anna Karanina* she transcribed several times. If the reader will pick up a copy of either of these novels, and think what it means to write out every word of them, the reader will understand the enormous labor performed by the wife of Tolstoï. If the reader will then reflect that these two novels are only a portion of his voluminous work, some dim comprehension will be secured of the world's debt to this silent partner of the most famous man the Slav race has produced, excepting only Peter the Great.

And this is only a portion of her labors. She it is who prevented Tolstoï from transferring every foot of his estates to the pcasantry and leaving himself and his family without a roof of their own. She it is who personally manages his still considerable holdings. She it is who attends to every item of the Count's finances. She it is who sees to the income from the literary product of her famous husband's amazing mind. For it must be known that if Tolstoï could have his way every word he writes would be given to the world without the slightest reward. Tolstoï thinks that no man has a right to put a price upon his thought. Keeping in the background, doing her work with patience and in silence, the wife of Tolstoï is not only his helpmeet, in the marital sense of that term, not only his amanuensis, his financier, his comforter; she is his very preserver.

Whether she agrees or disagrees with her husband's views is not known, except that she bitterly resents the action of the Greek Orthodox Church in excommunicating him, not so much on account of the excommunication itself as on account of its results. But whether this glorious woman is in agreement or antagonism with her husband's opinions and life, the love, aid, comfort, and protection with which she has surrounded him form one of the noblest and most beautiful stories afforded by the household life of any great man of the nineteenth and twentieth centuries.

The statement had been published throughout the United States in 1901 that Count Tolstoï was banished. Of course, this was not true. He lives at his home in the country, some miles beyond Tula, goes to town when he likes, to Moscow when he wishes, and in general, so far as could be observed, has as perfect personal liberty of movement and even speech as is enjoyed by a citizen of the United States. He was excommunicated by the Church; but denying, as he does, and with violence, every teaching of that institution—denying even the divinity of Christ—it appears to the impartial inquirer that the Church could take no other action. As has been remarked in another chapter, the same thing has been done many thousands of times by the various denominations of the United States, where their members dissented from their doctrines, for a much milder offence and on far less material points than is the case with Tolstoï and the Greek Orthodox Church. Believing nothing that the Church teaches, asserting even, with all the fearlessness of his volcanic nature, that its teachings are false in fact and ruinous in practice—teaching this in every way and on every occasion, how could the Church itself retain him as a member?

Such is the Autocrat of Protest in Russia. But he is not popular even among those who are in favor of improvement in many features of the Russian government and generally feel that the continuance of the advanced ideas begun by Alexander the Liberator is desirable. For example, an informing conversation occurred among several Russian gentlemen; but whether liberal or reactionary, there was general condemnation of Tolstoï's theories. "He is erratic, impossible, impracticable, and thus delays by unwise insistence upon fanatic propositions any real practical advance," said a brilliant man who was himself a liberal. "His power among extremists is due to the fact that because of his outspokenness and radicalism his name has become the flag of revolt," was the way a highly educated officer put it. Thus, the current of talk among Russians who would like to see some things bettered cannot be said to be favorable to Tolstoï. Nevertheless, all concede his splendid abilities, and it is easy to see that all Russians are proud of this the greatest intellect the Slav race has produced. Even where you will hear emphatic dissent from Tolstoï's more violent opinions, you will be astonished to find that the very man who thus denounces the views of Tolstoï the dreamer is a warm and even affectionate friend of Tolstoï the man.

"Oh yes, we all know here that Tolstoï is down on the Saviour," said one of the most accomplished women of the empire—one of the inner circle of the highest nobility, and, of course, a stanch adherent of the government.

"It is said, you know, that Tolstoï is jealous of Christ. It will end with him trying to establish a religion of his own."

This keen and witty woman's observations are a very fair reflection of the opinion the cultivated class entertains of Russia's greatest writer.

"Oh," said a wealthy young merchant of Moscow, "Tolstoï is impossible. We pay no attention to him here." Several peasants expressed utter indifference to him, and knew little or nothing about his teachings. Here and there you will find a Russian of the common people who knows something of him, but from such information as could be gathered it appeared that he has not yet reached even the fringe of the vast masses of Russians. Such, at least, was the result of the inquiries which the writer was able to make, which were too few, perhaps, and too superficial to be the basis of valuable judgment. On the other hand, it must be stated that others who have made more careful inquiry state that among the peasantry Tolstoï is beloved and reverenced as the "good old man" who is thinking of them and wants to help them. An incident was related by such an observer of a peasant who, upon being asked about Tolstoï, referred to him with childlike affection as "the father of the peasant," who knew what was best for them. But it is believed that so far as his name has penetrated into the homes of the Russian peasantry, it stands for some vague good, without any definite notions of what that good is.

But whichever view may be correct, it is certain that the influence of Tolstoï upon Russian thought and opinion is not yet so great as it is upon the thought and opinion of non-Russian nations, and especially the American people. As factors influencing Russian policy and Russian tendencies, it is doubted whether Tolstoï and his work are yet appreciable. Indeed, it is doubted whether Tolstoï himself thinks that he is accomplishing anything or will accomplish anything during the present generation or the next. He is looking to the future.

"All this wrong and folly are but passing phases," said he. "The people of the world two hundred years from now will be as much surprised that we endure many of the things which are now considered as admirable parts of our civilizations as we are amazed at many of the horrid practices of the dark ages."

As a force to be estimated in weighing Russian activities in the world at the present hour, this wonderful man may be left out of account. That he is a splendid dreamer of an ideal reign of peace and brotherhood over all the earth will be admitted even by his worst enemies in Russia itself. But his dreams are as yet nothing more than dreams. And so, with his dreaming, we may leave him to turn to the two other overpowering personalities of Russia, who are intellects of equal vigor, wills of equal dogmatism, and who, in addition, are the most effective present forces of the empire.

Of these let us first consider Sergius Witte — the incarnation of the practical, the personification of the business and commercial spirit of Russia, the business-man of the empire, the first modern, up-to-date financier and administrator Russia has yet produced. This is the man who took the almost Orientally disorganized finances of Russia in hand and reduced them, first, to a system along recognized lines of sound economics, and finally established the gold standard. This is the man through whose influence the government has become the owner and operator of more than two-thirds of the railroad mileage of the empire. This is the man who has adjusted tariffs on imports along the lines of radical protection for the purpose of building up Russian industry. This is the man who is determined that Russia shall herself manufacture everything the Russian people need. He it is who has taken in charge the monopoly of vodka. He is the chief inspiration of the "working-man's palace" in St. Petersburg and of similar movements throughout the empire. He is the controlling mind that directs the construction of the great Manchurian railway. He negotiates all the loans for the Russian government. His eye is upon every manufacturing establishment throughout the Czar's dominions. He is reforming the laws of mines and mining everywhere. It is Witte who has draughted the most comprehensive employer's liability law in Europe. Silent, taciturn, relentless, immovable, his personality has gradually grown upon the statesmen and financiers of other nations, until only two other men fill the imagination of Europe in equal measure.

This greatest dreamer of the present day will tell you that he has no use for dreams or dreamers; but by that he means those men who entertain theories which cannot be reduced to facts. "What can be done?"—that is his only question. Witte is the man who "does things" in Russia.

Perhaps there is no man in America so busy as he is; yet he does not appear hurried. He is a very tall man, very ungainly, and, though stiff in manner, is cordial with that genuineness which captivates.

The first thing that impresses you about Witte is perfect simplicity. This seems to be characteristic of all extraordinary men. A child or a backwoodsman or the most highly cultivated man of the world (and the manner of these three are almost the same) could not be simpler than this powerful minister. He speaks in a low voice, looking directly at you. What a steady eye! The freedom of his conversation, in view of your previous notions of Russia and Russians, astonishes you. There is not a cabinet officer in Washington who will talk with the apparent unreserve of this chief counsellor of the Czar. His eyes are large and brown, with an expression of patience and weariness about them which reminds you of what you read about the eyes of Lincoln. The eyes are not sharp or luminous, but have the speculative expression of those minds which are not content with things as they are, but are planning and dreaming of the things as they should be. His forehead is high, but not too high, of medium breadth; but between the ears the breadth is perceptibly greater, and the back-head, where resides the "drive" of the human intellect, is perfectly developed. His hair is brown, has a slightly waving effect, is of medium length, and is worn brushed back from the forehead. In his office he wears a common, unpretentious sack-coat, well-worn trousers, which bag at the knees, and shoes that show they do not receive overmuch attention. Everything reveals the characteristic indifference of great men for the details of personal appearance.

Where Tolstoï was interested in moral conditions, abstractly considered, Witte was interested in economic conditions reduced to actual facts. Particularly was he interested in those organizations of industry known in our country as trusts. Whether they were over-capitalized or had sufficient assets behind them was a matter to which he seemed to have given almost as much thought as he had given to problems affecting the Russian Empire itself. But Witte's interest in this feature of trust phenomena seemed to be only incidental to his general interest in the commercial possibilities of these aggregations of capital, especially in relation to foreign trade. How they were steadily to maintain prices appeared to him to be a matter of real concern. When it was suggested that he was able, by government purchases from steel organizations in Russia, and other methods, to influence, and indeed largely to maintain, prices, he replied: "Yes, but you forget that for any emergency we can immediately devise and put into operation a law which our world of people immediately obey"; and there spoke the true autocrat, this time the autocrat of finance and commercialism. Indeed, the three pre-eminent contemporary Russians—Tolstoï, Witte, and Pobyedonostseff—may each be called an intellectual autocrat—the Autocrat of Protest, the Autocrat of Commercialism, and the Autocrat of Orthodoxy.

It will be hard to find in America any one man who has so many enemies as this first of the Russians. But a traveller, listening to the assaults upon him from one end of the empire to the other, cannot but arrive at the conclusion that his enemies have been made by measures devised for the good of the whole Russian people, from adherence to which interested parties have not been able to shake him. The result of these hatreds is a swarm of calumnies, most, perhaps all, of which are declared by the best-informed men to be maliciously untrue. Certain it is that this greatest business-man ever called to the councils of the Czar is doing more to eradicate corruption from the Russian Empire than any one force in Russian history. He is doing this not by moralizing, but by the introduction of business method into the government's practical administration. A system of audits and counter audits is being effected which makes the pocketing of large sums of money by contractors very difficult, no matter how many officials connive at it.

When he becomes convinced of corrupt practices in any business or establishment, he does not hesitate to take special methods with reference to it. These arbitrary acts are, of course, very rare, the correction of nearly all abuses being left to the ordinary administration of rights and remedies in the courts of justice.

Witte is "a pessimist of conditions and an optimist of possibilities," to use the phrase of a brilliant writer. Indeed, his unpopularity began early in his ministerial career by his declaration that the abounding prosperity of Russia some years since was abnormal, and that a disastrous reaction was sure to follow. He plainly told investors that they were building great plants in Russia without reckoning with ultimate conditions. He discouraged rash enterprise everywhere. In conversation and public speech he proclaimed that the values of many corporations' shares, especially banking concerns, were swollen and fictitious. His maxim was, and is, that any prosperity which is unnatural is no prosperity at all, and that it is the sure and certain parent of disaster.

When he took office the Russian ruble was a more fluctuating currency than the Chinese tael. Gambling upon its changing value prevailed throughout the empire, and indeed all over Europe. Business was unsettled, investment excited and feverish, and the whole commercial world in that delirium of uncertain activity which comes from the expectation of unnatural profits and of the element of chance. Witte called in the circulation, reduced it to a limit, supplied the well-known principles of sound economics to the currency, and, finally, effected the *coup* of his career by placing Russia on the gold standard, together with the great commercial nations of the world. The brief limitations of this chapter do not permit even a summary of this extraordinary man's practical activity. These instances are given only as a hint of what he has done and is doing.

His most ambitious project, next to the establishment of the gold standard, is the scheme which is now being put into operation for taking over to the government the monopoly of vodka. Hereafter the government is to control the manufacture, and actually to conduct the sale, of this universally consumed national Russian drink. The conception was daring, its execution cautious. As in every radical reform in Russia, it was first tried in one province, and, succeeding there, it was gradually extended to others, being improved and remedied as experience and actual operation suggested. It has been said that the tax on vodka maintained the army and navy of Russia. This, of course, is an exaggeration, but it is probably no exaggeration that the profits which the government ultimately will derive from its sale will largely support the army and navy. Together with this reform, the government is introducing practical temperance measures. The instance cited in another chapter will be recalled, of minute instructions to the district officials upon the subject of temperance of the people, and the literature, brief and easily read, to be distributed to the people, found in the government offices of a country town. The active mind behind all of this is Witte.

The consequences of the Russian government's monopoly of the manufacture and sale of vodka are so numerous, far-reaching, and radically important that a chapter, or even a volume, might be profitably employed in their description. The best that can be done in these pages is to note the large general effects which are most striking to the observer's eye. First of all, the vodka-shop, which hitherto has been perhaps the most prominent feature of every Russian town or village, is disappearing, if, indeed, it has not already disappeared. These public-houses were at once the opportunity and the inducement for the peasant to drink. In these nests of congenial intoxication the peasants would gather, and, imbibing until their ready money was exhausted, would mortgage their belongings, and even their apparel, to purchase more of this Russian drink. The result was that these vodka-shops, scattered by the tens of thousands all over the empire, were centres not only of drunkenness but of poverty. All this is being abolished, if, indeed, the process is not now entirely complete. The peasant can no longer repair to these places of his fleeting joy and permanent ruin. He must buy vodka at government stores, and either take it home to drink, or at least consume it some place else than at the place where he purchases it.

Then, again, the peasant can no longer buy his vodka by the drink. He cannot buy less than a certain quantity fixed by the government. This quantity of vodka fixed by the government is bottled by the government and sealed by the government. Thus the temptation to loiter on the premises and to treat his fellows, which were the source of much of the drunkenness of the Russian people in former times, is taken away from the peasant.

In the third place, the vodka that the peasant buys under this government system of manufacture and distribution is comparatively pure. Indeed, it is claimed that it is entirely free from the poisonous adulterations which made the vodka consumed by the Russian peasant under the old system a terrible and maddening drink. The peasant may still become drunk on the vodka he purchases at the government stores, although the chances of his doing so are reduced to a minimum in comparison with the certainties existing under the old system; but if he does drink to intoxication, his health will not suffer, except as it is impaired by the alcohol itself, unmixed with other poisonous ingredients.

One unexpected result of the abolition of the vodka-shop, or saloon, as we would call it in this country, grows out of the peculiarly social nature of the Russian peasant. They must get together and talk. As has been noted, the Russian peasant is the least solitary of all human beings. Apparently, he cannot live alone even for a short time. It was this phase of his character which supported the vodka-shop as much if not more than the desire to drink. The public-house afforded the peasantry a common place of meeting and conversation. When these places were taken away from them their gregarious nature immediately sought a substitute. This has been found in other public-houses springing up in place of the vodka-shops, where tea, instead of vodka, is sold, served, and consumed. Thus the drinking of tea, already a national habit, is encouraged and increased. Thus, too, is the peasant more and more weaned from the vodka habit.

The national habit of tea-drinking suggests the next plan contemplated by this constructive Russian statesman. This plan is to make the sale and distribution of tea a government monopoly. Already this plan has been matured, although not yet put into practice. Already, too, it is arousing bitter protest, for the tea-dealers of Russia are numerous, and everybody consumes tea. From the highest nobleman to the humblest peasant the one necessity, next to bread itself, appears to be tea. It is probably true that a gallon of tea is consumed by the people of Russia to every pint of plain water they drink. Witte reasons that, from a moral point of view, the dealers have no more right to derive private profit from the necessity of the people than they have to enrich themselves by sale of common drinking-water. From a financial point of view, he reasons that in the sale of this common article of consumption the government could fill its treasury with an unfailing stream of taxation, which would not be felt by those who paid it. From the point of view of economics and human interest, he argued that a better quality of tea would be supplied by the government, at a cheaper price, to Russia's one hundred and forty millions than by irresponsible dealers, whose object, of course, is to sell the poorest article at the highest possible price. And so it is said to have been decided that the government of Russia will go into the tea business, just as it has gone into the liquor business, and just as it has gone into the railway business, except that the tea-houses which have taken the place of the vodka-shops are not to be abolished.

It is said by many that the tea monopoly will not be carried into practice, although plans for it have been perfected in minute detail. The best information, however, is that when the time arrives which the government thinks most suitable for introducing its plan, it will be put into effect in much the same manner that the vodka reform was consummated. If this is done, it will mean that the Russian government has gone into a business of stupendous proportions, even when compared with its other vast undertakings of a similar character.

The largest owner and operator of railways in the world, the largest dealer in alcoholic liquors in the world, Russia, will, if the tea monopoly is undertaken, become a greater buyer and seller of tea than all other dealers of the world put together. Should this process continue, it requires no seer to behold the development of Russia into a communistic state. But it is no dreamer, no enthusiast, no excited lecturer who is accomplishing these visions of socialism; it is the hardest-headed, clearest-eyed, most modern business-man that Russia has ever produced who is working out into practical results what the world has heretofore regarded as the idle fancies of pure imagination.

These are some of the monumental achievements of Sergius Witte in the realms of Russian practical statesmanship. Any one of them would be sufficient to establish the fame of any American public man. But these gigantic plans already accomplished are not the full measure of Witte's activities. The tariff protector of Russian manufacturing interests and their special champion, Witte is, possibly, even more concerned in the industrial welfare of the Russian agriculturalist. Observing the needs of the Russian peasant, only recently freed from slavery, Witte has established a reserve fund from which, time and again, the government has loaned the peasantry many millions of rubles each year, in those provinces where drought and failure of crops have reduced the peasant farmers to serious straits. It is said also that he is the inspiration of the commissions which of recent years have been studying the causes of Russian agricultural depression and attempting to devise remedies therefor. In short, where there are practical things to be done in the realms of finance, manufacturing, agriculture, transportation, empire building, Witte's mind and hand are present.

One of the defects of Russian administration has been the variances of the ministry. One minister's plans would interfere with those of another, and there were constant strife and contention, so that, instead of statesmanship with a common purpose and all forces in accord, there have been heterogeneous and confused adoption and execution of divergent schemes. It needed a strong hand and a master-mind to consolidate the ministry. This Witte has nearly accomplished, and that, too, by sheer force of reason. The Czar shows that rarest instinct of rulers, and that most necessary one, of knowing his wisest man and trusting him. Such is the relation said to exist between the Czar and Witte. While not given a free hand, it is seldom that his measures are disapproved. So great is the respect of his sovereign for this most resourceful of his advisers that it is said that Witte does not in an emergency follow the ordinary course of submitting his proposition to his fellow-ministers, but goes directly to the Czar for his approval.

So it is that Witte has brought system and solidarity to the cabinet of the Russian Czar, and in the same way he is bringing system and order into the complex chaos of commercial and industrial conditions throughout the Russian Empire. Nor does his activity stop there. It is said that Witte has eyes in every financial centre in the world. For example, it is not generally understood, but it is true, that he has an agent in Washington, not known as an attaché of the legation, who keeps him carefully and accurately informed on all financial conditions in this country. The movements of our corporations, trusts, politicians are all laid before this enterprising statesman of the Slav people. He is in the councils of every cabinet, in the sense that he follows all their decisions and policies carefully and instantly. He has agents in Paris, Berlin, Vienna. At every salient point in the Orient are the eyes of Witte. He is as carefully informed upon the financial conditions in London as the English statesmen themselves, and, indeed, more so, for he is more remorselessly industrious.

In short, Witte intends that Russia shall be in practical touch with all the rest of the world, which it is the ambition of every Russian statesman and the whole Russian people some day—perhaps in the far distance, but still some day—to dominate. It is a great work, in which all the energies of his life are consumed, for which he receives a financial reward that is comparatively contemptible, the hatred of active interests in the empire with whose schemes he interferes, the indifference of the vast mass of the people, who do not know of his connection with the work he is doing for them; and to balance all this, only the approval, confidence, and affection of his emperor, the admiration of the statesmen of other countries, and the final panegyric of history.[1]

It is interesting to note that this great mind, whom Tolstoï considers a surface and artificial juggler, is of Dutch origin, although this is strenuously denied by the Russians, who begin to see the mountainous proportions of the man, and who, with racial jealousy, are now claiming him all for themselves. Whether this is true or not, true it is that he has worked himself up, unaided, against obstacles that seemed almost insurmountable, from the humblest of positions to the greatest. There is not a life-work in America which more perfectly illustrates the power of merit in building a career than does the story of Sergius Witte, Minister of Finance, and practical Chancellor of the empire. He came from the people. It is true that some claim that Witte's family was noble; but if so, they were not of any practical consequence; and, besides, it amounts to nothing to be a nobleman in Russia, unless nobility is also accompanied by wealth or ability. From the time of Peter until now many of Russia's greatest public servants have been of comparatively lowly origin. The biography of Witte, briefly told, is as follows:

With a fair education he began as a clerk in one of the departments of the Odessa railroad, with headquarters at that port. Within a short time it was noted that he was the most competent man in the whole force. Accordingly, he was given more important work. Again,

[1] The recent rumors that Witte is not in as high favor as formerly should be accepted with caution. Even if temporarily "promoted up-stairs," it seems probable that his future power will be as great or greater than formerly. Indeed, it is seriously doubted that he has lost much influence even for the moment.

he did his work better than anybody else had done it before. And so, steadily and rapidly, he rose to the management of the road itself. In this position he proved the best railway administrator of a limited line who had yet appeared upon the field of Russia's railroad activities.

During the Turkish war his genius for organization is said to have saved the military situation. With the confusion of things then prevailing in Russia, and which still prevails to a considerable extent in spite of Witte's work, there was the very gravest danger of congestion in forwarding the troops. It appears that Witte had foreseen this difficulty, and had worked out in advance a system which, when the time arrived, he put into successful execution. He did this, too, without obtruding himself offensively upon the notice of anybody. Nevertheless, a work so important to the empire did not, of course, go unnoticed. It attracted the attention of the government and the admiration of the railway men of the empire and of Europe.

After the Turkish war a greater line than the Odessa road claimed his services. He was made managing director of this line, and he made it the best road in the empire. He became an expert on railroad tariffs. He improved the road-bed. He improved the rolling-stock. He introduced rigid system. He so economized that he turned channels of expenditure into channels of revenue. The government and all of Russia, and indeed the railroad world of Europe, could not but be impressed, and were impressed. And so Vyshnegradsky, then Finance Minister, offered him the head of the railroad department of the Ministry of Finance, because of his unrivalled knowledge and resource in the matter of railway tariffs. He accepted, and for a few months conducted this department with the same notable ability that had formerly marked his railway management. Then the position of Minister of Ways and Communications became vacant, and the Czar appointed Witte, who had made himself by effort and ability, and nothing else, the chief railway man of the empire, to this cabinet position. He held it for a year with brilliancy and distinction. Then fate yielded at last her entire favors to this man who could not be denied. The position of Minister of Finance became vacant, and the Czar looked over the heads of bankers, over theoretical financiers, over all, to the practical man of affairs, who knew how to create sources of revenue and how to spend economically that revenue after it had been collected.

Thus Witte mounted to the high place at the right hand of the Czar. Such is the story of this patient, sleepless, ceaselessly active, stern, and silent man. It is possible that he will continue for the remainder of his life the most powerful influence among the Czar's one hundred and forty millions of subjects. It seems to be on the cards of fate that more and more, as years go by, the name of Witte will be heard in every centre of finance and in every cabinet of every government on earth. He is scarcely more than fifty years of age. With his vast energies, his great daring, and his productive mind, tempered by a lifetime of practical experience, it is probable that his future work will be even more striking than his past activities. Should Sergius Witte die, or should he be the victim of court intrigue, and deprived of his power, Russia will have lost her ablest statesman and the Czar his most resourceful minister. To make Russia commercially and industrially modern; to make Russia absolutely self-supporting; to place Russia's treasury in as opulent a condition as the reproductive forces of her people, which are so great that she turns away from her military service every year almost five hundred thousand young men; and, finally, to impel Russia onward towards the mastery of the earth—this is the mission, this is the secret ambition of this most practical mind of that great world of men and human possibilities which we call the Russian Empire.

He is the chief exponent of the aggressive forces of order, system, and material advance, against which Tolstoï is the principal voice of protest.[1]

But Tolstoi is fiercer against the Church than he is against what he considers the gross commercialism of Witte. And the man upon whom his hatred is focused is Constantine K. Pobyedonostseff, Procurator of the Holy Synod. Upon his head, too, is poured all the discontent of every Russian who objects to the autocracy of the Greek Church, which, as has been pointed out, is a political as well as a religious organization. It is not possible, of course, to give a history of the Church, or even a sketch of Pobyedonostseff's ecclesiastical statesmanship. It is enough to say that it has been the rigid, unyielding maintenance of one general plan and purpose—namely, the inflexible solidarity of the Church establishment and its absolute identity with the government itself. It has been his ambition to make and keep the Church and the government as inseparable as are the soul and body of the living, thinking man.

Pobyedonostseff has sternly refused to submit to the fiercely demanded reform of permitting a person once a member of the Russian Church to leave. "Once an orthodox Russian, always an orthodox Russian." He has resisted all demands to revise the Church's creed. The ideal of his life is stability—authority; and to this ideal he is devoted with a passionate singleness of purpose which is the secret of most of his power. It is the claim of the Greek Church that as it is the purest and most ancient form of Christianity, so it is the only religious institution which never changes. Its priests boast that it is as much more permanent and unchangeable than the Roman Catholic Church as the latter is more permanent and unchangeable than the various Protestant

[1] Witte's devotion to the Czar is illustrated by the following striking sentence in his financial report for 1900: "To a Russian no obstacle is insurmountable when his Czar commands."

denominations. "Let the people have a fixed faith," says Pobyedonostseff. "The soul of the people, finding expression through the ages and from remote antiquity in the fundamental doctrines of the Church, is the surest proof of its auhenticity and of its real representation of the soul of the nation." This is his idea.

Against this adamantine character all the waves of reform have beaten in vain. With a terrible calmness he has denied every application for what protesters call relief. He has crushed at their first appearance all impulses of what reformers call advance, but what he calls degeneration. To his belief the fundamental truths are the things of vital, permanent, and eternal moment to the souls of the people. "Let them be taught the simple, the profound, and the everlasting truths," he exclaims. To believe with all your soul in one God, the Father of mankind; to believe without doubting and with all the passion of unquestioning faith in Jesus Christ, His Son, as the Saviour of the world; to learn the simple and fundamental difference between right and wrong, between good and evil; to make and keep the people simple, obedient, united; to guard the Church as the instrumentality through which all these shall be protected from all change, all innovation—these to Pobyedonostseff are the necessary things.

Thus the Church becomes to him the most precious of all institutions. To make the Russian people one people, to bind together Fin and Slav and Tartar and Circassian, and, finally, Chinamen too, by the invisible and unbreakable bonds of a simple and common faith the roots of which run back unbroken through the soil of the centuries —this is the vast ambition of this statesman of the Church. And so it is that Pobyedonostseff rules with an iron hand. So it is that, being the apostle of Russian patriotism, intensified into the white heat of religious passion, and thus in a sense the highest personification of the Russian nation, Pobyedonostseff has the mind and heart of his Czar.

And so it is that the object of all dissent, the person at whose breast is aimed every shaft speeded at the Church itself and its doctrine on the one hand, and on the other the visible and responsible head to which all officers, priests, and members of that enormous organization attribute all their misfortunes, fancied and real —so it is that Pobyedonostseff is the most hated man in Russia. But even Pobyedonostseff's bitterest foes in Russia gladly admit his absolute purity of character. His name has never been connected with scandal, although his fierce denunciation of the immorality of even the leading characters of Russian high life, fearlessly published, stings like a whip of scorpions and intensifies the already burning hatred felt for him. Retaliation by way of charge of dishonesty or immorality or any word or deed of a personally improper kind has never been possible. It is admitted, too, that he is totally without personal ambition, even by those who speak of him as bigoted and fanatical and cruel, and that he is actuated in all his policies and plans by a devoted and fervent, if narrow, ideal. The color of money has never stained his hand. Single-mindedness, simplicity, purity, intensity, fearlessness, and a determination that is fanatical—these are the elements of Constantine Pobyedonostseff's character.

Time and again you have read of him as the Tomas de Torquemada of the Russian people. More than once I have heard him described as the spirit of the Spanish Inquisition living and breathing the atmosphere of the twentieth century. So you would expect that, upon meeting him, you would find a relentless countenance at once a mask for, and an expression of, ferocity and fanaticism. And the conversation with him was looked forward to with keener interest than that with Tolstoï or even with Witte himself.

What of this man, then, and his surroundings? Unless you visit him in the office of the Holy Synod, you will find him in a very unpretentious building, which stands flush with the sidewalk on one of the streets of St. Petersburg. Upon entering you are in a hallway, wide and of medium height, with two soldiers standing at either side. Turning to the right, you mount three low, broad steps into another hallway or room, with lower ceiling than the first, where again two soldiers are motionless sentinels. One of these announces you, and a broad door is entered into a large, low room, full of shadow.

There are books by the score, by the hundred. The man who works here is a student—that is plain. You know that he has translated more than one English classic into Russian. You know, too, that our own Emerson is Pobyedonostseff's favorite author. So the regiments of books in several languages do not surprise you. At the extreme end, in still deeper shadow as it appears from where you enter the door, there is an ample, broad, heavy desk, made out of some dark wood. At this desk sits an old man whose shoulders droop with age—that thing you observe, although he is bending forward, lost to all other things in the writing in which he is engaged. He turns quickly, however, and advances towards you, and in a low, pleasant voice, full of all courtesy and kindliness, speaks, and makes you instantly at home. You see the face now and the head. The hair, now becoming scanty and quite gray, is cut as close as possible. It is a large and finely shaped head, with the regions of thought and reflection highly developed. The face is mild, even benevolent. The gray eyes are almost affectionate. The features are aglow with intelligence. The impression immediately produced is that of acute and profound mentality. In a photograph his face looks like that of the typical New England professor of twenty years ago. But, with the living man before you, it is the last face that you would have picked out as that of the ruthless autocrat of religious stability. His talk is mellow, alive, informing. His memory is sensitive and instantaneous.

Everybody knows of the visit of the late Charles A. Dana, of the New York *Sun*, to this kindred mind. Mr. Dana sought the interview, and, it is said, went to him with disapproval. He came away the captivated admirer of this prince of Russian religious permanency. The incident of Mr. Dana's visit being called to his attention, Pobyedonostseff remembered it instantly, and all of its details, and spoke of Mr. Dana with admiration and enthusiasm. "A wonderful man," he said, "so broad, so catholic, so well informed. His was a mind and spirit of true greatness."

Pobyedonostseff has the courage of his convictions in the most ultimate degree. He does not believe in democratic institutions. He does not apologize for Russian autocracy; he does not even defend it; he *asserts* that it is the only correct principle of government—asserts, asserts, asserts! The whole man is assertion!

"People who live in parlimentary governments flatter themselves that they govern themselves; but they do not. A small oligarchy governs them. I have studied that system well, Votes are influenced by the appeals of demagogues. Other votes are bought outright by actual cash. Still other votes are influenced by the unthinking force of party association; and all of this programme is arranged and operated by the few wire-pullers behind the scenes. These wire-pullers are the real rulers in democratic governments. And are they pure? Are they learned? Are they wise? Do they have the real interests of the people at heart, or is their own petty personal interest the thing that controls them most? And if this last is so, are they equal to the enlightened governing class at whose head sits a hereditary Czar, above corruption, above jealousies, above the mutations of party, and influenced under God only by the consideration of the welfare of the people for whom he is responsible to God? Sometimes elections turn upon the mere chance as to whether one party or the other gets the voters belonging to their organization out to the polls. In those instances chance rules. It is like throwing dice. Is there anything rational in such a government as this?" This, of course, is not a verbatim report of a consecutive conversation; but it accurately represents his views.

But perhaps there can be no better method of setting out the mental quality of this autocrat of Russian orthodoxy than to reproduce his own words from the book mentioned in another chapter, entitled *The Reflections of a Russian Statesman.* Let us take as our first example some paragraphs from his philippic against "The Press." We shall thus see what a universe of opposite and antagonistic thought rolls between the beliefs of this dominant Russian mind and our American conceptions of the character, work, and duties of that most active and omnipresent agent of our modern civilization, the newspaper. Says Pobyedonostseff:

"The newspaper has usurped the position of judicial observer of the events of the day; it judges not only the actions and words of men, but affects a knowledge of their unexpressed opinions, their intentions, and their enterprises; it praises and condemns at discretion; it incites some, threatens others; drags to the pillory one, and others exalts as idols to be adored and examples worthy of the emulation of all. In the name of public opinion it bestows rewards on some, and punishes others with the severity of excommunication. The question naturally occurs: Who are these representatives of this terrible power, public opinion? Whence is derived their right and authority to rule in the name of the community, to demolish existing institutions, and to proclaim new ideals of ethics and legislation?"

Then he answers his own questions:

"Any vagabond babbler or unacknowledegd genius, any enterprising tradesman, with his own money, or with the money of others, may found a newspaper, even a great newspaper. He may attract a host of writers and feuilletonists, ready to deliver judgment on any subject at a moment's notice; he may hire illiterate reporters to keep him supplied with rumors and scandals. His staff is then complete. From that day he sits in judgment on all the world, on ministers and administrators, on literature and art, on finance and industry. It is true that the new journal becomes a power only when it is sold on the market—that is, when it circulates among the public. For this talent is needed, and the matter published must be attractive and congenial for the readers. Here, we might think, was some guarantee of the moral value of the undertaking—men of talent will not serve a feeble or contemptible editor or publisher; the public will not support a newspaper which is not a faithful echo of public opinion.

"This guarantee is fictitious. Experience proves that money will attract talent under any conditions, and that talent is ready to write as its paymaster requires. Experience proves that the most contemptible persons — retired money-lenders, Jewish factors, news-venders, and bankrupt gamblers — may found newspapers, secure the services of talented writers, and place their editions on the market as organs of public opinion. The healthy taste of the public is not to be relied upon. The great mass of readers, idlers for the most part, is ruled less by a few healthy instincts than by a base and despicable hankering for idle amusement; and the support of the people may be secured by any editor who provides for the satisfaction of these hankerings, for the love of scandal, and for intellectual pruriency of the basest kind. Of this we meet with evidence daily; even in our capital no search is necessary to find it; it is enough to note the supply and demand of the news-venders' shops and at the railway-stations.

"Such a paper may flourish, attain consideration as an organ of public opinion, and be immensely remunerative to its owners, while no paper conducted upon firm moral principles, or founded to meet the healthier instincts of the people could compete with it for a moment."

Finally he delivers this last blow at what he considers the irresponsibility of the journalist:

"For the journalist, with a power comprehending all things, requires no sanction. He derives his authority from no election, he receives support from no one. His newspaper becomes an authority in the State, and for this authority no endorsement is required. The man in the street may establish such an organ, and exercise the concomitant authority with an irresponsibility enjoyed by no other power in the world. That this is in no way exaggeration there are innumerable proofs. How often have superficial and unscrupulous journalists paved the way for evolution, fomented irritation into enmity, and brought about desolating wars? For conduct such as this a monarch would lose his throne, a minister would be disgraced, impeached, and punished; but the journalist stands dry above the waters he has disturbed, from the ruin he has caused he rises triumphant, and briskly continues his destructive work.

"This is by no means the worst. When a judge has power to dishonor us, to deprive us of our property and of our freedom, he receives his power from the hands of the state only after such prolonged labor and experience as qualify him for his calling. His power is restricted by rigorous laws, his judgments are subject to revision by higher powers, and his sentence may be altered or commuted. The journalist has the fullest power to defame and dishonor me, to injure my material interests, even to restrict my liberty by attacks which force me to leave my place of abode. These judicial powers he has usurped; no higher authority has conferred them upon him; he has never proven by examination his fitness to exercise them; he has in no way shown his trustworthiness or his impartiality; his court is ruled by no formal procedure; and from his judgment there lies no appeal.

"Its defenders assure us that the Press itself heals the wounds it has inflicted; but any thinking mind can see that these are mere idle words. The attacks of the Press on individuals may cause irreparable injury. Retractions and explanations can in no way give them full satisfaction. Not half of those who read the denunciatory article will read the apology or the explanation, and in the minds of the mass of frivolous readers insulting or calumnious suggestions leave behind an ineffaceable stain. Criminal prosecution for defamation is but the feeblest defence, and civil action seldom succeeds in exposing the offender, while it subjects the offended to fresh attack. The journalist, moreover, has a thousand means of wounding and terrifying individuals without furnishing them with sufficient grounds for legal prosecution.

"It is hard to imagine a despotism more irresponsible and violent than the despotism of printed words. Is it not strange and irrational, then, that those who struggle most for the preservation of this despotism are the impassioned champions of freedom, the ferocious enemies of legal restrictions and of all interference by the established authority. We cannot help remembering those wise men who went mad because they knew of their wisdom."

This denunciation of the modern newspaper will reveal from what a different and hostile view-point the Russian, who is a fervent believer in orthodoxy and autocracy, looks upon things which to the American, or indeed the non-Russian European, mind are essential parts of modern progress. And yet this is only a phase of Pobyedonostseff's boundless antagonism to all forms and manifestations of what to us is liberty, but what to him is license. A single quotation from his essay, "The Great Falsehood of Our Time," directed against the English Electoral system, will throw a flood of light upon his views as well as reveal his method of thought and expression:

"Elections are a matter of art, having, as the military art, their strategy and tactics. The candidate is not brought into direct relations with his constituents. As intermediary stands the committee, a self-constituted institution, the chief weapon of which is impudence. The candidate, if he is unknown, begins by assembling a number of friends and patrons. Then all together organize a hunt among the rich and weak-minded aristocrats of the neighborhood, whom they convince that it is their duty, their prerogative, and their privilege to stand at the head as leaders of public opinion. There is little difficulty in finding stupid or idle people who are taken in by this trickery; and then, above their signatures, appear manifestoes in the newspapers and on the walls and pillars, which seduce the mass, eager always in the pursuit of names, titles, and wealth. Thus are formed the committees which direct and control the elections. They resemble in much public companies. The composition of the committee is carefully elaborated; it contains some effective forces—energetic men who pursue, at all costs, material ends; while simple and frivolous idlers constitute the ballast. The committees organize meetings, where speeches are delivered, where he who possesses a powerful voice, and can quickly and skilfully string phrases together, produces always an impression on the mass, and acquires notoriety—thus comes out the candidate for future election, who, with favoring conditions, may even supersede him whom he came to help. Phrases, and nothing but phrases, dominate these meetings. The crowd hears only him who cries the loudest, and who, with impudence and with flattery, conforms most artfully to the impulses and tendencies of the mob.

"On the day of polling few give their votes intelligently; these are the individual influential electors whom it has been worth while to convince in private. The mass of the electors, after the practice of the herd, votes for one of the candidates nominated by the committees. Not one exactly knows the man, or considers his character, his capacity, his convictions; all vote merely because they have heard his name so often. It would be vain to struggle against this herd. If a level-headed elector wished to act intelligently in such a grave affair, and not to give way to the violence of the committee, he would have to abstain altogether, or to give his vote for his candidate according to his conviction. However he might act, he could not prevent the election of the candidate favored by the mass of frivolous, indifferent, and prejudiced electors.

"In theory, the elected candidate must be the favorite of the majority; in fact, he is the favorite of a minority, sometimes very small, but representing an organized force, while the majority, like sand, has no coherence, and is, therefore, incapable of resisting the clique and the faction. In theory, the election favors the intelligent and capable; in reality, it favors the pushing and impudent."

It will be seen from these quotations that Pobyedonostseff is as intellectually intense, as mentally passionate, as he is in manners urbane and charming; but he is not always soothing and velvet-voiced even in personal talk and contact. At the close of the conversation the policy of the Church was mentioned. Instantly it appeared that every nerve of his sensitive organism had been touched into abnormal alertness. "Yes, what of the policy of the Church?" It was suggested that, when considered as a great cohesive force, whose purpose it was to bind together into a solid and substantial society scores of millions of people widely scattered, it was a coherent and reasonable policy, as viewed even by an ultra-republican. He answered, his form gradually straightening as he spoke, until he stood as erect as a man of twenty. The years rolled away from his virile shoulders, the light of youth blazed from his eyes, his voice grew more vibrant as he proceeded, until, at the last word, it rang as a trumpet. "Yes, yes," he said, "you are quite right about that. But, sir, you make one terrible mistake. You refer to Russia as a state. No! no! Russia is no state; *Russia is a world!*"

It was the most illuminating, as it was the most quotable, single sentence heard within the dominions of the Czar. There was the master word that unlocked all the complexities of Witte's statesmanship; there was laid bare the unspoken—almost unthought—aspiration of the Russian people, so profound as to be an instinct; there spoke the determination of the virile Slav race, which, despite frightful mortality, due to unhygienic living and conditions—despite the fact that no Russian child but the fittest survives—is yet adding to its numbers by over two million souls every year. This was the voice of the soul of Russia—Russia that ever waits, Russia that is ever patient, Russia that ever advances, Russia that never hurries, Russia that looks upon other peoples as disorganized communities and dying races and considers herself the heir of all the ages, Russia that believes and feels that she is not a state, but a world. "No! no! Russia is no state; *Russia is a world!*" So exclaims the apostle of Russian orthodoxy, so devoutly believe the Russian people, so plan the far-seeing Russian statesmen. All men estimating the thought and tendencies of nations, when putting Russia to the test of analysis, should, if they would truly understand as they analyze, repeat these words of Pobyedonostseff, Procurator of the Holy Synod of Russia's national Church: "*Russia is no state; Russia is a world.*" For these eight words express the feeling and the faith of the most numerous of modern peoples and the most extensive of modern empires.

APPENDIX

TREATY OF SHIMONOSEKI, BY WHICH SOUTHERN MANCHURIA WAS CEDED TO JAPAN

(Signed April 17, 1895; ratified at Chefoo, May 8, 1895.)

Article I. China recognizes definitely the full and complete independence and autonomy of Korea, and in consequence the payment of tribute and the performance of ceremonies and formalities by Korea to China in derogation of such independence and autonomy shall wholly cease for the future.

Article II. China cedes to Japan in perpetuity and full sovereignty the following territories, together with all fortifications, arsenals, and public property thereon:

(a). The southern portion of the province of Feng-t'ien within the following boundaries:

The line of demarcation begins at the mouth of the river Yalu and ascends that stream to the mouth of the river Anping; from thence the line runs to Feng Huang; from thence to Haicheng; from thence to Ying-Kow, forming a line which describes the southern portion of the territory. The places above named are included in the ceded territory. When the line reaches the river Liao at Ying-Kow it follows the course of that stream to its mouth, where it terminates. The mid-channel of the river Liao shall be taken as the line of demarcation.

This cession also includes all islands appertaining or belonging to the province of Feng-t'ien, situated in the eastern portion of the bay of Liaotung and in the northern part of the Yellow Sea.

(b). The island of Formosa, together with all islands appertaining to the said island of Formosa.

(c). The Pescadores Group—that is to say, all islands lying between the one hundred and nineteenth and twelfth degrees of longitude east of Greenwich and the twenty-third and two hundred and fortieth degrees of north latitude.

Article III. The alignments of the frontiers described in the preceding article, and shown on the map, shall be subject to verification and demarcation on the spot by a Joint Commission of delimitation, consisting of two or more Japanese, and two or more Chinese delegates, to be appointed immediately after the exchange of the ratifications of this act. In case the boundaries laid down in this act are found to be defective at any point, either on account of topography or in consideration of good administration, it shall also be the duty of the Delimitation Commission to rectify the same.

The Delimitation Commission will enter upon its duties as soon as possible, and will bring its labors to a conclusion within the period of one year after appointment.

The alignments laid down in this act shall, however, be maintained until the rectifications of the Delimitation Commission, if any are made, shall have received the approval of the governments of Japan and China.

Article IV. China agrees to pay to Japan as a war indemnity the sum of two hundred million Kuping taels. The said sum to be paid in eight instalments. The first instalment of fifty million taels to be paid within six months, and the second instalment of fifty million taels to be paid within twelve months after the exchange of the ratifications of this act. The remaining sum to be paid in six equal annual instalments as follows: The first of such equal instalments to be paid within two years; the second within three years; the third within four years; the fourth within five years; the fifth within six years; and the sixth within seven years, after the exchange of the ratifications of this act. Interest at the rate of five per centum per annum shall begin to run on all unpaid portions of the said indemnity from the date the first instalment falls due.

China, however, shall have the right to pay by anticipation at any time any or all of said instalments. In case the whole amount of said indemnity is paid within three years after the exchange of ratifications of the present act, all interest shall be waived and the interest for two years and a half or for any less period, if then already paid, shall be included as a part of the principal amount of the indemnity.

Article V. The inhabitants of the territories ceded to Japan, who wish to take up their residence outside the ceded districts, shall be at liberty to sell their real property and retire. For this purpose a period of two years from the date of the exchange of the ratifications of the present act shall be granted. At the expiration of that period, those of the inhabitants who shall not have left such territories shall, at the option of Japan, be deemed to be Japanese subjects.

Each of the two governments shall, immediately upon the exchange of the ratifications of the present act, send one or more commissioners to Formosa to effect a final transfer of that province, and within the space of two months after the exchange of the ratifications of this act such transfer shall be completed.

Article VI. All treaties between Japan and China having come to an end in consequence of war, China engages immediately upon the exchange of the ratifications of this act, to appoint plenipotentiaries to conclude, with the Japanese plenipotentiaries, a treaty of commerce and navigation and a convention to regulate frontier intercourse and trade. The treaties, conventions, and regulations now subsisting between China and European powers shall serve as a basis for the said treaty and convention between Japan and China. From the date of the exchange of the ratifications of this act until the said treaty and convention are brought into actual operation, the Japanese government, its officials, commerce, navigations, frontier intercourse and trade, industries, ships, and subjects, shall, in every respect, be accorded by China most favored-nation treatment.

China makes, in addition, the following concessions, to take effect six months after the date of the present act:

First. The following cities, towns, and ports, in addition to those already opened, shall be opened to the trade, residence, industries, and manufactures of Japanese subjects, under the same conditions and with the same privileges and facilities as exist at the present open cities, towns, and ports of China:

1. Shashih, in the province of Hupeh.
2. Chung-King, in the province of Szechuan.
3. Suchow, in the Province of Kiang-Su.
4. Hangchow, in the province of Chekiang.

The Japanese government shall have the right to station consuls at any or all of the above-named places.

Second. Steam navigation for vessels under the Japanese flag for the conveyance of passengers and cargo shall be extended to the following places:

1. On the upper Yang-tse River, from Ichang to Chung-King.
2. On the Woosung River and the Canal, from Shanghai to Suchow and Hangchow.

The rules and regulations which now govern the navigation of the inland waters of China by foreign vessels shall, so far as applicable, be enforced in respect to the above-named routes, until new rules and regulations are conjointly agreed to.

Third. Japanese subjects purchasing goods or produce in the interior of China or transporting imported merchandise into the interior of China, shall have the right temporarily to rent or hire warehouses for the storage of articles so purchased or transported without the payment of any taxes or exactions whatever.

Fourth. Japanese subjects shall be free to engage in all kinds of manufacturing industries in all the open cities, towns, and ports of China, and shall be at liberty to import into China all kinds of machinery, paying only the stipulated import duties thereon.

All articles manufactured by Japanese subjects in China shall, in respect of inland transit and internal taxes, duties, charges, and exactions of all kinds, and also in respect of warehousing and storage facilities in the interior of China, stand upon the same footing and enjoy the same privileges and exemptions as merchandise imported by Japanese subjects into China.

In the event additional rules and regulations are necessary in connection with these concessions, they shall be embodied in the Treaty of Commerce and Navigation provided for by this article.

Article VII. Subject to the provisions of the next succeeding article, the evacuation of China by the armies of Japan shall be completely effected within three months after the exchange of the ratifications of the present act.

Article VIII. As a guarantee of the faithful performance of the stipulations of this act, China consents to the temporary occupation by the military forces of Japan, of Wei-Hai-Wei, in the province of Shang-Tung.

Upon the payment of the first two instalments of the war indemnity herein stipulated for and the exchange of the ratifications of the Treaty of Commerce and Navigation, said place shall be evacuated by the Japanese forces, provided the Chinese government consents to pledge, under suitable and sufficient arrangements, the Customs Revenue of China as security for the payment of the final instalment of said indemnity.

It is, however, expressly understood that no such evacuation shall take place until after the exchange of the ratifications of the Treaty of Commerce and Navigation.

Article IX. Immediately upon the exchange of the ratifications of this act, all prisoners of war then held shall be restored, and China undertakes not to ill-treat or punish prisoners of war so restored to her by Japan. China also engages to at once release all Japanese subjects accused of being military spies or charged with any other military offences. China further engages not to punish in any manner, nor to allow to be punished, those Chinese subjects who have in any manner been compromised in their relations with the Japanese army during the war.

Article X. All offensive military operations shall cease upon the exchange of the ratifications of this act.

Article XI. The present act shall be ratified by their Majesties the Emperor of Japan and the Emperor of China, and the ratifications shall be exchanged at Chefoo, on the eighth day of the fifth month of the twenty-eighth year of Meiji, corresponding to the fourteenth day of the fourth month of the twenty-first year of Kuang Hsu.

In witness whereof, the respective plenipotentiaries have signed the same and have affixed thereto the seal of their arms.

Done at Shimonoseki, in duplicate, this seventeenth day of the fourth month of the twenty-eighth year of Meiji, corresponding to the twenty-third day of the third month of the twenty-first year of Kuang Hsu.

COUNT ITO HIROBUMI.
VISCOUNT MUTSU MUNEMITSU.
LI HUNG CHANG.
LI CHING-FONG.

SEPARATE ARTICLES

Article I. The Japanese Military Forces which are, under Article VIII. of the Treaty of Peace signed this day, to temporarily occupy Wei-Hai-Wei, shall not exceed one brigade, and from the date of the exchange of the ratifications of the said Treaty of Peace, China shall pay annually one-fourth of the amount of the expenses of such temporary occupation—that is to say, at the rate of 500,000 Kuping taels per annum.

Article II. The territory temporarily occupied at Wei-Hai-Wei shall comprise the island of Liu Kunk and a belt of land five Japanese ri wide along the entire coast-line of the bay of Wei-Hai-Wei.

No Chinese troops shall be permitted to approach or occupy any places within a zone five Japanese ri wide beyond the boundaries of the occupied territory.

Article III. The Civil Administration of the occupied territory shall remain in the hands of the Chinese authorities. But such authorities shall at all times be obliged to conform to the orders which the Japanese army of occupation may deem it necessary to give in the interest of the health, maintenance, safety, distribution, or discipline of the troops.

All military offences committed within the occupied territory shall be subject to the jurisdiction of the Japanese military authorities.

The foregoing Separate Articles shall have the same force, value, and effect as if they had been word for word inserted in the Treaty of Peace signed this day.

In witness whereof, the respective plenipotentiaries have signed the same and have affixed thereto the seal of their arms.

Done at Shimonoseki, in duplicate, this seventeenth day of the fourth month of the twenty-eighth year of Meiji, corresponding to the twenty-first year of Kuang Hsu.

COUNT ITO HIROBUMI.
VISCOUNT MUTSU MUNEMITSU.
LI HUNG CHANG.

MIKADO'S RESCRIPT WITHDRAWING FROM MANCHURIA. (*May* 10, 1895.)

We recently complied with the request of China, and in consequence appointed plenipotentiaries and caused them to confer with the plenipotentiaries appointed by China and to conclude a Treaty of Peace between the two Empires.

Since then the governments of their Majesties the Emperors of Russia and Germany and of the Republic of France have united in a recommendation to our government not to permanently possess the peninsula of Feng-t'ien, our newly acquired territory, on the ground that such permanent possession would be detrimental to the lasting peace of the Orient.

Devoted as we unalterably are and ever have been to the principles of peace, we were constrained to take up arms against China for no other reason than our desire to secure for the Orient an enduring peace.

Now the friendly recommendation of the three powers was equally prompted by the same desire. Consulting, therefore, the best interests of peace and animated by a desire not to bring upon our people added hardship or to impede the progress of national destiny by creating new complications and thereby making the situation difficult and retarding the restoration of peace, we do not hesitate to accept such recommendation.

By concluding the Treaty of Peace, China has already shown her sincerity of regret for the violation of her engagements, and thereby the justice of our cause has been proclaimed to the world.

Under the circumstances we can find nothing to impair the honor and dignity of our empire if we now yield to the dictates of magnanimity and, taking into consideration the general situation, accept the advice of the friendly powers.

Accordingly we have commanded our government, and have caused them to reply to the three powers in the above sense.

Regarding the arrangements by which we will renounce the

permanent possession of the Peninsula, we have specially commanded our government that the necessary measures shall be made the subject of future negotiations and adjustment with the government of China.

Now, the exchange of ratifications of the Treaty of Peace has already been effected, the friendly relations between the two Empires have been re-established, and cordial relations with all other powers are also strengthened.

We therefore command our subjects to respect our will; to take into careful consideration the general situation; to be circumspect in all things; to avoid erroneous tendencies; and not to impair or thwart the high aspirations of our empire.

[IMPERIAL SIGN MANUAL.]
[COUNTERSIGNED BY ALL MINISTERS OF STATE.]

THE (REPUTED) CASSINI CONVENTION

TEXT PUBLISHED BY THE NORTH CHINA "DAILY NEWS" AS THAT OF AN AGREEMENT CONCLUDED AT PEKIN BY COUNT CASSINI, THE RUSSIAN MINISTER, IN 1895

His Imperial Majesty, the Emperor of China, having received the various benefits arising from the loyal support of his Imperial Majesty, the Emperor of Russia, at the close of the late war between China and Japan, and being desirous that the communications between the frontier territories of their respective empires and the international commerce of the two countries should be managed to their mutual advantage, has commanded the mutual settlement of certain matters in order the better to consolidate the basis of friendship between the two empires. In this connection, therefore, his Imperial Majesty, the Emperor of China, has specially appointed the Imperial High Commissioners, the Princes and great officers of the Crown, composing the Imperial Chinese Ministry of War, with plenipotentiary powers, to confer and agree upon certain matters, at Pekin, with his Excellency, Count Cassini, Envoy Extraordinary and Minister Plenipotentiary of H.I.M., the Emperor of Russia, to the Court of China, concerning the connecting of the railway system of the three Eastern Provinces (Feng-t'ien, Kirin, and Hei-Lung-Kiang) with that of the Imperial Russian Railway in the province of Siberia, with the object of facilitating the transport of goods between the two empires, and of strengthening the frontier defences and sea-coasts. And, furthermore, to agree upon certain special privileges to be conceded by China to Russia as a response to the loyal aid given by Russia in the retrocession of Liaotung and its dependencies:

1. Owing to the fact that the Russian Great Siberian Railway is on the point of completion, China consents to allow Russia to prolong her railway into Chinese territories (a) from the Russian port of Vladivostock into the Chinese city of Hunchun, in the province of Kirin, from thence northwestward to the provincial capital of Kirin, and (b) from a railway-station of some city in Siberia to the Chinese town of Aigun in Hei-Lung-Kiang province, from thence southwestward to the provincial capital of Tsitsihar, and from thence to the town of Petunê in Kirin province, and from thence southeastward to the provincial capital of Kirin.

2. All railways built by Russia into the Chinese provinces of Hei-Lung-Kiang and Kirin shall be built at the sole expense of Russia, and the regulations and buildings thereof shall be solely on the Russian system, with which China has nothing to do, and the entire control shall be in the hands of Russia for the space of thirty years. At the end of the said period China shall be allowed to prepare the necessary funds wherewith, after proper estimation of the value of the said railways, she shall redeem them, the rolling-stock, machine-shops, and buildings connected therewith. But as to how China will at that date redeem these railways shall be left for future consideration.

3. China is now in the possession of a railway, which she intends to extend from Shanhaikwan into the provincial capital of Feng-t'ien — namely, Mukden (Shengking), and from Mukden to the provincial capital of Kirin. If China should hereafter find it inconvenient to build this road, she shall allow Russia to provide the funds to build the railway from the city of Kirin on behalf of China, the redemption of which road shall be permissible to China at the end of ten years. With reference to the route to be taken by this railway, Russia shall follow the surveys already made by China in connection therewith, from Kirin to Mukden, New-Chwang, etc.

4. The railway to be built by China, beginning from Shanhaikwan, in Feng-t'ien, to New-Chwang, to Kaiping, to Chinchou, to Lushunk'ou (Port Arthur), and to Talienhwan and their dependencies, shall follow the Russian railway regulations, in order to facilitate the commercial intercourse between the respective empires.

5. With reference to the railways to be built by Russia into Chinese territory, the routes along which the said roads shall pass

must be protected, as usual, by the local, civil, and military officials of the country. They shall, moreover, afford all facilities and aid to the civil and military officials of Russia at the various railway-stations, together with all the Russian artisans and laborers connected therewith. But, owing to the fact that the said railways will pass, for the greater part, through barren and sparsely inhabited territory, in which it will be difficult for the Chinese authorities to be always able to grant the necessary protection and aid, Russia shall be allowed to place special battalions of horse and foot soldiers at the various important stations for the better protection of the railway property.

6. With reference to the customs duties to be collected on goods exported from and imported into the respective countries by the said railways, they shall follow the regulations provided by the Treaty of Commerce between China and Russia, ratified in the first year of the reign of Tung Chin, fourth day, second moon (20th of February, 1862, O. S.), regulating overland transit of goods between the two empires.

7. There has always been in existence a rule prohibiting the exploitation of the mines in Hei-Lung-Kiang and Kirin provinces, and in the Ch'angpai mountains (Long White mountain range). After the ratification of this Treaty, Russians and subjects of the Chinese Empire shall be permitted hereafter to exploit and open any of the mines therein mentioned; but before doing so they shall be required first to petition the Chinese local authorities on the subject, who, on the other hand, shall grant the necessary commissions (huchas) in accordance with the mining regulations in force in China Proper.

8. Although there exist certain battalions of foreign-drilled troops (Lienchun) in the three Eastern provinces, yet the greater portion of the local territorial Army Corps thereof still follow the ancient regulations of the empire. Should, therefore, China in the future require to reform, in accordance with the Western system, the whole army organization of the said provinces, she shall be permitted to engage from Russia qualified military officers for that purpose, and the rules for the guidance of this arrangement shall be in accordance with those obtaining in the Liang-Kiang provinces in regard to the German military officers now engaged there.

9. Russia has never possessed a seaport in Asia which is free from ice and open all the year round. If, therefore, there should suddenly arise military operations in this Continent, it will naturally be difficult for the Russian Eastern Seas and Pacific Fleets to move about freely and at pleasure. As China is well aware of this, she is willing to lease temporarily to Russia the port of Kiaochou,

in the province of Shan-Tung, the period of such lease being limited to fifteen years. At the end of this period China shall buy all the barracks, godowns, machine-shops, and docks built there by Russia (during her occupation of the said port). But, should there be no danger of military operations, Russia shall not enter immediately into possession of the said port, or hold the important points dominating the port, in order to obviate the chance of exciting the jealousy and suspicions of other powers. With reference to the amount of rent and the way it is to be paid, this shall form the subject of consideration in a Protocol at some future date.

10. As the Liaotung ports of Lushunk'ou (Port Arthur) and Talienhwan and their dependencies are important strategical points, it shall be incumbent upon China to properly fortify them with all haste, and to repair all their fortifications, etc., in order to provide against future dangers; Russia shall, therefore, lend all necessary assistance in helping to protect these two ports, and shall not permit any foreign power to encroach upon them. China, on her part, also binds herself never to cede them to another country, but if, in future, the exigencies of the case require it, and Russia should find herself suddenly involved in a war, China consents to allow Russia temporarily to concentrate her land and naval forces within the said ports, in order the better to enable Russia to attack the enemy or to guard her own position.

11. If, however, there be no danger of military operations in which Russia is engaged, China shall have entire control over the administration of the said ports of Lushunk'ou and Talienhwan; nor shall Russia interfere in any way therein. But, as regards the building of the railway in the three Eastern Provinces, and the exploitation and opening of the mines therein, they shall be permitted to be proceeded with immediately after the ratification of this Convention, and at the pleasure of the people concerned therein. With reference to the Civil and Military officers of Russia and Russian merchants and traders travelling (in any part of the territories herein mentioned), wherever they shall go, they shall be given all the privilege of protection and facilities within the power of the local authorities; nor shall these officials be allowed to put obstructions in the way or delay the journeys of the Russian officers and subjects herein mentioned.

12. After this Convention shall have received the respective signatures of their Imperial Majesties (the Emperors of China and of Russia) the articles included therein shall go into immediate force, and, with the exception of the clauses regarding Port Arthur, Talienhwan, and Kiaochou, shall be notified to the various local authorities of the two empires. As to the place for the ex-

change of ratifications, it shall be left to be decided at some future time, but the exchange shall take place within the space of six months.

It has, furthermore, been agreed upon between the respective Plenipotentiaries of the High Contracting Powers to make this Convention out in three languages—namely, Chinese, Russian, and French, one copy of each language to be held by the respective High Contracting Parties, after the signing and sealing thereof. And it has, furthermore, been shown, upon comparison, that the contents of the documents, as given in the three languages aforesaid, tally with each other in all respects; but in case of dispute, in the future, the wording of the French copy shall be deemed the correct version.

THE RUSSO-MANCHURIAN RAILWAY AGREEMENT

STATUTES OF THE CHINESE EASTERN RAILWAY COMPANY

Section 1. On the strength of the Agreement concluded on the 27th August (8th September), 1896, by the Imperial Chinese Government with the Russo-Chinese Bank, a Company is formed, under the name of the "Eastern Chinese Railway Company," for the construction and working of a railway within the confines of China, from one of the points on the western borders of the Province of Hei-Lung-Kiang to one of the points on the eastern borders of the Province of Kirin, and for the connection of this railway with those branches which the Imperial Russian Government will construct to the Chinese frontier from Trans-Baikalia and the Southern Ussuri lines.

The Company is empowered, subject to the sanction of the Chinese Government, to exploit, in connection with the railway, or independently of it, coal-mines, as also to exploit in China other enterprises—mining, industrial, and commercial. For the working of these enterprises, which may be independent of the railway, the Company shall keep accounts separate from those of the railway.

The formation of the Company shall be undertaken by the Russo-Chinese Bank.

With the formation of the Company all rights and obligations are transferred to it in regard to the construction and working of the line ceded in virtue of the above-named Agreement of the 27th August (8th September), 1896.

The Company shall be recognized as formed on the presentation to the Minister of Finances of a Warrant of the State Bank, certifying the payment of the first instalment on the shares. In any case, such payment must be made not later than two months from the day of confirmation of the present Statutes.

The succeeding instalments on the shares shall be paid in such order of gradation that the shares shall be fully paid up at their nominal value not later than one year from the day of formation of the Company.

Owners of shares of the Company may only be Russian and Chinese subjects.

Section 2. In virtue of the Agreement with the Chinese government, the Company shall retain possession of the Chinese Eastern Railway during the course of eighty years from the day of the opening of traffic along the whole line.

Section 3. In recognition that the enterprise of the Chinese Eastern Railway will be realized only owing to the guarantee given by the Russian Government in regard to the revenue of the line for covering working expenses, as well as for effecting the obligatory payments on the bonds (sections 11, 16), the Company on its part binds itself to the Russian Government, during the whole term of the Concession, under the following obligations:

(A) The Chinese Eastern Railway, with all its appurtenances and rolling-stock, must be always maintained in full order for satisfying all the requirements of the service of the line in regard to the safety, comfort, and uninterrupted conveyance of passengers and goods.

(B) The traffic on the Chinese Eastern line must be maintained conformably with the degree of traffic on the Russian railway lines adjoining the Chinese line.

(C) The trains of all descriptions running between the Russian Trans-Baikal and Ussuri lines shall be received by the Chinese Eastern Railway and despatched to their destination, in full complement, without delay.

(D) All through trains, both passenger and goods, shall be despatched by the Eastern Chinese Railway at rates of speed not lower than those which shall be adopted on the Siberian Railway.

(E) The Chinese Eastern Railway is bound to establish and maintain a telegraph along the whole extent of the line, and to connect it with the telegraph wire of the Russian adjoining railways, and to receive and despatch, without delay, through telegrams sent from one frontier station of the line to another, as also telegrams sent from Russia to China, and conversely.

(F) Should, with the development of traffic on the Chinese Eastern Railway, its technical organization prove insufficient for satisfying the requirements of a regular and uninterrupted passenger and goods traffic, the Chinese Eastern Railway shall immediately, on receipt of a notification on the part of the Russian railways to augment its capacity to a corresponding degree, adopt the necessary measures for further developing its technical organization and the traffic on it. In the event of a difference of opinion arising between the above-mentioned railways, the Chinese Eastern Railway shall submit to the decision of the Russian Minister of Finances. If the means at the command of the Chinese Eastern Railway prove insufficient for carrying out the necessary work of its development, the Board of Management of the railway may at all times apply to the Russian Minister of Finances for pecuniary assistance on the part of the Russian Government.

(G) For all transit conveyance of passengers and goods, as also for the transmission of telegrams, there will be established by agreement of the Company with the Russian Government, for the whole term of duration of the Concession,

¶ Maximum Tariffs, which cannot be raised without the consent of the Russian Government during the whole term above referred to. Within these limits the Tariffs of direct communication, both for railway carriages and telegrams, will be fixed by the Board of Management of the Company on the strength of a mutual agreement with the Russian Minister of Finances.

(H) The Russian letter and parcels post, as also the officials accompanying the same, shall be carried by the Chinese Eastern Railway free of charge.

For this purpose the Company shall set apart in each ordinary passenger train a carriage compartment of three fathoms in length. The Russian postal authorities may, moreover, if they deem it necessary, place on the line postal carriages, constructed by them at their own cost; and the repair, maintenance (interior fittings excepted), as well as the running of such carriages with the trains, shall be free of charge and at the cost of the railway.

The above-mentioned engagements—by which, as already stated, the grant of a guarantee by the Russian Government is conditioned, and the consequent realization of the enterprise of the Chinese Eastern Railway—shall be binding on the railway until the same, after the expiration of the eighty years' term of the Concession shall, without payment, become the property of the Chinese Government (section 29). The redemption of the line from the Company before the above-mentioned term, in accordance with section 30 of the present Statutes, shall not in any way diminish the effect of the above-specified engagements, and these latter, together with the railway, shall be transferred to its new proprietor.

In the same manner, during the course of the whole eighty

years' term of the Concession (¶ 2), the following privileges granted to the railway by the Imperial Chinese Government shall remain in force:

(a) Passengers' luggage, as also goods, carried in transit from one Russian station (? to another) shall not be liable to any Chinese customs duties, and shall be exempt from all internal Chinese dues and taxes.

(b) The rates for the carriage of passengers and goods, for telegrams, etc., shall be free from all Chinese taxes and dues.

(c) Goods imported from Russia into China by rail, and exported from China to Russia in the same manner, shall pay respectively an import or export Chinese duty to the extent of one-third less as compared with the duty imposed at Chinese seaport custom-houses.

(d) If goods imported by the railway are destined for conveyance inland, they shall in such case be subject to payment of transit duty to the extent of one-half of the import duty levied on them, and they shall then be exempted from any additional imposts. Goods which shall not have paid transit duty shall be liable to payment of all established internal carrier and lits-zin (? likin) dues.

Section 4. In regard to the place of acquisition of materials for the requirements of the railway, the Company shall not be liable to any limitations. If materials be obtained beyond the confines of Russia, they shall, on importation through Russian territory, be freed from payment of Russian customs duties.

Section 5. The breadth of the railway track must be the same as that of the Russian lines (five feet).

The Company must commence the work not later than the 16th August, 1897, and conduct it in such a manner that the whole line shall be completed not later than six years from the time when the direction of the line shall be finally determined and the necessary land assigned to the Company.

When tracing the line of the railway, cemeteries and graves, as also towns and villages, must, so far as possible, be left aside of the railway.

When effecting the connection, in accordance with section 1 of these Statutes, of the Chinese Eastern Railway with the Russian Trans-Baikal and South Ussuri lines, the Company shall have the right, with a view to reduction of expenditure, of abstaining from building its own frontier stations and of utilizing the frontier stations of the above-named Russian lines. The conditions on which they shall be so utilized shall be determined by agreement of the Board of the Company with the Boards of the respective railways.

Section 6. The tariffs for the carriage of passengers and goods, as also for supplementary carriage rates, shall be determined by the Company itself, within the limits indicated in section 3.

Section 7. Crimes, litigation, etc., on the territory of the Chinese Eastern Railway shall be dealt with by local authorities, Chinese and Russian, on the basis of existing Treaties.

In regard to the carriage of passengers and goods, the responsibility of such conveyance, the lapse of time for claims, the order of recovering money from the railway when adjudged, and the relations of the railway to the public shall be defined in rules drawn up by the Company and established before the opening of the railway traffic; and these rules shall be framed in accordance with those existing on Russian railways.

Section 8. The Chinese Government has undertaken to adopt measures for securing the safety of the railway and of all employed on it against any extraneous attacks.

The preservation of order and decorum on the lands assigned to the railway and its appurtenances shall be confided to police agents appointed by the Company.

The Company shall, for this purpose, draw up and establish police regulations.

Section 9. The whole amount of the capital of the Company shall be determined according to the cost of construction calculated on the basis of estimates framed when the survey of the line was carried out. The foundation capital shall be charged with (a) the payment of interest and amortization of the foundation capital during the construction of the railway; (b) the purchase from the Russian Government of the results of the surveys of the direction of the railway to Manchuria which were made by Russian engineers; the sum payable for these surveys will be determined by agreement of the Russian Minister of Finances with the Company.

The capital of the Company shall be formed by the issue of shares and bonds.

Section 10. The share capital of the Company shall be fixed at 5,000,000 nominal credit rubles, and divided into 1000 shares at 5000 nominal credit rubles.

The shares are to be issued at their nominal value.

The guarantee of the Russian Government does not extend to them.

Section 11. The remaining portion of the capital of the Company will be formed by the issue of bonds. The bonds will be issued in measure of requirement, and each time with the special sanction of the Minister of Finances. The nominal amount and value of each separate issue of bonds, the time and condition of the issue, as also the form of these bonds, shall be subject to the sanction of the Minister of Finances.

The Russian Government will guarantee the interest on and amortization of the bonds.

For the realization of these bonds the Company must have recourse to the Russo-Chinese Bank, but the Russian Government reserves to itself the right of appropriating the bond loan at a price which shall be determinded between the Company and the Bank, and to pay to the Company the agreed amount in ready money.

Section 12. As payments are received for bonds guaranteed by the Russian Government, the Company shall be bound to keep such sums, or interest-bearing securities purchased with the same by permission of the Russian Minister of Finances, under the special supervision of the Russian Ministry of Finances.

Out of the above receipts the Company shall have the right to make the following payments:

(a) According to actual fulfilment of the work in progress and execution of orders, and at the time when various expenditures shall become necessary, such payments to be made on the scale and on the conditions specified in the working estimates.

(b) During the construction of the line, of interest, as it becomes due, on the bonds issued by the Company, subject to the conditions of their issue, and the Company shall pay the sums necessary for the above purpose within the limits of the amount realized by it in the emission of its bonds.

Section 13. On the payment of the first allotment on the shares, the founders shall receive temporary certificates, on which, subsequently, when the Board of Management of the Company shall have been formed, the receipt of the further instalments on the shares will be inscribed.

When the shares shall be fully paid up, the temporary certificates issued to the founders shall be replaced by shares.

The shares of the Company are issued to bearer, under the signature of not fewer than three members of the Board of Management. To the shares will be attached a coupon-sheet for the receipt once yearly under them of any dividend that may be payable. On the coupon-sheets becoming exhausted, new sheets will be issued. A dividend on the shares out of the net profits of any year, supposing such accrue, shall be payable on the adoption by the general meeting of shareholders of the annual report for that year, and the dividend shall be payable at the offices of the Company, or at such places which it may indicate.

The Company shall notify, for general information in the Official Gazette and in the *Finance Messenger*, as also in one of the Chinese newspapers, the extent and place of payment of the dividend.

Section 14. The reserve capital is destined

(a) For the capital repair of the railway, its buildings and appurtenances.

(b) For defraying extraordinary expenditure of the Company in repairing the railway and its appurtenances.

The reserve capital of the Company is formed out of annual sums put aside from the net profits of the working of the railway (section 17).

The reserve capital must be kept in Russian State interest-bearing securities, or in railway bonds guaranteed by the Russian Government.

At the expiration of the term of possession of the railway by the Company, the reserve capital shall be, first of all, employed in the payment of the debts of the Company, including among them sums due to the Russian Government, if such exist; and after the debts of the Company shall have been paid, the remainder of the reserve capital shall be divided among the shareholders. In the event of the redemption of the railway by the Chinese Government, the reserve capital becomes the property of the shareholders.

Section 15. The net revenue of the Company shall be the remainder of the gross receipts after deduction of working expenses. Under these expenses are classed:

(a) General outlays, including assignments towards pension and relief funds, if such be established on the line.

(b) Maintenance of the staff of the Board of Management, and of all the services, as also the maintenance of employés and laborers not on the permanent list.

(c) Outlays for materials and articles used for the railway, as also expenditure in the shape of remuneration for using buildings, rolling-stock, and other various requisites for the purposes of the railway.

(d) Outlays for the maintenance, repair, and renewal of the permanent way, works of construction, buildings, rolling-stock, and other appurtenances of the railway.

(e) Expenditure connected with the adoption of the measures and instructions of the Board of Management for insuring the safety and regularity of the railway service.

(f) Expenditure for the improvement and development of the railway, as also the creating and developing its resources.

Section 16. Should the gross receipts of the railway prove insufficient for defraying the working expenses and for meeting the yearly payments due on the bonds, the Company will receive the deficient sum from the Russian Government, through the Russian Minister of Finances. The payments referred to will be made to the Company as advances, at a rate of interest of six per cent. per annum. Sums paid in excess to the Company in consequence of its demands and on account of the guarantee will be deducted from succeeding money payments.

On the presentation to the general meeting of shareholders of the annual report of the working of the railway for a given year, the Company shall at the same time submit to the general meeting, for confirmation, a detailed statement of the sums owing by the Company to the Russian Government, with the interest that has accrued thereon. On the confirmation of this statement by the general meeting, the Board of Management shall deliver to the Russian Government an acknowledgment of the Company's debt, to the full determined amount of the same, and this acknowledgment, until its substitution by another, shall bear annually interest at the rate of six per cent.

The acknowledgment above mentioned, given by the Board of Management to the Russian Government, shall not be subject to bill or deed stamp tax.

Subjects of minor importance are dealt with in the following sections:

Section 17. Distribution of net profits of the railway.

Section 18. Functions of Board of Management, the seal of which will be at Pekin and St. Petersburg.

Section 19. Constitution of the Board, which is to consist of nine members elected by the shareholders. The Chairman is to be appointed by the Chinese Government. The Vice-Chairman is to be chosen by the members of the Board from among themselves.

Sections 20–28. Administrative details.

Section 29. In accordance with the Agreement concluded with the Chinese Government, the latter, after the expiration of eighty years of possession of the railway by the Company, enters into possession of it and its appurtenances.

The reserve and other funds belonging to the Company shall be employed in paying the money due to the Russian Government under the guarantee (section 16), and in satisfaction of other debts of the Company, and the remainder shall be distributed among the shareholders.

Any money that may remain owing by the Company to the Russian Government at the expiration of eighty years in respect of the guarantee shall be written off. The Russo-Chinese Bank will incur no responsibility in respect of the same.

Section 30. In accordance with the Agreement concluded with the Chinese Government, on the expiration of thirty-six years from the time of completion of the whole line and its opening for traffic, the Chinese Government has the right of acquiring the line, on refunding to the Company in full all the outlays made on it, and on payment for everything done for the requirements of the railway, such payments to be made with accrued interest.

It follows, as a matter of course, that the portion of the share capital which has been amortized by drawing, and the part of the debt owing to the Russian Government under the guarantee, and repaid out of the net profits (section 17) will not constitute part of the purchase money.

In no case can the Chinese Government enter into possession of the railway before it has lodged in the Russian State Bank the necessary purchase money.

The purchase money lodged by the Chinese Government shall be employed in paying the debt of the Company under its bonds, and all sums, with interest, owing to the Russian Government, the remainder of the money being then at the disposal of the shareholders.

ANGLO-RUSSIAN AGREEMENT RESPECTING SPHERES OF INFLUENCE IN CHINA

(*Signed April 28, 1899*)

SIR C. SCOTT TO COUNT MOURAVIEFF:

The undersigned British Ambassador, duly authorized to that effect, has the honor to make the following declaration to his Excellency Count Mouravieff, the Russian Minister of Foreign Affairs: Great Britain and Russia, animated by a sincere desire to avoid in China all cause of conflict on questions where their interests meet, and taking into consideration the economic and geographical gravitation of certain parts of the empire, have agreed as follows:

1. Great Britain engages not to seek for her own account, or on behalf of British subjects, or of others, any railway concession to the north of the Great Wall of China, and not to obstruct, directly or indirectly, applications for railway concessions in that region supported by the Russian government.

2. Russia, on her part, engages not to seek for her own account, or in behalf of Russian subjects, or of others, any railway concession on the basin of the Yang-tse, and not to obstruct, directly or indirectly, applications for railway concessions in that region supported by the British government.

The two contracting parties, having no wise in view to infringe in any way the sovereign rights of China on existing treaties, will not fail to communicate to the Chinese government the present arrangement, which, by averting all cause of complications between them, is of a nature to consolidate peace in the Far East, and to serve primordial interests of China itself.

(Signed) CHARLES S. SCOTT.

ST. PETERSBURG, *April 28, 1899.*

(A copy of the above note was signed at the same time by the Russian Minister of Foreign Affairs, "duly authorized to that effect.")

TREATY OF OFFENSIVE AND DEFENSIVE ALLIANCE BETWEEN GREAT BRITAIN AND JAPAN

(*Signed at London, January 30, 1902*)

The governments of Great Britain and Japan, actuated solely by a desire to maintain the *status quo* and general peace in the extreme East, being moreover specially interested in maintaining the independence and territorial integrity of the Empire of China and the Empire of Korea, and in securing equal opportunities in those countries for the commerce and industry of all nations, hereby agree as follows:

Article I. The high contracting parties having mutually recognized the independence of China and of Korea, declare themselves to be entirely uninfluenced by any aggressive tendencies in either country. Having in view, however, their special interests, of which those of Great Britain relate principally to China, while Japan, in addition to the interests which she possesses in China, is interested in a peculiar degree politically, as well as commercially and industrially, in Korea, the high contracting parties recognize that it will be admissible for either of them to take such measures as may be indispensable in order to safeguard those interests if threatened either by the aggressive action of any other power, or by disturbances arising in China or Korea, and necessitating the intervention of either of the high contracting parties for the protection of the lives and property of its subjects.

Article II. If either Great Britain or Japan, in the defence of their respective interests as above described, should become involved in war with another power, the other high contracting party will maintain a strict neutrality, and use its efforts to prevent other powers from joining in hostilities against its ally.

Article III. If in the above event any other power or powers should join in hostilities against that ally, the other high contracting party will come to its assistance and will conduct the war in common, and make peace in mutual agreement with it.

Article IV. The high contracting parties agree that neither of them will, without consulting the other, enter into separate arrangements with another power to the prejudice of the interests above described.

Article V. Whenever, in the opinion of either Great Britain or Japan, the above-mentioned interests are in jeopardy, the two governments will communicate with each other fully and frankly.

Article VI. The present agreement shall come into effect immediately after the date of its signature, and remain in force for five years from that date.

In case neither of the high contracting parties should have notified twelve months before the expiration of the said five years the intention of terminating it, it shall remain binding until the expiration of one year from the day on which either of the high contracting parties shall have denounced it. But if, when the date fixed for its expiration arrives, either ally is actually engaged in war, the alliance shall, *ipso facto*, continue until peace is concluded.

In faith whereof the undersigned, duly authorized by their respective governments, have signed this agreement, and have affixed thereto their seals.

Done in duplicate at London the 30th January, 1902.

[L. S.] LANSDOWNE,
His Britannic Majesty's Principal Secretary of State for Foreign Affairs.

[L. S.] HAYASHI,
Envoy Extraordinary and Minister Plenipotentiary of his Majesty the Emperor of Japan at the Court of St. James.

SPECIMEN OF THE REGULATIONS CONCERNING FOREIGN JOINT STOCK COMPANIES OPERATING IN RUSSIA

Conditions on which the English Joint Stock Company, under the name of "The South Russian Oil Company, Limited," is permitted to carry on its operations in Russia:

1. The English Joint Stock Company, under the name of "The South Russian Oil Company, Limited," begins its operations in Russia by working the lot of oil-bearing land acquired by the said

company from N. W. Schmelling, situated in the Kizlar district of the Terek Territory and occupying an area of 30 dessyatinas, 1261 square sagenes (84 acres).

2. The Company is subject to the laws and regulations in force in Russia and bearing upon the object of the Company's operations, and it is likewise subject to the regulations laid down in the Law of the Imperial Tax on Industry and Trade (*Gazette of Laws*, 1898, No. 76, art. 964), as well as any laws and regulations that may hereafter be passed.

3. The acquisition by the Company of any real estate in Russia, either by purchase or hire, is to be made in accordance with the general laws in force in the empire, and with the Imperial decree of March 14, 1887 (see p. 515), in particular. Moreover, real estate may be acquired solely for the requirements of the undertaking, after the local authorities of the province (or territory) have certified that the acquisition of such property is really necessary.

The acquisition by the Company, on any terms whatever, of oil-bearing land in the Caucasus, over and above that acquired by the Company under article 1, as well as any prospecting or obtaining of lots for working oil in the above-mentioned territory, is permitted only on condition of observing the regulations contained in note 1, article 547, and note 2, article 544, volume vii. of the Mining Code, edition of 1895 (see p. 514).

4. The real estate and movable property of the Company within the limits of the [Russian] empire, as well as all sums due to the Company, are to be used primarily to meet the claims rising out of the operations of the Company in Russia.

5. A special responsible agency is to be established in Russia for the management of the Company's business. This agency is to be fully empowered (a) to carry on all the general operations of the Company, including the right and duty of being defendant in any lawsuit that may arise in Russia in connection with the Company; and (b) in particular, to decide immediately and independently, in the name of the Company, all cases when claims against the Company are brought either by the Russian government or by private persons, whether the latter be unconnected with the Company, or in its service, operatives included. The Company is obliged to give notice of the address of this agency to the Minister of Finance, the Minister of Agriculture and State Domains, the civil governor of the Caucasus, and the provincial (or territorial) authorities of the place where the real estate of the Company is situated; moreover, the Company must advertise the address, for general information, in the "official magazines," the *Gazette of Finance, Industry, and Commerce*, in the official ga-

zettes of St. Petersburg and Moscow, and in the local provincial gazette, with the observance of existing regulations in reference to such advertisements.

All the book-keeping of the Company in connection with its operations in Russia is to be centred in the above-mentioned agency.

6. In the appointment of managers of oil-fields and managers of the Company's affairs, the Company is obliged to follow the regulations laid down in article 547 (note 1) and supplement to article 544 (note 2) of volume vii. of the Mining Code, edition of 1895 (see p. 514).

7. Under articles 102–104, 107 and 110 of the Imperial Tax on Industry Law (*Gazette of Laws*, 1898, No. 76, article 964), the responsible agents of the Company are obliged (a) within two months after the confirmation of the Annual Report by the general meeting, to file two copies at the Ministry of Finance (Department of Manufactures and Trade), and four copies at the local office of the Exchequer in the province where the agency has its offices—of the full reports and balance-sheets, both of the Company's operations in general and of its operations in Russia in particular, and likewise a copy of the protocol of the confirmation of the reports; (b) to publish in the *Gazette of Finance* the closing balance-sheet and summary of the annual return of the Company, showing in the summary of the operations carried on in Russia the amount of foundation capital for such operations, the reserve, etc., the profit and loss account for the last financial year, and the amount of net profit on the aforesaid operations; (c) to give the local office of the Exchequer or its manager any supplementary information that may be required and any explanations that may be necessary for the auditing of the returns, being responsible for non-observance of the requirements of this (7) article under articles 104 and 164 of the Imperial Industrial Tax Law; and (d) in the cases mentioned in article 110 of the aforesaid law, to submit to the demands of the local Exchequer office in regard to the examination and verification, with the object of ascertaining the net profit, of books and documents, as well as the premises of the Company.

8. The time and place of the general meetings are to be announced in the publications mentioned in article 5 at least a month before the date of the meeting, and such announcements are to contain an explanation of the subjects to be discussed, and the name and address of the bank in Russia where the shares of the Company must be presented in order to obtain the right of taking part in the general meeting.

9. Any disputes that may arise between the Company and

government institutions or private persons, in regard to the operations of the company in the empire, are to be settled according to the laws in force in Russia by a Russian court of law.

10. The operations of the Company in Russia are exclusively restricted to the objects mentioned in article 1 of these conditions, and for the amalgamation or union with other similar companies or undertakings, as well as for any alteration or supplementing of the statutes (in particular, the increase or decrease of capital and the issue of debentures), the company is first obliged to obtain the sanction of the Ministry of Finance, of Agriculture and State Domains in Russia; in case of liquidation the company must inform the same ministries.

11. In regard to the cessation of its operations in Russia, the company is obliged to submit to the laws and government regulations now in force or which may hereafter be enacted.

THE END